UNIVERSITY LIBRARIES

Tin Pan Opera

Tin Pan Opera

Operatic Novelty Songs in the Ragtime Era

LARRY HAMBERLIN

OXFORD
UNIVERSITY PRESS

Oxford University Press

Oxford University Press, Inc., publishes works that further
Oxford University's objective of excellence
in research, scholarship, and education.

Oxford   New York
Auckland   Cape Town   Dar es Salaam   Hong Kong   Karachi
Kuala Lumpur   Madrid   Melbourne   Mexico City   Nairobi
New Delhi   Shanghai   Taipei   Toronto

With offices in
Argentina   Austria   Brazil   Chile   Czech Republic   France   Greece
Guatemala   Hungary   Italy   Japan   Poland   Portugal   Singapore
South Korea   Switzerland   Thailand   Turkey   Ukraine   Vietnam

Published by Oxford University Press, Inc.
198 Madison Avenue, New York, New York 10016

www.oup.com

Oxford is a registered trademark of Oxford University Press

Publication of this book was supported by a grant from the
H. Earle Johnson Fund of the Society for American Music.

This volume published with generous support from the Gustave Reese
Publication Endowment Fund of the American Musicological Society.

Library of Congress Cataloging-in-Publication Data
Hamberlin, Larry.
Tin Pan Opera : operatic novelty songs in the ragtime era / Larry Hamberlin.
p.   cm.
Includes bibliographical references.
ISBN 978–0–19–533892–8
1. Popular music—United States—History and criticism.
2. Opera—United States—20th century.   3. Opera in popular music.
I. Title.
ML3477.H34 2010
782.421640973—dc22   2008053836

1 3 5 7 9 8 6 4 2

Printed in the United States of America
on acid-free paper

Acknowledgments

This book has benefited from the keen critical eye of Judith Tick, whose insights have improved much of what I say and write, and not only in these pages. Alan Keiler, Jessie Ann Owens, and Joanna Bowen Gillespie also offered valuable advice in the project's early stages, as did the anonymous reviewers for Oxford University Press at a later stage. Paul Charosh, Charles Hamm, Leta Miller, W. Anthony Sheppard, Wayne Shirley, and Mary Simonson put hard-to-find materials at my disposal and were helpful sounding boards for ideas. Several librarians and archivists have also given indispensable aid; my thanks in particular to Darwin Scott, then at Brandeis University; Holly Callahan, Cynthia Requart, and Kelly Spring at Johns Hopkins University; Lucinda Cockrell at the Center for Popular Music, Middle Tennessee State University; Francis Lapka at Indiana University's Lilly Library; Christine Windheuser at the National Museum of American History; Thomas Lisanti at the New York Public Library; and Rachel Szatlowski at UCLA.

I am deeply appreciative of the generous support this book has received from the H. Earle Johnson Fund of the Society for American Music and the Gustave Reese Publication Endowment Fund of the American Musicological Society. Grateful acknowledgment is made as well to *American Music* and to the *Journal of the American Musicological Society* for permission to reproduce material that first appeared in those journals in somewhat different form.

At Oxford University Press I have had the good fortune of working with the expert team of Suzanne Ryan, Norm Hirschy, Madelyn Sutton, Jennifer Kowing, and Michael Philoantonie, whose patience and good humor sustained the project through the rough patches. My thanks to Timothy Woos for preparing the musical examples. As a former long-time copy editor myself, I particularly appreciate the meticulous work of Robert Milks, who saved me from numerous embarrassments. It's a humbling experience to be on the receiving end for a change.

To the many friends and family members who have sustained me through this long project, I can only offer my love and gratitude.

Contents

Tin Pan Opera

Introduction

> It's a complex thing being an American, and one of the responsibilities it entails is fighting against a superstitious valuation of Europe.
>
> —Henry James

- Harpo Marx is swinging from a rope high above the stage, creating comic mayhem while the romantic couple below, soprano and tenor, sing the Miserere from Verdi's *Il trovatore*.
- A young folklorist named Alan Lomax sets up his recording equipment while an older man sits at the piano, reminiscing about his childhood in New Orleans and playing sweet music. The aging musician identifies the melody as the "Miserere from *El travador*," then swings into a lively jazz version.
- A housepainter hears a German band passing by, recognizes the band's operatic music, and in his ecstasy falls from his scaffold, shouting Verdi's name. The ragtime song that tells his story sets the scene with a quotation from *Il trovatore*—the Miserere.

These three vignettes—from *A Night at the Opera*, Jelly Roll Morton's Library of Congress recordings, and Ted Snyder and Irving Berlin's song "That Opera Rag"—give some idea how a single operatic fragment can turn up in unexpected corners of American popular culture, including movies, jazz, and lowbrow stage comedies such as the one that featured Snyder and Berlin's song. Well into the twentieth century, popular songs in particular—unpretentious products of Tin Pan Alley—often made reference to the operatic repertory, usually to make a satirical or topical point. These songs, and the way they incorporate bits of borrowed high culture, can tell us much about the people who sang them and listened to them, and in particular how they saw themselves in relation to others, including the Europeans whose music they borrowed.

Though the distance between opera and popular music seems immense today, that has not always been the case. The time period that is the focus of this book, roughly 1900 to 1920, saw a gradual transition between nineteenth- and twentieth-century ways of thinking about the relationship between the two kinds of music. It is scarcely an overstatement to assert that in nineteenth-century America, opera *was* popular music. Much of that music was heard, naturally, on the operatic stage.[1] But Americans also brought the music into their homes. Excerpts from French

3

and Italian operas, issued as sheet music by the publishers of the nascent
popular music industry, graced the music rack of many a parlor piano, and
bel canto composers exerted a powerful influence on native songwriters
such as Stephen Foster.[2] Moreover, operatic music figured in an astonish-
ing range of social activities; Katherine Preston has noted the presence of
operatic excerpts

> on programs from instrumental and vocal concerts, to be sure, but also
> among the entre-act compositions performed by theater orchestras; on
> dance cards from masquerade balls, hops, and soirées; among the works
> played by brass bands marching in parades; as part of the repertory for col-
> lege commencement ceremonies; [and] as music performed by wind and
> string ensembles to entertain excursionists on Potomac River steamers.[3]

One important measure of opera's popularity in antebellum America was
the performance of operatic burlesques, most of them part of blackface
minstrelsy. Renee Lapp Norris has shown that the humor of blackface
burlesques such as *Lucy Did Sham a Moor* or *He Fries and Shoots!* depended
on a surprisingly intimate familiarity with the originals.[4] The inescapable
conclusion is that a significant part of the audience for minstrelsy was also
the audience for opera—that is, that the separation of the American pop-
ulace into "highbrows" and "lowbrows" had not yet taken place.

The methodology of scholars such as Preston and Norris—namely, of
examining operatic allusions in antebellum popular culture to explore
audiences' knowledge of and attitudes toward opera—has greatly influenced my own work, which treats early Tin Pan Alley songs in a similar
way. These songs reveal that opera's role in the popular culture of the
early twentieth century was only scarcely less extensive than in the nineteenth century. But America before the Civil War and America in the
years leading up to World War I are two quite different places. Among the
differences so keenly represented in these songs are two: the dichotomy
between highbrow and lowbrow just alluded to, and the growing sense
that the culture of the United States, long seen to be inferior to that of
Europe, was ready to take its place on the world stage.

It was in the early years of the twentieth century that the terms *highbrow* and *lowbrow* came into common use, thanks to an influential 1915
essay by Van Wyck Brooks.[5] Lawrence Levine has traced the growth of
this conception of two distinct cultural levels in a process he calls "sacralization," which was fueled by the idea that high art and literature (read:
imported European culture) must be kept pure from contamination by
vulgarity (read: native-born American culture). The sacralization of opera
was well under way before 1900, according to Levine. "By the end of the
nineteenth century," he writes, opera

> was no longer part and parcel of the eclectic blend of culture that had char-
> acterized the United States. More and more, opera in America meant for-
> eign-language opera performed in opera houses like the Academy of Music
> and the Metropolitan Opera House, which were deeply influenced if not

controlled by wealthy patrons whose impresarios and conductors strove to keep the opera they presented free from the influences of other genres and other groups.[6]

For Levine, the progression from the antebellum ubiquity noted by Preston to the exclusivity of the Metropolitan Opera in the 1890s runs parallel to similar currents that by the century's end had removed symphonic music, Shakespeare, and the visual arts from the general public and secluded them in temples of the arts, real or metaphorical, reserved for the privileged few.

But the corralling of opera into the opera house was by no means complete by 1900. Just as their nineteenth-century forebears had played and sung operatic music around the parlor piano, Americans early in the twentieth century avidly consumed opera excerpts in all the ways described by Preston, and in at least two other important ways as well. One of these was the phonograph, which decades after its invention in the 1870s had become a moderately priced mass-produced staple of even lower-income households. The growth of the phonograph industry and the special role of opera in the production of commercial records greatly influenced the careers of such operatic celebrities as Enrico Caruso. The other important new medium for opera was vaudeville, a purveyor of all manner of entertainment to audiences across the continent. Although vaudeville today is commonly thought to have been thoroughly lowbrow, many vaudeville bills included, among the dog acts and acrobats, a fair sampling of operatic music. The soprano Rosa Ponselle got her start in vaudeville, established stars such as Emma Calvé toured the vaudeville circuit, and one-act "condensed" versions of full operas were presented as featured vaudeville attractions.

If these new media for disseminating opera were merely extensions of nineteenth-century means such as sheet music and band concerts, then what was genuinely new was the slowly growing perception that opera, despite the Victrola and vaudeville, somehow belonged in the opera house—or worse, belonged to the rich patrons who occupied the boxes. Although opera was still widely consumed outside the opera house— excerpted, arranged, sung in English or played instrumentally—in the Tin Pan Alley songs about opera one can detect a growing sense that to consume opera in these ways somehow constituted a "desecration," to quote the title of a popular ragtime medley of operatic music, Felix Arndt's 1914 "Operatic Nightmare: Desecration no. 2." Even if sacralization was by no means complete, a rift had opened between popular and elite musical cultures that would widen dramatically in midcentury. As Joseph Horowitz writes in the postlude to his study of the Wagner cult in New York in the late nineteenth century, "it was after World War I that sacralization metastasized into an insidiously popular movement—a midculture based on snob appeal—which rejected contemporary culture, enshrined celebrity performers, and canonized aged European masterworks."[7] Focusing on the period immediately following Horowitz's, and examining an entirely different cultural phenomenon—popular song—I reach a similar conclusion in the chapters to follow, namely, that the mixing of operatic and popular genres remained lively through the World War I era, but always with an awareness that two distinct musical styles, with their evocations of two distinct social strata, were being juxtaposed in ways often comical and always problematic.

By combining operatic quotations with popular musical idioms such as ragtime, the writers of these songs found a new way to take part in a long-standing tradition of opera criticism in the United States. That tradition, which took its cue from Joseph Addison's and Richard Steele's denunciations of Handel in the *Spectator*, began in antebellum New York newspapers that derided both elite operagoers and opera itself as frivolous, effeminate, and infatuated with what is foreign and hence intrinsically inferior.[8] In contrast, a new cultural current, reaching the United States in the 1840s, saw music as part of the transcendent culture famously summed up by Matthew Arnold as "the best which has been thought and said in the world." The two modes of criticism were not mutually exclusive, however; although Walt Whitman, in his music journalism, began firmly in the earlier camp, he later came to recognize "the power and worth of complex music" but at the same time "distanced himself from the economic and social elites with which [opera] had long been associated."[9]

By the end of the century, the Arnoldian cultural critics, in response to the economic inequities of the Gilded Age, ever more emphatically defined high culture as transcending commercial pursuits. Separating the old Addisonian antielitism from its disdain for music, the new attitude equated high culture (including "good" music) with authenticity and associated wealth with its opposite, artificiality. In an ironic updating of the *Spectator* critics, writers such as George William Curtis (1824–92), an editor of *Harper's* magazine, could once again link the frivolous rich with Italian opera, which now could be portrayed as a threadbare and debased art form in comparison with the more "authentic" music dramas of Wagner. Yet, as Karen Ahlquist notes, whereas these critics "succeeded in isolating themselves from the socioeconomic elite above them," they also failed to make "the great leap to the democracy below."[10] Although by century's end Wagner came to enjoy the cult status that Horowitz describes, the songs discussed in the chapters to follow demonstrate that Italian and French operas remained the favorites of the social and economic extremes; dozens of allusions to Italian opera composers dwarf the rare allusions to Wagner. The songs confirm that the Wagnerian critics had little influence on either the wealthy elite or the masses.

In a brilliant essay on opera in the Gilded Age, Ahlquist concludes with an indication of a new cultural force that in the twentieth century would fundamentally alter the critical debate about opera: "The growth in the late nineteenth century and into the twentieth of an economically strong, self-consciously popular music shows how much cultural influence would come from other sources [besides the Arnoldian critics]. This growth brought—and brings—an 'outsider' approach toward opera to the fore, in turn magnifying the anti-elite critique."[11] Ahlquist pinpoints the phenomenon that I have chosen to explore: the rise of a countervailing cultural trend, one that early on came to be seen as the United States' "answer" to Europe's high cultural legacy, in the popular music industry, nicknamed "Tin Pan Alley" after the stretch of West Twenty-eighth Street in New York City where many music publishers had their offices.[12] In contrast to nineteenth-century opera criticism, this new way of thinking about music was worked out not exclusively or even primarily in journalistic writing but in the music itself. In both their music and their lyrics, these songs, by mixing operatic themes with vernacular genres such as ragtime, transform the debate about opera into a debate over its merits in relation to popular music, and thus into a debate over the relative merits of European high culture and vernacular American culture, a topic I examine in depth in chapter 7.

If these songs display an "outsider" approach, as Ahlquist argues, then it is a complex one; like their minstrel burlesque predecessors, the songs testify to the general public's widespread knowledge of and love for at least the most familiar operatic excerpts. Evident throughout the book, and especially in part I, is a sense that the notion of opera as the exclusive property of the social and economic elites was hotly contested. Whether or not audiences were enjoined to view the opera-loving African, Irish, Italian, and Jewish American protagonists of these songs as outsiders, those characters do not see themselves that way; they simply love opera. At the same time, there is no mistaking the songs' antielitism; the upper classes are repeatedly skewered, continuing a vein of operatically inspired social satire extending from Addison through Curtis and the Tin Pan Alley songsmiths to the Marx Brothers and Bugs Bunny. But unlike mid-twentieth-century operatic burlesques such as *A Night at the Opera* (1935) and "What's Opera, Doc?" (1957), these songs poke fun at the snobbery of high-class opera patrons without poking fun at opera itself. Thus they maintain the distinction, ignored by Addison but carefully delineated by Curtis and the other Gilded Age critics, between admiration for opera as cultural legacy and disdain for operagoing as social spectacle.

These operatic popular songs also situate themselves within a prominent strain of American literature, theater, and journalism concerned with, in the words of the literary critic William Spengemann, "America's perennial love-hate relation with Europe and all its attendant feelings of cultural inferiority and moral superiority, of parricidal guilt and newborn innocence, of nostalgia for the old home and the urge to destroy it."[13] Constance Rourke, in her classic *American Humor: A Study of the National Character* (1931), outlines an archetypal story in which a rough-hewn American claims moral superiority over a suave, fashionable, but deceitful European. This "Yankee fable," as she calls it, runs throughout American literature and folk humor in countless instances, beginning with Royall Tyler's Revolutionary-era play *The Contrast* and including *Our American Cousin*, the play Lincoln attended at Ford's Theater the night of his assassination; Mark Twain's *Innocents Abroad*, an account of his participation in an organized cruise in 1867 that may be considered the first instance of cultural tourism; and the novels of Henry James, of which Rourke focuses on *The American* (1876–77). Early on, this archetypal fictional American took on three characteristic forms: the rustic New England Yankee (Brother Jonathan, who metamorphosed into Uncle Sam), the frontier backwoodsman (Davy Crockett and his ilk), and the southern Negro of minstrelsy (Jim Crow). Later in the nineteenth century, immigrant characters—Rourke discusses Irish, German, and Jewish immigrants, to which I would add Italians—"wore the same air of masquerade"; that is, characters drawn from these marginalized segments of society were made to speak for the whole. Together these figures constituted "popular oracles," embodiments of a distinctive national character who were able to comment humorously on topical matters and who remained a lively part of the popular theater well into the twentieth century.[14] Parts I and III of this book explore how Italian immigrants and African Americans, respectively, serve as "popular oracles" in songs that express what Spengemann calls "the collision of disruptive American energy with repressive European tradition."[15]

My interest in these "grand-opera-popular songs," to use the phrase found on one sheet music cover,[16] is an outgrowth of research into the uses of European classical music in early jazz. One example, Jelly Roll Morton's 1936 interviews at the Library of Congress with the folklorist Alan Lomax, has already been cited. Another is Louis Armstrong's virtuosic use in his improvised solos of quotations from *Rigoletto* and *Pagliacci*; years later, Armstrong enthusiastically described his purchase as a teenager of a windup Victrola and phonograph records by Caruso, Luisa Tetrazzini, Amelita Galli-Curci, and other singers, testimony to the phonograph's role in disseminating opera among a diverse range of listeners.[17] Both Morton and Armstrong, with little formal education and coming from underprivileged backgrounds, were familiar with at least a sampling of the operatic repertoire. While studying these two figures I came to surmise that if exposure to opera was a part of their upbringing, then the same was probably true for many Americans at the turn of the century, not just the socioeconomic elite.

At the same time, while perusing Charles Hamm's critical edition of early Irving Berlin songs, I came across "That Opera Rag" (1910), whose pastiche of operatic quotations demanded explication beyond the brief mention in Hamm's biography of Berlin.[18] While investigating *Getting a Polish*, the play in which that song premiered as an interpolation, I recognized Rourke's Yankee fable and saw how the song distills the play's preoccupation with European and American difference. Here, in a thoroughly demotic genre—a ragtime song in Negro dialect, sung before the audience at a lightweight farce-comedy—was a manipulation of operatic music to address themes of national and racial identity that reach deep into the American psyche.

If similar songs could be found, I suspected, then it might be possible to reach an understanding of how opera—European in origin, to be sure, but thoroughly naturalized—functioned as a part of American popular culture. In time, thanks to published popular song bibliographies, library catalogs, and in particular the new phenomenon of online digitized sheet music archives, I was able to amass a database of songs that reference opera or other forms of European high culture, of which some 150 figure in this book.[19] Such a quantity makes possible at least a first effort at assessing the workings of operatic music in American popular songs.

Although historians of popular music have long noted the presence of quotations, only in recent years has this particular aspect of Tin Pan Alley songs been the subject of scholarly inquiry. Of the 190 songs that Irving Berlin published between 1907 and 1914, Hamm lists 27 that quote other musical sources, of which 4 quote operas.[20] J. Peter Burkholder, in his exemplary study of quotation in the music of Charles Ives, describes some of the methods and meanings of quotation in Tin Pan Alley songs, which, he argues, served as models for at least one type of quotation in Ives.[21] For instance, the use of four different patriotic tunes in George M. Cohan's "The Yankee Doodle Boy" (1904) constitutes what Burkholder calls a "patchwork," the stitching together of several tunes to create a new melody. Cohan uses all four tunes to reinforce a single aesthetic goal, the expression of patriotic nostalgia; the nostalgic tone is heightened by the contrast between the musical style of the eighteenth- and nineteenth-century tunes and the ragtime idiom of the newly composed connective tissue, a contrast no doubt stronger in Cohan's time than in ours.

Similar stylistic contrasts have musical meanings in the operatic pop songs. Moreover, the songwriters capitalize on the contrasts not only between quoted operatic tunes and the overall ragtime-influenced style of the songs themselves but also among multiple quotations, which unlike Cohan's "The Yankee Doodle Boy" may be drawn from radically different repertories. An example treated in depth in chapter 2 is "My Cousin Caruso," a song that quotes, in addition to fragments of Verdi and Leoncavallo, an emphatically lowbrow song about exotic dancers at Coney Island. As first performed in a musical comedy, the operatic snippets would have been heard as incongruously highbrow for the performance context; but just as importantly, the "hootchy-kootchy" quotation would have been heard as incongruously lowbrow and risqué. In "My Cousin Caruso," as in many other songs, the operatic quotations convey meaning not in isolation but in relationship to the musical styles and social functions of other quotations and the song itself.

The great majority of operatic popular songs that I have collected were published in the first two decades of the twentieth century. This time period coincides exactly with Burkholder's observations about the rise and fall of quotations in Tin Pan Alley songs in general.[22] There are several reasons why that should be the case. Although the occasional satirical song about opera appeared in the nineteenth century, not until Tin Pan

Alley's increased production of songs in the 1890s was this or any other type of song published in great numbers.[23] Also, the end of the nineteenth century saw a fledgling American appreciation for the Parisian-style topical revue, a stage entertainment consisting of short comic sketches and musical numbers, many devoted to topical satire. Annual revues, notably the *Ziegfeld Follies* and the *Passing Show*, were enormously popular in the early twentieth century, both in New York and in the broad swaths of the country covered by touring road companies; it was in these and similar revues that many of the operatic popular songs were first performed.[24] Although the topical revue never disappeared, its popularity gradually declined in the 1920s as the "book" musical (i.e., one with characters and a plot) came into its ascendancy. The revue created a taste for topical humor in popular song that spilled over to other performance venues as well, as can be seen in the songs discussed herein that were first performed not only in revues but also in vaudeville, musical comedy, and even occasionally in operetta.

Another reason why these songs flourished in the first two decades of the century and then passed out of fashion concerns the United States' shifting relationship with Europe in those years. The Spanish-American War of 1898, the first time the United States defeated a European military power on foreign soil, marked the emergence of the United States as an imperialistic world power. Americans at the turn of the century were thus engaged in a self-examination of their relationship not only with Europe but also with the Far East, a subject I explore further in chapter 5. Twenty years later, with World War I, the United States defeated a European military power on *European* soil and confirmed its military, if not its cultural or moral, superiority over what former secretary of defense Donald Rumsfeld, displaying a recurrent trope in American thought, called "old Europe." If the psychic power fueling the Yankee fable had been anxiety over Americans' inferiority to Europe, then U.S. participation in the Allied victory in World War I seems to have at least temporarily quelled that anxiety. Chapter 7 details that shift in thinking, which eventually obviated the need for songs that probed the old anxiety by means of operatic quotations.

Because quotations of opera in popular songs trail off rapidly after World War I, I carry my examination forward only to 1921, the last year for which I have multiple examples. Nevertheless, lowbrow opera burlesques certainly retained their vitality for decades to come. To the Marx Brothers and Bugs Bunny examples mentioned earlier one might add opera parodies by Spike Jones, Anna Russell, Andy Griffith, even the rock group Queen's "Bohemian Rhapsody," from their 1975 album *A Night at the Opera*.[25] These parodies distinguish themselves from their pre-1920 antecedents in two ways. One, as already mentioned, is their ridiculing not only of opera snobs but of opera itself; like the eighteenth-century *Spectator* critics, they fail to separate the music from the social practices that surround it. The other is their assumption that audiences have little or no knowledge of the opera being parodied. Back in 1910, when the would-be connoisseur in "That Opera Rag" hears a snippet from *Carmen* and identifies the composer as Verdi, audiences could spot him as a poseur; the joke hinges on the listener's knowing that the correct composer is Bizet. By midcentury, in contrast, Bugs Bunny and Elmer Fudd could send up Wagnerian opera in a manner hilarious to audiences regardless of their familiarity, or lack thereof, with the *Ring* cycle; recognizing the sources of the quotations, in fact, does little to heighten the comedy. By the late twentieth century, putting a horned helmet on a fat lady was all it took to get a laugh at opera's expense.

All of this is to suggest how one may track opera's changing position in American society by looking not at opera itself but at its reflections in popular culture. I have chosen to focus on the early twentieth century, still a time of widespread familiarity with the operatic warhorses but also a time when a new, native-born music—a thoroughly commercialized popular music rooted in the African-derived idiom of ragtime—was making the first serious inroads against European music's cultural hegemony. At the same time that some Americans were beginning to suspect that the United States would make its greatest musical impression on the international scene with just such popular forms, large-scale demographic shifts— a massive influx of immigrants, a new demand for equal rights on the part of African Americans and women—were changing fundamental ideas about exactly who the "typical American" might be. Because the operatic popular songs express all of these cultural currents, this book is organized not around the operatic sources and their treatment but around the social situations on which they comment.

Part I treats the songs' representation of Italian Americans. Chapter 1 surveys songs in which lowbrow Italian immigrants assert a right of ownership to opera more authentic than that of the social elite that aspired to such ownership. The songs in chapter 2 describe the celebrity status of Enrico Caruso and Luisa Tetrazzini from the viewpoint of the working-class Italian immigrants whom these stars attracted to the Metropolitan and Manhattan opera houses; they highlight the contrast between those immigrants' sincere but noisy appreciation of opera and the more refined but less genuine response of elite operagoers.

The songs in part II use opera, an arena in which women had come to exert some degree of autonomy, to comment on the first wave of feminism. The fictional women portrayed in the songs in chapter 3 study singing, aspire to be on the musical stage, or already sing professionally; the students are portrayed as naïve victims of male music teachers, and the professionals and would-be professionals are vain and empty-headed at best, conniving and duplicitous at worst. Much of the animus directed toward professional singers had to do with the supposed indecency of feminine self-display in public. No opera put that self-display in the foreground as provocatively as did *Salome*. Although much has been written about the "Salomania" that Strauss's opera inspired in the United States, little has been written about the songs that contributed to that mania; those songs, the subject of chapter 4, reveal that much of the uproar was not so much about the opera's indecency as it was the association of that indecency with "hootchy-kootchy" dancers at Coney Island and similar places of lowbrow amusement. Even more influential on popular culture than Salome was Cho-Cho-San, the title character of *Madama Butterfly*. Chapter 5 surveys the large repertoire of Butterfly songs, which, like the opera, allegorize the United States' flexing of imperialistic muscle in the Far East as a love story between a powerful American man and a power-less Japanese woman. Unlike the opera, the songs explore a wide range of alternative readings of that allegory, from validating Pinkerton as hero, not villain, to empowering Cho Cho San and giving her a chance to redress her wrongs.

In this era, popular culture often racialized tensions between highbrow and lowbrow culture, expressing them as tensions between white and black America. Part III treats songs that use opera in this way. In contrast to the other chapters, each of which surveys a large number of songs, chapter 6 is an in-depth case study of a single song, Ted Snyder and Irving Berlin's "That Opera Rag." Through a close reading of the music and lyr-ics, an examination of the song's use in a stage comedy, and a consider-ation of the stage persona of the actress who interpolated the song in that comedy, I demonstrate how contemporary audiences could perceive mul-tiple levels of meaning that interact in a complex piece of social and musi-cal commentary. Chapter 7 surveys more songs about black opera lovers, as well as songs that address the emerging sense that in its popular music the United States was developing its own musical culture worthy of stand-ing alongside the high cultural legacy of Europe—a legacy that, in the form of opera, had long been and would continue to be a vital part of American culture.

Part I

CARUSO AND HIS COUSINS

Chapter 1

The Operatic Italian American

Two opposing forces shaped cultural life in the United States at the turn of the twentieth century, forces that have been termed *sacralization* and *popularization*.[1] On the one hand, high culture (read: European culture) was increasingly treated with near-religious reverence, which included a tendency to isolate artworks in museums, concert halls, and other spaces devoted entirely to their contemplation. On the other hand, a vigorous new commercial culture, typified by newspapers, vaudeville theaters, and the nascent music industry nicknamed Tin Pan Alley, fostered an environment in which cultural products were merely another kind of consumer item over which the average citizen could exercise choice through purchasing power.[2] Opera, which in the nineteenth century had been a feature of such informal venues as the outdoor band concert and the parlor piano duet, now became a battleground on which these opposing forces faced off.

Nowhere did the contradictions between sacralization and popularization play themselves out more dramatically than in the use of opera in popular ragtime songs. By quoting operatic music or making verbal reference to operatic characters or performers, popular songs could allude to the social tensions surrounding sacralization while themselves embodying the very essence of popularization. A good way to begin investigating these tensions is by considering songs that comment on one of the most important factors then influencing opera's status in American society: the massive influx of immigrants from opera's homeland, Italy. Because the American public, not surprisingly, drew a close connection between Italian opera and Italian ethnicity, the "problem" of working-class Italian immigrants complicated opera's movement toward high cultural status. Proceeding from the earliest Tin Pan Alley depictions of Italian immigrants and continuing to songs that portray immigrant opera lovers and singers, we can observe how, in the songs' contrast between elitist opera patrons and working-class immigrant operagoers, the forces of sacralization and popularization take on a human face.

ITALIAN IMMIGRATION AND THE ITALIAN DIALECT SONG

Approximately 2 million Italian immigrants arrived in the United States between 1900 and 1909, with another 1.2 million in the next decade, making Italians the largest immigrant group in the United States during those years.[3] Italians constituted a major portion of the roughly 1.3 million immigrants from southern and eastern Europe who made New York City their home between 1900 and 1920; by 1910 three quarters of New York City's population consisted of immigrants and their children. Over the space of three decades, the city underwent a massive "Italianization": in 1890, New York was home to 40,000 Italian immigrants; at the turn of the century, 140,000; in 1910, 340,000; and by 1920, there were more Italians in New York City than in Florence, Venice, and Genoa combined—most of them rural southerners with little education and less money.[4] Home for many Italian Americans was Little Italy, an area in the Lower East Side neighboring the Bowery and bounded by Houston, Canal, and Lafayette Streets.[5] Many of these new U.S. residents at least occasionally made the trip uptown to the Metropolitan and Manhattan opera houses.[6]

Although they had escaped crushing economic oppression back home, these immigrants faced new discrimination from Americans who considered them "dirty, lazy, ignorant and prone to violence."[7] Moreover, they arrived in the United States at a time when huge waves of European immigration triggered what one historian has called "a fracturing of whiteness into a hierarchy of plural and scientifically determined white races," in which swarthy Mediterraneans ranked low. Thus an 1890s Californian labor boss, asked by a journalist if an Italian was a white man, could reply, "No sir, an Italian is a Dago." Victims of lynchings in the South, immigrant Italians occupied a rung of society only slightly above that of African Americans. Not until the 1920s and later, after more restrictive immigration laws eased the sense of crisis, would the notion of a unified "Causasian" race, embracing formerly distinct racial categories such as "Mediterranean," "Hebrew," "Slav," and the like, become a dominant part of American thinking about race.[8]

Acting as a barometer of social change, popular music reflected both the immigrant experience and the nativist reaction. Comic "novelty" songs in Italian dialect constituted a significant part of the many songs relying on ethnic humor. The characters depicted in these songs and on their illustrated covers display familiar stereotypical images: their names are Tony or Maria (or the latter's peasant diminutive form, Mariuccia); they wear traditional costumes, the women in peasant skirts and blouses, the men sporting long mustaches and earrings; they play mandolins and street organs; and the men work as fruit or peanut vendors, street cleaners, or barbers. The lyrics use a stereotyped "Italian" dialect: a final - a is added to some words, final syllables are dropped especially from words that end in vowels (thus Maria becomes Marie), and th- is changed to d-.

The connection between Italian immigrants and opera already makes an appearance in the earliest popular song in Italian dialect I have found: "Niccolini," by Charles Daniels (using the pseudonym Neil Moret) and James O'Dea, an interpolation in two 1905 musicals, Fantana and The Earl and the Girl. The title character is an organ grinder and singer of Neapolitan songs whose sweetheart will marry him only if he switches to the more respectable trade of peddling fruit. He agrees, bidding his monkey a tearful good-bye:

> Good-a-by Jock I kiss you de farewell,
> Instead of us going to play,
> Cavalier Rusticana I sell de banana.[9]

The association of mechanical instruments and opera is an old one, dating back to the eighteenth century and reaching a saturation point in the nineteenth. In 1878 the Bostonian John Sullivan Dwight printed in his *Journal of Music* this report from a correspondent in Newport, Rhode Island: "To-day I have heard '*Casta Diva*' seven times; four times with the monkey [played on the hand organ], and three times without (i.e., sung in houses); on the whole I prefer it with the monkey."[10] Niccolini, however, plays not Bellini but a still-current operatic hit: the famous Intermezzo from Pietro Mascagni's *Cavalleria rusticana*.

The U.S. premiere of *Cavalleria rusticana* on 9 September 1891 at the Philadelphia Grand Opera had been a part of that opera's rapid worldwide dissemination after its first performance in Rome in 1890. The New York Metropolitan Opera had offered four performances in the 1891–92 season, with Emma Eames as Santuzza. When Emma Calvé brought her smoldering interpretation of that role to the Met, the number of performances increased to seven per season for 1893–94 and 1894–95.[11] The opera's popularity in other U.S. cities as well may be seen in the publication before 1900 in Boston and Chicago of two independent adaptations of the opera's Intermezzo to the words of the Ave Maria.[12] The continued popularity of the Intermezzo in particular is evident in a piano reduction published in Philadelphia in 1914 or later with an illustrated cover more typical of popular music—a cover in which a Venetian gondola stands in for all things Italian, despite the opera's southern Italian setting (see fig. 1.1).[13] Even freer treatments were made by ragtime composers; the back cover of a 1902 song lists, among the publisher's stock, a fifty-cent "collection of New and Original Rag Time pieces by the best Rag Time Players in America, including a Rag Time Arrangement of…the Intermezzo from Cavalleria Rusticana."[14]

Black Italians

The interactions between highbrow European opera and lowbrow American ragtime were many and complex. Beyond the musical interest resulting from the wedding of lyrical, Italianate melodies to earthy African American rhythms, these interactions carried social implications as well. In the wider culture, operatic melodies and ragtime syncopations each signified the sort of people who created them and, by extension, the sort of people who enjoyed listening to them. The contrast between the two musical styles, then, was also a contrast between two cultural subgroups. Opera represented, if not solely the elite, then also those who aspired to

Figure 1.1. Mascagni, Intermezzo from *Cavalleria rusticana* (Philadelphia: Eclipse [ca. 1914]), cover

elite status. Ragtime, on the other hand, was in its early years strongly associated with the black underclass. The extension of ragtime as a signifier of not just black Americans but all Americans grew slowly during the first two decades of the twentieth century, and the chronicling of that growth is one theme of this book. A first step in that process was the association of ragtime with non-African lower-class groups. One way to explore that association is by considering the ways popular songs used African American tropes to signify Italian American immigrants.

It helps here to remember that the lines dividing Italians from other racial categories now subsumed under the label "white" were stronger then than they are today, while the lines separating Italians from categories now labeled "black" were weaker. For instance, in 1922 the Alabama Circuit Court of Appeals overturned a black man's conviction for miscegenation on the grounds that the state had failed to establish that the woman in question, a Sicilian, was white. While this decision did not establish that the woman was definitely nonwhite, the historian Matthew Frye Jacobson points out, it did indicate that "she was not the sort of white woman whose purity was to be 'protected' by that bulwark of white supremacism, the miscegenation statute."[15] At a time of fluid and multiple racial categories, Sicilians, like mainland Italians, occupied a position in close proximity to blacks.

The complex linking of Italian Americans and African Americans in the popular mind can be traced in three songs by the Boston songwriter Thomas S. Allen. The sheet music cover for Allen's "Any Rags?" (1902) depicts the song's subject, a "big black rag picker," in conventional "coon song" caricature (fig. 1.2), and the song's syncopated rhythms label the subject as African American. Two years later, Allen's "Scissors to Grind"— billed on its cover as a companion song to "Any Rags?"—includes a performer inset of Cooper and Robinson, an African American duo apparently patterned after Bert Williams and George Walker's successful combination of a handsome straight man in stylish clothes and a clown in blackface.[16] And like Williams and Walker's material, the song relies on ragtime syncopations and stage Negro dialect ("'taint no rags," "don't leave none behind") to project a black ethnic identity. Yet the cover's main illustration portrays the song's subject, a scissors grinder, with the stereotypical long mustache and felt hat of the Italian immigrant (fig. 1.3). Here, one year before the advent of Italian dialect songs, popular songs had already marked the unassimilated immigrant as culturally "black."[17]

This link between Italian American and African American identities underlies the ragtime syncopations of Allen's 1909 "Strawberries (Here Comes the Strawberry Man)," in which a strawberry vendor becomes an unlikely opera singer (fig. 1.4).[18] The lyrics, although they identify the protagonist as Michael Tony Angelo, who "came here from sunny Italy," make little use of Italian or any other dialect. While we cannot know if Belle Travers, the performer featured on the sheet music cover, made use of Italian mannerisms in her stage performances of this song, Arthur Collins, in a period recording, sings "Strawberries" in a pseudo-Italian accent, with no trace of the stage Negro dialect he used in other recordings.[19]

Michael Tony Angelo has no need of a bell such as that used by the wandering tradesman on the cover of "Scissors to Grind": his voice is loud enough to attract customers from "a mile away." "Pete" Mascagni chances to hear Michael sing, and "right away he said that man for me." Intriguingly, the only bit of written dialect is assigned not to the fruit peddler but to a respected opera composer. When Michael finally walks onstage in a suit of armor after five years of preparation, however, he is no better equipped to sing opera than he was at the beginning:

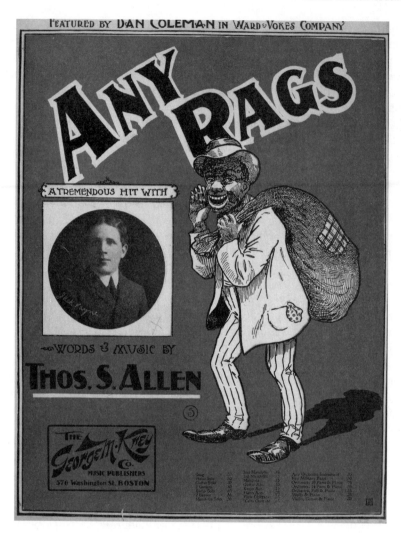

Figure 1.2. "Any Rags?" cover

> He stepped out to sing they said he'll be the rage.
> But Michael forgot himself and yelled.
> [chorus] Strawberries,
> Strawberries,
> Nice juicy
> Strawberries.

Once a street vendor, always a street vendor, or so the song would have us believe.

An item in a 1904 joke book carries a punch line that bears a strong resemblance to the chorus of "Strawberries." The story, "Beecher's Tact,"

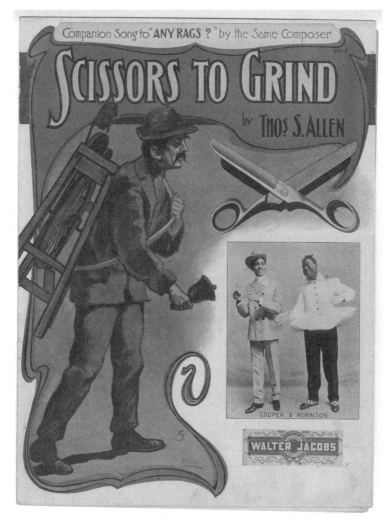

Figure 1.3. "Scissors to Grind," cover

concerns the famous clergyman Henry Ward Beecher, suggesting that the joke was rather an old one, Beecher having died in 1887:

> A very little girl was taken by her parents to a prayer meeting at Plymouth Church, presided over by Mr. Beecher. In giving out a hymn, Mr. Beecher requested every person present who could sing to do so.
>
> The response not having been sufficiently hearty during the first verse, Mr. Beecher, before the second, again exhorted all to sing.
>
> "Come, brethren, if you have the grace of God in your hearts, let it come out in your voices. Sing! All together now! Sing!"
>
> The little girl took this as a personal appeal, and hastily bethought herself of the song dearest to her heart, the cry of a fruit vender who often

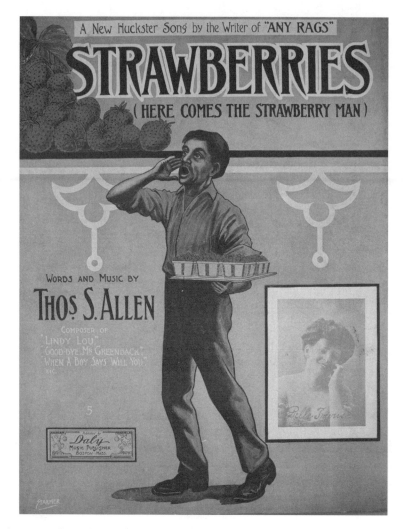

Figure 1.4. "Strawberries (Here Comes the Strawberry Man)," cover

brought fruit to her home. Accordingly, when the verse began she let forth her voice in a shrill cry of "Straw-ber-ries! Straw-ber-ries!" The congregation faltered, stopped and laughed, but Mr. Beecher, not at all disconcerted, called out: "That's right, little girl. That's right. If you can't praise God in anything but strawberries, then sing strawberries."[20]

The story suggests that at least some audience members might have responded to the hapless fruit vendor in "Strawberries" with patronizing indulgence rather than ridicule.

It is significant that Pietro Mascagni's presence in "Strawberries"—to my knowledge, his only appearance as a character in a popular song—

should occur in a publication by a Boston house, Daly Music. Although Mascagni's 1902–3 U.S. tour had begun triumphantly in New York in September, by the time his badly managed troupe reached Boston in November it was coming apart at the seams. A performance of his short operas *Cavalleria rusticana* and *Zanetto* on 3 November went well, but two days later, just before the curtain was to rise on the composer's *Guglielmo Ratcliff*, the unpaid orchestra members walked out in protest. The tour's American impresario had a warrant executed on Mascagni to prevent his fleeing the country with unpaid bills.[21] Most of the orchestra players, writes Mascagni's biographer Alan Mallach, "remained in Boston, staying in cheap boardinghouses in the Italian North End, playing in cafés to earn enough to eat, and living on Mascagni's promise that, one way or another, he would get them home." Mascagni, released on bail "with the help of a few prominent Bostonians...organized a series of benefit concerts with his reduced orchestra, a local chorus, and the handful of singers who had decided to remain with him." By the end of November the composer and his musicians were able to continue the tour, albeit on a much more modest scale than that with which it had begun.[22] Though "Strawberries" was not published until seven years later, the song, which represents the composer as recruiting new singers from the lowest rungs of Italian immigrant society, suggests that local memory of Mascagni's stay in Boston, at the nadir of his U.S. tour, had not faded. Perhaps the song's portrait was not far from the truth.

The Americanization of Mascagni

Two other Italian dialect songs juxtapose Mascagni's music and ragtime to comment on Italian immigrants' first tentative steps toward assimilation. In both songs, fictional immigrant narrators, or personae, react to ragtime Intermezzo performances; their contrasting reactions, though, reveal contradictions in how these immigrants were becoming Americanized. Most importantly, ragtime idioms position the immigrants at the bottom of the social hierarchy, along with African Americans.

Al Piantadosi and Thomas J. Gray's "Rusty-Can-O Rag" (1910) was issued with a sheet music cover again using a gondola to invoke a picture postcard image of Italy (fig. 1.5). The verse praises Mascagni's music to a tune adapted from the Intermezzo's opening measures, music that is also heard in the opera's big choral moment, the Easter Hymn (ex. 1.1 a, b).[23] The argument that the United States had yet to produce music as grand as that of the European classical tradition was hardly new, but hearing it uttered in a stage version of Italian dialect must have been something of a novelty for the song's vaudeville audiences. The song's immigrant persona (i.e., its first-person narrator) backs his statements with some authority, being a compatriot of

Figure 1.5. "Rusty-Can-O Rag," cover

Mascagni's, though he lacks the cultural authority wielded by the era's arbiters of taste.

Undermining the seriousness of his assertion, though, is the music's insistent syncopations, which align the singer with ragtime's African American originators. This becomes even more evident in the chorus, when the song's persona offers an organ grinder encouragement. Ragging the big tune of Mascagni's Intermezzo, he mixes "coon song" vocabulary lifted from a current hit, "Wild Cherries (Coony, Spoony Rag)," with a fake Italian exclamation that extends the musical phrase into a woozy ninth measure, with a break in tempo just before the last word (ex. 1.1 c, d).[24] The song's rapturous paeans are inspired not by a complete opera house performance of *Cavalleria rusticana* but by a hand organ's serenade. And the mechanical instrument plays not Mascagni's Intermezzo but a ragtime

Example 1.1. (a) Piantadosi and Gray, "Rusty-Can-O Rag," verse, mm. 1–4; (b) Mascagni, *Cavalleria rusticana,* Intermezzo, mm. 1–4; (c) "Rusty-Can-O Rag," chorus, mm. 1–9; (d) *Cavalleria rusticana,* Intermezzo, mm. 20–23

Example 1.1 (*continued*)

(d)

Example 1.1 (*continued*)

travesty of it. Far from criticizing, the song wholeheartedly approves of the Americanizing of Mascagni's music. The persona, by implication, has been affected by his residence in the United States; he responds to the "Rusty-Can-O Rag" not as an Italian but as an Italian American.

Not all Italian immigrants embraced Americanization as enthusiastically, however, judging by Egbert Van Alstyne and Harry Williams's 1910 "Cavalier' Rustican' Rag." Here the song's Italian immigrant persona has had quite enough of ragtime versions of the Intermezzo, as the first verse makes clear:

> Mister, won't you please-a come and stop de ban?
> Stop-a quick! Stop-a quick!! Stop-a quick!!!
> When dey play de Cavalleria Rustican,'
> I'm a-sick! I'm a-sick!! I'm a-sick!!!

In the correct performance situation, Mascagni's music is pleasing, but out of context it raises a music lover's ire:

> Many times I hear him sing by Cousin Carus,'
> He sing him right,
> Mos' ev'ry night,[25]
> By a ragtime orchestra he sound like de deuce,
> And I feel-a much-a fight.

The chorus, once again to the big Intermezzo tune, riffs on the Negro dialect in "Rusty-Can-O Rag" ("spooney" and "looney" become "rippy," "trippy," "dippy"), now to suggest annoyance rather than intoxication (ex. 1.2). Ironically, this Italian immigrant expresses his distaste for ragtime

Example 1.2. Van Alstyne and Williams, "Cavalier Rustican' Rag," chorus

Example 1.2 (*continued*)

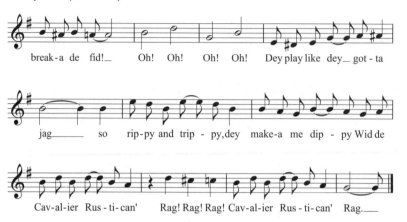

in the very language of ragtime, both musically, in the syncopations, and verbally, in the stylized vocabulary and repeated interjections ("Oh! Oh! Oh! Oh!") of the Negro dialect song. Willingly or not, he is undergoing the same process of Americanization enthusiastically embraced by his fellow *contadino* in "Rusty-Can-O Rag." What the two hold in common is their veneration for their home country's opera. Where they differ is in their response to opera's adaptation to the New World. And in both songs, ragtime idioms suggest that these immigrants occupy a place in the social order near that of African Americans.

IMMIGRANT SINGERS IN ITALIAN DIALECT SONGS

If ragtime idioms position the immigrant personae in Italian dialect songs at the bottom of the social hierarchy, then the presence of operatic allusions point to Italy's paradoxical role in American culture as a source of both elite culture and plebian workforce. Both "Rusty-Can-O Rag" and "Cavalier' Rustican' Rag" presented vaudeville audiences with the incongruous image of low-status characters who opine with some authority on the right and wrong ways to perform opera. Heightening the social contrast, a number of songs depict Italian immigrants who go one step further and aspire to take their place on the operatic stage.

Three Songs by Gus Edwards

If Michael Tony Angelo was an unwilling recruit for opera, the same cannot be said for the ambitious soprano who sings Gus Edwards's 1909 "I'm After Madame Tetrazzini's Job" (fig. 1.6).[26] Featured in Florenz Ziegfeld Jr.'s *Follies of 1909*, the song was published with a cover carrying a photo

inset of Belle Wynn, the singing actress who had introduced Victor
Herbert's "Toyland" in *Babes in Toyland* 1903. Yet Wynn was not a part of
the cast for the 1909 *Follies*; presumably she sang the song in her vaudeville act. There she might have turned the song into a miniature dramatic
scene by impersonating an aspiring singer who enters in a breathless rush,
singing her sixteenth notes so quickly that she trips over the name of
Oscar Hammerstein, whose Manhattan Opera Company had introduced
Luisa Tetrazzini to American audiences in January 1909:

> Please tell me have you seen dear Mister Op'rasteen
> I got a see-a heem queek

Figure 1.6. "I'm After Madame Tetrazzini's Job," cover

Here in the paper wrote, there is one little note
Says Tetrazzini she's seek.

Only one newspaper article around the time of the song's composition reported the diva's indisposition, which was no more than acute gastritis, caused by a meal of Boston baked beans and sardines that delayed her departure from New York for London in April 1909.[27] Yet this slim pre-text is enough to give the singer, appearing in Ziegfeld's summer revue, hopes of deposing Tetrazzini before her return in the fall for her second season in Manhattan.

The fictional singer's purpose in seeking out Hammerstein, then, is to offer herself as a replacement for the ailing prima donna. In the chorus, she promises and pleads to a pastiche consisting of the Barcarolle from Offenbach's *Tales of Hoffmann*, "Quando m'en vò" from Puccini's *La boheme*, and "The Last Rose of Summer" from Flotow's *Martha* (ex. 1.3).

The music of the chorus suggests that the singer does indeed know familiar opera excerpts, and the second verse lists operas by Verdi, Bizet, and Donizetti that she feels ready to sing. Yet all the music quoted and mentioned could have been heard in vaudeville and on phonograph records—there is no evidence that she has studied singing or even heard any of these operas in their entirety. Why, then, does this singer think that she stands a chance of actually getting Madame Tetrazzini's job? Her

Example 1.3. Edwards, "I'm After Madame Tetrazzini's Job," chorus

Figure 1.7. "Rosa Rigoletto," cover

grammar and vocabulary suggest that she is a poorly educated immigrant or first-generation Italian American. In 1909 such a person's prospects in the world of opera would strike audience members at Ziegfeld's *Follies* as extremely poor. Her ambition, like her lack of reticence in expressing it, would mark her as an object of ridicule. Less than a decade later, however, such a story would not seem quite so ludicrous. In 1918 a young woman, the daughter of southern Italian immigrants, would take a day off from her job singing as one-half of a vaudeville duo, the Ponzillo Sisters (billed as "Those Tailored Italian Girls"), to audition for Enrico Caruso. Six months later, with no European training or previous operatic experience, she would debut at the Met as Leonora in Verdi's *La forza del destino*. The career of

Example 1.4. Edwards and Madden, "Rosa Rigoletto," chorus

Rosa Ponselle would prove that a successful opera singer could indeed emerge from such unpromising circumstances.[28] In 1909, however, such a success story could only be told as pure fiction, and as comedy at that.

Likewise, in 1910 Edwards, now working with the lyricist Edward Madden, would tell a similar story in "Rosa Rigoletto" (fig. 1.7).[29] Here the hyperbolic boasting is the work not of the singer but of her besotted boyfriend, who seems fixated more on his beloved's looks than on her singing. "Beautiful-a Rose," he declares,

> Got-a fac-a on her like Italian Madonna,
> With-a same style like Venus De Mile,
> She's-a got-a figga mak you want-a dance de jigga.

The chorus turns to the topic of her singing, but even here the narrator veers back to her appearance, asserting that she "mak-a Tetrazzini sing de scene behind de screen." The music quotes, appropriately, the famous Quartet from act 3 of Verdi's *Rigoletto* (ex. 1.4). As a marker of his over-flowing enthusiasm, Rosa's lover sings not only the soaring melody of the Duke of Mantua's flattering words "Bella figlia dell'amore" (Fairest daugh-ter of love) but also a rapid figure that suggests the staccato notes of Maddalena's sarcastic reply: "Ah! ah! rido ben di core, chè tai baie costan poco" (Ha! ha! That really makes me laugh; talk like that is cheap enough). These lover's words, the melody tells us, are idle boasting.

The comparison of Rosa with Luisa Tetrazzini seems to be more about the two singers' respective looks than their voices—in competition with Rosa, Tetrazzini would choose to hide her stout figure behind a screen. The only other singer invoked for comparison is Lina Cavalieri, a soprano more widely admired for her striking beauty than for her rather small voice. Rosa has "got-a pretty face like Cavalieri," but her voice resembles not the great Tetrazzini's nor even Cavalieri's but that of a "sweet canarie." The closing lines reinforce this suggestion that her voice may have less than operatic strength: "When she sings Lucee"—to an appropriate snippet of the Sextet from Donizetti's *Lucia di Lammermoor*—Rosa "make you climb up a tree." The love-besotted suitor is no competent judge of Rosa's musical abilities. Rosa may be as beautiful as Cavalieri, but Tetrazzini's job is in no danger.

Poor judgment separates another immigrant persona from his lofty artistic goals in 1911's "Italian Romeo," in which Gus Edwards returned to writing both words and music (fig. 1.8).[30] Drawing a parallel between the balcony scene in *Romeo and Juliet* and his own serenade to his sweetheart, the first-person narrator thinks more highly of his singing ability than does his audience, as the second verse makes clear:

> I sing Gran Op. so well
> But the neighbors yell
> oh go to bed
> Things the[y] begin to drop
> Juliet yell "wop
> If you love a me a stop
> Get a wis-a and forget all about a Rigolett
> we don't want a hear Lucia but we like a mariutch
> If you want to win a me a sing a chirra birra bee."

This suitor is no more an opera singer than he is a Shakespearean hero, and the music underlines that comic point by steadfastly abstaining from

Figure 1.8. "Italian Romeo," cover

any operatic quotation. On the contrary, the one quotation is from a Negro dialect song popularized nine years earlier by Lillian Russell in a Weber and Fields burlesque, *Twirly-Whirly*.[31] The chorus of that song, "Come Down Ma Evenin' Star," consists of twelve measures—not a blues chorus, but rather an eight-measure period that ends with a lover's plea, "So come down from dar, ma evening' star," followed by a four-measure extension that intensifies the plea: "Come down! Come down! /Come down from dar, ma evening' star" (ex. 1.5 a).

The chorus of "Italian Romeo" consists of twenty measures—sixteen measures (in cut time, corresponding to the eight measures of common time in "Come Down Ma Evenin' Star") ending with a similar plea, "don't frown, but come down / Beside your burning beau" (ex. 1.5 b). The closing four-measure tag is an intensification: "O won't you come down, / Come down to your Italian Romeo." Melodic similarities—the cadence on the fifth scale degree just before the extension, the falling fifth on "come down," now a more poignant diminished fifth, thrice stated—clinch the resemblance. Attempting to present himself as both operatic and Shakespearean, the would-be Italian Romeo comes across as no more than a "coon song serenader," appropriately so for an audience that constructed the immigrant as black.

Between Opera and Popular Song: "Ciribiribin"

Along with the operatic allusions in "Italian Romeo" is a reference to a song that spawned its own small subgroup of answer songs with operatic overtones, "Ciribiribin," by the Neapolitan songwriter Alberto Pestalozza. Three American editions, all published in 1909, attest to the popularity of

Example 1.5. (a) Stromberg and Smith, "Come Down My Evenin' Star," refrain, mm. 6–12; (b) Edwards, "Italian Romeo," chorus, mm. 12–20

(a)

Example 1.5 (*continued*)

(b)

this "big song craze," and one associates it with "the world's greatest tenor, Enrico Caruso," whose photo dominates the cover (fig. 1.9).[32] Thus the song, though not operatic, was evidently associated closely with Caruso in particular and operatic culture in general.

Such associations between popular songs and opera singers were not uncommon in the era before electric amplification, when popular vocal

Figure 1.12. "When My Marie Sings Chilly Billy Bee" cover

called "ragging the classics." That is, though not itself a classic, it was deemed a suitable target for ragging, much like the Intermezzo from *Cavalleria rusticana*. Thus Lewis F. Muir's instrumental "Chilly-Billy-Bee Rag" (1910) bases its first strain on the chorus of "Ciribiribin" (fig. 1.11).[38] That strain in turn became the basis of the chorus of Muir's "When My Marie Sings Chilly-Billy-Bee," with words by Ed Moran, a song issued in the same year by the same publisher, and with cover art derived from that for the piano rag (fig. 1.12).[39]

In the first verse for this new song, a geographically inaccurate "valse espagnol," two famous divas are jealous of the singing of a working-class Italian immigrant:

foolish in the feet." Lest anyone wonder exactly which Italian tune is being alluded to, the final eight measures quote the chorus of "Ciribiribin" with the new words:

> That's the melody
> "Chili Billi be"
> That's Italian Serenade.[37]

Unlike other Neapolitan songs, however, and because of its association with Caruso (who, ironically, never recorded it), "Ciribiribin" occupied a social position somewhere between high-class opera and low-class popular song. As such, it was ripe for the teasing downward pull of genres

Figure 1.11. "Chilli-Billi-Bee Rag," cover

Figure 1.13. "Night Time in Little Italy," cover

reference, at the words "sweet-a macaroni he's a growing on the vine," to the opening line of the familiar 1896 "plantation lullaby" "Kentucky Babe": "Skeeters am a hummin' on de honey suckle vine."[45] As in the "spooney, looney" vocabulary of the *Cavalleria rusticana* songs, the complex ethnic associations of "Strawberries," and the allusion to a Negro dialect song in "Italian Romeo," the allusion here to "Kentucky Babe" once again uses an African American trope to situate Italian immigrants at the low end of the social order.

At a historical moment when partisans of Italian opera were aiming to consolidate its elite status in American culture, these popular songs reveal the wider culture's reluctance to separate lower-class Italian immigrants

Figure 1.14. "Night Time in Little Italy," back cover

thoroughly from the high culture that shared their place of origin. If fictional immigrant singers such as Rosa Rigoletto made easy targets for humorous songs, a much more complicated target was presented by actual opera singers, such as Enrico Caruso and Luisa Tetrazzini, who embodied the contradictions in American attitudes toward Italian opera and Italian immigrants.

Chapter 2

Mister Pagliatch and Miss Tetrazin'

Though Lawrence Levine considers the years before World War I the high-water mark of sacralization, even he recognizes that "opera was not [yet]...totally divorced from popular culture—as witness the great popularity of such singers as Caruso."[1] The public's adulation of opera singers—rarely matched by any other phenomenon before the advent of movie stars—marked the area of greatest congruence between operatic and popular cultures. For precisely that reason, it is here, in the popularity of Enrico Caruso and Luisa Tetrazzini, that we may explore opera's continuing role in American popular culture of the early twentieth century. As in the songs we've encountered in chapter 1, the novelty songs that mention these two singers use Italian immigrant personae to highlight the social tensions generated by the two opposing forces of sacralization and popularization. To place these songs in context, this chapter considers Caruso's early critical reception in the United States before examining his musical portrayals, then finishes up with a comparison of those songs with others that allude to Tetrazzini.

CARUSO'S EARLY RECEPTION IN THE UNITED STATES

Already an operatic celebrity from Montevideo to Moscow, Enrico Caruso arrived in New York in November 1903, more than two years after the retirement of Jean de Reske, the handsome Pole who had been the Metropolitan Opera's principal singer of Italian, French, and later German tenor roles. De Reske's trim figure, elegant manners, and refined vocal delivery had created a set of expectations against which the new tenor was to be measured; for many opera lovers de Reske remained "the beau ideal of aristocratic grace and vocal refinement,...the perfect symbol of opera as an elegant and elitist entertainment in New York during the 1890s."[2] Although reports of Caruso's spectacular success at Covent Garden had preceded him, and press coverage of his first days in New York were kindly disposed toward him, reporters could not resist noting his ample proportions and simplicity of manner, so much in contrast to de Reske's aristocratic bearing. A typical notice appeared in the *New York Telegraph:* "He is a wholesome good-looking person, this young Neapolitan. Deep-chested, full-throated, square-shouldered, a fine upstanding specimen of a man.... He looks as if he ate and fully digested three square meals a day, besides a snack at bedtime."[3]

Despite the journalistic buildup, Caruso's U.S. debut in *Rigoletto* on 23 November 1903 made little impression on the critics, who were caught up in the glitter and pomp of opening night at the Met. But reviews of the next evening's performance took more notice of the new tenor, especially of his appearance and acting, which the critics found to be no match for his predecessor. A reviewer for the *Musical Courier* found Caruso to be "stout and slow in his movements. His acting was conventional, which means that it was unexciting. Up to date, all memories of Jean de Reske are not effaced." More blunt was the reviewer for the *Commercial Advertiser:* "He is short and squat, with little or no neck." Said the *Herald:* "Disappointment that he should own so generous a girth could be read on many faces." Even those who admired his singing, such as the critic for the *Post*, could not be distracted from his physique: "His voice is of rare beauty, but he is stout."[4]

Though on the whole much more positive, the critical comments on Caruso's singing reveal an undercurrent of anti-Italian dismissal. While W. J. Henderson, in the *Sun*, considered Caruso's "pure tenor" voice to be "smooth and mellow...without the typical Italian Bleat," the *Tribune's* Henry Krehbiel disagreed: "Signor Caruso has many of the tiresome Italian vocal affectations, and when he neglects to cover his tones, as he always does when he becomes strenuous, his voice becomes pallid." Likewise, Richard Aldrich, in the *Times*, found Caruso to be "an Italian in all his fibre, and his singing and acting are characteristic of what Italy now affords in those arts. His voice is purely a tenor in its quality, of high range, and of large power, but inclined to take on the 'white' quality in its upper ranges when he lets it forth."[5] As we will soon see, this mention of a pallid or "white" tone—the use of falsetto that can be heard in Caruso's early recordings—betrays a perception of nationalistic difference.

Already in this, Caruso's first Met performance to receive serious critical attention, at least one reviewer complained that Caruso "exaggerated" his third-act aria's "catchpenny effect by his vocal flourishes at the end."[6] The reviews of his next appearance, in *Aida* on 30 November, make clear that the Met audiences were eager to applaud his performances. The *Herald* noted that "he had not sung halfway through the '*Celeste Aida,'* tenderly phrased, before the audience was impatiently waiting for him to finish, that it might break into applause. The last note had not ended before 'bravo!' rang out from all parts of the house." The *Press* agreed that the acclaim was virtually unanimous: "Thunderous was the applause that came from every part of the crowded auditorium." Yet the *Times* observed a difference in levels of enthusiasm: "It was an admirable performance and commanded not only the enthusiastic plaudits of the cooler portions of the audience, but also the frenzied 'bravos' of his compatriots who were present in large numbers."[7]

This veiled class distinction between Italian American operagoers and the "cooler portions" became overt in reviews of Caruso's next performance, a *Tosca* on 2 December. Again, the aristocratic ghost of de Reske loomed over Caruso the actor. The *Times* complained of the Italian's "bourgeois air, with little distinction of bearing." Henderson, in the *Sun*, concurred: "Mr. Caruso's Cavaradossi was bourgeois….His clothes were without distinction and his carriage was less so." "Caruso sang Mario excellently," Henry T. Finck conceded in the *Evening Post*, "but dramatically he hardly filled preconceived conceptions of the part. There was something common about it. It lacked, altogether, aristocratic flavor."[8] Yet this shortcoming posed no problems for Caruso's compatriots, sniffed the *Press:* "He indulged frequently in the *'voix blanche,'* dear to the Italians but disagreeable to the Americans. He achieved some fine climaxes, however…and so worked upon the feelings of the Italian contingent in his audience that he was forced to repeat a whole passage, greatly to the detriment of the dramatic integrity of the scene. The applause continued even after his concession to popular feeling and it was several minutes before the orchestra could be heard."[9]

The effect of Caruso's popularity on the staid atmosphere of the Metropolitan Opera House is evident in Gustav Kobbé's recollection of a *Lucia di Lammermoor* on 8 January 1904: "As for Caruso, rarely have I witnessed such excitement as followed the singing of the sextet the evening of his first appearance as Edgardo at the Metropolitan Opera House. It is a fact that the policeman in the lobby, thinking a riot of some sort had broken loose in the auditorium, grabbed his night stick and pushed through the swinging doors—only to find an audience vociferously demanding an encore."[10] These moments of delirium, in the critics' eyes, did not necessarily correspond with the artistic high points in Caruso's performances. Of his rendition of "Una furtiva lagrima" in a 23 January 1904 *L'elisir d'amore*, the *Times* commented, "Rapture is no fitting expression for the state of mind into which it threw the audience, and he was instantly called upon to unfold that tale of amorous longing again." Yet the critic found his singing on the same evening of "Quanto è bella" to be "given in a less exaggerated, and hence in some ways more artistic style."[11]

In sum, the critical response to Caruso's first season at the Metropolitan reveals a network of classist and racist attitudes. Behind the complaints about his visual appearance is a comparison, sometimes covert but always present, with de Reske, a non-Italian predecessor seen to be his superior in manners and bearing. Mixed in with strong approval of Caruso's singing is a note of reserve regarding his use of falsetto, which is reported to be favored by Italian operagoers but held in contempt by the "cooler portions" of the audience. Moreover, Caruso is seen to lower his own dignity by occasionally pandering to the less discriminating members of his audience with "catchpenny" vocal flourishes, a practice that draws the strongest response from his Italian compatriots. And most damning of all, the vociferous applause of those compatriots has lowered the dignity of the Metropolitan Opera House itself, creating such pandemonium that a police officer might mistake it for a riot.

These complaints suggest that Caruso's presence in New York posed a problem for the patrons seated in the Metropolitan Opera House's boxes, the fabled Diamond Horseshoe. Yet the obvious solution—not to renew Caruso's contract after the first season—was never seriously considered. For in fact, Caruso's appeal extended not only downward to the immigrant working class but also upward to the most discriminating connoisseurs. My journalistic sample leaves out the lengthy and often rapturous paeans written by even the crustiest critics to the man who soon came to be called "the world's greatest tenor." Enthusiasm for Caruso's singing brought together elite operagoers, whose box at the Met confirmed their high social status, and nonelite Italian American opera lovers, for whom Verdi was an emblem of nationalistic pride. For the elite, whose attitudes found voice in the newspaper critics, Caruso was a paradox. There seemed to be no way to separate the consummate artist from the popular performer of humble Neapolitan origins.

If Caruso paradoxically united and polarized the upper and lower fringes of the Met audience, then what was his effect on the middle—that is, on those who frequented both the opera house and the city's less elevated places of amusement yet saw themselves as socially superior to the working-class Italian immigrants in the cheapest seats? The answer to that question may be found not in the operas they heard at the Met but in the Italian dialect novelty songs they heard in roof gardens and vaudeville houses. Those songs mirror the conflicting attitudes of the middle-class audiences in those venues: on the one hand, a disdain for the Italian immigrants whose presence disrupted the propriety of opera performances, and on the other hand, a recognition that the same immigrants evinced a genuine love for opera, on which they possessed a cultural claim whose authenticity could only be envied by elite Anglo-Americans.

"MY COUSIN CARUSO": AN EMBLEMATIC OPERATIC NOVELTY

Although Caruso's popularity reached great heights already in his first New York season, 1903–4, he did not achieve that era's quintessential marker of public notoriety, caricature in a topical revue, until 1907, the year after the infamous monkey house incident, in which the tenor was arrested for making improper advances to a woman in the monkey house of the Central Park Zoo. Although Caruso was found guilty and levied the minimum fine, ten dollars, improprieties in the handling of the case had generated for Caruso more sympathy than outrage among the public, which eagerly consumed the press's sensationalistic coverage. When the following summer saw the first of Florenz Ziegfeld Jr.'s annual *Follies*, which billed itself as "another one of those things in thirteen acts," one of the thirteen segments portrayed Caruso "tried on stage (by a jury of twelve beauties) for his then famous antics at the Central Park monkey house."[12]

Notably missing in this skit was a song tweaking the tenor. (As we will see in chapter 4, a song did feature in the *Follies'* satire of another bit of operatic news that year — the disastrous New York premiere of Richard Strauss's *Salome*.) That oversight would be corrected in the fall of 1908, when the first and most important song about Caruso made its appearance onstage. "My Cousin Caruso," with music by Gus Edwards and lyrics by Edward Madden, inaugurates the string of novelty songs about Caruso.[13] Although Edwards's publishing company issued the song with a copyright date of 1909—the same date as the autographed self-portrait of Caruso on the cover (fig. 2.1)—the song made its debut in a 1908 musical comedy produced by Ziegfeld, *Miss Innocence*, where it was sung by the comedian Charles Bigelow. Probably because of its success in *Miss Innocence*, Ziegfeld also used the song the next summer in the 1909 *Follies*. (The same edition of the *Follies* also included Edwards's "I'm After Madame Tetrazzini's Job," described in chapter 1, as well as Edwards and Madden's other hit of that year, "By the Light of the Silvery Moon.")

The title alludes to a then-current Italian dialect song, "My Brudda Sylvest,'" whose sheet music cover portrays a stereotypical southern Italian *contadino*, with not only the characteristic earring and long mustache but also the ragged clothing and *paesano's* hat associated today with Chico Marx, the only Italian dialect comic to make the transition into the sound film era and thus the only one familiar to present-day audiences.[14] The song's persona boasts of his brother's prodigious strength with outlandish hyperbole: Sylvest,' who has "Got a chest a measure forty sev'n a feet," is said to "Kill a fifty thousand Indians out west" and "With a one a punch a sink a da ship." Only passing mention is made of his humble trade: he has "a peanut stand on Mulberry Street," the Little Italy address of many Neapolitan immigrants.[15] The song lampoons what has been called "the basic unit of Southern [Italian] cultural life, the family and its honor (*onore della famiglia*)."[16] Although the extended family functioned as a safety net for immigrant relatives, the protective family dynamic also tended to isolate the new arrivals from nonimmigrant society.[17] Non-Italians often viewed these kinship ties in a negative light. Social researchers found intense family loyalty to be an educational barrier for Italian immigrants, who reportedly viewed school as "a direct challenge to family values and parental control"; in the years 1908–10 more than one-third of Italian American schoolchildren in New York City were held back one or more grades, and not until World War I did high school enrollment among Italian American children climb above 1 percent.[18] Thus the song underlines a perceived connection between Italian Americans' family fidelity and willful ignorance.

As in "My Brudda Sylvest,'" the persona in "My Cousin Caruso" brags about a kinsman, though his faulty English inadequately explains the family connection: "His-a mudd' she's my fadder's brud, / Dat-a mak' him ma cousin Carus." Madden's lyrics make topical reference to the unsuccessful attempts of Oscar Hammerstein, the director of the Manhattan Opera

Figure 2.1. "My Cousin Caruso," cover

Company, to woo Caruso away from his competitor, the Metropolitan Opera Company; Hammerstein's offer had been the subject of intense rumors early in 1908.[19] Moreover, Madden uses the conventions of the Italian dialect song to comment not only on Caruso's great popularity but also on the perception that he had introduced a vulgar tone to opera performances in New York. Here again is the hyperbolic boasting: when Caruso "cut loose, / Dat Op'ra House just-a shak-a like-a dis-a like dat."

Though the trope of boasting is borrowed from "My Brudda Sylvest,'" the specific language here evokes another Italian dialect song, the 1907 "Mariutch (Make-a the Hootch-a ma Kootch) Down at Coney Isle," by Harry Von Tilzer and Andrew B. Sterling.[20] "Mariutch Down at Coney

Isle" presents a persona who believes that his sweetheart Mariutch (a corruption of Mariuccia, a southern Italian diminutive of Maria) has taken a steamboat back to Italy.[21] Attending a sideshow at Coney Island, he makes the surprising discovery that she has left him not to return to the home country but to take up a new career as an exotic dancer; now "Mariutch she make-a de hootch a ma kootch down at Coney Isle, / Make me smile, / she go like-a this, like-a that, like-a this."

In "My Cousin Caruso," the opera house reacts to Caruso's singing with the same motions that Mariutch makes when doing an erotic dance; it "shak-a like-a dis-a like dat." Madden thus draws a connection between the indecency of hootchy-kootchy and the supposedly vulgar emotional nakedness of Caruso's onstage deportment—or better, he sees the audience as debased by Caruso's singing just as Mariutch is debased by her seamy profession. The invocation of Coney Island is also significant; middle-class writers at the turn of the century deplored the new amusement parks as escalations of the new mass culture over the earlier genteel tradition. James Gibbons Huneker, an esthete but certainly no prude, denounced Coney Island in 1910 as "a disgrace to our civilisation," noting that "when you are at Coney you cast aside your hampering reason and become a plain lunatic." For Huneker, the human nature revealed at Coney Island was not only unattractive but even dangerous: "After the species of strait-jacket that we wear in every-day life is removed at such Saturnalia as Coney Island, the human animal emerges in a not precisely winning guise.... Once en masse, humanity sheds its civilisation and becomes half child, half savage.... It will lynch an innocent man or glorify a scamp politician with equal facility."[22]

For Huneker and other writers, furthermore, the animalism of the Coney Island crowds was linked to the high proportion of immigrants. Huneker waxed nostalgic for a golden age before New York had become "the dumping-ground of the cosmos." Fearing that "a new population was displacing 'native American stock,'" an article in the *New Republic* complained that "the hair on most heads along Coney Island's beach was black."[23] The cover of "Mariutch Down at Coney Isle" (fig. 2.3) emphasizes the immigrant presence at Coney Island by depicting a stereotypical *campesino*, with earring, bandanna, and long mustache, against a background silhouette of Luna Park.[24] By linking Caruso's immigrant fans in the upper gallery to the coarse crowds at Coney Island, "My Cousin Caruso" suggests the threat of debasement posed to the Metropolitan Opera by an influx of swarthy foreigners.

The music of both "My Brudda Sylvest'" and "Mariutch Down at Coney Isle," like that of many Italian dialect songs, differs little from other Tin Pan Alley genres. Occasionally a song will allude to folk dance rhythms such as the tarantella; more often, the musical allusions are to Italian opera.[25] Such associations, present from the very beginning, take on added significance after the advent of the most famous southern Italian to take up residence in the United States, Enrico Caruso. If Edward Madden's

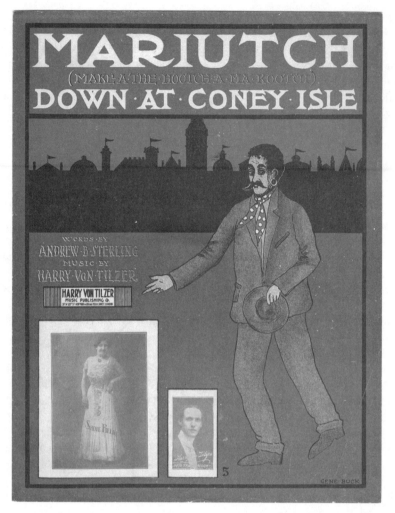

Figure 2.3. "Mariutch (Make-a the Hootch-a ma Kootch) Down at Coney Isle," cover

lyrics capture the tension surrounding Caruso's reception in New York by reaching down to images of Coney Island dancers and the low discourse of Italian dialect comedians, then Gus Edwards's music heightens that tension by reaching both upward and downward. Writing in a ragtime idiom, with its syncopated rhythms, foursquare phrasing, and rigid sectional construction, Edwards manages to work in quotations from two highbrow operatic sources—thus the cover's "apologies to Leoncavallo and Verdi." Without the cover's tip-off, it would be easy to miss the veiled reference to the Anvil Chorus at the opening of the song's chorus (ex. 2.1).[26] The choice of a tune from *Il trovatore* is apt, since Caruso had first sung the role of Manrico earlier that year, on 26 February 1908, at the

Example 2.1. (top) Verdi, *Il trovatore*, Anvil Chorus (transposed); (middle) Edwards and Madden, "My Cousin Caruso," mm. 27–34; (botom) Von Tilzer and Sterling, "Mariutch Down at Coney Isle," mm. 46–48

Metropolitan Opera. Edwards disguises the quotation by beginning with the sixth note of Verdi's melody and reinterpreting it as the fifth scale degree rather than the first; the cadence thus becomes a modulation to the dominant rather than a simple tonic cadence, while the opening bears a resemblance to Bizet's "Toreador Song."[27] Embellished with chromatic neighbors in a ragtime syncopation, the quotation incorporates at its end an inversion of Von Tilzer's melodic setting of Mariutch's swiveling hips—altogether, a simultaneous evocation of high and low musical styles worthy of Charles Ives.[28]

A 1909 phonograph recording of "My Cousin Caruso" by the popular Victor Talking Machine Company artist Billy Murray reveals another Verdi quotation not evident in the sheet music.[29] At measures 9–12 of the chorus (ex. 2.2), the orchestra accompanies the vocal melody with a snippet of Maddelena's opening phrase from the act 3 Quartet in *Rigoletto*, the opera in which Caruso had made his U.S. debut in 1903. The *Rigoletto* Quartet is a favorite operatic excerpt that we have already encountered in "Rosa Rigoletto" and "Night Time in Little Italy"; removed from its original context, in which it acts as a comic rejoinder to the Duke of Manuta's high-flown "Bella figlia d'amore," Maddelena's melody recurs in American popular culture as a comic deflation of operatic pretense in general.[30]

Yet another operatic quotation cites "Vesti la giubba" from Leoncavallo's *Pagliacci*, which Caruso had already recorded three times for Victor's Red Seal label, once in 1904 and twice in 1907.[31] Although three performances of *Pagliacci* had immediately preceded the February 1908 *Trovatore* performances, the reference in "My Cousin Caruso" would no doubt have more strongly reminded the audiences at *Miss Innocence* and the *Follies of 1909* of Caruso's extraordinarily popular recordings.[32] By doing so the song invoked the Victor Company's complex program of positioning recorded music as an emblem of social status, in which highbrow Red Seal records of opera singers sold for as much as five dollars apiece, in contrast to seventy-five cents for lowbrow Black Seal comedy and band records.

Example 2.2. Edwards and Madden, "My Cousin Caruso," mm. 34–36; the upper staff of the accompaniment shows the orchestra obbligato audible on Billy Murray's recording but not notated in the sheet music

Example 2.3. (a) Leoncavallo, *Pagliacci,* "Vesti la giubba," mm. 26–33; (b) Edwards and Madden, "My Cousin Caruso," mm. 39–46

Example 2.3 (*continued*)

The higher price was part of Victor's efforts to reposition as a medium of genteel culture the still-new phonograph, which had quickly become associated with low culture through the placement of coin-operated machines in saloons and other places of mass entertainment such as Coney Island.[33] On phonograph records, even more than in the opera house, Caruso's status as a representative of high art was placed in question.[34]

In both the first and second choruses of "My Cousin Caruso," the *Pagliacci* quotation accompanies lyrical references to the sound of Caruso's voice: "His voice so sad-a / Drive de ladies all mad-a"; "His voice so dream-a / Lak'a peaches and cream-a." The reference to one of Caruso's most popular recorded selections intensifies the evocation of his vocal sound, as opposed to his physical presence onstage. The unusual (for Tin Pan Alley) expression mark *"rit. con espressione"* (*"rit. appassionato"* in the piano)—echoing the original's *"con grande espressione"*—invites the performer to treat the audience to his or her best imitation of Caruso's vocal style (ex. 2.3).[35] After four measures the direction *a tempo* suggests a return to the song's normative popular style, and the return of ragtime syncopation in the penultimate measure distances us still further from the evocation of an operatic aria. As in songs by George M. Cohan and Charles Ives discussed by J. Peter Burkholder, the juxtaposition of older and more contemporary musical styles allows us to hear the latter as if the singer "is speaking in his own voice."[36] Although the song's lower-class Italian immigrant persona boasts about his cousin Caruso, his own musical dialect is that not of the opera house but of the vaudeville stage.

For present-day listeners, sensitized to ethnic humor's potential for cruelty, the inclination is to read "My Cousin Caruso" as hostile to Caruso and the Italian immigrants portrayed stereotypically. Yet the cover art, by Caruso himself, hints that the tenor took no offense at Edwards and Madden's parody. That Edwards and Caruso knew each other and were on good terms is confirmed by an unpublished memoir by Georgie Price, a vaudevillian described as "a kind of combination Eddie Cantor and Al Jolson" who made a number of Victor records and Vitaphone shorts in the 1920s and 1930s.[37] Born in a Yiddish-speaking Lower East Side household, Price was a child singer in barrooms and on streetcars who graduated to winning amateur nights. Price's neighbor Herman Timberg was a performer in *Gus Edwards' School Days*, Edwards's vaudeville act employing child entertainers and capitalizing on his 1907 hit "School Days." At a party for Herman's eighteenth birthday, Price had the opportunity to meet not only celebrities associated with *School Days* but also Enrico Caruso himself:

> Herman took me across the room to meet Gus and Mrs. Edwards, saying, "Mr. Edwards, I want you to hear this little boy sing. I never heard him myself, but Mamma has been raving about him." I stood in the center of the room and without accompaniment I sang. What an audience. What a reception. Caruso said, "The leetla boy is only sixa year olda and evena now, he singsa better as me." I got hugs and kisses from the ladies, and Mr. Edwards sat me on his lap. He asked me how I would like to sing with Mr. Caruso and himself. I said I would and I did. He arranged with Mom for us to come to his apartment for luncheon the next day. He taught me the song "My Cousin Caruso," a comedy number which he had written in tribute to his great friend. Several hours later we were seated in a box at Wallack's Theatre, where a benefit performance was given for [the family of] Detective Petrosini, the chief of the New York squad handling the Mafia and Black Hand gang cases. Petrosini had been killed while performing his dangerous duties, leaving his family in dire circumstances. The house was packed, and the applause was thunderous when Caruso finished. He then introduced Gus Edwards. Gus sang "My Cousin Caruso." The audience howled at the catch lines, and Caruso screamed louder than anyone else at Gus's efforts to satirize him. Then Gus introduced me simply as "Little Georgie." I imitated him giving an imitation of Caruso. After many encores, I pulled my little mother-and-the-flag recitation and Caruso carried me off the stage on his shoulder.[38]

Price's memoir documents a friendship between Edwards and Caruso that has otherwise gone unrecorded.

An even greater sign that Caruso took no offense at "My Cousin Caruso" is his 1918 silent film *My Cousin*, produced by Jesse Lasky's Famous Players Company—the same Jesse Lasky who wrote the words to "My Brudda Sylvest.'" The short film, loosely based on "My Cousin Caruso," casts the tenor as an impoverished artist in Little Italy whose romantic fortunes depend on proving that he is indeed the cousin of the great opera star Caroli, also played by Caruso. Moviegoers apparently had little interest in seeing but not hearing Caruso, and the film was such a failure that a second film, shot at the same time as *My Cousin*, was never released in the United States.[39]

Both *My Cousin* and Price's recollection lead us to read "My Cousin Caruso" as poking only the gentlest fun at the singer. If the song was intended as biting satire, then the target lay elsewhere. For those persons among the middle-class audiences at *Miss Innocence* and the *Follies of 1909* who also attended Met performances, the song would bring to mind both the demonstrative Italian Americans in the cheapest seats and, indirectly, the disapproving "cooler portions" in the Diamond Horseshoe, who found those demonstrations so distasteful. By indirect means, then, "My Cousin Caruso" superficially satirizes lower-class Italian Americans while on a deeper level satirizing the upper-class snobs who resented their undermining of the project of sacralizing opera. This preoccupation with class and ethnicity remains a feature of almost all the subsequent songs about Caruso.

CARUSO IN LATER NOVELTIES

The success of "My Cousin Caruso" inspired Edwards and Madden to create a number of similar operatic novelties, among them another Italian dialect song focusing on Caruso, "Mister Pagliatch" (1912).[40] The persona is an operagoer seated "in de top-a gal'ry" whose response to Caruso's performance as Canio is openly demonstrative. The first verse ends by setting up the chorus, in which the persona can address Caruso directly:

> And when his voice come up to-a me
> I weep, so deep, you would take-a da swim
> That's when I yell-a to him,

The chorus melody incorporates the opening of "Vesti la giubba," not the climactic "Ridi, pagliaccio" phrase, which turns up in so many other songs. By interspersing eighth-note patter between each phrase, the melody takes on the character of a dialogue; it is as if Caruso and the spectator are singing to each other (ex. 2.4).

As in "My Cousin Caruso," the target of the satire is ostensibly the loud Italian Americans in the upper balcony of the Met. At the same time, though, the song celebrates that audience's genuinely heartfelt response to opera and indirectly criticizes those who are incapable of being deeply moved. Like many Tin Pan Alley songs of this period, "Mister Pagliatch" is an expression of immigrant culture; Edwards had arrived in the United States from Germany with his family at an early age, and many other songwriters were immigrants or children of immigrants. And like much ethnic humor in the hands of ethnic minorities, this song subverts stereotypes devised to assert a dominant social group's sense of superiority, redirecting the satirical barbs toward the mocking upper classes. The song's persona, like an Italian Mr. Dooley, can exploit his own outsider, greenhorn status to deflate the pretensions of the mighty.[41]

Unlike "My Cousin Caruso," "Mister Pagliatch" takes a few swipes at Caruso's unimpressive appearance and notorious appetite for food, drink, and tobacco, once again invoking the lowbrow image of hootchy-kootchy dancing in "Mariutch Down at Coney Isle":

> Pagliatch, he's short and the fat
> And when he walk, he shake like dis a-like dat.
> …
> He train voice on chiante, spaghett,
> He smoke-a forty cigarette.

But those shortcoming are outweighed by his musical abilities:

> He look a-like one great big clown.
> But when he sing he knock you down.
> …
> Can't stop dis wop, he sing-a better each night.

Example 2.4. (a) Leoncavallo, *Pagliacci,* "Vesti la giubba," mm. 1–4; (b) Edwards, "Mister Pagliatch," mm. 26–33

Example 2.4 (*continued*)

(b)

For elite critics who compared Caruso unfavorably with memories of the aristocratic tenor Jean de Reske, the most forceful rejoinder is a reference to the singing itself.

A distinctly more hostile tone toward Caruso is evident in Al Piantadosi and Billy Dunham's "Good-bye Mister Caruso" (1909; fig. 2.4).[42] Here an Italian American barber (another stereotypical occupation) is upset over reports that Caruso can no longer sing:

My head is goin' dip,
I think I got the pip,
Since I read about Caruso:
Ev'rything I was a-stop
no more work the barber shop,
When I hear his voice he los-a.

In fact Caruso had canceled several performances in the 1908–9 season, which had followed a difficult summer in which the press had gleefully reported his traumatic abandonment by his longtime mistress, Ada Giachetti. The *New York Telegraph* summarized the rumors that

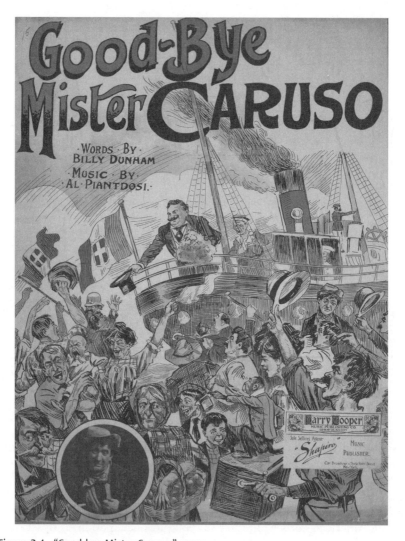

Figure 2.4. "Good-bye Mister Caruso," cover

had surrounded the tenor that year: "that Caruso was suffering from a most grievous infection of the throat, that his voice had gone, that his career was finished, that the earthquake in San Francisco, the famous court trial in which he was engaged three seasons ago, his losses of money in the panic of 1907, and his recent domestic troubles had dealt a series of blows." Most stunning was the *Times'* announcement in mid-April that Caruso would cut short his season and depart immediately for Milan, where in May he would undergo an operation for the removal of a vocal node.[43]

In response to these developments, Piantadosi and Dunham's barber advances his own explanation, which contains a verbal (but no musical) reference to the sobs and laughs in Caruso's renditions of "Vesti la giubba":

> He sing to[o] much-a song,
> 'Till something it go wrong,
> But he was-a only laugh-a,
> He love-a his own voice
> and he make to[o] much-a noise,
> In the big-a Phona-ma-graph-a.

The implication is that Caruso's greed—his notoriously large fees for performing and recording—has led to his undoing. The beneficiary of his misfortune is the Manhattan Opera Company, though the barber has little use for Florencio Constantino, the Spanish tenor who had debuted that season with Hammerstein's company, declaring that "Spanish op'ra good for nothing." In the meantime, Caruso's indulgence in tobacco and women has brought him down to the level of the common Italian immigrant:

> No more he sing in Opera grand,
> He's gone-a back to Italy to peddle banan
> He was one big-a chump
> Smoke-a cigarette and make-a fool with the monk.

The "monk" not only raises the specter of the monkey house incident but also associates Caruso with a stereotype of Italian dialect songs, the organ grinder with his monkey. With its less-than-genial tone, "Good-bye Mister Caruso" suggests that the singer's bad publicity was affecting at least some of his audience.

A comparison of the tenor with a fictional singer is the conceit of "My Irish Caruso," also from 1909.[44] Such a comparison is rarely found in songs about male singers, although it is common in songs about female singers, such as "Rosa Rigoletto"; the next chapter will suggest why. Here the Irishman James Caruso Murphy changes "the good old Murphy name for one with foreign frills" and eschews the familiar Irish ballads for "some Grand Op'ra tune…with all the shakes and trills." Despite the resemblance, this fictional tenor is probably not meant to represent John

McCormack, who was little known in the United States before his November 1909 debut with the Manhattan Opera Company; not until the next year would he begin the series of Victor recordings that would make him a household name. Although it is not impossible that "My Irish Caruso" came out at the very end of 1909 and was an extremely quick response to McCormack's U.S. debut, it is more likely an attempt to graft the name of the popular Italian tenor to a venerable vaudeville standby, the Irish character song.

Caruso Murphy's sweetheart considers him to be both a source of nationalistic pride—"He is my Irish Caruso / He is the finest ever seen"— and an emblem of ethnic shame—"Sure he could make old Ireland happy, / If he'd sing the wearin' of the green." The chorus then departs from the opening cakewalk rhythm to quote "Anges pur" from Gounod's *Faust*: "But he is always singing this song, and tho' it sounds real good to me"; then, to a new melody: "If he would only sing the Tanyard side, how happy I would be" (ex. 2.5).

The new melody, though it does not coincide with any tune I can locate, fits the closing words of the traditional Irish song "Down by the Tanyard Side," an apt choice here, since that song is sung by a "wandering hero" (corresponding to the socially mobile Caruso Murphy) who travels

Example 2.5. Allen, "My Irish Caruso," chorus

across the ocean but promises to remain true until he comes home to his sweetheart, "And I will roll her in my arms again / Down by the Tanyard side." Less happy is the quotation from *Faust*. Although Caruso sang this opera at the Met from 1906 to 1910, he was never considered well suited to the role; even worse, the number that the Irish Caruso is always singing is for Marguerite, not Faust. The writer of "My Irish Caruso" displays a better knowledge of Irish music than of opera.

Caruso's popularity is not the direct topic of this song; rather, the mere presence of his name testifies to his celebrity status, no less than the "name-checking" of rap stars in hip-hop. After a flurry of name-checking in the years 1908–13, Caruso is absent from popular songs until the final year of his life, when two last songs put the singer back in the spotlight.[45]

THE LAST TWO CARUSO SONGS

Although Caruso continued to be an enormously popular performer throughout the second decade of the century, none of his performances in those years could be considered truly newsworthy until, at the end of his career, he took on a new role, that of Eléazar in Halevy's *La Juive*. Caruso's first performance in that role, on 22 November 1919, was in Irving Kolodin's words not only "the artistic event of the year" but also "without doubt the most striking artistic triumph of his career."[46]

One sign of the public's renewed interest in Caruso at this time is the appearance, for the first time since 1912's "Mister Pagliatch," of a popular song that takes the singer as its primary topic. Unlike its predecessors, however, Abner Silver's "When Caruso Comes to Town" (1920) does not use Italian dialect.[47] Indeed, it takes as its model not the earlier Caruso songs but one that references Irish songs, the 1915 "When John McCormack Sings a Song," a vehicle for Nora Bayes.[48] That song depicts Caruso's younger contemporary entirely in his role as a singer of Irish ballads, not as an opera singer; McCormack seems to have been widely regarded in those years as a singer of popular (i.e., Irish) songs who occasionally appeared in opera, whereas Caruso was considered the opposite. The song allowed Bayes, née Goldberg, to bring out the Irish in her listeners by incorporating snippets of McCormack's Irish repertoire, culminating with the couplet "Sure you get a glimpse of heaven where all Irish hearts belong, / When John McCormack sings a song."

The verse of "When Caruso Comes to Town" is a catalog of ethnic types that begins with the Irish and ends with the Italians (the tune begins with an echo of "The Wearing of the Green"):

> Sure the Irish like McCormack when he sings an Irish song
> They cheer and they applaud him quite a lot.
> The Americans all praise the voice of Nora Bayes
> And the Hebrews think there's none like Rosenblatt[49]

> The Italians have their one and only one
> When he sings a song their joy is first begun.

Here "Americans" implies Anglo-Americans, an indication that Bayes's Jewish identity was not a prominent part of her public persona.[50] The use of the term also indicates that the song views Caruso and his fans from a normative "American" perspective. Indeed, the emphasis in the chorus is not on Caruso but on his Italian American audience:

> When Caruso sings a song,
> All the bootblacks hum along,
> Once again they seem to be in Napoli
> All the ice cream parlors close,
> [E]ach banana peddler goes
> To buy a ticket in the gallery.
> All the street cleaners are gay
> It's their legal holiday
> The opera house is packed for blocks around.

Then, to the requisite musical quotation of the climactic "Ridi, pagliaccio" melody from "Vesti la giubba":

> And ev'ry Broadway Blazer[51]
> [H]as to use his safety razor,
> For it's hard to find a barber when Caruso comes to town.

Like the nineteenth-century critics described in the introduction who strove to differentiate between opera as an art form and opera as a social practice of the wealthy, this song's persona, evidently no opera lover, does not associate an operatic performance with the sacralizing upper classes. Instead, he associates it with working-class Italian immigrants. From this point of view, the day of a Caruso performance promises only the inconvenience of being without the services provided by Italian American tradesmen.

A young man at the time he wrote this song, Abner Silver (1899–1966) displays only the most rudimentary knowledge of opera and no particular sympathy for it. The *Pagliacci* quotation is the most obvious choice conceivable; otherwise, the only nod to operatic style is the use of *Luftpausen* to indicate Caruso's characteristic rubato. Ironically, operatic quotation occurs again in one of Silver's last songs, "Tonight Is So Right for Love," a number based on the Barcarolle from Offenbach's *Tales of Hoffmann* and sung by Elvis Presley in the movie *G.I. Blues* (1960).

"When Caruso Comes to Town" made a belated appearance onstage in *The Passing Show of 1921*, where it was sung by the Howard Brothers. This comedy team—Willie Howard was a leading "Hebrew comedian," Eugene the straight man—made something of a specialty of opera parodies; in 1917's *Show of Wonders* they spoofed Puccini with "My Yiddisha Butterfly" and in the 1918 edition of the *Passing Show* they sang "The Galli-Curci Rag" and performed their travesty of *Rigoletto*.[52] After skipping the 1920 edition of their long-running annual summer revue, the producers Lee and J. J. Shubert brought out the 1921 edition on the unlikely date of 29 December, a sign, as Gerald Bordman notes, that "all was not what it once had been for the big annuals."[53] Owing to the delay, perhaps, the song had already lost some of the topicality it might have had at the end of the 1919–20 season. Instead, its premiere in the *Passing Show* came five days after Caruso's last performance.

At the opening of the 1920–21 season, Caruso was a sick man. Exhausted from a barnstorming tour of eleven cities in September and October, he sang well enough when he opened the Met season on 14 November with *La Juive* but was in noticeably poor form three nights later for Donizetti's *L'elisir d'amore*. December began ominously when, suffering from pains in his side, he blacked out during a performance of *Pagliacci*; despite the continuing pain, and against his doctor's advice, he sang all his scheduled performances in December, culminating in his final performance, a torturous 24 December *La Juive*. On Christmas Day he was diagnosed with pleurisy; on 2 August 1921, after several surgical interventions, Caruso died.

Before the year was out, a tribute song appeared, Jack Stanley and George A. Little's "They Needed a Song Bird in Heaven (So God Took Caruso Away)."[54] Based on an "idea suggested by Geo. Walter Brown" and "respectfully dedicated to the memory of our beloved Caruso," the song is a lugubrious *valse lente* that would have seemed old-fashioned a decade earlier, with maudlin lyrics along the lines of "Gone is a flower that we learned to love, / To bloom for the Master and Maker above!" Issued with a sober monochromatic cover featuring a photo of Caruso in formal pose, this negligible song is of interest only for the complete absence of the Italian American stereotypes endemic in the comic Caruso novelties. Granted, such stereotypes would be inappropriate in a posthumous tribute; that such a tribute was written and published indicates that by the end of Caruso's life at least some of the class conflict for which he had acted as a flash point had dissipated. With the institution of more stringent immigration laws, the number of arrivals from southern Italy decreased dramatically, and with them the popularity of Italian dialect songs. Moreover, after seventeen Met seasons, the Caruso phenomenon had established a new norm for opera in New York. No longer was the loud acclaim of the upper balconies the source of controversy it had been in 1903. A new generation of operagoers had grown up with Caruso and his cousins.

NOVELTIES ABOUT TETRAZZINI

Should there be any doubt that popular songwriters equated operatic stardom with Italian ethnicity, one need only look beyond the Caruso novelties to songs about other opera singers. The tremendously popular sopranos Mary Garden and Geraldine Farrar turn up on occasion as passing references but never as title subjects. To my knowledge, only three sopranos rated popular songs that put their names in the title, and all three are Italian: Adelina Patti, with a single song; Amelita Galli-Curci, with two; and by far the most significant, Luisa Tetrazzini, with at least six songs naming her in the title and countless others that reference her in passing.[55] Like the Caruso songs, the Tetrazzini novelties illustrate the close connection for the American public between Italian culture in general (including its lower-class aspects) and opera in particular.

On 15 January 1908, the same year in which "My Cousin Caruso" set off the string of Caruso songs, Luisa Tetrazzini made her U.S. debut with Hammerstein's Manhattan Opera Company, causing a delirium among New York operagoers. Before the year was out she figured in the titles of two popular songs. The first, "When Tetrazzini Sings," was featured in *The Mimic World*, a revue that opened at the Casino on 9 July and starred George M. Cohan; despite its title, however, Tetrazzini plays a small role in this song about a fictional singer. The second, "The Tetrazzini Family," is listed in the playbill for *The Boys and Betty*, a musical comedy vehicle for Marie Cahill that opened at Wallack's Theatre on 2 November, but does not appear to survive in sheet music form. Only in 1909 do we find a song that gives Tetrazzini her due, "My Sist' Tetrazin,'" in which songs about Tetrazzini and songs about Caruso intersect.

"My Sist' Tetrazin'" is billed on the sheet music cover as "another grand-opera-popular song by the author of 'My Cousin Caruso.'"[56] Here, though, the lyricist Edward Madden has teamed up not with Gus Edwards but with a different composer, Anatol Friedland. The more malicious tone of the first verse suggests that Edwards's friendship with Caruso may have accounted for the earlier song's gentler spoofing. Here the satire is closer to that of "Good-bye Mister Caruso":

> What's de matta with that great big fatta fellow
> Mista Enrico Caruso,
> Gone-a craze with all the ladies praise,
> He sing so much his voice he goin-a lose oh!

The song's Italian American persona, upholding *onore dell' famiglia*, recommends a family member as a replacement for the prematurely washed-up tenor. Caruso

> Won't be missed a when they hear my Sist
> She got a voice that tickle Hammerstein,
> Sing from Verdi, lak a littly [*sic*] birdie,
> That's my sist, Miss Tetrazin![57]

For the chorus, in the mode of hyperbolic boasting familiar from "My Brudda Sylvest'" and its descendants, Friedland travesties the Intermezzo from *Cavalleria rusticana*, an act of thievery that the sheet music cover ameliorates by giving "due credit to Mascagni." When Tetrazzini sings

Mascagni's opera, the chorus asserts, "all the crazy 'wop' holler 'Don't let her stop'" (ex. 2.6).

The only problem with this scenario is that Tetrazzini never sang *Cavalleria rusticana* onstage or for recordings—apart from a single *Pagliacci* and a handful of *Bohèmes,* all sung before she came to the United

Example 2.6. Friedland and Madden, "My Sist' Tetrazin,'" chorus, mm. 1–8 (voice only)

States, Tetrazzini stayed away from the verismo repertory.[58] The mismatch between subject and musical quotation may simply reveal Friedland's ignorance of the operatic world; of his many songs, this is the only one to touch on an operatic subject, and his choice for quotation, as we have already seen, was a tremendously popular melody. Or are we to attribute the ignorance to the song's persona? Verse 2 refers to *La traviata*, in which Tetrazzini had made her spectacular U.S. debut and which she performed again during the 1908–9 season in New York, Baltimore, and Boston; but the reference is vague, alluding to a time when Tetrazzini "had to sing that ver-a sadda thing, that make you cry from Traviata." The specifics seem not to have made much of an impression on the great singer's sibling.

"My Cousin Caruso" makes multiple quotations from operas that Caruso had sung at the Met in the preceding year—*Pagliacci, Rigoletto, Il trovatore*, and *Carmen*. "My Sist' Tetrazin'" makes a single extended quotation that is irrelevant to its subject. While this probably indicates the contrast in ability or knowledgeability between Gus Edwards and Anatol Friedland, it may also reflect a difference between the performance venues for the two songs. On the one hand, "My Cousin Caruso" was part of two Ziegfeld productions, a musical comedy and a topical revue. Ziegfeld was noted for the elegance of his productions, and in the early years the *Follies* attracted the smart set as much with their up-to-date topical satire as with their much-touted chorus girls. On the other hand, "My Sist' Tetrazin'" was interpolated into *The Midnight Sons*, a Lew Fields production in a genre that his biographer Jason Rubin has called "vaudeville-musicals."[59] Though equipped with a slender book, *The Midnight Sons* was basically a vehicle that allowed favorite vaudeville performers to do familiar turns, and these changed frequently during the show's run. Audiences came for the performers and little else. Rubin notes that "most of the critics praised the performances, although they bemoaned the lack of plot, wit and humor," and he quotes the theater historian Richard Kislan: "No art here, just commerce."[60] Perhaps the subtle references in "My Cousin Caruso," so pleasing to Ziegfeld's more sophisticated audience, would have been wasted on Fields's less discriminating crowd, for whom the generalized allusions of "My Sist' Tetrazin'" would suffice.

The song's third verse, though, is surprising in this context. It uses a class argument to criticize Tetrazzini and Caruso for making records:

> Phonograph he's goin-a kill the graft,
> she sing-a song in one, what mak her do so?
> Save expensa, now for five-a centsa,
> hear Miss Tetrazin' and fat Caruso,
> What's da use they kill the golden goose
> Caruso betta marry Tetrazin'
> Bimeby maybe there's a littly baby,
> They can call him Caruzine.

The argument appears to be that records cheapen opera by making it available to those who cannot afford to attend full performances. Moreover, records relocate the sound of opera from the opera house to the nickelodeon, part of the lowest class of public amusements. (The verse does not refer to the home phonograph; a nickel would not buy a record but simply allow one to hear it once on a coin-operated machine.) This "sacralizing" third verse gives voice not to the lower-class Italian immigrants that the dialect implies but to the upper-class operagoers who objected to sharing opera with those immigrants.

Class consciousness also pervades a song in which Tetrazzini plays a secondary role, Irving Berlin's "Yiddisha Nightingale" (1911), whose title riffs on Tetrazzini's nickname, "the Florentine Nightingale." Once again, a fictional singer is compared to an actual opera star, though Berlin's music undermines his lyrics' comparison by setting the diva's name to a minor-key melody with a prominent "Jewish-sounding" augmented second, implying that Minnie sounds more Jewish than Italian (ex. 2.7).[61]

Example 2.7. Berlin, "Yiddisha Nightingale," mm. 7–14 (voice only)

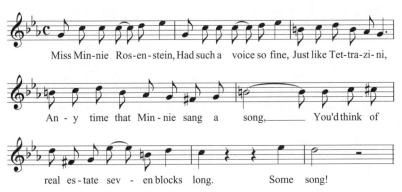

Miss Min-nie Ros-en-stein, Had such a voice so fine, Just like Tet-tra-zi-ni,

An-y time that Min-nie sang a song,____ You'd think of

real es-tate sev-en blocks long.   Some song!

Minnie's beau, Abie Cohn, is more concerned with status than with art, as becomes clear in the second verse, when he makes a prediction about the role of music in their married life:

> I'll go and learn to play on the piano, say,
> you'll sing while I'm playing,
> People will be saying,
> As they pass,
> And they look in through the windowpane glass,
> Some class!

The mercantile trope common to Jewish novelty songs is extended in the chorus when Abie tells Minnie:

> I'd give a dollar to hear you, my queen,
> I wouldn't give a nickle [*sic*] to hear Tettrazini.[62]

Unlike his fellow immigrants from Italy, Abie Cohn evinces little pleasure in music for its own sake. Constrained by the narrowness of ethnic
stereotype, he can judge Minnie's singing only as a commodity and is deaf
to its intrinsic value. Ironically, in this respect he has more in common
with many of the patrons in the Metropolitan Opera House's Diamond
Horseshoe than with the working-class opera lovers in the upper balcony;
like the frivolous rich decried by the previous century's Arnoldian critics,
he values music only for the social status it endows. Yet he lacks the necessary wealth to purchase an opera box and thus lay claim to a higher social
ranking. Beyond his means, Tetrazzini does not offer the same potential to
enhance his social standing that Minnie does; his Yiddisha nightingale is
indeed worth a dollar to the Florentine Nightingale's nickel.

As in "Yiddisha Nightingale," Tetrazzini's nickname inspires avian comparisons in Berlin's "Ragtime Mocking Bird" (1912), in which the bird of
the title is called a "feathered Tetrazzin," and a decade later, in George
Gershwin and Irving Caesar's "Nashville Nightingale," whose title refers
not to a bird but to "a sweet singing lady down in Tennessee" who is a
"Darktown Tetrazzini."[63] As these songs indicate, the use of Tetrazzini as
an emblem of a great singer was not restricted to Italian dialect songs but
extended to songs with Jewish and African American characters as well.
That her name should be so frequently used, while that of such a celebrated opera singer as Geraldine Farrar should not, points to the close
connection for most Americans at this time between opera and Italian
ethnicity. At the same time, these songs, like "Rosa Rigoletto" and "I'm
After Madame Tetrazzini's Job," raise questions about the depiction of
women in popular songs of the ragtime era. The next chapters explore
how popular songs could use operatic culture, with its adoration of the
diva, to probe anxieties over the changing status of women at the beginning of the twentieth century.

Part II

SALOME AND HER SISTERS

Chapter 3

Scheming Young Ladies

"As late as the 1920's," wrote Jacques Barzun in his midcentury *Music in American Life*, "untutored popular sentiment regarded the playing of music as the occupation of wretched professionals and scheming young ladies."[1] True, many professional musicians at that time were underpaid and underappreciated, and thus "wretched." But why musical "young ladies" should be characterized as "scheming" is a topic worth investigating. A perusal of ragtime-era novelty songs about female singers confirms Barzun's recollection of "untutored popular sentiment"; moreover, analysis of those songs provides some clues as to why such a negative stereotype was both widespread and long-lived.

Because the ragtime era coincided with the peak of the women's suffrage movement, which culminated in the passage in 1920 of the Nineteenth Amendment, it is easy to attribute the popularity of songs that ridicule female singers to antisuffragist backlash. A characteristic frequently lampooned in these songs is the ambition women display in their quest to become professional singers. The freedom to pursue a career in music, with its promise of financial and artistic independence at its apex, came at a high social cost. It is the unseemliness of their ambition that makes these presuffrage women appear "scheming."[2]

Yet the ridicule of women singers, and especially sopranos, certainly did not end with the suffrage movement; indeed, it is still with us. Among the singer jokes currently accessible from the American Musicological Society's website, jokes about sopranos outnumber those about altos, tenors, and basses combined.[3] Why are sopranos more often the targets of humor than other singers? Perhaps the humor is related to questions of power—sopranos have always been the primary object of diva worship, and their power over audiences may ignite resentment among those who cannot wield it. Thus the popularity of soprano jokes among musicians.

Moreover, the soprano voice itself may be an object of psychological discomfort that male listeners might want to defuse with humor. Several critics in recent years have articulated psychological interpretations of the experience of listening to opera. Drawing on the perspectives of Jacques Lacan, Michel Poizat has advanced a view of opera that privileges musical sound over verbal meaning, in which the voice of the diva inspires in the (male) listener a *jouissance* "in which the listener himself is stripped of all possibility of speech."[4] That *jouissance* is dramatized in film operettas in which Jeanette MacDonald's displays of vocal prowess reduce Nelson Eddy to a state of passive receptivity.[5] Lawrence Kramer reads a similar infantilized response to the soprano voice in Walt Whitman's poetic descriptions of opera. For example, in *Song of Myself* the "train'd soprano" leaves the poet "steep'd amid honey'd morphine, my windpipe throttled in fakes of death," a line that for Kramer

> suggests the satiation of the infant "steeped" in the mother's breast that soothes away all bitter and angry wounds.... But music as honey'd (mellifluous?) heal-all is also music as sweetened poison. It must register as poisonous because by reducing Whitman to a helpless, preverbal state, it doubly suspends his subjectivity. It gags him both as a speaking subject and as a poetic voice.[6]

For Whitman, this artistic evocation of the preoedipal state is simultaneously alluring and discomfiting, a source of both pleasure and pain. That paradoxical blend of attraction and repulsion may have something to do with opera itself, which Carolyn Abbate describes as "a genre that so displaces the authorial musical voice onto female characters and female singers that it largely reverses the conventional opposition of male (speaking) subject and female (observed) subject."[7] When the soprano can render the words she sings semiotically powerless, engulfed in sheer sound, logocentric male listeners may find the experience of listening to be both exhilarating and profoundly disturbing.

Whether these Lacanian approaches to interpretation accurately describe what happens when most men hear opera is open to question. Pleasure in hearing a beautiful voice can indeed be mixed with annoyance that the words are hard to understand—an inevitable distortion of vowel formants when sung on high pitches. And when those distorted vowels are sung by a less-than-beautiful voice, annoyance rises, and there is no need to look back to early childhood to explain why. Male discomfort in the soprano voice may have several causes, the arousing of preoedipal feelings being only one possibility. As for the songs examined in this chapter, a likely reason for that discomfort is resentment of the professional singer's financial independence, which presents a threat to patriarchal norms. Yet another is an association of female display with less reputable entertainments such as the burlesque or hootchy-kootchy show—self-display, even on the operatic stage, some songs imply, is intrinsically indecent.

Because so many of these songs focus on "unfeminine" ambition, aspiring singers, including voice students, feature prominently among the protagonists. This chapter considers in turn portraits of voice students, amateur singers, and professional singers, tracking the increasingly negative portrayals of women's aspirations, and concludes by comparing these songs with a few novelties about male singers. In all of these songs, operatic references ground these satirical portraits in a shared musical culture.

STUDENT SINGERS

Songs that characterize a student singer as young, immature, and naïve invite the listener to patronize someone in an inferior position. Sometimes the presence of a predatory teacher highlights the student's vulnerability. In the first verse of Sam M. Lewis's lyrics for "My Music Teacher" (1912), for instance, the persona attempts to assure her jealous boyfriend that her music lessons are entirely proper:

> Maybe some one told you some one's calling on me,
> Maybe you are wond'ring who that some one can be,
> I won't cry to you,
> I won't lie to you,
> I'll just tell you what's true.[8]

In the chorus, her worshipful description of her teacher is not likely to set her young man's mind at ease:

> He is my music teacher, he's such a lovin' creature,
> I get an hour ev'ry day,
> My heart is fairly bumpin' because I'm learning somethin,'
> It's such a blessin,' to get a private lesson
> His touch is so magnetic, his ways are so pathetic,
> I'm pickin' things up mighty fine.

The implication that the teacher is taking liberties with his impressionable student—her bumping heart and his magnetic touch should send up a red flag—becomes stronger in the second verse. The teacher insists there be no interruptions during the lessons:

> Ev'ry time I make mistakes he squeezes my arm,
> Ev'ry squeeze he gives me seems to have such a charm.

Near the end of the chorus, the teacher's seduction is camouflaged as a promise of operatic initiation (ex. 3.1). George Meyer's musical setting encourages us to read the reference to *Il trovatore* as an erotic symbol. The syncopated rhythm of the words "show me how, show me how" suggests a quickening of breath, just as the word repetition suggests rising excitement.[9] Then the word "Trovatore" is harmonized with a major triad on B natural, a chord distant from the tonic E-flat. Rather than quote any specific music from Verdi's opera, Meyer makes a generic operatic-sounding gesture, the movement to the lowered submediant (here written enharmonically). Susan McClary, writing about Donizetti, characterizes this harmonic motion as "a sudden, dramatic shift into what is perceived as an alien region: a realm of fantasy, illusion, nostalgia, unreason, or the sublime, depending on semiotic context."[10] To McClary's list of alien regions may be added erotic initiation.

This song, then, is an enactment of taboo behavior between teacher and student. The listener, however, is not encouraged to join in the boyfriend's jealous anger. Instead, the persona's coquettish language ("baby, dear, /

Example 3.1. Meyer and Lewis, "My Music Teacher," mm. 34–44

Example 3.1 (*continued*)

learn-ing more, learn-ing more, From that mus-ic teach-er of   mine._____

Come over here"), coupled with saucy ragtime syncopations, focuses our gaze through the eyes of the music teacher, who no doubt rationalizes his advances toward his student by reading her language as encouragement. Written by men for an implied male audience, the song ventriloquizes a male fantasy of the compliant victim of seduction.

At what sort of music lesson does this seduction take place? The song lyrics and the cover illustration (fig. 3.1) give two different answers. The lyrics clearly describe a piano lesson. The student hopes to learn to "*play the music from Il Trovatore*"—a reference to the operatic medleys arranged for piano that were a mainstay of nineteenth-century amateur pianism and were still being published early in the next century.[11] Similarly, a decade before "My Music Teacher," another comic song had featured a female pianist playing *Il trovatore* under the influence of an older male musician:

> Since Sister Nell heard Paderewski play
> She's at the grand piano night and day
> And when she plays Il Trovatore
> The people on the second floor
> Get down upon their knees and pray and pray.[12]

Moreover, the teacher's habit of squeezing his pupil's arm suggests a piano teacher's corrective gestures. Yet the cover illustration, a tinted photograph, shows a young woman *singing* to the accompaniment of an older longhaired musician. He is turned about forty-five degrees away from the keyboard, as if ready to pounce upon the young woman, who is dressed in what appears to be southern European peasant costume. The illustrator's mistake, if it is a mistake, raises the possibility that the song's scenario, with its naïve student and lecherous or otherwise dishonest teacher, was associated in the popular mind with singing lessons.[13]

Pecuniary motives underlie a voice teacher's false praise in Irving Berlin's "Tra-La, La, La!" (1913).[14] Told by her teacher that her voice is

Figure 3.1. "My Music Teacher" (cover)

"very canary," Mabel Beecher (her name labels her as a "normal" American, i.e., an Anglo-American) "scrapes the money somehow" for two singing lessons a week.[15] Other auditors, however, do not agree with her teacher's assessment of her vocal ability. When "all day long she's singing 'Tra, la, la, la!'" to a tune derived from the Barcarolle in Offenbach's *Tales of Hoffman* (ex. 3.2), "ev'rybody hollers, 'Tie a can-o to her Soprano!'"[16]

On a 1913 Edison cylinder, Billy Murray departs from the sheet music in subtle ways that bring out the song's humor.[17] He delivers the verses in a *parlando* style that gives primacy to storytelling over singing. Then, at the chorus, although no tempo change is indicated in the score, he slows down into a broad *moderato* that, with an accompanimental cello doubling

Example 3.2. Berlin, "Tra-La, La, La!" chorus, mm. 1–16

the vocal line in thirds, emphasizes the *cantabile* quality of the Offenbach allusion. Two measures later, Murray sings Mabel Beecher's "Tra, la, la la!"—the song depicts her as singing nothing but this phrase—in a cracked, out-of-tune voice. By slowing the tempo and adding the cello, with its high-class connotations, the recorded performance heightens the comic contrast between Mabel Beecher's artistic aspirations and her vocal incompetence.

The lyrics suggest that the negative reaction to Mabel's voice is shared by men and women:

> All her aunts and uncles
> When they heard her,
> Holler'd "Murder!"

The cover illustration, however, masculinizes the response, contrasting the singing woman with a man covering his ears in exasperation (fig. 3.2). Mabel Beecher's mouth is a grotesque black hole, transforming her face into a Gorgon's mask, whose "monstrously maternal throat/vagina" represents the Gorgon's terrifying cry.[18] And just as Athena, in Pindar's Twelfth *Pythian Ode*, transforms the Gorgon's primal lament into the civilized music of the flute, so too must the popular song use ridicule to rob the soprano voice of its sheer sonic power.

The song's title divorces the sound of Mabel's voice from any verbal meaning embedded in her song. The distinction is one that Roland Barthes, modifying the terminology of Julia Kristeva, makes between pheno-song and geno-song, which Leslie Dunn and Nancy Jones define as the song's "verbal or cultural content" and "the purely sonorous, bodily element of the vocal utterance," respectively.[19] Geno-song—the sheer sound of the voice—triggers in some male listeners the infantile regression that Kramer finds in Whitman's poem. Here, vocables—to use the ethnomusicologist's term for nonsemantic syllables such as *tra la la*—indicate that the soprano's usurpation of textual meaning is a source of discomfort that must be dispelled through humor.

Likewise, the flirtatious persona of "The Soubrette's Secret," a number from the 1909 comedy *The Midnight Sons*, dismisses the wise sayings of Shakespeare and Emerson, "Greek and Latin sages," Mark Twain and Mister Dooley, even the Rosicrucian writers Elbert Hubbard and Ella Wheeler Wilcox. In their place she offers to an attentive male chorus her own simpleminded philosophy:

> Tra la, la, la, la, la, la, la, la, la, la,
> This motto daily
> I warble gaily.
> Tra, la la la
> You'll find Tra la, la la
> The best prescription
> For ev'ry trouble
> Tra la la la la.

Figure 3.2. "Tra-La, La, La!" (cover)

The seductive soubrette erases from men's minds the words of great think-
ers and replaces them with empty vocables. As Bram Dijkstra writes of the
mythological sirens portrayed in nineteenth-century paintings, she
"personifie[s] the regressive, bestial element in woman's nature."[20]
"Midnight sons," the cigar-smoking bon vivants depicted on the sheet music
cover in evening dress, pay heed to her siren song at their own risk.[21]

Vocables also occur in Harry Von Tilzer and Jack Mahoney's "When
Priscilla Tries to Reach High C" (1916).[22] Here the singer Priscilla Lee—
again, her name labels her an Anglo-American—studies with Professor
Beany, who mixes praise and ridicule: "Her teacher said 'I think your
throat is full of music, but, / 'Twould be much better if you had it cut.'"

Undeterred, Priscilla is "rehearsing for the stage"; unlike Mabel Beecher, she has declared her professional ambitions and thinks herself the equal of Tetrazzini and Patti. The chorus incorporates her vocalises in the form of scales on "ah ah ah" and octaves on "Gobble Gobble Gobble Gobble," associating her singing not with the usual nightingale or canary but with a turkey. Verse 2 extends the avian metaphor:

> Her ah ah ah's and tra la la's
> Scare all the birds away
> They think it is a sea gull or a vulture.

And the chorus extends the imagery further into the rest of the animal kingdom when it says that "back yard cats are jealous" of her singing.

Like "Tra-La, La, La!" this song was issued with a cover that caricatures not only a female singer—here her mouth is a distended oval, her closed eyes suggesting her self-absorption—but also a discomfited male, here an accompanist seated at a bucking piano (fig. 3.3). Cartoon eighth and quarter notes, their stems drooping in displeasure, sport masculine faces of pain and outrage. The chorus's opening couplet, "In the morning when you're dreaming / She will wake you with her screaming," draws a parallel between Priscilla's annoyed listeners and the sleep-deprived parents of a newborn baby, strengthening the psychological tie that Poizat and others posit between the cultivated soprano voice and the preverbal cry of the infant.

The popular duo of Ada Jones and Billy Murray recorded "When Priscilla Tries to Reach High C" not once but twice for Edison in 1916.[23] Their Diamond Disc recording adheres closely to the printed sheet music version, with a substantial change only in the penultimate measure, where Jones inserts a cadenza with flute obbligato parodying the Mad Scene in *Lucia di Lammermoor*. The cadenza in *Lucia*, which ironically is not Donizetti's but has become a part of the opera's performance tradition, took on a life of its own in the later nineteenth century and beyond. Its imitators are legion, ranging from Emilio Arrieta's 1855 zarzuela *Marina* (where the cadenza, again, is a traditional interpolation and not the composer's own) to Gilbert and Sullivan's *Pirates of Penzance* (1879) and *Ruddigore* (1887). Although *Ruddigore* retains the context of the mad scene—the libretto labels the moment "an obvious caricature of theatrical madness"[24]—most other imitations efface the element of insanity; in *Marina*, for instance, the interpolated cadenza caps the zarzuela's happy ending. Shorn of its original meaning, the soprano cadenza with flute obbligato went on to become an icon of operatic vocal display in early- and middle-twentieth-century popular culture. Jones and Murray interpolate such a cadenza into both of their recordings of "When Priscilla Tries to Reach High C," as does Marguerite Farrell in her Columbia disc of 1916.[25] Al Jolson adds a similar cadenza in his 1913 recording of "The Spaniard That Blighted My Life," after which he asks, "Ain't I the darned fool?" in a voice that must have been the model for Bugs Bunny's.[26] As low

Figure 3.3 "When Priscilla Tries to Reach High C" (cover)

as this humor might be, perhaps the lowest point for the *Lucia*-style cadenza occurs in a midcentury Three Stooges short, *Micro-Phonies* (1945), where Curly, dressed in drag as "Señorita Cucaracha," lip-synchs it as the climax of Strauss's "Voices of Spring."[27]

Jones and Murray's other Edison recording of "When Priscilla Tries to Reach High C," a four-minute Blue Amberol cylinder, departs further from the sheet music, adding an extra chorus and interpolated comic bit, climaxing in a more complete travesty of the *Lucia* cadenza. The nature and extent of the changes illustrate how songs such as this one could be altered in performance. The performers stick close to the sheet music through the introduction, the first verse, and well into the first chorus. Eight measures from the end, they substitute a couplet from the sheet music's second chorus ("Once a copper heard her / And thought it was murder"); it will become clear why they reserve the original couplet for later. Taking the first ending, they repeat the chorus with new lyrics not in the sheet music:

BOTH: In the morning when you're dreaming
   She will wake you with her screaming.
JONES: Tra la la la la la la la
MURRAY: Gee her pipes are full of rust
JONES: Gobble Gobble Gobble Gobble
MURRAY: Something's going to bust
BOTH: She sings like an old kiyoodle[28]
   You'd think someone kicked her poodle
JONES: Tra la la la la la la la
   Gobble Gobble Gobble Gobble
MURRAY: Children weep and strong men wabble [sic]
   Once they thought they had her
   Someone brought a ladder[29]
BOTH: When Priscilla tries to reach high C.

Murray and Jones then sing the printed second verse and chorus as written until the eighth measure from the end, when the excised couplet from chorus 1 finally appears, now setting the scene for an interpolated comic dialogue:

JONES: And the neighbors tells us
   Back yard cats are jealous (Sound effects: cat fight; next bit is spoken)
JONES: I told you so (Soprano vocalise [not Ada Jones])
MURRAY: Ha! There's Priscilla (out-of-tune Lucia cadenza, with barking
   dogs instead of flute, culminating in dogs, cats, and an overturned garbage
   can)
MURRAY: Ha! Now that's what I call very artistic
JONES: Artistic? Why it's something awful
MURRAY: What is?
JONES (singing):   When Priscilla tries to reach
BOTH (singing):   high C.

The dissociation of the Lucia cadenza from its dramatic point of origin is complete: from the pairing of coloratura soprano and flute to indicate madness, to the use of cadenzas for soprano and flute to indicate vocal display with no textual content, to the substitution of fighting cats and dogs in place of the flute to indicate a negative response to female vocal display. Jones and Murray, on the Diamond Disc recording but even more emphatically on the Blue Amberol cylinder, demonstrate how certain selections from nineteenth-century opera continued to carry cultural meaning in twentieth-century America, though in ways far removed from their original meanings.

AMATEUR SINGERS

Songs that portray women as amateur singers continue the negative response to female vocality found in the songs about student singers. Even more apparent is the theme of foolish ambition, as many of the amateur singers aspire to professional status. For example, in "My Gal's Another Gal like Galli-Curci" (1919), by Felix Arndt and Louis Weslyn, a persona admires an amateur singer who, in his view, rivals Amelita Galli-Curci and Geraldine Farrar.[30] Her former teacher, "Signor Del Pye," seems to lack the predatory features of the music teachers already discussed, being simply "some musical guy." Del Pye's lessons "come awfully high," however, raising the possibility that, like Mabel Beecher's and Priscilla Lee's teachers, he preys economically on foolish, untalented young women. Slang-filled language hints at the disparity between the singer's ambitions and her current social status. She has "got a lot of ambish," and though not yet a professional,

> Someday she's gonna be a prima donna,
> Oh, boy, how proud of her I'll be,
> Gee!

The love-struck persona ignores, however, the implications of other listeners' reactions: "When she sings 'Home Sweet Home' / Ev'rybody starts to cry."[31] Their response suggests that this singing amateur is no better than Mabel Beecher or Priscilla Lee.

Early stage performances added a new wrinkle to the song's gender implications. Although the song's persona is male, the sheet music cover highlights no fewer than three women who performed the song "with success": Leonora McDonough, Sally Taylor, and Lillian Lane.[32] Judging by this and other period covers, women performers commonly sang songs with male personae, including songs that, like this one, are in the first person throughout. Most male performers, in contrast, apparently sang songs with female personae only when a third-person verse sets up the persona's first-person chorus; a classic example is "Bill Bailey, Won't You Please Come Home?" (1902).[33] An exception, of course, would be female impersonators such as Julian Eltinge. Because women could easily slip into and out of a male persona, a woman's performance of "My Gal's Another Gal like Galli-Curci" could at times suggest the boyfriend narrator, at other times the would-be diva herself. Such a performance may have been the songwriters' intent, in fact; in measures 5–6 Arndt provides, instead of the usual instrumental vamp, an opportunity for the singer to give an "Imitation of Soprano's Vocal exercise"—in other words, to embody not the male admirer but the female object of his affections. As in "My Music Teacher," with its female persona, masculine disdain for women musicians could be ventriloquized through a female performer.

The same disdain appears in Irving Berlin's "I Love a Piano" (1915), sung by a pianist persona who prefers "long-haired" music.[34] Clarinets, trombones, and violins come in for disparagement, but the strongest criticism is reserved for the amateur soprano:

> When a green Tetrazine starts to warble,
> I grow cold as an old piece of marble;
> I allude to the crude little party singer, who don't know when to pause,
> At her best I detest the soprano.

The soprano irritates not only because she is inexperienced but also because she makes a "crude" display of her ambition—she "don't know when to pause."

Overreaching ambition is also the theme of Bert Williams and George Walker's "She's Getting Mo' like the White Folks Every Day" (1901), which describes the changes that have come over Miss Sally Horn since she started working as a maid at a big hotel and became acquainted with elite Euro-American culture:

> She got herself some irons she's been working on her hair
> She's got herself some kalsomine to help to make her fair
> Now she can sing "The Swanee river" like it never was sung before
> But since she's worked in that hotel she warbles "Il Trovatore."[35]

Opera here is the musical equivalent of hair straighteners and whitewash, the instruments of Sally Horn's vain attempt to deny her African heritage.[36]

References to opera and Stephen Foster also mix in Bert Grant and Joe Young's "Serenade Me Sadie with a Rag-time Song" (1912), which may be thought of as an inversion of Gus Edwards's "Italian Romeo," from the previous year.[37] Even the cover reverses the gender roles of the serenader and the recipient of the song (fig. 3.4; cf. fig. 1.8); here a young woman, offering a rose, sings in the moonlight to a cigar-smoking, top-hatted man sitting on a balcony, wineglass nearby. And where the persona of Edwards's song is the serenader, here it is that of the person being sung to. What the two songs share is a scenario in which a singer aspires to opera but is encouraged by a lover to sing lighter fare. Where the Italian Romeo's Juliet would rather hear "Ciribiribin," here Abie Schwarz wishes his sweetheart, Sadie Klein, would sing a ragtime song.

Sadie's voice is a "number nine," probably a reference to dress or shoe sizes. The former, which connotes the stereotypical Jewish tailor's trade, implies that her voice is of middling (i.e., nonoperatic) size; the latter interpretation would equate her big voice with big feet, implying awkwardness. Though she aspires to sing opera, Sadie is flighty and gives up the pursuit too easily; she

> Left her happy home to study op'ra grand;
> Went to Sunny Spain, but came back again,
> 'Cause the language there she couldn't understand.

When Abie visits her on her return, he is not pleased with what he hears:

Figure 3.4 "Serenade Me Sadie with a Rag-time Song" (cover)

Sadie in the parlor was singing Traviata;
Abie hollered stop her
I don't care for Op'ra.
[Chorus] Serenade me, Sadie, with a ragtime song,
Give me something, baby, that won't last so long.

As in "She's Getting Mo' like the White Folks Every Day," opera here
stands in contrast to an African American musical idiom. But the different
ethnic context changes the meaning of that contrast. Abie doesn't want
Sadie to sing opera, but neither does he want her merely to sing lighter
music that might be considered appropriate for a nice Jewish girl. Instead,

he wants her to sing and dance in a sexually suggestive manner associated with African American entertainers:

> Sing about the Swanee river,
> Make sure that you shake and shiver,
> Snap the fingers like they do in 'Frisco town;
> Holler, oh you bear cats! bend yourself way down.

The reference to Lewis F. Muir and Fred Watson's "Oh, You Bear Cat Rag" (1910) links this song as well to the answer song "Stop That Bearcat Sadie" (1912), in which a Jewish father despairs over the coarse language and behavior his daughter has adopted since visiting San Francisco.[38] Both songs allude as well to George Botsford and Irving Berlin's "Grizzly Bear" (1910), with its references to San Francisco and the then-scandalous "animal" dances, with their African-derived motions, which were superseding in popularity the more sedate ballroom dances.[39] "Stop That Bearcat Sadie" also cites another Berlin song, "Alexander's Ragtime Band" (with its own "Swanee River" allusion). Similarly, "Serenade Me Sadie" parodies the choppy exhortations of Berlin's ragtime songs: "Sing Abie, look a here, look a here, come along."

Abie's request for ragtime instead of opera signals more than just his musical tastes, as verse 2 makes clear:

> Sadie Klein, had a wedding fine,
> Married Abie, and that night at half-past nine,
> Husband got a note that some girlie wrote;
> Said, come hear a song that's called the ragtime goat.
> Abie yelled, if that's the case, I'll have to leave at once.
> Sadie cried, Oi Abie please, don't be a ragtime dunce.
> Then she sang a yoodle and Abe went off his noodle,
> Sounds like a Kioodle,
> Stop or I'll skidoodle.

Abie's willingness to leave Sadie on their wedding night for "some girlie" implies that he is not looking for respectability. Underlying his complaints about her singing is a wish to have her join him in a disreputable lifestyle associated with ragtime and animal dances. Sadie's upward social trajectory, halted when she capriciously abandoned her opera studies in Spain, has taken a downward turn with her marriage to Abie.

Ridicule of the ambitious but frivolous would-be operatic soprano worked its way up from vaudeville and revue to the pinnacle of the popular musical hierarchy in Victor Herbert and Harry B. Smith's 1911 operetta *The Enchantress*. Although the show's title character is an opera singer, it is not her but the Princess Stellina, an aristocratic amateur, who sings "Art Is Calling for Me" (also known as "The Prima Donna Song" and sometimes identified by its subtitle, "I Want to Be a Prima Donna").[40] For Stellina, an operatic career represents not a climb up the social ladder—as royalty, she is already at the pinnacle—but a means of escaping the "dull dreary" life at the top. Her resemblance to professional opera singers, however, is more physical than vocal; her "figure's just like Tetrazzini's," and she has "the embonpoint / To become a queen of song." Though she claims that "Melba I'd oust / If I once sang in 'Faust,'" her voice causes reactions not as positive as she would like to think:

> I've roulades and the trills
> That would send the cold chills
> Down the backs of all hearers of my vocal frills.
> …
> Girls would be on the brink
> Of hysterics, I think,
> Even strong men would have to go out for a drink.

Stellina is attracted to opera for two reasons: she sees it as a way for an overweight woman to gain positive attention and as an escape from the restrictions placed upon her by her social position:

> I want to be a screechy, peachy cantatrice,
> Like other plump girls that I see,
> I hate society
> I hate propriety,
> Art is calling for me.
> …
> I long to hear them shouting "Viva" to the diva,
> Oh, very lovely that must be,
> That's what I'm dying for,
> That's what I'm sighing for,
> Art is calling for me.

Like Priscilla Lee and Sadie Klein, Stellina aspires to be on the operatic stage. Unlike those other women, though, she sings about her ambition in music untouched by ragtime syncopations, and for two reasons: the low-brow musical idiom would be alien to her royal position, and ragtime was foreign to Herbert's style, a well-crafted amalgam of French and Viennese operetta.[41] Thus she sings sparkling music reminiscent of Offenbach and Lehár. Though her royal status places Stellina in a much higher social position than those other fictional singers, she shares with them an operatic ambition that is superficial, frivolous, egotistical, and not backed up with genuine musical ability.

OPERATIC MAIDENS

A realist might argue that these negative characterizations merely reflect the fact that student and amateur voices seldom meet professional standards of quality. If these singers were any good, this line of reasoning suggests, they would not be open to attack. But even professional singers are shown in novelty songs to be empty-headed at best and vain or avaricious at worst.

Victor Herbert's sharpest satire of sopranos, "An Operatic Maiden," occurs in what is simultaneously his "lowest" and one of his most sophisticated compositions, the 1906 one-act burlesque *The Magic Knight*.[42] The comedy team of Joe Weber and Lew Fields, despite their many overtures to Herbert, never persuaded him to write music for their decidedly lowbrow productions, which typically paired a one-act musical comedy (or "comic opera," in the parlance of the day), with a one-act burlesque, or extended satire, of a current theatrical hit.[43] Once the two comedians had broken up their act and each was on his own, however, Herbert's attitude apparently softened. For Weber he agreed to write the music for *Dream City*, a spoof on Long Island real estate speculation with a book by Edgar Smith, a longtime writer for the Weber and Fields shows.[44] *Dream City*, which opened at Weber's Music Hall on 25 December 1906, cast Joe Weber as Wilhelm Dinglebender, a Long Island farmer whose dreams of developing his real estate at Malaria Center into a grand metropolis are the basis for comic spectacle.[45] Among the features of his imaginary Dream City is an opera house, but Dinglebender's fantasy visit there disillusions him; if being rich means having to spend time at the opera, he would rather remain a farmer.

This skeletal story line suggests that the visit to the opera house be treated as a burlesque play-within-a play, a format Weber and Fields had developed in their earlier hit *Hoity-Toity* (1901).[46] However, Herbert's treatment of the operatic travesty grew to such proportions that it broke loose from *Dream City* and became an independent afterpiece, *The Magic Knight*. Thus the entire evening consisted of two related yet somewhat independent pieces, both scored by Herbert. His parody of Wagner boasts a continuous musical score, with recitative in place of spoken dialogue, that makes heavy use of motives from *Lohengrin*. Dropped into the musical texture are numbers in a more popular style, including "An Operatic Maiden," sung by Elsa, described in the program as "a typical grand-operatic maiden in the usual distressing predicament." The role, which requires an accomplished coloratura soprano, was first performed by Lillian Blauvelt, a successful recitalist and Victor recording artist.[47]

Elsa is more interested in singing about herself than about her "distressing predicament." Her list of attributes in the verse tucks a single line about her voice in the midst of her description of her own physical appearance—eyes, blush, hair, voice, lips—before observing that her "kind of unaffected air / Is off the stage exceeding rare." In other words, her perfection is artificial, not to be found in real life. At the chorus, as the meter changes from common to waltz time, she suggests that her modest demeanor may have a less innocent subtext:

> There's a chance, I'm afraid
> That this shy, modest maid,
> May be called by the ribald, a "fairy."

The reference is to the fairy theme of early burlesques and extravaganzas such as *The Black Crook* (1866), in which actresses appeared in tights, fairy wings, a bit of gauze, and little else.[48] These shows grew in popularity along with the Victorian fascination with fairies, often portrayed in the graphic arts with a discomfiting combination of the erotic and the child-like.[49] Simply by appearing onstage, even in opera, the song suggests, a woman makes herself vulnerable to charges that she is engaging in titillating self-display and, by extension, willing to prostitute herself.[50]

The same association between operatic ambition and burlesque display occurs in a 1908 song, "When Tetrazzini Sings," which describes not the Florentine Nightingale but an aspiring diva who, although she knows "ev'ry opera score, from Salome to Trovatore," has to settle for work in a backwoods touring company of *The Black Crook*.[51] Likewise, the title character in "Henrietta, Dainty Henrietta" (1901) is a singer not in opera but in lowly burlesque, a job she acquires by going to dinner (a common sexual euphemism) with the company's manager.[52] With her "full three octave appetite," she soon grows so stout that she descends still further from burlesque to the circus, where she becomes first a lion tamer with "a gilded cage" and ultimately the lion's dinner. Henrietta shares several negative attributes with the other singers we have encountered: she is vulnerable to the false encouragement of scheming men (the voice teachers in other songs here become a burlesque manager); though her physical attributes are at least as impressive as her voice (like Elsa's), she becomes too heavy (like Stellina's Tetrazzini-like figure); and her professional independence is impugned by the implication that she supplements her income by selling sexual favors (like the woman whose "beauty was sold / For an old man's gold" in the 1900 weeper "A Bird in a Gilded Cage," an implication shared by the description of Elsa as a "fairy").

Elsa's vocal agility affords her protection—or financial safety, at least—against such slander:

> But it cannot harm me,
> While I have my high C
> And make good as a human canary.

Up to this point in the song there has been no display of vocal prowess. But Herbert has cunningly prepared for such fireworks from the very beginning. The melody of the verse comprises four phrases, all beginning on the lowest notes of the verse (D–C-sharp–D). The first three phrases rise identically to the F-sharp at the top of the staff, immediately descending to midstaff; the fourth phrase, however, rises to a high A, held for two and a half beats. This bit of vocal display, though slight, occurs ironically as Elsa refers to her "unaffected air."

The chorus, a thirty-two-measure ABAC structure, varies the verse's rising melodic contour (ex. 3.3). The two A phrases extend the low note down to B and rise only as high as the fourth-space E, which lasts for

Example 3.3. Herbert and Smith, "An Operatic Maiden," chorus (melody only)

Tempo di Valse. Lento.

There's a chance, I'm a-fraid That this shy, mod-est maid, May-be called by the

rib-ald, a "fair-y,"_____ But it can-not harm me, While I have my high

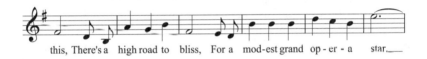

C And make good as a hu-man ca-na-ry._____ In a case such as

this, There's a high road to bliss, For a mod-est grand op-er-a star._____

accel.

_____ Who can cure all her ills, With a vol-ley of

trills Ah_____ And a

rit.   *ff*

sky-rock-et note on Ah Ah._____

merely a single beat the first time and is held for five beats the second time. The final phrase, which begins *accelerando*, decorates a chromatic climb from A to the final G, with two notable exceptions. On the word "trills," the melody leaps over the expected C sharp to the same climactic E that ended the previous phrase, now trilled and held with a fermata. A cadenza on the neutral syllable "ah" follows. The closing section, now marked *pesante* and *molto rit.* in the accompaniment (not shown in the example), continues the chromatic ascent, decorated with a penultimate *fortissimo* high B. The highest (and loudest) note of the entire song is thus reserved for this bravura ending.

Significantly, the lyric devolves into meaninglessness just as the vocal pyrotechnics begin. Wrapped up in self-regard, this "modest grand opera star" concludes her song with coloratura display that dissolves words into vocables. At the end, her song has no meaning apart from the sheer sound of her voice.

OPERATIC GENTS

All of the songs discussed so far express a masculine discomfort with the spectacle of the female singer. Three possible reasons for that discomfort have suggested themselves. It may have its roots in the sheer power of the soprano voice to override logocentric rationality, suggested by the prominent occurrence of vocables. Or it may be a response to the threat to the patriarchal social order presented by women who, through singing, have become independent professionals or otherwise are able to flout convention. Finally, that discomfort may be associated with the very act of self-display, a behavior at that time associated with nonlegitimate entertainment and tinged with scandal.

But not all comic songs about singers target women. At the AMS website mentioned earlier, tenor jokes come in a distant second in number to soprano jokes, which outnumber them two to one. Extrapolating back a century, one might expect to find comic songs about fictional tenors during this period that generated so many songs about fictional sopranos, and indeed a few exist—very few. An examination of them supports the observation that the humor in the preceding songs is so sharply barbed precisely because their targets are women. Furthermore, although all but a few of the songs about female singers are narrated in the third person by an implicitly male persona, all of the songs about male singers surveyed here are sung in the first person.[53]

A logical place to look for a song that spoofs a tenor would be *The Magic Knight*, Victor Herbert's Wagnerian travesty that includes "An Operatic Maiden." That song is "Ta! Ta! My Dainty Little Darling," sung by Lohengrin, described in the program as "a professional rescuer of distressed maidens."[54] Because the role was written for Maurice Farkoa, a musical comedy star who was capable of operetta but was certainly no heldentenor, this number lacks the vocal display of Elsa's song.[55] Rather, it is a Gilbert-and-Sullivanesque patter song, broadening only at the end for a fermata on the antepenultimate note—merely an F, not the high B of Elsa's song. For the same reason, perhaps, the lyric focuses not on singing but on stereotypical tenor foibles—vanity, impracticality, ostentatious gallantry—as well as Lohengrin's penchant for departing by swan boat at inconvenient moments. Lohengrin's passing reference to his "tenor stunts" is sandwiched between mention of his "valiant deeds" and "efforts ama-tory" and thus could as easily be nonvocal as vocal. Missing is the element of vocality found in virtually all of the songs about female singers.

Among the interpolated songs in the 1902 musical comedy *The Wild Rose* was "I Sing a Little Tenor," introduced by Albert Hart, a popular character actor in musical comedy and operetta.[56] The song, an extended boast about the singer's wide vocal range, mentions three pieces of music, none of them operatic: textual and musical quotations from the nine-teenth-century religious songs "Rocked in the Cradle of the Deep" and "The Palms" are followed incongruously by "A Hot Time in the Old Town Tonight," an 1896 hit that still would have been fairly fresh in 1902.[57] The citations imply that the song's persona is willing and (in his own opinion) able to sing almost anything. In the second verse he auditions for all the parts in a vocal quartet, boasting that as a one-man quartet he would "stand alone."

This comic device, in which a persona's boasting words can be read in the opposite way by the audience, is by now a familiar one. The audition-ing singer in "I'm After Madame Tetrazzini's Job" brags that her voice will "put Tetrazzini to sleep." Likewise, when Rosa Rigoletto "sings Lucee / Make you climb up a tree." When the gal who is like Galli-Curci "sings 'Home Sweet Home' / Ev'rybody says 'Goodnight!'" Missing in this song about an auditioning tenor, though, is any description of listeners' displea-sure. With the single exception of "An Operatic Maiden," all of the songs about women singers include the negative response of a (male) audience. Here, in contrast, the portrayal of a conceited male singer carries no impli-cation that he cannot in fact sing rather well.

A particularly interesting case because of its gender ambiguities is "I Want to Sing in Opera," a 1910 British music hall song with an unusual American incarnation. As published in the Commonwealth, the lyrics and music are credited to Worton David and George Arthurs. As the cover pro-claims, the song was popularized by the comedian Wilkie Bard, whose act included female impersonations. In Bard's 1910 phonograph recording, which reproduces the song much as printed, the song's persona is clearly female, although Bard sings in his usual light baritone and not in falsetto.[58]

When the song was interpolated the following year in the Broadway production of Leo Fall's operetta *The Siren*, with a new book by Harry B. Smith, it was sung by Will West, in the role of a horse doctor named Hannibal Beckmesser. Perhaps because female impersonation did not fit the character, an unlikely suitor of the leading lady, small changes were made in the lyrics for the U.S. sheet music publication and presumably for the New York performance. The changes were not made because American audiences objected to female impersonators; Julian Eltinge, one such impersonator, was then such a popular success that in 1912 he had a Broadway theater named after him, the Eltinge Theatre on Eighth Avenue and Forty-second Street.[59]

These lyric changes are the only substantial difference between the two publications. Intriguingly, the American edition carries a triple authorship: added to the names of David and Arthurs is that of Jerome Kern, the composer of the show's other interpolated songs. If Kern had a part in "I Want to Sing in Opera," his must have been the unlikely job of creating alternative lyrics for another composer's music.

An alteration in verse 2 shifts the persona's gender from female to male:

British edition:	U.S. edition
I'd like to play Carmen, I just love the part,	I would like to wriggle in sweet Rigoletto,
The music's so awfully sweet!	The music's so awfully neat
And all prima donnas I'd beat	And all leading tenors I'd beat
If in "Faust" I played sweet Marguerite	If as "Faust" I loved fair Marguerite

Even as revised, however, the lyrics borrow from the feminine lexicon; to "wriggle in sweet Rigoletto" is to engage in physical self-display, an activity coded as female.[60]

In both British and U.S. versions, gender ambiguity also marks the song's chorus. Shifting from the verse's rapid-fire 6/8 meter to a *tempo di valse*, the chorus contains a feature noted in chapter 1 in relation to songs about Caruso (i.e., masculine songs): a quotation of the "Ridi, pagliacco" line from *Pagliacci's* "Vesti la giubba." Although the notated melody, over *sostenuto* chords that contrast with the surrounding waltz accompaniment, does not match Leoncavallo's, Wilkie Bard sings the lyrics "Signor Caruso / Told me I ought to do so" to the familiar tune, which is doubled by the accompanying instruments (i.e., the quotation must have been written in the arrangement). The waltz accompaniment then resumes for the feminine closing lines: "That's why I want to sing in op'ra / sing in op-pop-pop-pop-e-ra! Hoorah!" As in "An Operatic Maiden," the song ends with a lyric that devolves into meaningless vocables—an emphasis on vocality that marks the song as female.

"I Want to Sing in Opera" emphasizes self-display and the primacy of the sound of the voice over the text—quintessential elements of songs portraying women singers. Significantly, its lyrics underwent a somewhat piecemeal and only partially successful revision to accommodate a masculine persona. Even in songs ostensibly about men, the figure of the vain, incompetent singer is to be construed as essentially feminine.

Chapter 4

Visions of Salome

A great number of fin-de-siècle artists, writers, and musicians found inspiration in the biblical story of Salome's dance before Herod and the beheading of John the Baptist, a story that offers up a potent mixture of decadent obsessions: murder, incest, female sexuality, and the mysterious Orient.[1] Oscar Wilde's 1892 play *Salomé* and Richard Strauss's 1905 operatic adaptation of it form the dual high points of the Salome literature, which critics have treated as a unitary "cultural text" of the late nineteenth and early twentieth centuries. Although the story's Middle Eastern setting supports a reading of that "text" as a part of that era's orientalism—namely, the West's strategies for, in Edward Said's words, "dominating, restructuring, and having authority over the Orient"—such an interpretation is only the beginning. Lawrence Kramer describes Salome as "not [merely] a monstrous sexual icon but…a focal point for the representation of a bundle of instabilities produced by the *fin-de-siècle* gender system." The turn-of-the-century fascination with Salome, then, may be more profitably viewed as a manifestation of an overlapping but distinct cultural phenomenon, namely, exoticism, which Gilles de Van defines as "an impetus toward the other which becomes a mirror of the self…the quest for the different that sends us back to the same."[2] In other words, the continual retelling of the Salome story in the decades around 1900 reflects a desire, unconscious or not, to probe not the Eastern but the Western psyche.

Exoticism as a screen for psychological projection, then, is a unifying element in the many specific versions of the Salome "text." Because of the wide geographic dispersal of those versions, however, historians have discerned distinct national trends among them. For example, Sander Gilman has noted in German Salomes (including Strauss's) a Central European association of Jewishness with sexual perversion, moral depravity, and disease. Davinia Caddy's study of Parisian theatrical dance suggests that in France the Salome theme brought artistic and social respectability to female display onstage by "resituat[ing] strip-tease for upper-class audiences." And in England, Amy Koritz argues, the spectacle of a Western woman dancing in veils upheld a British colonial discourse that, in Homi Bhabha's words, "produces the colonized as a fixed reality that is at once 'other' and yet entirely knowable and visible."[3]

Little musicological work has been done, however, on American versions of the Salome "text."[4] This chapter attempts to fill that gap somewhat by arguing that American musical representations of Salome at the turn of the century differ from their French, German, and British counterparts in two ways. First, despite such notable compositions as George Whitefield Chadwick's lyric drama *Judith* (1901) and Henry Hadley's tone poem *Salome* (1905–6), the orientalist femme fatale makes her U.S. appearance most vividly in popular artifacts, and especially in the works of Tin Pan Alley songwriters.[5] Second, the dominant trope of those songs is the very artificiality of the exoticist conceit. In song after song, the alluring oriental dancer reveals herself, as the last veil drops, to be a rather mundane Western woman indulging in playacting. While sharing with European exoticism a tendency to use the East as a screen on which to project a Western subjectivity, these American popular songs focus a critical eye on that act of projection. They satirically deflate the exoticist impulse by puncturing the illusion on which it depends. The "otherness" of the Orient is reduced to Barnumesque hokum. Nowhere is that critique more pointed than in popular songs that make reference to Salome.[6]

Those songs first appear shortly after the U.S. premiere of Strauss's opera, and this chapter begins by placing that 1907 premiere in its American theatrical context. Further contextualization of the ensuing fad, which the *New York Times* dubbed "Salomania," requires a flashback to the 1893 World's Columbian Exposition in Chicago, where Middle Eastern dance exhibitions sparked widespread imitations elsewhere and gave rise to the personification called Little Egypt. In turn, Salomania effected changes in social attitudes that may be measured by the very different reception given the second U.S. production of Strauss's *Salome*, in 1909, with Mary Garden in the title role. Finally, this chapter traces the demise of Salome as a figure in popular song, a decline temporarily offset by a brief cinematic efflorescence. Although by midcentury this cultural icon had lost its potency, for a short time Americans were fascinated by the unsettling femme fatale who, by making herself the object of the male gaze, not only gets her man but also gets his head served on a platter.

1907: SALOME COMES TO THE UNITED STATES

One of the rockiest moments in the history of the Metropolitan Opera was its premiere of *Salome* on 22 January 1907.[7] Though many new operas have had short initial runs at the Met, none has been shorter than the first run of *Salome*—a single performance. At the same time, that ill-fated production was one of the Met's most expensive; the complexity of Strauss's score and the size of his huge orchestra demanded extra players and extra rehearsals, driving costs up to the then-exorbitant sum of twenty thousand dollars.[8] The combination of elaborate and expensive preparations for performance (with their attendant media hype) and a hasty withdrawal of the work after its opening night made for juicy gossip and fed the rumor mills for months to come.

The most persistent rumor, which eventually was substantiated, was that the production was shut down more or less single-handedly by J. P. Morgan, who wielded considerable financial influence over the Met's board of directors.[9] Yet Morgan had not even seen the opera; he raised his objections on the advice of his daughter, Louisa Morgan Satterlee. It remains unclear whether Mrs. Satterlee attended the opening night or the open dress rehearsal two days earlier, on Sunday, 20 January.[10] That rehearsal was conducted before an audience of one thousand, a remarkably large crowd whose presence indicates the high degree of anticipation that the European debate over Strauss's opera and Wilde's play had generated in the United States. Many audience members, coming directly from church, were in precisely the wrong frame of mind to watch Olive Fremstad, who sang Salome, exulting over the severed head of John the Baptist.[11] Her kissing of the head became an object of controversy even more than the Dance of the Seven Veils, which was executed not by Fremstad but by a Met ballerina, Bianca Froelich.[12]

If advance publicity had drawn an unusually large audience to the dress rehearsal, then word of that rehearsal added a buzz that drew to the opening night what the *Times* critic Richard Aldrich called "a vast audience, tense with a sort of foreboding expectancy."[13] His review focused on the music rather than the "abhorrent" subject matter or the audience's reaction; the latter was the topic of a sidebar with the eloquent headline "How the Audience Took It: Many Disgusted by the Dance and the Kissing of the Head." Despite exceptionally high ticket prices ranging from two to ten dollars,[14] Metropolitan staff and "ten extra policemen were required last night to handle the crowds," according to the sidebar. Tickets quickly sold out, and the ticket booth turned away customers after standing room was gone. The report of this capacity audience's reaction to the opera is worth quoting at length:

> After the curtain went up on "Salome" there was no sensation until the dance began. It was the dance that women turn away from, and many women in the Metropolitan Opera House last night turned away from it. Very few men in the audience seemed comfortable. They twisted in their chairs, and before it was over there were numbers of them who decided to go to the corridors and smoke.
>
> But when, following the lines of Wilde's play, Mme. Fremstad began to sing to the head before her, the horror of the thing started a party of men and women from the front row, and from Boxes 27 and 29 in the Golden Horseshoe two parties tumbled precipitately into the corridors and called to a waiting employe [sic] of the house to get their carriages.
>
> But in the galleries men and women left their seats to stand so that they might look down upon the prima donna as she kissed the dead lips of the head of John the Baptist. Then they sank back in their chairs and shuddered.[15]

   Three important distinctions are made here. First of all, the dance
apparently caused at least as much discomfort for men as for women. The
phrase "the dance that women turn away from" was by this time a stock
euphemism for belly dancing, originating in descriptions of the Midway
dancers at the Chicago world's fair of 1893. Though women turned away
from the dance, now it was men who got up and left, if only to retreat
temporarily to the corridors. This is an important point for understanding
the rash of songs inspired by Salome, a discomfiting object for the male
gaze, in contrast to the paucity of songs about Little Egypt and world's
fair–style belly dancing, which was generally enjoyed by men and abhorred
by women.[16] The second distinction is between the reactions to the dance
and to the "kissing of the head"; it was the latter that drove some operagoers from the hall. The presence of the severed head distinguishes depictions of Salome from generic oriental dancers and makes her a more
disturbing, and thus more potent, cultural icon than Little Egypt.
   The third distinction is one of class: whereas operagoers in the expensive front row and boxes got up to leave during Salome's final monologue,
those in the galleries, both men and women, got up not to leave but to get
a better look. As the kiss took place on a darkened stage and thus was
virtually invisible to the audience (per Strauss's stage direction), the occu-
pants of the cheap seats apparently craned their necks to get their money's
worth, just as if they were at a Coney Island sideshow or a Barnum-style
dime museum. They had bought their tickets expecting to be shocked,
and it was with an air of satisfaction, no doubt, that many "sank back in
their chairs and shuddered."
   If the gallery gods had had their say, *Salome* might have enjoyed a long
and profitable run at the Met. Indeed, a later *New York Times* story repeats a
rumor that, in the wake of Morgan's shutdown, the Met's general manager,
Heinrich Conried, had considered moving the production to a number of
other theaters, including the cavernous Hippodrome, in which circuses and
other spectacles could be staged for an audience of five thousand.[17] Whether
true or not, the rumor not only reflects the large expense that Conried was
now unable to recoup but also suggests that he might have been able to put
the production in the black by filling the Hippodrome with thousands of
operatic thrill-seekers.[18] As it turned out, Americans would not see another
operatic *Salome* for two years and would not see the opera at the Met for
another twenty-seven years. In the meantime, though, Salome managed to
find her public in other venues. In fact, on the very evening of the Met premiere she was already appearing on two other New York stages in quite
different theatrical contexts. Those two Salome plays tell us much about the
milieu in which Strauss's opera had its U.S. premiere.[19]

A Salome with Uplift

On Saturday, 19 January 1907, the day before the Met's dress rehearsal of
Salome, a spoken drama on the same biblical subject opened at the Shubert

brothers' Lyric Theatre. This highbrow production of *John the Baptist*, by the German naturalist playwright Hermann Sudermann, featured the respected husband-and-wife Shakespearean team of E. H. Sothern and Julia Marlowe in the roles of John and Salome respectively. An ad in the preceding Sunday's *New York Times* indicates the mix of moral edification and voyeurism aimed for by the Shuberts, equal parts Sunday school teacher and sideshow barker: "Produced in Berlin by order of the German Emperor setting aside 'the suppression edict' issued by the censor. Approved by Baptist ministers in Philadelphia. In Act V of *John the Baptist* Miss Marlowe as Salome will be seen in the extraordinary 'Dance of the Seven Veils.'"[20]

Although the opening performance was considered to be "one of the most important of the season," a review did not appear in the *Times* for some days (generally a bad sign), and then it ran under a headline that telegraphed the general tone of the review with the words "uninspired" and "drab monotone."[21] Sudermann had written a play that "can hardly be regarded as of any vital importance to the drama, though it can scarcely fail, considering the theme, to have a certain sort of interest." The playwright's decision to focus the play on John's interior spiritual struggle not only betrayed a poor dramatic sense but also caused the reviewer to question Sudermann's "honesty of purpose," since the only "genuinely dramatic" scenes were those involving Salome. That is to say, the play's religiosity struck a false note. And even the livelier scenes were vitiated by casting as Salome a forty-year-old actress "who has hitherto been regarded as something other than a disciple of Terpsichore." Her Dance of the Seven Veils could "hardly be said to give occasion for the breathless rapture prophesied in advance reports." A publicity photo in the previous Sunday's paper, showing a heavily veiled Salome posed statically before Herod, supports a columnist's recollection, a year and a half later, that Julia Marlowe had merely "swayed somewhat ponderously."[22] In short, the play's pretensions to moral uplift were only a smokescreen to disguise its prurient appeal, albeit one that fooled the Philadelphia ministers, while as titillating spectacle it fell disappointingly short. Insufficiently shocking, *John the Baptist* failed critically for reasons precisely opposite to those that shut down Strauss's *Salome*.

Salome Goes West

Also opening one night earlier than the Met's *Salome* dress rehearsal was a play that, remarkable as it may seem, transposed elements of the story to frontier California. *Salomy Jane* was a dramatic adaptation by Paul Armstrong of Bret Harte's short story "Salomy Jane's Kiss," which had appeared in his 1898 collection *Stories in Light and Shadow*. Living in London from 1885 until his death in 1902, Harte had continued to write stories whose Californian hues appealed to British audiences long after the U.S. enthusiasm for such works of the 1860s as "The Luck of Roaring Camp" and "The Outcasts of Poker Flat" had cooled. Internal evidence in "Salomy Jane's Kiss" suggests that Harte, while in London, had got hold of a copy of Oscar Wilde's *Salomé*, no doubt in the small edition printed there by John Lane in 1894. (The play was not staged in England until a private performance in 1905.) However Harte came to know Wilde's play, that work has several parallels in the strikingly different "Salomy Jane's Kiss."

Salomy Jane Clay is "a tall, handsome, lazy Kentucky girl" who "thought no small potatoes of herself"; in the short story she is first seen "lean[ing] against the doorpost, chewing gum"—in those days, a signal of bad breeding at best and loose morals at worst.[23] The house of her cattleman father, compared to the neighboring cabins in their California settlement, is "a superior dwelling" boasting "a sitting-room and a parlor organ." As mistress of this palace, Salomy Jane is consumed with "a large, protecting admiration for her father, for some years a widower." Harte, toning down the incest in Wilde, conveniently dispenses with a parallel character for the problematic Herodias and establishes a father-daughter relationship that, though intense, is nonsexual: "As for Mr. Clay, he accepted [Salomy Jane] as housewifely, though somewhat 'interfering.'"

Salomy Jane is shaken from her routine by a chance encounter with a captured horse thief, "a stranger there," as he is being led by a band of vigilantes to a necktie party. Acting on a momentary "grotesque idea," the stranger asks Salomy Jane for a good-bye kiss. In response, "she paused; her shy, fawn-like eyes grew bold, and fixed themselves upon his. She took the chewing-gum from her mouth, wiped her red lips with the back of her hand, by a sudden lithe spring placed her foot on his stirrup, and, bounding to the saddle, threw her arms about his neck and pressed a kiss upon his lips." The immediate result of her action is that she becomes the object of the vigilante party's masculine gaze: "SHE was the focus of all eyes,—she only!" But a farther-reaching reaction is stirred in the stranger, who returns the kiss "like a man." Soon after, he slips free of his captors and becomes a fugitive from frontier justice.

Speculating on what has become of the horse thief, Salomy Jane later recalls him as "a young man with very bright eyes, a flushed and sunburnt cheek, a kind of fixed look in the face, and no beard." If the bright eyes and fixed look only faintly suggest Wilde's Jokanaan, the parallels become stronger when the two protagonists meet again on "a fine moonlit night" when "the moon added a vague elusiveness to everything"; Harte's emphasis on moonlight in this scene resembles a similar emphasis throughout Wilde's play, which had prompted Wilde facetiously to call the moon the main character. At a moment of supernatural stillness, when "even the moonbeams appeared no longer tremulous," the stranger "stepped into the moonlight....He looked as white and spirit-like in the moonlight, dressed in the same clothes, as when she saw him last."[24] The imagery resembles Salome's first declaration of love for Jokanaan: "Thy body is white, like the lilies of a field that the mower hath never mowed. Thy body is white like the snows that lie on the mountains of Judæa, and come down into the valleys....There is nothing in the world so white as thy body."[25]

This Jokanaan has been lucky enough to receive his kiss just before his planned execution: "That kiss you gave me put life into me—gave me strength to get away. I swore to myself I'd come back and thank you, alive or dead." Far from ordering his head removed, she has "put the heart in" him. Fully in love, the two share another, longer kiss. All that remains for Salomy Jane is to learn the stranger's name: Jack. Both Salome/Salomy and Jokanaan/Jack escape tragedy when, after a series of melodramatic events, they elude the vigilantes and escape to a happy ending in Kentucky bluegrass country. There Jack becomes the "best judge of horse-flesh in the country," and Salomy Jane can be seen "rigged out in the latest fashion" so that "you'd never think she had ever lived out of New York or wasn't the wife of one of its millionaires."

Paul Armstrong's stage adaptation of Harte's short story introduced many changes, generally weakening the parallels with Wilde's *Salomé*. The play's action begins with a quite different kiss, forcibly stolen from Salomy Jane by a new character, a gambler/villain, who receives his comeuppance from the stranger, now known simply as "the man," not as Jack. No longer the ambiguous outlaw antihero, this do-gooder is falsely accused of horse stealing after taking in a stray, and only late in the play does Salomy Jane's last-minute kiss save him from the noose.[26] With its leading role for "an attractive girl type," *Salomy Jane* was a success, playing for 122 performances from January to May 1907 and returning in September for an additional 33. Armstrong's play was brought to the silent screen in 1914 and again in 1923; a 1932 sound version, *Wild Girl*, starred Joan Bennett and Ralph Bellamy.

Harte's short story marks an important stage in the Americanization of Salome. A work of light popular fiction, it sustains a tone of romantic adventure, not travesty or parody. But like the more comic versions to come, its revisions defang the unsettling aspects of the standard "text." Harte also removes all trace of exoticism (or more accurately, he replaces the exoticism of the East with that of the Wild West). While later American treatments would retain orientalist trappings, they generally highlight the Western presence behind the exotic Eastern veil. Such is the case in the first popular Salome song to appear in the wake of Strauss's opera, a mere six months later.[27]

Salome Goes to the *Follies*

The 1906–7 season had not been an easy one for the Metropolitan Opera. In addition to January's *Salome* debacle, the previous autumn had seen not only Enrico Caruso's highly publicized monkey house scandal but also the launching of the Met's most formidable rival, Oscar Hammerstein's

Manhattan Opera Company. For all of these reasons, the Met presented an irresistible target for a satirical new entertainment that opened that summer. The owners of the New York Theatre, hoping to promote their roof garden during the hot summer months, hired Florenz Ziegfeld Jr. to create something appropriate, and at the suggestion of his French wife, Anna Held, he renamed the roof garden the Jardin de Paris and mounted there a Parisian-style topical revue, something New York had not seen since the brief run of Casino Theatre revues in the 1890s.[28] The *Follies of 1907* was the first of what would prove to be a quarter-century-long series of annual revues (Ziegfeld would append his name to the title beginning in 1911). The first *Follies* took potshots at everything and everyone from Theodore Roosevelt to John D. Rockefeller, the Metropolitan Opera being a prominent target.

The *Follies of 1907* comprised thirteen scenes, loosely tied together by the conceit of a visit to modern New York by Pocahontas and John Smith (a reference to 1907's Jamestown Exposition, a world's fair whose heavy-handed militaristic and colonialist propagandizing had drawn controversy).[29] Years later, Harry B. Smith, the author of the revue's slender book, recalled skits in which "the rival impresarios, Oscar Hammerstein and Heinrich Conried, fought an operatic duel supported by their respective companies; and in a court scene Caruso was found guilty of misdemeanor on account of his much advertised adventure at the Central Park monkey house."[30] Smith failed to mention that at least two numbers alluded to *Salome*. The ballerina Mlle. Dazie (a.k.a. Daisy Peterkin from Detroit) performed her version of the Dance of the Seven Veils with, according to a *New York American* critic, "all the grace and abandon that characterized Mlle. [Bianca] Froelich's performance in 'Salome' at the Metropolitan."[31] If the Metropolitan ballerina was the first to perform a Salome dance in the United States, then Mlle. Dazie was apparently the second.

In addition to Mlle. Dazie's dance, the *Follies* featured its headliner, Nora Bayes, who sang Harry Von Tilzer and Vincent Bryan's "When Miss Patricia Salome Did Her Funny Little Oo La Palome."[32] Using the habanera rhythm of Sebastián Yradier's 1859 "La Paloma" (Yradier's Cuban tune appears in the vamp and in the last eight measures of the chorus), the song tells the story of Bridget McShane, an Irishwoman who poses as a Spanish dancer with the stage name Patricia Salome.[33] An Irishman in the audience recognizes Bridget and calls her bluff; the scenario resembles Von Tilzer's Italian-dialect song "Mariutch (Make-a the Hootch-a ma Kootch) Down at Coney Isle," also from 1907, and will recur in Irving Berlin's 1909 "Sadie Salome (Go Home)," both discussed later.

The music sets Patricia's last name with the accent on the second of two syllables, to rhyme with "home." This pronunciation and a three-syllable version that rhymes with "show me" are the standard ones for Salome songs; one often finds both pronunciations in the same song.[34] And though this song has no strong tie to Strauss's opera, it does touch on

Figure 4.1. "When Miss Patricia Salome Did Her Funny Little Oo La Palome," cover

themes that recur, singly or together, in later Salome songs: a use of the habanera rhythm, which connects Salome with another operatic femme fatale, Carmen; an association of theatrical dance with scandalous or unethical behavior (nothing new here); a female dancer who pretends to be someone she is not; and a male character who voices his objection to (or sometimes his delight in) her dance—an allusion to J. P. Morgan's notorious act of running Salome off the Metropolitan stage?[35]

"Patricia Salome" is, to my knowledge, the first popular novelty song to mention Salome and the only such song from 1907 that is extant. There was at least one other, from *The Gay White Way*, a revue that opened in the autumn of 1907 the Casino Theatre; the song, now apparently lost, was called "You've Got to Do That Salome Dance."[36] Though one can only speculate on the song's content, the title supports a conclusion confirmed by other evidence: in the wake of the Met uproar, plenty of women were doing that Salome dance.

1908: AN OUTBREAK OF SALOMANIA

A fad for stage representations of Salome and her Dance of the Seven Veils, often incorporating the severed head of John the Baptist, began in 1907 and reached its zenith in 1908 in what the *New York Times* called "Salomania." Previous scholarly writings about the Salome craze in the United States have treated it either as an epiphenomenon of the public fascination with belly dancing that began with the 1893 Chicago world's fair or as a peripheral aspect of a similar fad for Salome dancers in Europe.[37] In this section I first go back to the dancers at the 1893 fair and the songs they inspired, then consider the later rise of Salome dancers and the quite different songs associated with them. By the end of this chapter it will be clear that American Salomania differed from its European counterpart largely because the 1893 Chicago fair set a precedent that shaped Americans' responses to Strauss's opera.

Chicago, Little Egypt, and the Streets of Cairo

At the 1893 World's Columbian Exposition in Chicago, the American public came into contact with representatives of the world's cultures in unprecedented numbers. Some 27 million people visited the fair, almost all of them spending time on the Midway Plaisance, where lighter entertainments leavened the serious tone of moral elevation that characterized the educational exhibits in the White City, the fair's model of idealized architecture, art, and engineering (so named for the uniform color of its buildings). And just as the White City purported to represent civilization's highest achievements, so it was left to the mixed attractions of the Midway to represent what in white-supremacist terms would be considered inferior manifestations of humankind, such as the Native American, African, and Middle Eastern "villages."[38] At three such "villages" fairgoers could witness authentic Middle Eastern dance, hitherto virtually unknown in the United States. Performers at the Algerian Village presented the traditional handkerchief dance, while those at the Turkish Village showcased folk dances of various countries under Ottoman rule. Most popular was an exhibition called "A Street in Cairo," or simply Cairo Street, where *ghawazi*, professional Egyptian dancers in elaborate costumes, performed a dance that featured virtually no footwork but much shoulder shaking and "rhythmical, then spasmodic, movement of the abdominal region."[39] This was the dance that became known in the United States as belly dancing.

Sharing the Midway Plaisance with the ethnological villages were openly commercial amusements such as bandstands, hot-air balloon rides, and the original Ferris Wheel. Complicating the picture for all but the most sophisticated fairgoers were attractions that occupied a zone between ethnology and exploitation. Among them were the Moorish Palace (a dime museum) and the Persian Palace, where Parisian music hall dancers shook tambourines and executed can-can-style high kicks in recreation of the highly inauthentic exotic dances that had sprung up in Paris following that city's 1889 Exposition universelle. Compounding the fairgoers' cultural confusion was the physical placement of these fake orientalist attractions among the more genuine Middle Eastern villages. One contemporary observer made no distinction between the Persian Palace's dancers and the *ghawazi* of Cairo Street in terms of the female audience members' response: "No ordinary Western woman looked on these performances with anything but horror, and at one time it was a matter of serious debate in the councils of the Exposition whether the customs of Cairo should be faithfully reproduced, or the morals of the public faithfully protected."[40] This comment alludes to a request made in August 1893 to Director-General George R. Davis by the exposition's Board of Lady Managers, a group of notable members of Chicago society, that the dancing on the Midway Plaisance be cleaned up. Focusing on the Persian Palace, Davis ordered its closure, but the palace's management obtained a court injunction that allowed it to remain in business. And thanks to the publicity generated by the attempted closing, business was booming.

After the exposition concluded in October, many of the Midway dancers, widely referred to as "nautch" or "cooch" dancers, remained in the United States, where they found work in traveling carnivals, circuses, and vaudeville and burlesque theaters, as well as at the new amusement parks inspired by the world's fair, such as Steeplechase Park at Coney Island. By 1895 Coney Island boasted an attraction called the "Streets of Cairo," which featured cooch dancers. Some were authentic, according to Donna Carlton, who considers the Coney Island dancer filmed in 1897 by Thomas Edison to be the real thing.[41] Others were merely striking exotic poses, like the young woman in "Mariutch (Make-a the Hootch-a ma Kootch) Down at Coney Isle."

New York's most famous cooch dancer was an Algerian named Ashea Wabe, who may have been at the Chicago fair and who subsequently became famous under the stage name Little Egypt. Wabe's presence at a private gentlemen's dinner that was raided by the police in 1896, along with her subsequent appearance for questioning before a grand jury, gained her a notoriety that was capitalized on by the impresario Oscar Hammerstein, who booked her into his Olympia Theatre on Broadway for a highly profitably two-month run in vaudeville.[42] Her stage name was "borrowed" by countless other dancers, each claiming to be the original, and in short time Little Egypt became not a specific woman but a generalized personification of belly dancing—"the dance that women turn away from"—and of the illicit, and masculine, pleasures associated with it.

Of the popular songs that memorialize the Midway and its exotic dancers, one anticipates the dominant theme of the later Salome songs, namely, the revelation of the artifice behind exoticist fantasy. James Thornton's 1895 "The Streets of Cairo, or The Poor Little Country Maid" is based on the tune that seems always to accompany the "exotic" pseudo-oriental dancer or snake charmer (fig. 4.2).[43] The lyrics describe not a Middle Eastern dancer but a seemingly naïve young American woman. One young man who takes her out to dine is now "sorry that he met her / And he never will forget her, / In the future he'll know better." But the danger she presents to men is not just financial:

(a)

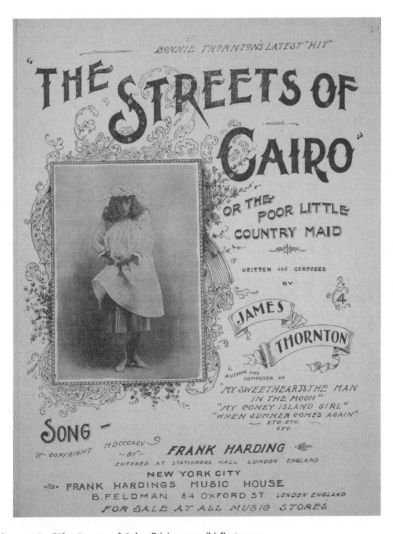

Figure 4.2. "The Streets of Cairo," (a) cover; (b) first page

(b)

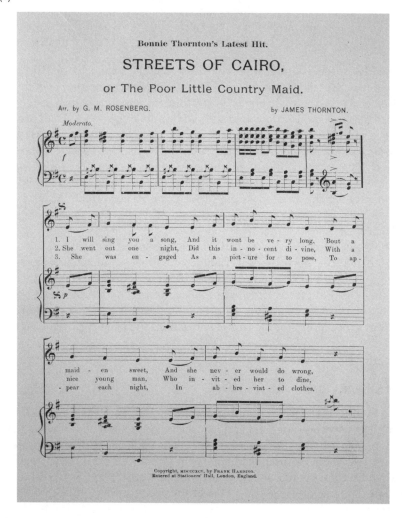

Figure 4.2. (*continued*)

> She was engaged
> As a picture for to pose,
> To appear each night,
> In abbreviated clothes,
> All the dudes were in a flurry,
> For to catch her they did hurry,
> One who caught her now is sorry,
> Poor little maid.

What the dude "caught" is presumably a sexually transmitted disease.

Ironically, the chorus emphatically denies any connection between this country maid and belly dancing:

> She never saw the streets of Cairo,
> On the Midway she had never strayed,
> She never saw the kutchy, kutchy,
> Poor little country maid.

When Thornton's wife, Bonnie Thornton, sang the song in vaudeville, presumably in the "rube" costume in which she is pictured on the sheet music cover, she probably enlivened her performance with a parody of cooch dancing, her inappropriate costume adding to the humor. That performance would have implicitly underlined the song's message that girls who appear to be innocent may be the opposite and indeed pose a threat to unwary men. A native-born femme fatale can be dangerous enough without the exoticist trappings of a hootchy-kootchy girl. The tremendous popularity of "The Streets of Cairo" thus forms an important backdrop for Americans' skeptical reception of Salome, the sixteen-year-old oriental virgin capable of decapitating a holy man.

Notably absent in this and other songs inspired by the Chicago fair dancers is Little Egypt herself. Fascinated as many Americans appear to have been with the Middle Eastern dancing introduced at the 1893 Chicago fair, not until a U.S. performance of Strauss's *Salome* in 1907 did Americans have a character who could galvanize that fascination and serve as a focal point for the complex reactions the dance provoked. When that character arrived, the result was Salomania.

The Salome Craze

The action that precipitated Salomania was one that crossed the boundary between high art and low entertainment. The ballerina who had presented the Dance of the Seven Veils at the Metropolitan Opera's single performance of *Salome* in January 1907, Bianca Froelich, subsequently took her act to vaudeville, appearing first at the Lincoln Square Theatre on Broadway. Her interpretation was a milder version of the artistic Salome dance being developed in Europe; looking back at the Met performance two years later, she remarked, "I did it in the European way at rehearsal but was told to tone it down."[44] Initially successful, her highbrow rendition was quite tame in comparison to the lowbrow Salome dances soon to come, and a year later she would be "hooted off the stage in Yonkers."[45] In the meantime, the imitation of Froelich's dance in Florenz Ziegfeld's *Follies of 1907* met with such success that Mlle. Dazie opened a "school for Salomes" that produced 150 graduates a month.[46]

An even better education in Salome dancing than Mlle. Dazie's was the one financed by Oscar Hammerstein's son Willie, who in early 1908 bankrolled a trip to London for Gertrude Hoffmann, a chorus girl who had begun to attract attention with her comic impersonations of popular entertainers. The object of Hoffmann's study was Maud Allan

(1873–1956), a Canadian who had grown up in San Francisco and traveled to Berlin in 1895 to study piano with Ferruccio Busoni.[47] Berlin offered greater opportunities for dancers and artist's models than for pianists, and in 1903 Allan began dancing professionally, taking her inspiration from Isadora Duncan, Ruth St. Denis, and Loie Fuller. Each of these American women in Europe, by choreographing her own unconventional solo dances, was creating a unique idiom; later their individual styles would coalesce, to greater or lesser degrees, to form what became known as modern dance. Duncan was inspired by ancient Greece, and St. Denis based some of her work on Indian sacred dancers. In 1907 Allan presented in Berlin an original piece that also had religious overtones, "The Vision of Salome," thereby not only emulating her successful predecessors but also capitalizing on the popularity in Germany of Wilde's play and Strauss's opera. For several months she toured the European continent, during which time she performed for King Edward VII of England, a notorious rake whose acquaintance she had made through the American operatic soprano Lillian Nordica. Acting on Edward's suggestion, Allan arrived in London in February 1908, where, for the first time, her high-class dance shared the bill with variety performers: comedians, jugglers, even an animal act. Her engagement at the Palace Theatre, where she was initially booked to play two weeks, would eventually extend until October 1909. At some point early in this twenty-month run, Gertrude Hoffmann observed Allan's act.

An ace mimic, Hoffmann came back to the United States with a dance evidently modeled on Allan's. Studio portraits show Hoffmann in an orientalist costume clearly patterned on the one Allan herself had designed for "The Vision of Salome": breastplates encircled with pearls and jewels, chains of more pearls and jewels draped from her breasts and hips, and an ankle-length transparent skirt revealing otherwise bare legs and feet (fig. 4.3). Allan's costume owes more to nineteenth-century Salome paintings by Gustave Moreau and other French exoticists than to actual Middle Eastern dancers.[48] Brought to the United States by Hoffmann, it and other close imitations would become the norm in Salome dances and can be seen on the covers of several Salome songs. Also borrowed from Allan's act was a notable prop, a papier-mâché head of John the Baptist. Allan's "Vision of Salome" combined the two most shocking moments in Wilde/Strauss's *Salome:* the Dance of the Seven Veils and the closing scene with its necrophiliac kiss. A new element was the ending; instead of dying under the shields of Herod's soldiers, Salome collapses in fear and, it is implied, remorse.[49]

Hoffmann called her version of Allan's dance "A Vision of Salome," the title differing from Allan's only in the change from definite to indefinite article. Her dance premiered on 9 July 1908 at Hammerstein's Victoria Theatre on Forty-second Street (owned by Oscar, managed by Willie) and played to sold-out houses for twenty-two weeks, its popularity helped along when Willie Hammerstein arranged to have Hoffmann arrested for indecency as a publicity stunt.[50] The New York run led to a twenty-five-week tour of the United States. Some cities banned her performance, and Des Moines responded by passing an ordinance that prohibited women from kicking their legs at an angle higher than forty-five degrees from the floor.[51] Hoffmann apparently livened up Allan's artistic dance by throwing in a bit of can-can, like the Parisian dancers at Chicago's Persian Palace.

(a)

Figure 4.3. (a) Maud Allan and (b) Gertrude Hoffmann as Salome: studio portraits from 1908; originals in New York Public Library

(b)

Figure 4.3. (*continued*)

No descriptions of Hoffmann's act describe the music in any detail. She possibly used a piece by J. Bodewalt Lampe published in the same year by Remick with a title identical to that of Hoffmann's dance: "A Vision of Salome."[52] Although the cover does not mention Hoffmann, its illustration depicts a dancer in Hoffmannesque costume, the first of many such illustrations to appear on sheet music covers in the ensuing years (fig. 4.4). A dramatic synopsis printed in its entirety as a preface and repeated, sentence by sentence, in the score suggests that the music was composed to accompany a dance that bore more than passing resemblance to Allan's. Lampe's music begins in triple meter and includes a lengthy section in waltz tempo, somewhat like Strauss's "Dance of the Seven Veils." Yet its most familiar tune is in a ragtime-era duple meter, marked "dance tempo," and combines the minor mode, a tonic pedal, and a raised fourth, all standard orientalist tropes (ex. 4.1).[53] This tune remained popular for decades and no doubt served as accompaniment for many stage Salomes, as well as other exotica such as circus tiger acts.[54]

By October 1908 there were twenty-four Salome dancers in New York City alone, each one prancing in pearls and kissing a papier-mâché head,

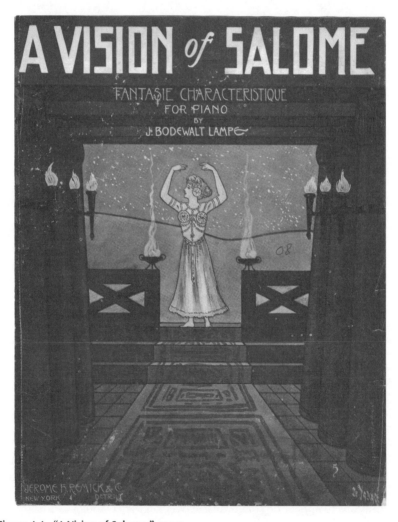

Figure 4.4. "A Vision of Salome," cover

Example 4.1. Lampe, "A Vision of Salome," mm.12–17

according to a contemporary journal article with a telling title: "The Vulgarization of Salome."[55] One Salome, with the stage name La Sylphe, appeared for three weeks at Keith and Proctor's 125th Street Theater, then moved to the Fifth Avenue Theatre with a revised act, "The Remorse of Salome."[56] Another dancer was Eva Tanguay, who three years earlier had introduced her signature song "I Don't Care" in *The Sambo Girl*, which had also included a drinking song in which she poured a bottle of champagne over her head. When Tanguay presented her version of a Salome dance at the Alhambra Theatre, she thereby furthered her stage persona of unbridled impetuosity.[57]

A *New York Times* writer lampooned the growing Salome craze in an August 1908 article whose lead sentence refers as well to the other dance craze of that year: "In spite of rumors which have been prevalent of late, it is extremely improbable that a 'Salome' dance will be substituted for the 'Merry Widow' waltz at the New Amsterdam." So strictly did the producer of *The Merry Widow* supervise his cast, the article goes on to report, that the leading lady "complained that she couldn't so much as take off her hat without arousing suspicion." The tongue-in-cheek article denies rumors that Salome dances would be added to forthcoming productions of *Hamlet* and *A Doll's House* but asserts that Oscar Hammerstein planned to add them to every production at the Manhattan Opera House in the next season, including *Götterdämmerung*. As we shall see, that last joke proved to be not as much of an exaggeration as the writer probably intended.[58]

Journalistic use of such terms as *vulgarization* and *Salomania* indicate that Maud Allan's high-minded Salome dance, which had begun its downward slippage in February 1908 when she accepted a spot in London variety, had quickly come crashing down to the level of burlesque in the United States that summer. If, as Caddy argues, Parisian dancers had used the Salome theme to gain respectability, then New York dancers had no such luck.[59] Instead, as Toni Bentley writes, "Salomania represents a jewel-like example of good old American enthusiasm grasping an icon of serious European art, stripping it of all pretense, and popularizing it for everyman—at least for every man who could get a ticket."[60] Further documenting Salomania's trajectory from opera house to cooch show are the Salome songs of 1908.

Salome Songs in 1908

A summer revue at the Casino, *The Mimic World*, featured a "Salome Dance" with music by Melville Ellis. The dancer there was Lotta Faust, who in 1903 had spiced up the stage version of *The Wizard of Oz* with her saucy number "Sammy," a love song sung to an unsuspecting audience member. In the autumn she would reprise her *Mimic World* Salome dance as an interpolation when she rejoined the cast of the British musical comedy *The Girl behind the Counter*.[61]

September saw the opening of *Fluffy Ruffles*, a musical comedy based on a series of *New York Herald* cartoons. Among its songs was "Salome," by William T. Francis and John E. Hazzard.[62] A conventional cakewalk with a touch here and there of tonic-dominant drone to suggest the exotic East, the song expresses longing for "my oriental sweet." Only repeated references to moonlight connect "Salome dear, my moonbeam dream" to Wilde's (and Strauss's) femme fatale.

Of the other extant Salome songs from 1908, two were apparently performed in vaudeville, and the third was part of a musical comedy that opened just before the year was out. The first of these, "My Sunburned Salome," is the work of Gus Edwards and Will D. Cobb, who the previous year had written the mammoth hit "School Days."[63] The barefoot Salome on the cover wears a costume clearly derived from Maud Allan's original (fig. 4.5), but the lyrics confuse Salome with Little Egypt. Over minor-key music whose chromatically decorated dominants signal an orientalist topic, the verse sets the scene as "the land of Cleopatra." The song's persona declares:

> It was on the streets of Cairo,
> With her dark Egyptian art,
> She danced herself into my open heart one day.

The setting is not Cairo but "the streets of Cairo," that is, the ersatz Orient of a carnival sideshow. This Salome is probably no more authentic than the dancers at the Coney Island "Streets of Cairo" attraction. Likewise, the persona himself indulges in exotic disguise to act out an orientalist fantasy:

> And when the sun retires for the night,
> Beneath her window in a turban white,

> I twang a bar, on my guitar,
> And sing to eyes that shame the evening star.

The music he sings is represented by the major-key chorus, in which he entreats Salome to come to the United States and claim success as a popular entertainer:

> Don't put on your shoes and stockings,
> Leave your clothes at home,
> And you'll top the bill in Vaudeville
> My Sunburned Salome.

In the fifteen years since the World's Columbian Exposition, it would appear, Americans had become more savvy about the "genuine" Middle

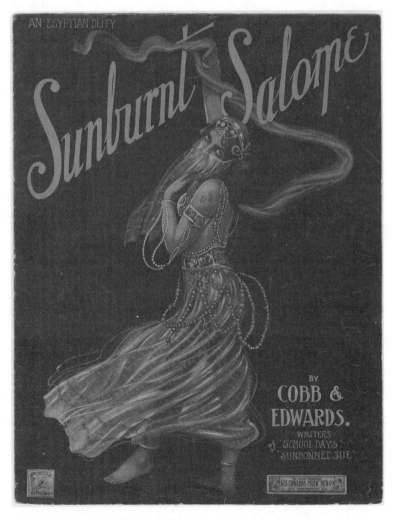

Figure 4.5. "My Sunburned Salome," cover

Eastern dancers who seemed to be everywhere. "My Sunburned Salome" winks knowingly, revels in the inauthenticity of the Salome craze, and acknowledges that vaudeville audiences were willing to accept patently phony orientalism for a choreographed glimpse of female flesh.

For "I'm Going to Get Myself a Black Salome," the lyricist Stanley Murphy (in 1909 he would write "Put on Your Old Gray Bonnet") teamed up with the comedian Ed Wynn, whose twenty-two-year-old visage, smoking a long-stemmed pipe, stares at us from the cover's photo inset (fig. 4.6).[64] The cover illustration shows not only a dancer in Allanesque costume but also a male audience member who gazes delightedly; both are African American.

Wynn's music contrasts a verse in the conventional style of ragtime songs with a chorus built on orientalisms: a minor key, the fifth scale degree ornamented with chromatic lower neighbors, and heavy downbeat accents suggesting the throbbing drumbeat that accompanied hootchy-kootchy dancing. Anticipating these orientalisms is the vamp, which is not to be ignored: here is an early occurrence of what would come to be known as the "Salomy melody." All the instances of this minor-key tune described in this chapter share a three-note structural core, $\hat{1}$–$\flat\hat{7}$–$\hat{5}$, often embellished with a dominant anacrusis, a supertonic neighbor note, or both (ex. 4.2a). Here the anacrusis is absent, the neighbor note is present, and the melody is extended with an extra $\hat{5}$–$\flat\hat{7}$ (ex. 4.2b). In most appearances (though not here) the Salomy melody has a rhythm of long-short-short-short-long; it appears in that rhythm in the vamp of a 1907 song mentioned earlier, "Mariutch (Make-a the Hootch-a ma Kootch) Down at Coney Isle," which also adds a pickup note on $\hat{5}$ that sometimes recurs in other songs (ex. 4.2c). The vamp is a typical place for a quotation to occur (e.g., the quotation of "La Paloma" in the vamp of "When Miss Patricia Salome Did Her Funny Little Oo La Palome"); my hunch is that both "Mariutch Down at Coney Isle" and "I'm Going to Get Myself a Black Salome" are quoting some earlier piece that by 1907 had become associated with pseudo-oriental dancing. Its presence in "Mariutch Down at Coney Isle" implies that only over time did it come to connote Salome dancing, and a song considered at the end of this chapter suggests that it never entirely lost its Little Egypt overtones. Nevertheless, its appearance here is the first of several that we shall observe in the Salome novelties from 1908 and after.

Big Bill Jefferson, the protagonist of "I'm Going to Get Myself a Black Salome," complains that his girlfriend spends too much of his money on fashionable clothes. The chorus switches to the first person to reveal his solution:

> I'm going to get myself a black "Salomee"
> A Hootchie Kootchie dancer from Dahomey
> All that she'll wear is a yard of lace
> And some mosquito netting on her face

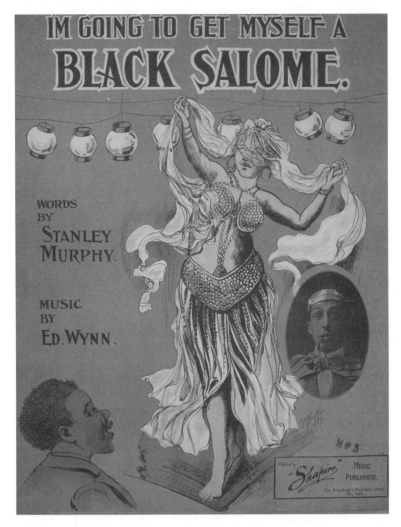

Figure 4.6. "I'm Going to Get Myself a Black Salome," cover

Example 4.2. The Salomy melody, (a) Structural outline; (b) "I'm Going to Get Myself a Black Salome," vamp melody (mm. 6–7); (c) "Mariutch (Make-a the Hootch-a ma Kootch) Down at Coney Isle," vamp melody (mm. 7–8); (d) "The Dusky Salome," chorus, mm. 1–4; (e) Joyce, "Vision of Salome," mm. 1–4, 9–12; (f) "Fatima Brown," chorus, mm. 1–4; (g) "Becky from Babylon," chorus, mm. 25–28; (h) "When They Play That Old 'Salomy' Melody," verse, mm. 1–4; chorus, mm. 1–8; (i) "Moonlight on the Nile," verse, mm. 1–4; chorus, mm. 25–28; (j) "Queen of Sheba," chorus, mm. 1–8; (k) "Fat, Fat, Fatima," chorus, mm. 25–28

(a)

Example 4.2 (*continued*)

Example 4.2 (*continued*)

(h)

d: 1̂   ♭7̂   5̂

Far   a - way   up - on the streets of Cai - ro,   When they

d: 1̂   2̂ 1̂ ♭7̂   5̂

play that old "Sa - lo - my" mel - o - dy,_____ Then my

g: 1̂   2̂   1̂ ♭7̂   5̂

heart be - gins a   throb - bing lov - ing - ly,_____

(i)

c: 1̂   ♭7̂   5̂

Long_____   a - go_____

d: 1̂   ♭7̂ ♭5̂ ♭7̂   4̂

Moon -   -   light   on   the   Nile_____

(j)

d: 1̂   ♯7̂ ♭6̂ ♯7̂   5̂

Queen_____   of She - ba,   mine_____

a: 1̂   ♯7̂ ♭6̂ ♯7̂   5̂

I_____   kneel   at your   shrine_____

(k)

g: 1̂ 2̂ 1̂   ♭7̂ 5̂   1̂   2̂ 1̂   ♭7̂ 5̂

That is just___ a guess, may be more___ or less,

A whole new outfit costs about a cent,
And then she can wiggle out of paying rent,
There's no use of talking,
I'm tired of my home,
So I'm going to get myself a black Salome.

In verse 2 Bill meets a Coney Island dancer who is wearing only "a smile / oriental earrings and a string of pearls." Knowing that she "surely was the Queen of the Salome girls," he takes her to a fancy ball:

She hadn't hardly started in to wiggle about,
When ev'ry colored gentlemen [*sic*] began to shout. Oh
[chorus] I'm going to get myself a black "Salomee."

Whereas Big Bill wants to "get" a Salome dancer only to relieve his financial distress, the other "colored gentlemen" desire her because of her sexualized dancing. Unlike the legion of Little Egypts, each of whom purported to be a genuine Middle Eastern dancer, this Salome makes no pretense of authenticity. Bill is looking for a Hootchie Kootchie dancer not from the Middle East but from the West African nation of Dahomey (present-day Benin). The reference might be to the Chicago fair's Dahomey Village, just a short way down the Midway from the Middle Eastern villages, but more likely is to the 1903 all-black musical comedy *In Dahomey*, by Will Marion Cook and Paul Laurence Dunbar.[65] The reason for citing that musical in a Salome song will become clearer after we consider the last of the extant 1908 Salome songs, Ben M. Jerome and Edward Madden's "The Dusky Salome."

The last new musical of 1908, *Mr. Hamlet of Broadway*, opened on 23 December at the Casino Theatre. In the cast was the comic singer Maude Raymond, who introduced "The Dusky Salome."[66] Unlike the two vaudeville songs just discussed, this novelty focuses not on the male admirer but on the dancer herself. To a minor-key tune accompanied by a habanera rhythm like that in "When Miss Patricia Salome Did Her Funny Little Oo La Palome," Edward Madden's lyric describes Evaline, a "ragtime queen" who "sighed for a chance at a classical dance with a movement oriental." When "lovesick coons" serenade her with ragtime, she counters, "I'm goin' to dance Salome." But she needs a partner who can meet her demands for music that is better than ragtime: "I want a coon who can spoon to the tune of Salome." Ironically, the music of the chorus that sets this line abandons the habanera style not for ragtime syncopations, and certainly not for anything that sounds like Strauss, but for a simple pentatonic melody with a melisma on the word "Salome" that hints at the "Salomy melody" (ex. 4.2d). Evaline may want a highbrow accompaniment for her dance, but, the music suggests, she lacks the sophistication to sing it herself.

In the second verse a "musical coon" accepts her challenge. Impressed by her dancing, he offers her his heart and hand, but she wants only his

head: "I'll dance Salome to it." Although newspaper accounts of vaudeville Salome dances frequently mention the papier-mâché head of John
the Baptist, here, to my knowledge, is the head's sole appearance in a
Salome song—or, in an etiolated rendition, on a sheet music cover
(fig. 4.7). The "composite" cover, used for all the published songs from
Mr. Hamlet of Broadway, depicts the show's star, Eddie Foy, in his Hamlet
costume. But in a possible reference to Salome he holds instead of Yorick's
skull a fully fleshed head, apparently Shakespeare's. With this one exception, popular songs eliminate the most unsettling part of the Salome figure, her ability to decapitate (Freud would read it as castrate) the man
who frustrates her primal lust. While some songs include men who object
to Salome's dance (we have seen this in "Patricia Salome" and will encounter it again in "Sadie Salome"), their objection has to do with the dancer's
claim to be someone other than who she is, especially someone of a different ethnicity. And while songs such as "The Streets of Cairo" associate
hootchy-kootchy dancing with a femme fatale who can rob a man of his
money and health, "The Dusky Salome" is the only song that portrays a
woman who openly says that she wants her man's head served à la carte.

The Genuine Black Salome

Songs about African American women who aspire to highbrow culture
and reject suitors who prefer lowbrow entertainments date as least as far
back as "When Mister Shakespeare Comes to Town, or I Don't Like Them
Minstrel Folks" (1901) and are often associated with Shakespeare.[67] The
comic figure of an overambitious black woman was definitely a stock
character type early in the century. In the case of both "The Dusky Salome"
and "I'm Going to Get Myself a Black Salome," however, it is probable
that the target of satire was one specific woman, a popular dancer who
attempted to use Salome as a means of raising her artistic status.

Aida Overton Walker (1880–1914), a chorus member in Black Patti's
Troubadours while in her teens, became famous as the choreographer and
leading lady for the Williams and Walker company, which produced the
first full-length musical comedies written and performed exclusively by
African Americans.[68] Built around the comic duo of Bert Williams and
George Walker (Aida's husband), who had risen from minstrelsy and
vaudeville to the legitimate stage, the company had its first great success
with *In Dahomey*, which in February 1903 became the first full-length all-
black show to play on Broadway. Although critical praise for *In Dahomey*
tended to focus on Bert Williams, one of the funniest performers of his era,
much attention went as well to Aida Walker, as in this review during the
production's tour of England later that year, a tour that included a com-
mand performance at Buckingham Palace for Edward VII: "Aida Overton
Walker is a delightful lady and a brilliant dancer. She...is a born actress,
and could shine in serious parts, and even Shakespearian drama. But singing and dancing are her great points."[69] The irony is that in 1903 no African

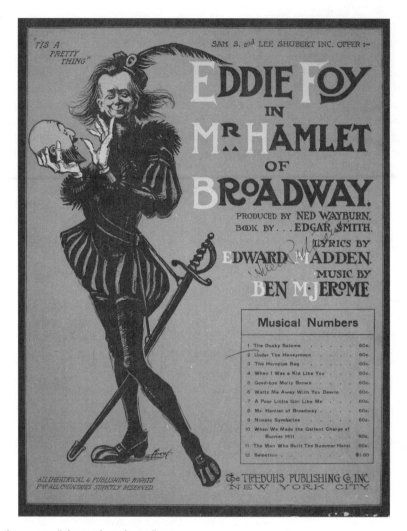

Figure 4.7. "The Dusky Salome," cover

American woman could hope to "shine in serious parts," much less in Shakespeare. One of her *In Dahomey* numbers was "I'd Like to Be a Real Lady," in which her character longs to be rich enough to hire Emma Calvé and Sarah Bernhardt to entertain at her private parties; for the London production she substituted Harry Von Tilzer and Vincent Bryan's "I Wants to Be a Actor Lady," in which Carrie Brown, a young woman who works in a dry goods store, sings about her aspiration to be on the stage.[70] Walker's very presence onstage showed that such an aspiration could be achieved in musical comedy, but the possibility of playing Shakespeare was just as remote for Aida Walker as it was for Carrie Brown.

Yet Walker saw in modern dance an opportunity to assert herself as a serious highbrow performer. The avenue in which she chose to make that assertion, Salome, was one fraught with hazards. As David Krasner has noted, African American female dancers early in the twentieth century had little chance of escaping the "paradigm of the black exotic" and at best could hope only to manipulate that paradigm to further their own artistic ends. For Walker the social pressures on her creation of a Salome dance included the black middle class's pursuit of "racial uplift," a pursuit that included "the 'policing' of the black woman's body, a rejection of any indication of sexuality in favor of self-restraint." Yet to emulate white Salome dancers was to emphasize a "primitive" sexuality that audiences were only too ready to ascribe to black women. Krasner argues that Aida Walker responded by

> suppress[ing] the erotic component of her dancing. As a result, her chore-ography, although notable for its grace, was also known for its propriety....The cultural influences that informed her performance exerted considerable and contradictory pressures....On the one hand, she stressed the abstract, hiding her sexuality and casting off the visibility of her body. On the other hand, she emphasized the sensual and the exotic, which puts [*sic*] the body in full view.[71]

Promotional material for Walker's appearance in Boston in September 1908 shows her in a costume unrelated to the revealing Maud Allan/ Gertrude Hoffmann outfit that had become the norm for Salome dancers (fig. 4.8). Walker models her exotic yet relatively modest costume in a defiant stance that contrasts with typical serpentine cooch-dancer poses. A *Boston Globe* critic echoed several others in praising her "very properly draped Salome," which nonetheless "is interesting because of the rare grace and skill of the performer." A Chicago reviewer saw in her dancing "a few wild figures, and much is made of the sinuous parade which most dancers conceive to have been characteristic of the foul-minded daughter of Herodias, but there is nothing of the hoocha-ma-cooch effect which adds a suggestion of sensuality to the exhibitions of other Salomes."[72] Even her treatment of the obligatory severed head was restrained; rather than fondling the head lasciviously, she had it separated from her by a curtain, where a sudden ray of light illuminated it at the climax of the dance.[73]

Unfortunately, the dance's theatrical context undermined its serious effect. Williams and Walker's current offering, *Bandana Land*, had opened on 3 February 1908 and was enjoying a long run. As *Bandana Land*'s leading lady, Aida Walker incorporated her Salome dance into that musical comedy in August, when Salomania was at its height.[74] At the same time, Bert Williams added his cross-dressed burlesque of the Salome craze, a juxtaposition that must have frustrated Walker's attempts to position herself as a highbrow artist. In this way the show resembled the previous year's *Follies*, in which Mlle. Dazie had performed a balletic Dance of the Seven Veils modeled on the Metropolitan Opera's version and Nora Bayes had sung the deflating comic song "When Miss Patricia Salome Did Her Funny Little Oo La Palome."

Figure 4.8. Aida Overton Walker as Salome; Billy Rose Theatre Collection, New York Public Library

Not until 1912, the year after her husband's death, was Aida Walker able to present her Salome outside the context of Williams and Walker's clowning. That summer, after a sixteen-week vaudeville tour, she played Hammerstein's Victoria Theatre, the same venue in which Gertrude Hoffmann had earlier set ablaze the fad for lowbrow Salome dances. Despite the public's waning interest—over five years had elapsed since the Metropolitan *Salome* had sparked Salomania—Walker's Victoria Theatre performances were politely received. At that time, near the very end of the Salome craze, Robert Speare of the *New York Telegraph* noted significantly that Walker was "the only colored artist who has ever been known to give this dance in public."[75]

In other words, Aida Overton Walker was not just a black Salome—she was *the* black Salome. Two of the three extant 1908 Salome songs, then, through their use of African American imagery, may well be making direct reference to her performances in *Bandana Land*. If so, then they signal an unwillingness for many in her audience to take seriously her attempt to align herself with the classical dance. Every distinction she made between herself and the lowbrow Salomes—her relatively modest costume, restrained gestures, downplaying of the gruesome head, and understated eroticism—disappears in "The Dusky Salome" and "I'm Going to Get Myself a Black Salome."

Unlike Maud Allan and her Parisian imitators, Walker had little success using Salome as a springboard to artistic legitimacy. In 1908, at the height of Salomania, theatergoers had rejected her highbrow Salome. In January 1909, though, Oscar Hammerstein would see to it that they accepted a new one.

1909: SALOME RETURNS TO THE OPERA HOUSE

When Hammerstein announced that the Manhattan Opera Company's 1908–9 season would include Strauss's *Salome*, he knew that much preparation would be needed if his production were to meet with success. His preparations concerned not only artistic matters but also public relations. Planning to take the opera to Philadelphia and Boston as well as New York, he laid the groundwork in Philadelphia in the fall by presenting Saint-Saëns's *Samson et Dalila* in that city's first stage performance (an oratorio-style performance had preceded it by two years) and including in the audience approximately four hundred clergymen, specially invited guests of the management. When they expressed their approval of that opera on a biblical subject, Hammerstein surmised that they would voice no objection to *Salome*.[76] Perhaps he had taken his cue from the 1907 production of Sudermann's *John the Baptist*, whose ads boasted that the play had been "approved by Baptist ministers in Philadelphia."

In New York the publicity took a lighter tone. Part of the buildup to the opera's opening night was a full-page article in the preceding Sunday's *New York Times* with the headline "What It Means to Present 'Salome.'" The unsigned article gives humorous descriptions of the elaborate rehearsals and scenic preparations. An especial object of anticipation was the heckelphone, "that weirdly mysterious instrument, caught and tamed by Richard Strauss himself." On actual acquaintance, the reporter found the reality to be a "disappointment, as it is merely a modest, unassuming oboe....It is played by a young man with a moustache, who already looks tired." Along with the usual promotional photos of the principal singers, the article was illustrated with some of the less pornographic of Aubrey Beardsley's illustrations for Wilde's play—hardly a prudent choice if the purpose had been to stress *Salome*'s propriety.

When the opening night arrived on 28 January 1909, the focus of critical and popular attention was not the indecency of the plot but the characterization of the prima donna, Mary Garden. Of Scottish birth but reared in Chicopee, Massachusetts, Garden had begun her career in France and, at Hammerstein's invitation, had returned to the United States in 1907 as an interpreter of the modern French operatic repertoire. In November of that year she debuted at the Manhattan Opera House in a signature role, as Massenet's Thaïs; in January 1908 she brought to New York another role she had made famous, Charpentier's Louise; and in February she gave the U.S. premiere of Debussy's *Pelléas et Mélisande*. For her second season in New York, Hammerstein asked her to depart from her customary French repertoire to take on Strauss's Salome. She spent the summer in Paris not only learning the role (in French) but also studying with the Paris Opéra's *première danseuse*. Although no soprano had at that time both sung and danced the role, Strauss himself had told Garden that such was his original intent, and she was determined to be the first to realize it.[77]

Unlike the Met performance two years earlier, the Manhattan Opera Company's French-language production was well received by critics and audience, not so much for Strauss's music as for Garden's performance—and the latter not so much for her singing as for her acting and, yes, her dancing. W. J. Henderson of the *New York Sun* called "*Salome* with Mary Garden...a dance with commentary, for the plain truth must be admitted that Miss Garden cannot sing a phrase of Strauss's music." Henry Krehbiel of the *Tribune* called her characterization "a conception of incarnate bestiality...a dreadful thing to contemplate....There is a terrible intensity in her acting...[that] is absolutely nerve racking to persons susceptible to music. Her dance is remarkable for its grace and voluptuous charm....Through it all she is a vision of loveliness."[78]

Salome had a run of ten performances in New York.[79] Things did not go as smoothly in Philadelphia, where disgruntled clergy persuaded Hammerstein to withdraw the opera after three performances in February and March, even though ticket sellers were turning customers away from the sold-out house. And in Boston the opera was not performed at all, prompting a *Musical America* cartoonist to note the acceptability of Salome dancing in Boston's burlesque halls but not the opera house (fig. 4.9). In November 1910 Garden brought her Salome to the Chicago Opera, where it was shut down after Police Chief Leroy T. Steward, acting in the line of duty, attended the second performance and reported that "Miss Garden wallowed around like a cat in a bed of catnip." When Hammerstein heard about the controversy, he remarked, "I don't know just what could be done to 'tone down' *Salome*, especially the head scene, unless, maybe they'd give the head a shave and a haircut."[80]

Two factors might explain New Yorkers' mild response to *Salome* in comparison to that of audiences in Philadelphia, Boston, and Chicago. One, of course, is that the shock had worn off from the Metropolitan's sensational 1907 premiere. A related but equally important explanation, moreover, is the Salome craze that had followed, a phenomenon that Percival Pollard, writing in the *New York Times* in 1908, had traced directly to the

Met performance.[81] Exposure, and ultimately overexposure, to Salome dancers had framed the question of *Salome*'s immorality in different terms, terms that may be explored by examining the novelty songs that followed Mary Garden's performances of Strauss's opera.

Salome Songs in 1909–10

In 1909 appear the first signs that the public's fascination with Salome and her dance was beginning to wane. The Salome novelties of 1909 and 1910 document how Salomania reached its peak and started its decline in those years.

The sheet music cover for one of these songs, Orlando Powell and John P. Harrington's "Salome," describes it as "Clarice Vance's big song success," and a large photo of Vance dominates the cover.[82] Vance apparently chose this song not only for its topicality but also for the opportunity it afforded her to exploit her large size for comic effect. Self-described as "six feet tall and quite wide," Clarice Vance (1871–1961) was a singer of Negro dialect songs—in the language of her time, a "coon singer." Like the more famous May Irwin, Vance used Negro and other dialect humor to project an uninhibited persona that opened routes to the stage closed to women whose looks did not conform to conventional notions of beauty.[83] In 1908 she described the development of her stage persona thus:

Figure 4.9. "The 'Salomé' Situation in Boston" (*Musical America*, 10 April 1909)

I was too big to play a leading part. Imagine a man making love to me on the stage. It would have been hilariously funny....Well, I could have kept on playing character parts. But what is there for a character woman? She starts as one and ends as one, and...the most she gets out of it at death is a few posies and a paragraph in the newspapers. I decided that I couldn't afford to waste my time at that line of work, so I branched out, and...have been singing dialect songs. If I'd been a sweet little thing, they would have been paying two dollars to see me and my name would have been printed in big letters on the billboards—maybe.[84]

Sterling Morris summarizes Vance's press clippings in the Locke Collection at the New York Public Library:

In 1909 it was reported in the theatrical press that "Miss Vance has first choice of all songs submitted to Remick Music for her exclusive use in vaudeville." In fact, Clarice found a song called *Salome* and thought it might be a big hit but it needed work. Mose [Gumble, her husband and a Remick manager] did not care for the song but he re-wrote it and it *was* a hit. One night Clarice got so enthusiastic during an encore of the song that she threw her "sixth and seventh vertebrae out of alignment." A cartoon in *Variety* caricatures her as a hilarious blur of squiggles and circles as she performs this number. At the same time it was noted that Clarice was stealing Eva Tanguay's audience with a "more refined manner"![85]

The last comment was no doubt tongue-in-cheek. Unlike Tanguay, who did an actual Salome dance, Vance did a parody of a Salome dance. And whereas the amply proportioned Tanguay, through sheer force of personality, could convince audiences to accept her as a sex symbol, Vance used her large size to spoof the popular figure of Salome as a serpentine seductress.

Though published by Remick, a New York company, "Salome" is the work of two British songwriters.[86] It thus reflects the British fascination with Maud Allan, whose dance "The Vision of Salome" was still packing the house at the Palace Theatre in London and inspiring imitators in England as well as in the United States. Vance probably sang "Salome" at London's Palace of Varieties (not the same as the Palace Theatre), where she played a twenty-seven-week run in 1909.[87] As did the Remick company, she no doubt found the song suitable as well for U.S. audiences, who were intrigued by Allan and familiar with her transatlantic imitators.[88]

"Salome" begins with a grandiose instrumental introduction, an "operatic" tenor-range melody under high *tremolando* chords, whose mock-serious tone is a foil for the following cakewalk rhythm. Verse 1 speculates on the theatrical Salome's low origins ("She may have been a waitress, she may have been a [diminished seventh chord, *forzato*, punctuates a blank in the lyrics]"). The closing couplet, using the first person plural to speak in the voice of the audience, comments on the ubiquity of Maud Allan imitators: "On ev'ry bill we see:—/ S-A-L-O-M-E!"

The chorus, surprisingly, quotes not *Salome* but Mendelssohn's "Spring Song." Interpretive dances to this classic were commonplace; Allan had danced one at her professional debut in Vienna in 1903.[89] Its quotation here may be intended to poke fun at "artistic" dancing in general or to ridicule the inappropriate music used by some Salome dancers. Verse 2 extends that ridicule to the bodies of Salome dancers:

> Girls thin and fat
> Round chests and flat!
> Pose as Salome, you see;
> Show their ability!

This verse culminates in a shift to the first person singular in which Vance directs the satire to her own body: "I'd make a fine Salome! / You ask the folks at home!" In performance these lines surely led into an interpolated comic dance, possibly to Mendelssohn's music and probably concluding with a reprise of the chorus.

Toni Bentley's account of the British version of Salomania emphasizes a way in which it differed fundamentally from the American variety: Maud Allan's British imitators were by and large amateurs, many of them women in the higher ranks of society. Men were not invited to the exclusive "Maud Allan" parties at which, according to a *New York Times* report on goings-on across the Atlantic, "when the coffee and cigarette stage had been reached, some of the most graceful members of the party demonstrated that they not only succeeded in matching Miss Allan's costume, but had learned some of her most captivating movements." In England, Salome was a personification of feminine power, not only for women but also for men, who found her display of power unsettling—hence this satirical song. A theatrical lampoon, *Salome and the Suffragettes*, made a connection between Salome's sexual voracity and women's demands for political equality.[90] Perhaps for that reason "Salome" ends with the couplet "All the fellows, it is true, have seen quite enough of you! / So, wherever you come from—'Go Home!'"

Back home in the United States, on 2 April 1909 Irving Berlin submitted for copyright protection two songs that allude to the Salome craze. The lesser of the two efforts, with music by Ted Snyder, is "No One Could Do It Like My Father!" Its third verse suggests that perhaps the British "Maud Allan" parties had a lower-class counterpart in the United States after all:

> One night, papa went in to see that great Salome dance.
> You talk about attention, say! he gave her ev'ry glance.
> He has my mother dancing now, her brain is in a whirl,
> And only here last week he came home with a string of pearls.
> [Chorus] No one could do it like my father!
> Ever clever, stunning, cunning father!
> Now he always stays at home.
> Mamma has learned that dance Salome:
> No one could do it like my dad![91]

But this is not a dance of empowerment by women for women, like the British amateur Salome dances. If the lowbrow American Salome dancers represented a debasement of an operatic figure, then Mamma's domestic dance may be no more than a poor man's burlesque. Still, in one possible reading of the lyrics Mamma gains the upper hand: her husband now stays at home instead of carousing, and there is a chance that the string of pearls he brings home is not a theatrical prop but the real thing.

A quite different male response characterizes the second of the 2 April 1909 songs, "Sadie Salome (Go Home)," which Berlin wrote in collaboration with Edgar Leslie.[92] Here, Sadie Cohen leaves home

> To become an actress lady,
> On the stage she soon became the rage,
> As the only real Salomy baby.

At a time of multiple Salomes, Berlin and Leslie invoke Little Egypt, whose many impersonators all claimed to be the "original," much as Sadie claims to be "the only real" Salome. At the same time, the music makes no reference to orientalist dance music; indeed, with its minor-key verse and ragtime-influenced chorus, it is stylistically indistinguishable from Berlin's other Jewish dialect songs.

When Sadie's sweetheart, Moses, comes to visit her at the theater, he is unprepared for what he sees:

> But he got an awful fright
> When his Sadie came to sight,
> He stood up and yelled with all his might:
> [Chorus] "Don't do that dance, I tell you Sadie,
> That's not a bus'ness for a lady!
> 'Most ev'rybody knows
> That I'm your loving Mose,
> Oy, Oy, Oy, Oy,
> Where is your clothes?["]

Moses's negative reaction is not shared by the theater audience; instead, when "the crowd began to roar, / Sadie did a new encore." The implication is that Salome dancing is acceptable as long as the dancer is not one's sweetheart. Although Moses's objections are voiced in the mercantile language common to the Jewish dialect song (Sadie's dance is "no bus'ness for a lady"), the scenario is not specifically Jewish; in fact, we have already encountered it in two 1907 songs, the Irish-themed "Patricia Salome" and the Italian-themed "Mariutch (Make-a the Hootch-a ma Kootch) Down at Coney Isle." In the latter, the song's Italian American persona jumps onto the stage "'cause that dance it make-a me sick." But that reaction is delayed; his first response to Mariutch's dance is delight: "Mariutch she make-a de hootch a ma kootch down at Coney Isle, / Make me smile." Perhaps it takes him a moment to recognize the exotic dancer as his estranged sweetheart; only then is he outraged. Common to both songs, then, is an objection to Salome dancing only when the dancer is known to the observer and thus not an anonymous woman on whom sexualized orientalist fantasies may easily be projected. This is a theme that we will see again in post-Salomania songs.

Charles Hamm notes that for Tin Pan Alley songs at this period "copyright and publication took place simultaneously"; that is, registration for copyright occurred at virtually the same time that a song was made commercially available.[93] Various copies of "Sadie Salome" have covers bearing photo insets of Troy Barnes, Rhoda Bernard, Bobby North, and Frank Ross, indicating that those singers were among the first to perform it publicly, probably very near the song's April 1909 copyright date. Not appearing on the cover was another singer who at that time was too obscure to generate many sheet music sales but who would be famous only a year later, when she would debut in Florenz Ziegfeld's *Follies of 1910*. Eighteen-year-old Fannie Brice's rise from burlesque began with a benefit concert for which she needed specialty material. Bernard Sobel recounts how Brice told the story:

> "Then I rushed out frantically to the music publishers: Berlin, Waterson and Snyder.[94]
> "'Hello, Irving,' I cried, 'I want two songs to sing at a benefit.'
> "'What kind of songs?'"
> The question flabbergasted her to whom songs then, were just songs.
> "I leave it to you, Irving."
> Surmising her inability, Irving walked over to the piano and took out two songs, "Cherry Rag" [i.e., "Wild Cherries"] and "Sadie Salome." He sang them; the "Salome" with a Jewish accent.
> Up to this time Fannie had never done a line of dialect. Automatically she followed the composer's lead and sang as he did.
> "That was a crucial moment in my life," she declares, "though I didn't know it, I suppose. If he had given me an Irish song and done it with a brogue, I would have been an Irish comedienne forever."[95]

Singing the songs in an incongruous white sailor suit, Brice made a strong impression. Upon returning to New York after a burlesque tour, she received a telegram from Ziegfeld offering her a contract. When she reprised her "Sadie Salome" for the 1910 *Follies*, both the song and the singer were hits.

Like the 1907 edition of Ziegfeld's revue, the *Follies of 1910* alluded to Salome not once but twice, in both a comic song and a "serious" dance number. Whereas Maud Allan had originated "The Vision of Salome" and Gertrude Hoffmann had modified it as "A Vision of Salome," the *Follies of 1910* version was titled simply "Vision of Salome."[96] The music was by "the English waltz king," Archibald Joyce (1873–1963), whose popular "Songe d'Automne" (1908) would be one of the tunes played by the ship's orchestra as the *Titanic* sank in 1912.[97] To strengthen the connection between Strauss's opera and this high-tone Salome music, Joyce's U.S. publisher issued the waltz with a cover modeled exceedingly closely on the composite cover used by Strauss's Berlin publisher for the opera's separate numbers (fig. 4.10).[98]

"Vision of Salome" has two important features. The first occurs in the four-measure introduction, which at first acquaintance is merely standard-issue orientalism; an unaccompanied, modal-sounding, ornament-laden melody in D minor is answered by choppy repeated open fifths in the bass, which can signal any exotic Other, whether Japanese, Chinese, or American Indian.[99] But a more specific reference may be intended: the melodic fragment in measure 1 and repeated in measure 3 is the "Salomy melody" (ex. 4.2e).

(a)

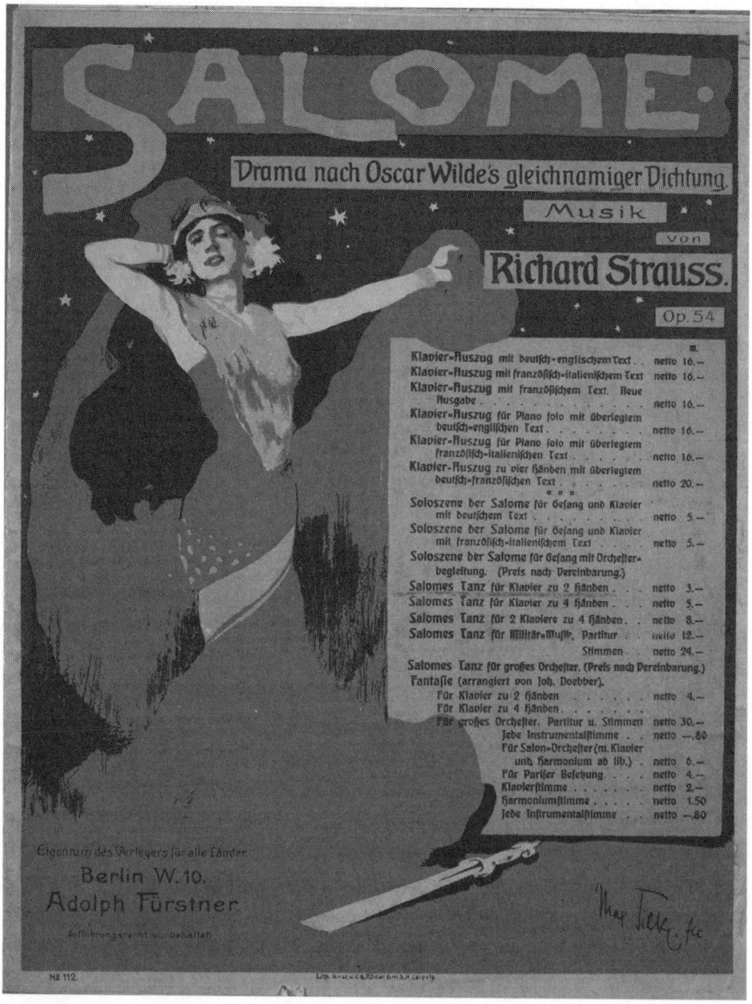

Figure 4.10. (a) Strauss, *Salome*, "Dance of the Seven Veils," cover of Berlin edition; (b) Joyce, "Vision of Salome," cover of New York edition

When the waltz proper commences, we hear the second important feature of "Vision of Salome": an imitation of the "Dance of the Seven Veils," at the very moment where Strauss descends most deeply into kitsch.[100] Joyce's waltz begins with a tunefulness that takes Strauss 127 measures to reach: a broad, thirty-two-measure, modal-sounding tenor melody (in Strauss the corresponding melody begins eight measures before rehearsal letter Q; see ex. 4.3). Moreover, Joyce is making a direct quotation not of Strauss but of the Salomy melody; at the very moment that the harmonies, melodic range, and texture of this salon music point

(b)

Figure 4.10. (*continued*)

up the musical hierarchy toward Strauss's opera, the specific tune points downward to hootchy-kootchy music. After new melodies in B-flat and, adventurously, B-flat minor, a wrenching dominant seventh plunges us into D major, where a voice (that of the dancer?) makes a startling entrance, intoning "Vah, vah" on a chromatically ornamented dominant— more standard-issue orientalism, inspired perhaps by the first theme in Strauss's dance, which an oboe begins by ornamenting the dominant with both upper and lower chromatic neighbors (three measures before letter C).[101]

Joyce likely had Maud Allan in mind rather than any of her U.S. imitators, and his waltz underlines the connection between her dance and Strauss's opera. By using Joyce's music in his *Follies*, Ziegfeld extended that line to the American Salome dancers. With its combination of high-class British kitsch and low-class Jewish dialect humor, the *Follies of 1910* marked the end of Salome's moment in the American spotlight. The remainder of her history in the United States traces her slow effacement and her refusal to fade away altogether.

1910 AND AFTER: SALOME RIDES SLOWLY INTO THE SUNSET

In January 1910, when Maud Allan finally completed her run of performances at London's Palace Theatre and made a long-delayed return to the United States, she found that Salomania had dulled the effect she and her dance might have made had she come back earlier, during the height of the craze in the summer of 1908, or even in January 1909, when Mary Garden was singing and dancing *Salome* at the Manhattan Opera House. As it was, her first U.S. performance left Boston audiences disappointed— no doubt because she omitted "The Vision of Salome," U.S. immigration officers having confiscated John the Baptist's papier-mâché head. On 29 January she added her most notorious number (sans severed head) for her New York debut at Carnegie Hall, but she had come too late—Carl Van Vechten, then a *New York Times* critic, wrote that "New York has seen so many dances of this sort by now that there were no exclamations of shocked surprise, no one fainted, and at the end there was no very definite applause."[102] In eighty-five performances over three months, Allan received a strong ovation only in her hometown, San Francisco. Another North American tour in 1916 was even less successful, despite the services of a young composer named Ernest Bloch as her conductor.[103] Then in 1918, in the waning days of World War I, she lost the highly publicized libel suit she had brought against Noel Pemberton-Billing, an extreme right-wing member of the British Parliament who had insinuated that she was a lesbian. Although Maud Allan would manage to keep performing into the 1930s, the so-called Black Book Case, for some time considered England's "trial of the century," had effectively brought her career to an end.

Example 4.3. Strauss, "Dance of the Seven Veils," waltz theme

   In late-stage Salomania, all artistic pretense falls away. As references to
Salome dwindle after the *Follies of 1910*, we are left with items such as a
1911 *Variety* review of a vaudeville dancer named Aleta whose act
included a "rag-time Salome."[104] In 1912 "That Pipe Organ Rag" declares
that ragtime played on the pipe organ "makes you feel so happy when you
find you're at home / You're trying hard to dance the dance that's called
the salome."[105] In this context the lukewarm but respectful reviews for
Aida Overton Walker's more restrained 1912 Salome are remarkable.
Though blasé—one reviewer called her "good without being great"—the
critics spared her the derision that sooner or later met the early "artistic"
Salomes such as Maud Allan and Bianca Froelich.[106]

Post-Salomania: The Last Salome Songs

In 1912 Archibald Joyce attempted a sequel to his 1909 "Vision of
Salome." His new waltz covers much the same ground as the earlier one:
a portentous introduction (this time with gong), an opening modal waltz
tune in the tenor range, and a climactic major-key tune emphasizing a
chromatically ornamented dominant. In the "Vision" that climax had a
voice singing "Vah, vah"; the sequel remains instrumental but labels the
section "Eastern Chant (Pastorale)." The name of the new waltz, "The
Passing of Salome," was prescient: Salome's moment in the center of the
public's attention had indeed passed.[107] As far as I can determine, eight
years would elapse before another song would refer to Salome by name.

But if temporarily nameless, Salome nevertheless made her presence subtly felt. For instance, two somewhat later songs allude to the Dance of the Seven Veils; both songs retail the "Sadie Salome" scenario of a hometown girl who becomes an exotic dancer.

In the first of the two, Jimmie V. Monaco and Joe McCarthy's "Fatima Brown" (1915), the title character starts out as a modest performer of the "butterfly dance" (possibly a reference to Loie Fuller's specialty). But after leaving town with a shady actor, she becomes a Salome dancer: "Now she dances the seven veils, / But six veils must be shy."[108] The chorus is based on the "Salomy melody," which is stated three times (chorus mm. 1–4, 13–16, and 23–24; see ex. 4.2f for the first statement).

The second song, Abner Silver and Alex Gerber's Yiddish-inflected "Becky from Babylon" (1920), was introduced by Willie and Eugene Howard in *The Passing Show of 1921*, the same show in which they sang "When Caruso Comes to Town." The song's persona sees a dancer, Princess Oyvayismeer, at an "oriental show":

> When she removed all of her veils
> I recognized her face,
> This Hindoo lady was a Yiddish baby.[109]

The last eight measures tell us that "She's no daughter of the Pyramids, / Her right name is Becky Bifkowitz," and that she hails from Babylon, Long Island.[110] The music here is the Salomy melody, stated first on D and then on A (ex. 4.2g).

"Becky from Babylon" mixes up the Dance of the Seven Veils with all the other orientalist claptrap of Little Egypt dancers and silent movie vamps, from snakes to Theda Bara (who in 1918 played Salome on film). And whereas the cover of "Fatima Brown" shows the title character in a costume whose chains and breastplates are derived from Maud Allan's Salome costume (by way of countless vaudeville imitators), five years later the cover of "Becky from Babylon" depicts an oriental dancer not so easily identified with Salome (fig. 4.11). By the end of the decade, the current of Salomania had merged into the broader stream of orientalist fantasy.

Another instance of Salome's effacement is the Viennese operetta composer Robert Stolz's 1919 song "Salome, schönste Blume des Morgenlands," which was published in the United States in 1920 as "Sal-O-May"—the phonetic spelling a too-late attempt to promote a Germanic pronunciation over the two ubiquitous American pronunciations, "Suh-LOAM" and "Suh-LOH-mee."[111] The English lyrics by Bartley Costello describe a "young chieftain on Araby steed" who sings to his "Rose of the Desert…Beautiful Sal-o-may." In musical style and lyrical content this song is of a piece with such contemporaneous "oriental fox-trots" as "Dardanella," "Egyptian Moonlight," and "Karavan" (all 1919), in which Arab lovers woo while their camels rest in the shadow of the pyramids—part of a fascination with the romantic Middle East that would find its

apotheosis in Rudolph Valentino's 1921 movie *The Sheik*.[112] In none of
the oriental fox-trots do the lyrics mention dancing, a key aspect of the
Salome figure. Again, the characteristics that define Salome have become
blurred in a generalized orientalist fantasy.

Also from 1920 is Richard Howard's "When They Play That Old
'Salomy' Melody."[113] Unsurprisingly, the Salomy melody is heard immediately in the introduction and again eight measures from the end, both
times over a tonic drone with chromatic ornaments. The vamp and
the opening of the verse use the most basic, three-note form (ex. 4.2h).
The melody occurs again, now with the neighbor note, at the beginning of

(a)

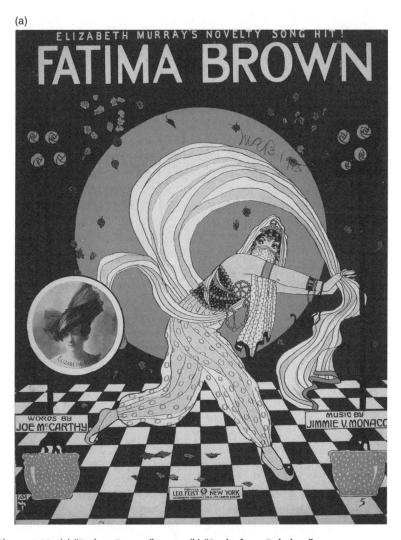

Figure 4.11. (a) "Fatima Brown," cover; (b) "Becky from Babylon," cover

(b)

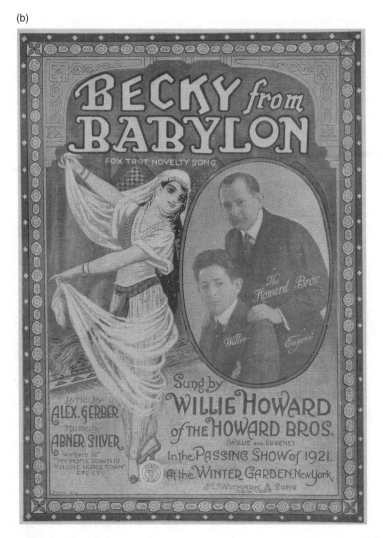

Figure 4.11. (*continued*)

the chorus, first on D (like the others) and then on G; it is harmonized in F major (the D functioning as an added sixth), thus sounding less "oriental," but even here the accompaniment's chromatic ornaments on the dominant (not shown in the example) suggest the exotic East. Apart from references to the tune itself, however, the lyrics have nothing to do with Salome. Instead, we have a standard orientalist fantasy: "Some fine day I'll travel back to Cairo....I'll ask for the hand of my sweet Oriental rose."[114] The song's Western persona is nostalgic not for the actual Egyptian city, however, but for "the streets of Cairo," where "girlies sway"; in other words, he longs to return to the exotic dancing venues at the Chicago fair or Coney Island. That earlier (and tamer) avatar of belly dancing, Little

Egypt, after nearly three decades in the United States, has emerged trium-
phant, overshadowing Salome, with her disturbing severed head and vir-
gin/vamp dichotomy. The exotic dancer, transformed into the demure
maiden portrayed on the cover (fig. 4.12), is now so thoroughly domesti-
cated that when the persona hears the Salomy melody he "seems[s] to
hear sweet wedding bells."

Variants of the Salomy Melody in Three Non-Salome Songs

Three songs from 1919–21 document Salome's absorption into the generalized orientalist romances of that era. None mentions Salome by name,
but all three use variants of the Salomy melody, and one sports a cover
illustration of what we now can confidently identify as a Salome dancer.

In 1919 the lyricists Gus Kahn and Bud De Sylva teamed up with the
composer Julius Lenzberg to write "Moonlight on the Nile."[115] Although
the lyric is in the exotic-nostalgic mode of orientalist romances (the last
line is "Moonlight and the Nile will always bring me memories of you")
with no mention of dancing, the cover shows a dancer in a costume
derived from that of Maud Allan, whose jewel-encircled breastplates and
chains of pearls provided the model for many Salome dancers (fig. 4.13).
The verse begins with the simplified Salomy melody also found in "When
They Play That Old 'Salomy' Melody." Eight measures from the end of
the chorus—a common moment for musical allusion—a variant of that
melody, beginning on the supertonic, lowers the third note a half step; the
resulting tritone, A-flat to D, intensifies the sense of exotic Otherness
(ex. 4.2i). The melodic contour resembles the "fate" motive from Bizet's
Carmen, a locus classicus of the femme fatale.

In fact, the *Carmen* "fate" motive is used verbatim in Ted Lewis and
Frank Ross's 1921 "Queen of Sheba" (with Grieg's "In the Hall of the
Mountain King" as a spooky countermelody; see ex. 4.2j). By 1921, apparently, the minor-key diatonicism of the Salomy melody was no longer
strong enough to conjure up the exotic femme fatale. Fortunately Bizet
had provided popular musicians with more suitable ready-made goods,
which in this context may be construed as a variant of the Salomy
melody.[116]

One last appearance of the unadulterated Salomy melody clinches
Salome's newfound domesticity. Sigmund Romberg's 1921 musical comedy *Love Birds* includes a scene in a Persian harem, where an emir sings a
"jazz rag" song about his favorite wife, "Fat, Fat, Fatima."[117] If in this harem
"avoirdupois…furnishes joy," then Fatima furnishes the most:

> The ladies never come too fat for me
> She weighs two hundred or maybe it's three
> That is just a guess, may be more or less

The last line quoted is set to a double iteration of the Salomy melody
(ex. 4.2k), beginning on $\hat{5}$ and harmonized with a dominant seventh. The

Figure 4.12. "When They Play That Old 'Salomy' Melody," cover

use of the tune here is no doubt intended to conjure up the image of the exotic oriental enchantress, comically juxtaposed with the image of the emir's obese wife. We have come a long way from the sixteen-year-old virgin/vamp of Wilde's play and Strauss's opera.

A CINEMATIC CONCLUSION

Around the time that Salome was fading from popular music, she made a few appearances in Hollywood.[118] Two notable examples are Theda Bara's 1918 *Salome* and Alla Nazimova's 1923 *Salome*, the latter with Beardsley-

Figure 4.13. "Moonlight on the Nile," cover

inspired sets and costumes designed by Natacha Rambova, Rudolph
Valentino's wife. A 1925 comedy, *Stage Struck*, starred Gloria Swanson as
a waitress who dreams of becoming a great actress. In an opening
Technicolor fantasy sequence she plays Salome, dressed in a Maud Allan–
style costume. A quarter century later, Swanson would demonstrate
Salome's continuing influence on the American imagination in *Sunset
Boulevard* (1950), playing Norma Desmond, an aging and delusional silent
movie actress who plans a comeback starring in her self-written screen
adaptation of *Salome*. For older audience members in 1950 her choice of
subject would have conjured up distant memories of Theda Bara and even
of the earlier Salomania, thus underlining Norma Desmond's unrealistic

living in the past. But the film as a whole suggests that the figure of Salome still conveyed a sexual and theatrical frisson, even as a fiftyish femme fatale who, if she cannot have her man alive, will have him dead. The score, by Franz Waxman, is full of allusions to Strauss's *Salome;* for instance, when William Holden looks up to see Swanson silhouetted in a window, the soundtrack quotes the opera's opening, in which the love-struck Narraboth is gazing at Salome. And at the movie's end, as Norma Desmond descends her palatial staircase, the music moves rapidly from a tango (evoking 1920s Hollywood) to a generalized exoticism, and finally to a quotation of the brutal chords with which Strauss accompanies Salome's death, chords that end both the opera and the film.[119] Lost in her fantasy world, thinking that she is indeed playing Salome, Norma Desmond dresses for her last scene in an off-the-shoulder costume similar to that worn by Mary Garden in her 1909 *Salome.* Whether in Billy Wilder's 1950 vision or in Andrew Lloyd Webber's 1993 musical version, Norma Desmond personifies the staying power of Salome in the popular consciousness.

Salomania allowed Americans to be shocked, then entertained, and ultimately bored by scantily clad pseudo-oriental dancers, one aspect of an increasing sexualized popular culture. After a sensational beginning in 1907, by the summer of 1908 indignation over Salome was turning to amusement, as humorous newspaper pieces indicate, and by 1910 audiences yawned when they finally got a chance to see Maud Allan's Salome dance. The 1910 *Musical America* cartoon about *Salome* in Boston suggests that, for many Americans, the proper place for Salome was the burlesque house, not the opera house. Thus the objections to Strauss's opera had to do not so much with its indecency as with its subject's lowbrow associations; for American operagoers, the Dance of the Seven Veils brought burlesque into the opera house. As one vaudeville comedian, John Hymer, had commented back during the Salomania of 1908 in his Negro dialect song "De Sloamey Dance":

> Dey say its classic—I don't know,
> But from all that I can see
> Dat thing dey call de Sloamey dance
> Looks like old Hooch a kooch to me.[120]

The United States lacked a cultural space for the highbrow eroticism of religious-themed orientalist dances such as those by Maud Allan, Isadora Duncan, and Ruth St. Denis—American dancers who found European audiences much more receptive than those back home. In the United States, the Dance of the Seven Veils was hootchy-kootchy, relegated to the bottom rungs of the cultural hierarchy.

Chapter 5

Poor Little Butterfly

Of all operatic heroines, Cho-Cho-San, the title character in Giacomo Puccini's *Madama Butterfly*, plays the largest role in American popular song—greater even than that of Salome.[1] Two factors account for the special place of *Madama Butterfly* in American popular culture. First, it was composed in the first decade of the century and, as an example of contemporary high culture, made a suitable subject for topical novelty songs. Second, the opera addressed topics of exoticism and femininity that were already much in the public consciousness; in that respect it engaged in a broad dialogue that was under way well before its U.S. premiere. In this case, then, as with Salome, a European opera entered a preexisting pop-cultural current that not only affected the opera's reception by American audiences but also was in turn affected by the opera. In other words, popular culture's interest in the exotic and the feminine influenced how Americans heard Puccini's opera, and that opera then influenced how those topics were subsequently represented in the popular culture. Much as cultural critics have come to view the many treatments of the Salome story as a sort of "text," it is time to view Puccini's opera as one part of a "Butterfly narrative" that also encompasses fiction, spoken theater, film, and popular song.[2]

The public's obsession with the exotic and the feminine was spurred by two cultural and political developments in this period. The first was U.S. expansion overseas, largely a result of the Spanish-American War, which inspired a fascination with Pacific Rim cultures that was entwined with anxieties about the United States' newfound role as an imperialist world power. The second development consisted of a changing American society's challenges to long-established gender roles, which reached a high-water mark in the attainment of universal suffrage in 1920 with the ratification of the Nineteenth Amendment. Unrelated as these two developments may seem, they find common expression in popular songs, plays, and works of fiction that depict the encounter between a masculinized West and a feminized East, thus providing a pop-cultural context for *Madama Butterfly*.

This chapter explores some of the numerous popular songs that use Puccini's heroine to probe, however tentatively, the unsettling theme of American imperialism in the Pacific. I begin by outlining the historical and cultural background of the Butterfly narrative and tracing its transformations as it passed from American short story and play to Italian opera. That outline serves as a backdrop for understanding the opera's early reception in the United States. Next I consider turn-of-the-century popular songs on Japanese topics, including songs based on the opera's American predecessors, as groundwork for the bulk of the chapter. I then examine several *Madama Butterfly* songs, dividing them chronologically into those that precede and those that follow the most successful and influential of all the songs about Cho-Cho-San, "Poor Butterfly" (1916). My examination aims to illuminate not only the process by which Puccini's opera was absorbed into the general culture of the United States but also how the American public appropriated the opera to enrich an ongoing self-examination that continues to the present day.

More than any opera that preceded it, *Madama Butterfly* was received by U.S. audiences as uniquely American—arguably more so than such Indianist operas as Frederick Shepard Converse's *The Pipe of Desire*, which had been performed at the Met two years before *Butterfly*. Whereas Converse and his fellow Indianist composers made use of Native American legends and music that by the turn of the twentieth century were remote from the experience of most Americans, Puccini and his Italian librettists created an opera whose leading tenor and baritone roles were contemporary Americans, caught up in a situation that had already drawn the fascination and censure of American audiences. And although the opera was not set in the United States, it took place in a country that was of vital interest to Americans in those years, a country that came to be personified in the figure of Cho-Cho-San.

To understand why *Madama Butterfly* had such a profound effect on American popular culture, it helps to consider briefly the United States' relations with Japan in the years preceding the opera's U.S. premiere. In those years the first American writings about Japan appeared, including the short story and play that became the basis of Puccini's opera. By tracing the American origins of *Madama Butterfly*, we can appreciate why U.S. audiences received it so warmly, and we can begin to apprehend why Cho-Cho-San should become a significant figure in two decades of popular song.

THE BIRTH (AND DEATH) OF BUTTERFLY: LONG'S STORY, BELASCO'S PLAY, PUCCINI'S OPERA

Admiral Matthew Perry's "opening of Japan," formalized in the 1854 Treaty of Kanagawa, marked the beginning of the United States' diplomatic relations with Japan. Throughout the late nineteenth and early twentieth centuries, the American public's interest in Japanese art and crafts grew steadily. Pavilions that displayed artifacts of Japanese culture figured prominently in the era's world's fairs, such as the 1876 Centennial Exposition in Philadelphia, the 1893 World's Columbian Exposition in

Chicago, the 1904 Louisiana Purchase Exposition in Saint Louis, and the 1915 Panama Pacific International Exhibition in San Francisco.

Interest in Japan also increased as the United States became involved in the affairs of that and other Pacific nations. The use of Japanese contract laborers on American-owned sugar plantations, beginning in 1885, played a crucial part in the exploitation of Hawaii by U.S. corporations. In June 1898 Congress passed a resolution to annex Hawaii, and President McKinley's signature the following month formalized politically what had for some years been an informal yet thorough economic domination of the islands. In the same year, the Spanish-American War resulted in Spain's granting the Philippines, Puerto Rico, and Guam to the United States in exchange for $20 million. McKinley's successor, Theodore Roosevelt, alarmed by the threat of Japan's overtaking the Philippines, instituted a plan of appeasement intended to win favor with a nation that he saw to be poised on the verge of becoming an important world power. In 1905 Roosevelt mediated a peace agreement between warring Russia and Japan, and he presided over the treaty signing in Portsmouth, New Hampshire—an act that added to the U.S. presidency the new and important role of international peacemaker. In recognition of his efforts, Roosevelt was awarded the Nobel Peace Prize, the first U.S. president so honored.

It was in this political context that the first American writings about Japan appeared. The journalist Lafcadio Hearn, who lived in Japan from 1890 until his death in 1904, fed the American appetite for things Japanese with his books *Glimpses of Unfamiliar Japan* (1894), *Exotics and Retrospective* (1898), *In Ghostly Japan* (1899), *Shadowings* (1900), *A Japanese Miscellany* (1901), *Kwaidan* (1904), and *Japan: An Attempt at Interpretation* (1904). But by far the most influential and popular literary work about Japan was a short story by the Philadelphia lawyer John Luther Long published in *Century Illustrated Monthly Magazine* in January 1898. Long's "Madame Butterfly" drew on earlier French treatments for its story of a Western man's encounter with an alluring geisha, who accepts his eventual abandonment with self-sacrifice. Unlike its most influential predecessor, Pierre Loti's *Madame Chrysanthème* (1887), however, the American story shifts the reader's sympathy away from the Western sailor and toward the geisha; a mere fifteen years old when she marries Lieutenant Pinkerton, Long's Cho-Cho-San, unlike Loti's cynical and mercenary Chrysanthemum, is the naïve victim of a cruel and capricious American whose disdain for his host country is much more pronounced than in Puccini's milder version of the character.[3] Written in the same year in which such prominent and diverse Americans as Andrew Carnegie, William James, and Samuel Clemens formed the Anti-Imperialist League to oppose the annexation of the Philippines, Long's "Madame Butterfly" may be read as an expression of anxiety over the United States' exercise of power in the Pacific and imperialism's potential to corrupt both oppressor and oppressed. Long's Pinkerton recalls the depiction in abolitionist literature, such as the writings of Frederick Douglass, of bestial slave owners drunk with "the fatal poison of irresponsible power."[4] And as we shall see, it is in the depiction of Pinkerton, even more than of Cho-Cho-San, that later treatments of Long's story most heavily revise his indictment of American imperialism.[5]

Whereas Loti's French sailor is gulled, albeit willingly, into a marriage of convenience by a crafty Japanese woman who is last seen testing his money to make sure it is not counterfeit, Long reverses the roles of victim and victimizer. His Pinkerton is singularly disagreeable, coarse in manner and disliked by his compatriots; as a result, Cho-Cho-San's devotion to him betrays a barely credible naïveté. Her fractured English, heavily spiced with the crude slang Pinkerton has taught her, increases our sympathy, in that it demonstrates Pinkerton's corrupting influence on her, while at the same time it distances us from her, in that the reader sometimes feels encouraged to laugh at the jokes of which Pinkerton has made her the unknowing butt; the dialect spellings resemble the stage patois of blackface minstrelsy. Although Long tips the scale in Cho-Cho-San's favor, his heavy-handed treatment ultimately reduces both of his protagonists to sordid stereotypes. Nonetheless, by directing the reader's sympathy toward an Asian woman in opposition to a Western man at a time when such a theme was unknown in American popular literature, Long earns his self-description later in life as "a feminist and proud of it."[6]

Without freeing itself of the same charge of stereotyping, David Belasco's one-act stage adaptation *Madame Butterfly: A Tragedy of Japan* (1900) tips the scale still farther in Cho-Cho-San's direction. Belasco confines the action to a forty-eight-hour period two years after Pinkerton has left Nagasaki; the centerpiece is Butterfly's dusk-to-dawn vigil as she awaits the sailor who has broken his promise to return when she sees the robins nesting. By keeping Cho-Cho-San onstage almost the entire duration of the play, the playwright focuses on her psychological drama, which in the hands of a capable actress becomes the opportunity for a bravura performance. At the same time, Belasco reduces the lieutenant's role to barely more than a walk-on part near the end of the play. Apart from a brief exchange with the American consul, Mr. Sharpless, during the one short period that Cho-Cho-San is offstage, Pinkerton does no more than enter (at the insistence of his American wife, Kate) after Butterfly's act of suicide, uttering a shocked "Oh! Cho-Cho-San!"—the cue for the heroine's dying words and the play's closing line, "Too bad those robins didn' nes' again."[7]

Advertised as "Belasco's charming Japanese romance,"[8] *Madame Butterfly* opened at the Herald Square Theatre on 5 March 1900 and received a generally positive review in the next day's *New York Times*. Praising "its daring admixture of European realism in the dramatic art with some of the conventional Oriental stage customs," the anonymous reviewer nevertheless felt that the play offered "just a little too much of 'Mme. Butterfly'" while giving nothing of substance to "the returned lover[,] who serves no real purpose at all." Still, the play afforded the actress Blanche Bates "another chance to show the serious side of her talent," in contrast to her comic acting in the first half of the bill, Belasco's farce *Naughty Anthony*.[9]

A London performance of Belasco's play in the summer of 1900 inspired Giacomo Puccini to undertake an operatic version—one that would further soften Pinkerton's villainy. The composer instructed the librettists Giuseppe Giacosa and Luigi Illica, who had collaborated on *La bohème* and *Tosca*, to turn to Long's story for the additional material needed for a full-length opera. The resulting libretto's first act depicts Cho-Cho-San's marriage to Pinkerton, while the second act (later divided into second and third acts) corresponds more or less to Belasco's play. Giacosa and Illica stretched to three years the interval between Pinkerton's departure and return, which Belasco had already increased from Long's single year to two years, thus allowing the couple's child, Trouble, to be played onstage by a toddler. The night-long vigil, which the play had treated as a fourteen-minute display of state-of-the-art lighting effects as Cho-Cho-San sat motionless, became the famous Humming Chorus and orchestral interlude linking the two large sections of act 2.[10]

More important, though, is the opera's representation of the two principal characters. By allowing the audience to witness Butterfly's transformation from a superficial and naïve fifteen-year-old child bride to a deeply suffering eighteen-year-old mother who takes her life just as she reaches adulthood, Puccini and his collaborators intensify Belasco's focus on her psychological state. Also, by wisely refraining from any attempt to create an Italian equivalent to the original's pidgin English, they restore her dignity and remove an obstacle to a Western audience's empathy with the tragic heroine.

At the same time, however, the opera reverses Belasco's effacement of Pinkerton, which the anonymous *Times* critic had perceived to be a structural weakness in the one-act play. Here the changes may be attributed to the generic conventions of Italian opera, which include the demand for a sympathetic tenor role with plenty of stage time and a big aria or two. By beginning his act 1 with a lengthy scene for Pinkerton and Sharpless, Puccini achieves an effective musical architecture that balances the second act's opening scene, for women's voices only, with a long stretch of music for male voices in the first act. But that architecture also reinforces a view of the opera's action through Western eyes by establishing a Euro-American norm against which Japanese characters and evocations of Japanese music are perceived as exotic additions. Moreover, Pinkerton, while retaining many of the negative attributes of Long's original, sings music that imbues him with some of the positive aura that seems intrinsic to the operatic tenor, so that he comes across as a dashing, devil-may-care rogue.[11] The great love duet that concludes act 1 resists interpretation as an expression of mere lust on Pinkerton's part. Instead, Puccini's operatic treatment induces us to regard Pinkerton as Cho-Cho-San's passionate lover—something never suggested by either Long or Belasco—and his subsequent abandonment of her as a tragic character flaw, a flaw that makes him a victim as well: Cho-Cho-San's death is *his* punishment for inconstancy.

Pinkerton is Aeneas to Butterfly's Dido, but this Aeneas returns to Carthage to witness his lover's suicide. And although Butterfly brings the opera to its conclusion with a long death scene addressed to her child ("Piccolo Iddio!"), Pinkerton literally has the last word, singing "Butterfly! Butterfly! Butterfly!" offstage before entering and kneeling over Cho-Cho-San's dying body as Sharpless takes the child and the curtain falls. Just as the opera begins with the image of an American's taking possession of property in Nagasaki, it ends with one American's taking possession of a Japanese-American child while another stakes his claim as a victim in this Japanese-American tragedy.

By softening Long's indictment of colonialist arrogance—Long's uncaring Pinkerton holds little regard for the life he is ruining—Puccini's opera opened the door to revisionist versions of the Butterfly narrative that in one way or another shift the blame away from Pinkerton and thereby implicitly absolve the United States of imperialist guilt. As we shall see, many of those revisionist Butterfly stories are told in popular songs.

Puccini's more sympathetic Pinkerton certainly did nothing to estrange the opera from the large audiences that enthusiastically greeted Henry W. Savage's touring company when it brought the United States its first *Madama Butterfly* (in English translation). Still, this Pinkerton—who is onstage much more than Belasco's had been—caused discomfort. In a lengthy *New York Times* preview to the opera's New York premiere on Monday, 12 November 1906, Richard Aldrich called Pinkerton the opera's "American Lieutenant hero—if hero that inexpressible cad may be termed."[12] His Tuesday review again finds the role of Pinkerton to be a "very unsympathetic part....He is set down as a cad by the librettists, and [the tenor] Mr. [Joseph] Sheehan allows him few redeeming points. It must be said that his singing is not one of them, for it sounded last evening hard and without intelligent modulation for his powers." Aldrich acknowledged, in other words, that a more capable tenor might have made the character more appealing. Alternatively, some of the blame might fall on the English translation, which had "been prepared more for the purposes of the singers than for the gratification of the audience; and it seemed as if a more skillful treatment of it could be made."[13]

If Savage's humdrum casting and pedestrian singing translation gave Aldrich pause, the same was not true when, later in the same season, *Madama Butterfly* received its Metropolitan Opera premiere on 11 February 1907 with a star-studded cast led by Geraldine Farrar and Enrico Caruso in a production sung in Italian and blessed by the personal appearance of the composer himself. An unsigned review, clearly the work of Aldrich, who recycled choice phrases from his November pieces, praised Farrar's performance at length; though Caruso was "not the man to impart distinction to" the unsympathetic role of Pinkerton, the part seemed to Aldrich "as though written for his voice and fits him to perfection, and of such music he is the very man to make the most." No doubt owing to the first-rate cast and the presence of the composer, the premiere drew "an enormous audience, with all the glitter and sumptuousness of the Monday night tradition" (new productions generally opened on Monday evenings).[14]

Yet it was not for musical reasons alone that *Madama Butterfly*'s Metropolitan Opera premiere was received with such intense interest. The opening night took place at the height of tensions between the United States and Japan. Already disgruntled over what it considered the unfair conditions of the 1905 Treaty of Portsmouth, the Japanese government had recently taken umbrage over the San Francisco school board's policy of placing the city's many Japanese children in a segregated school. That policy had been instituted under pressure from the Asiatic Exclusion League, a group opposed to California's steadily rising numbers of Japanese immigrants. At the White House, a series of meetings between President Roosevelt and San Francisco officials led to the so-called Gentlemen's Agreement, whereby San Francisco desegregated its schools and, in exchange, the Japanese government discouraged further emigration to California. Those meetings were still under way when, on Sunday, 10 February, the same edition of the *New York Times* that announced the next day's Met premiere of *Madama Butterfly* also carried such headlines as "No Decision Reached on Japanese Question" and "Japanese Look Down on Us: Regard the Action of San Francisco as Indicating Inferiority." An editorial cartoon that day identified Roosevelt's motivation for negotiating a settlement: fear that a provoked Japan might invade the Philippines (fig. 5.1). The Gentlemen's Agreement was reached on the same day that Puccini's opera opened, and the next day's *Times* carried not only the review but also a story, under the headline "Mikado's Envoy in Peace Talk," about a friendly, congratulatory dinner at Delmonico's for U.S. and Japanese trade officials.

Madama Butterfly could not have seemed a more timely offering. Indeed, it had an immediacy and political relevance stronger even than such late twentieth-century operas as *Nixon in China* or *The Death of Klinghoffer*—it pertained to events so current as to be in the headlines of the same newspapers that carried the opera's notices. Such immediacy was fortuitous, of course, since Puccini, when he began planning the opera in the summer of 1900, had surely given no thought to how U.S. audiences would receive his work six and a half years later. Now that relevance, combined with the U.S. origin of the opera's source material, guaranteed that American audiences would take *Madama Butterfly* to their hearts to a degree unmatched by any other European opera.

In this respect—its relevance to current headline news—Puccini's opera resembled not so much other works of high culture as the topical novelty songs and skits of the musical stage, though without those

Figure 5.1. "Stealing His Pet ('Twas Only a Nightmare)," editorial cartoon, *New York Times*, 10 February 1907

products' trivializing humor. Thus *Madama Butterfly* entered a stream of popular culture that had begun with Long's 1898 short story and was already in progress before the opera's U.S. premiere. To assess how popular culture affected the opera's reception, and vice versa, we may now turn to the first popular musical portraits of Cho-Cho-San.

THE FIRST BUTTERFLY SONGS

Unique among operatic characters, Cho-Cho-San was the subject of popular songs in the United States before she became the subject of an opera. What sparked the pre-Puccini Butterfly songs was David Belasco's stage version of John Luther Long's short story. Theatrical hits were common targets for topical burlesques and revues, and the one-act *Madame Butterfly* was no exception. The first Butterfly songs originated in such a burlesque, *Hoity-Toity*, which opened at the Weber and Fields Music Hall on 5 September 1901. One of its stars, the "coon singer" Fay Templeton, appeared as a music hall actress named Zaza DuBarry, who at one point in the evening dons Japanese costume to portray "Choo Choo San" in a burlesque of Belasco's hit of the previous season.[15] The connection between the parody and its target may have been lost, however, on the inattentive *Times* critic who wrote of the opening night: "Miss Templeton was a plump Japanese girl from 'The Geisha,' or some other musical farce, and she had the most bewitching accent, which was a mingling of Anna

Held's French and her own 'coon.'"[16] One result of the burlesque would have been the erasure of distinctions between Belasco's spoken tragedy and the sung comedy of Sidney Jones's 1896 British comedy *The Geisha*.[17]

Templeton's song in *Hoity-Toity*'s Butterfly burlesque, at least when the play opened, was John Stromberg and Edgar Smith's "My Japanese Cherry Blossom" (later in the show's run Templeton interpolated other songs, as was her wont).[18] The verse, in Cho-Cho-San's voice, uses the crude dialect that Belasco retained from John Luther Long's original story:

> I have what you callee "sweetheart," he's Unite' States man;
> Big moustache like this,
> It allee samee nicee, little Cho Cho San;
> Tickle when he kiss.

The music has none of the orientalisms of earlier pseudo-Japanese songs such as Reginald de Koven's "Japanese Lullaby" (1890) or Clayton Thomas's "Japanese Love Song" (1900): droning tonic-dominant fifths and pentatonic melodies, often in a tinkling upper register and with staccato repeated notes in short-short-long rhythm (or a common variant, four shorts and two longs).[19] The reason for their absence becomes clear when we reach the chorus, where, over ragtime piano figuration, the voice switches to Pinkerton's and the vocabulary mimics the minstrel song:

> "I love you my Jap'nese cherry blossom,
> Your lips are sweeter than pone and possum,
> Nestle close against your ragtime' Meli'can man,
> You can't shake me my cho cho San."[20]

Here the song echoes a moment in both Long's story and Belasco's play where Cho-Cho-San sings a song taught to her by Pinkerton:

> I call her the belle of Japan—of Japan,
> Her name it is O Cho-Cho-San, Cho-Cho-San!
> Such tenderness lies in her soft almond eyes,
> I tell you, she's just "ichi ban."[21]

Similarly, in both Long's and Belasco's version she sings to her child a lullaby that Pinkerton had sung to her:

> Rog'—a—bye, bebby,
> Off in Japan,
> You jus' a picture,
> Off of a fan.[22]

The use of lowbrow humorous songs to denigrate a Japanese character thus begins not with a burlesque of Belasco's play but with Long's short story itself.

With "My Japanese Cherry Blossom" begins a long series of songs about romances between American men and Japanese women.[23] In Bob Cole and James Weldon Johnson's "My Lu Lu San" (1905), an American sailor,

practicing "love making on the Yankee plan," pleads for Lu Lu San to
"come leave Japan / Quick as you can."[24] His sly expression on the sheet
music cover reveals him to be the manipulative, uncaring Pinkerton of
Long's original story (fig. 5.2). Likewise, when the "gently wooing"
American sailor in Dolly Jardon and Edward Madden's "Lotus San" gets
no more than a laugh from his geisha, he returns in the company of his
crew and steals her away as his comrades steal the other geishas, in a reenactment of the mythological rape of the Sabine women.[25]

Quite a different point of view characterizes Harry O. Sutton and Jean
Lenox's "Kokomo" (1904), which begins with a third-person verse, followed by a first-person chorus in the American's voice.[26] The second
verse disrupts this pattern, however, when the title character, knowing

Figure 5.2. "My Lu Lu San," cover

that "her heart would surely grieve" if she were to leave Japan, tells her lover, "I always will be true, / If in turn you will promise here to stay." The American "had to agree, / For he loved her you see," and he remains in Japan.[27] This revisionist Butterfly narrative, in which the Pinkerton figure is faithful and the assertive Kokomo resembles the new "emancipated woman," is the work of the obscure lyricist Jean Lenox, one of a handful of female songwriters on Tin Pan Alley, and it seems likely that she performed this song herself in vaudeville.[28] The song's happy ending is all too rare in the Butterfly songs that were to follow.

A dominant theme in Butterfly songs is that of the persona's nostalgia for the girl he left behind in the Orient. It first emerges rather late, in 1914, and in a song not obviously related to *Madama Butterfly* (beyond its Japanese theme). "I Want to Go to Tokio," by Fred Fisher and Joe McCarthy, describes a Japanese man, presumably in the United States, who longs for his Yo-san and plans to rejoin her in Tokyo.[29] Two 1915 songs take this theme of nostalgia for Japan and put it in the mouths of Western personae. Anita Owen's "In Japan with Mi-Mo-San" expresses a Western man's longing once again to "wander 'mong the flow'rs" with Mi-Mo-San, who in his dreams lures him to return to Japan, where "behind her fan I'd steal a kiss."[30] The subjunctive mood (instead of "I'll steal a kiss") tells us that the stance is one of idle fantasizing, not purposeful resolve. Here, as in the turn-of-the-century operas described by Gilles de Van, exoticism expresses "a desire for escape" from restrictive reality, an "escape into dreams."[31]

Similarly dreamlike is Will E. Dulmage and E. J. Meyers's "Poppy Time in Old Japan," in which a westerner woos a Yokohama geisha until "one sunny day I had to sail away."[32] But the close of verse 2 takes a surprising turn:

> And when I came back to the land of flowers
> I found you had vanished like the morning dew.
> The world seems blue, dear, without you, dear,
> For you took the sunshine, too.

Here it is the geisha, not the Pinkerton figure, who has departed without explanation. All blame rests on her head, and the male persona is absolved of guilt. He *had* to sail away, and he did come back for her, after all—not to witness her suicide but to find that she had simply "vanished." With a clean conscience, this Pinkerton is free to revel in gentle nostalgia.

Barely present in the songs discussed so far is any representation of the Butterfly figure's psychological perspective; only in "Kokomo" does she speak, and even there her words are few in comparison to the Pinkerton figure's. Not until 1916 would Cho-Cho-San's point of view become the principal focus, and then it is found in no fewer than three songs. One of them, "Poor Butterfly," was a huge hit whose success is the subject of the next section. The other two, minor songs by major Tin Pan Alley songwriters, are important here because they introduce another major theme: the

Butterfly figure as an abandoned victim who deserves our sympathy. Before considering "Poor Butterfly" at length, I will look briefly at these two songs and suggest why all three should have emerged within a five-month span in 1916.

Conflating Chinese and Japanese orientalisms, Egbert Van Alstyne and Gus Kahn's "My Dreamy China Lady" follows the basic outline of the Butterfly narrative but makes both protagonists Chinese.[33] Ching Lo "must sail away / Far across old China Bay" and "will never return" to his "little China girl," for reasons not divulged; but the nameless lady of the title "still in dreams…seems to hear / His love song ringing near," an excuse for a return of his first-person chorus. In contrast, Irving Berlin's "Hurry Back to My Bamboo Shack" give the first-person chorus entirely to the geisha, as she entreats her absent lover to return, though verse 2 makes clear that the "handsome sailor boy / Who sailed across the sea / Will soon forget his broken toy."[34] When Berlin registered the song for copyright on 30 June 1916, his company issued the sheet music with a decorative cover depicting a geisha watching a ship on the horizon (fig. 5.3). The absence of a performer inset signals that the song failed to be taken up by a performer in musical comedy, revue, or vaudeville.[35] Likewise, no evidence suggests that the song met with commercial success or was ever recorded. The music is pedestrian; in places it seem to be a pallid reworking of Berlin's December 1915 song "The Girl on the Magazine," and the pentatonicism that opens the verse is well within Berlin's normative style and probably is not a conscious orientalism. Still, it is the first of many songs that focus on a Japanese woman as a perpetually waiting victim of abandonment.

What might explain this shift in Butterfly songs in 1916, a decade after *Madama Butterfly's* U.S. premiere, toward a more sympathetic portrayal of Cho-Cho-San? Neither "My Dreamy China Lady" nor "Hurry Back to My Bamboo Shack" shows the least influence from Puccini's opera. If anything, their change in attitude could have more to do with the then-current film version of *Madame Butterfly* starring Mary Pickford in the title role. Shot in a Japanese-style garden in Plainfield, New Jersey, and released in November 1915, the film was promoted as a version of Long's story, not Belasco's play (and, by implication, not Puccini's opera).[36] Though the claim may have had more to do with contractual obligations than with artistic influences, audiences no doubt would have received the film as a part of the generalized depiction of the Butterfly narrative in popular culture, a blend of magazine fiction, illustration, play, film, opera, and popular song. By starring America's sweetheart, clearly recognizable despite her Japanese costume, the film may well have encouraged filmgoers to consider Cho-Cho-San in a more sympathetic light. As the next section suggests, a new development in operatic performances may have offered similar encouragement as well.

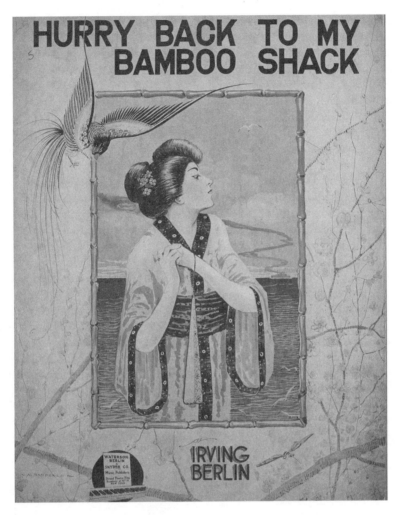

Figure 5.3. "Hurry Back to My Bamboo Shack," cover

THE QUINTESSENTIAL BUTTERFLY SONG: "POOR BUTTERFLY"

Although Puccini's *Madama Butterfly*, at its 1906 U.S. premiere, had failed to have the immediate effect on Tin Pan Alley that Mary Pickford could exercise, that effect finally came a few years later with the arrival of the first Japanese soprano to sing the title role, and indeed to have a career of any consequence in the West, Tamaki Miura.[37] After singing Santuzza in her native Japan, Miura traveled first to Germany and then to England in 1914, where she sang her first Cio-Cio-San. She made her U.S. debut in that role with the Chicago Grand Opera in 1915 and later that year sang

Butterfly with the Boston-based San Carlo Opera Company and with the Boston Grand Opera Company.[38] Miura made her New York debut when the latter organization presented *Madama Butterfly* at the Manhattan Opera House on 2 November 1915.[39] New York audiences apparently approved of Miura's performance; in the 1918–19 season she sang the role at the Met. More important here, though, is a New York revue in which she did not sing but in which appeared a song written for her: "Poor Butterfly."

The venue for that show was not any ordinary theater but the enormous Hippodrome, a "gigantic toy" for the masses built in 1905 by Frederic W. Thompson and Elmer S. Dundy, the creators of Coney Island's Luna Park.[40] Gerald Bordman lists the many splendors of this theater-cum-circus, which seated five thousand customers and employed a ballet of two hundred, a chorus of five hundred, and a technical staff of over one thousand. The space was too huge for any but the grandest spectacles; its unsuitability for ordinary musical entertainments caused the lyricist John Golden to complain, "The Hippodrome was so big that audiences could never hear the lyrics."[41]

From the beginning, the Hippodrome offered a mixed bill of fare built around exotic ballets, circus acts, and militaristic scenes of carnage. The Hippodrome's first show, in 1905, was a double bill; the musical comedy *A Yankee Circus on Mars* combined the first two elements (including horses jumping into water tanks and elephants pulling automobiles), while a "tableauxdrama" called *The Raiders*, about the Confederate prison camp at Andersonville, provided the third element, in the form of a fully staged Civil War battle reenactment. For three decades the most significant change in the formula was the elimination of the military theme after World War I. The last show to play the Hippodrome, Rodgers and Hart's *Jumbo* (1935), still relied on the same combination of song, dance, acrobatics, and animal acts found in *A Yankee Circus on Mars*, even if the setting had become somewhat more realistic.[42]

When the Broadway impresario Charles Dillingham took over the theater from Lee and J. J. Schubert in 1915, he brought in R. H. Burnside, a successful writer and director of musical comedies, who revamped the shows to emphasize star performers. His first presentation, *Hip-Hip Hooray!* was a revue that featured John Philip Sousa's band.[43] After December's *Mammoth Midwinter Circus Supreme*, the next show to play at the Hippodrome was a revue simply called *The Big Show*, which opened on 31 August 1916. To the usual blend that made up Hippodrome spectacle Dillingham added a new element: highbrow culture. Bordman describes this extravaganza:

> For the audiences that came to see [*The Big Show*] during its 425 performances, the main attraction was almost certainly the great ballerina, Anna Pavlova, dancing an abbreviated version of Tchaikovsky's "Sleeping Beauty" (with Leon Bakst scenery). Charlotte [a single-named celebrity] skated on ice, elephants played ball, and the ensemble participated in a gigantic

minstrel show. The edition also contained the one song to become a popular standard out of all the music the Shuberts and Dillingham introduced at the house. "Poor Butterfly" was, moreover, the prolific Raymond Hubbell's single claim to lasting fame. Its lyrics were by John Golden, who in a few years became one of New York's most successful and best-loved producers. This lament for Madame Butterfly was written when Dillingham thought he had secured the services of a then famous Japanese soprano, Tamaki Miura. The arrangements fell through. On opening night a Chinese-American vaudevillian introduced the song, but she was so bad she was hastily replaced.[44]

Despite the lack of a star performer and the unsympathetic acoustics of the cavernous Hippodrome, the song written for Tamaki Miura, "Poor Butterfly," became a huge hit. Of all the operatic novelties considered in this book, it is the only one to enjoy any longevity as a pop standard. The many recordings of "Poor Butterfly"—one discography lists 326 jazz versions alone—include records by artists as varied as Fritz Kreisler and Frank Sinatra; played on the Hammond organ, the tune also served as the theme song for *Myrt and Marge*, a popular 1930s radio soap opera.[45] In addition to its long recording history, another measure of its success is the large number of "answer" songs it inspired. In so doing, it kept Cho-Cho-San alive as a figure in popular culture for many more years.

Although "Poor Butterfly" was popular as an instrumental number, part of its effectiveness as a song lies in John L. Golden's lyrics.[46] Those lyrics focus on Cho-Cho-San as she waits for Pinkerton to return, much as Belasco's play had made her overnight vigil into a famous fourteen-minute stretch without dialogue and Puccini's opera had made of it a set piece comprising the Humming Chorus and an orchestral interlude. The song's Miss Butterfly is "a sweet little innocent child" until "a fine young American from the sea / To her garden came"; no mention of her work as a geisha tarnishes her pre-Pinkerton image. From him she learns "to love with her soul," but after he "sail[s] away with a promise to return," time freezes; Miss Butterfly remains constant as "the moment[s] pass into hours / The hours pass into years." Although the first verse and the first half of the chorus are in the third person, at midchorus the lyrics change to the first person and Miss Butterfly speaks with a trace of the old pidgin:

> The moon and I know that he be faithful,
> I'm sure he come to me bye and bye.
> But if he don't come back
> Then I never sigh or cry
> I just mus' die.
> Poor Butterfly.

Does Cho-Cho-San speak that last line, or is it a third-person commentary?[47] Either way, the maudlin lyrics unmistakably paint Cho-Cho-San as a sympathetic victim. The focus on Butterfly's vigil tightens the story's timeline even more narrowly than had Belasco's play. Nothing hints at Pinkerton's return, with or without an American wife. The passive

Butterfly stands frozen in a static tableau of unrequited fidelity. She seems incapable of even so decisive an action as suicide; instead, it is the very act of waiting that is slowly killing her. Already "her heart is growing numb."

By 1916 U.S. audiences were open to more sympathetic portrayals of Madame Butterfly, whether one attributes that change of attitude to Mary Pickford, Tamaki Miura, or any of the other early operatic Butterflies such as Geraldine Farrar. Nevertheless, "Poor Butterfly" would have had no effect on the public without a compelling musical setting. Even more than the lyrics, the music marks a significant departure from the earlier Butterfly songs. That it should do so is remarkable, given that the composer was Raymond Hubbell. A perusal of even a few of Hubbell's many songs confirms Alec Wilder's impression that, this one song excepted, his work is that of a prolific, technically competent, but uninspired hack.[48] Wilder considers "Poor Butterfly" to be

> one of the loveliest ballads I've ever heard. It is extraordinary that a man who revealed such talent in this song should have failed to write anything [else] of nearly its quality....
>
> There's not a word of criticism I can conceive of for it. Its verse is written in a deliberately oriental manner, and though its purpose is strictly exposi-tional, nevertheless it creates a proper mood for the chorus without in any way revealing what is to come. After three "held" pick-up notes the melody falls on the fourth interval [i.e., degree] of the scale....It is the very best example I know of the romantic potential of this interval, which under unromantic circumstances should never be stressed simply because it then comes off as a weak note....
>
> There isn't a suggestion of contrivance in this melody. It flows as freely as sometimes a song does from the pen of one who is truly inspired.[49]

This is high praise indeed from Wilder, who cares for very few songs writ-ten before the 1920s, and his comments are as good a place as any from which to begin a close look at "Poor Butterfly."

Perhaps because he intended the song to be sung by an operatic soprano, Hubbell not only makes greater-than-usual demands on the singer (the vocal range is nearly two octaves) but also sprinkles the page liberally with tempo and expression markings unusual in popular song: "dreamily," "slightly quicker," "poco animato," "con passione," "quasi recitativo." Moreover, unlike the composers of the earlier Butterfly songs, Hubbell attempts to incorporate some aspects of Puccini's musical style, especially in the realm of harmony. The song's success lies in these Pucciniesque ele-ments, and that success, by engendering imitations, was to enrich the American popular song in profound and far-reaching ways.

The influence of Puccini can be heard in the music for the verse, which is indeed orientalist, as Wilder notes. The verse begins with a tonic-domi-nant drone in the bass and a quasi-pentatonic melody, both of which were already well-established tropes in orientalist popular songs. Here, how-ever, the melody is harmonized in parallel triads, generating a rich texture of added-sixth chords and seventh chords that need not resolve in a conventional manner (ex. 5.1a). By comparison, Puccini harmonizes the Japanese folk tune heard at Butterfly's first appearance onstage (and which becomes a recurring motive throughout the opera) with a tonic drone and chords with added sixths and sevenths (ex. 5.1b).

Example 5.1. (a) Hubbard and Golden, "Poor Butterfly," mm. 4–11; (b) Puccini, *Madama Butterfly,* act 1, rehearsal number 41

(a)

Example 5.1 (*continued*)

(b)

The verse's first departure from the tonic-dominant drone occurs at the words "They met 'neath the cherry blossoms ev'ry day," as the lyrics turn from scene setting to narrative. Here a modal-sounding progression alternates minor triads on the mediant and supertonic (ex. 5.2a). Similar stepwise progressions characterize Butterfly's first exchange with Pinkerton, when she narrates her forced decision to become a geisha. Modal harmonies also underpin a melody notably similar to the verse of "Poor Butterfly," with its rocking minor thirds, when, a short time later, Butterfly declares her resolve to "forget her people" for Pinkerton's sake (ex. 5.2b).

If the verse imitates *Madama Butterfly* in several specific ways, then the chorus is a more generalized evocation of Puccini's rich harmonic palette. A thirty-two-measure ABAC form, the chorus comprises nine phrases; all the phrases begin with short pickup notes that lead to a sustained down-beat note (see ex. 5.3). In the A and C sections, quicker notes in midphrase lead to another held note; the contrasting B section ("The moment[s] pass into hours…") is a rising sequence on shorter phrases in which the held note is ornamented with a written-out trill beginning on the upper neighbor. Apropos the chorus's first sustained note, Wilder is correct in observing that a held note on the fourth scale degree is unusual in popular ballad style, especially as a beginning; what also makes this prominent note unusual is its emphasis of a dissonant harmony—it is the seventh in a dominant seventh chord. In fact, most of the sustained notes in the chorus form dissonances with the underlying harmony. Of the sixteen sustained notes labeled in example 5.3, twelve form a dissonant interval with the harmonic root, whether a ninth (seven notes), a seventh (two notes), an augmented fifth (two notes), or a suspended fourth (one note). Of the other four sustained notes, two occupy structurally important positions: the midpoint of the chorus is marked by a half cadence with a sustained consonant fifth above the root of the dominant, and the entire chorus ends, unsurprisingly, with the melody on the root of the tonic harmony. The other two sustained consonances, both in the B section, begin with the upper-neighbor ornament, which forms a ninth above the root.

The high incidence of phrases that end on the ninth of the harmony makes "Poor Butterfly" an extremely unusual song for the period before 1920. By comparison, the chorus of Art Hickman's "Rose Room" (1917)—another in the small repertory of pre-1920 songs that remained favorites of jazz performers in the following decades, largely because of its

Example 5.2. (a) "Poor Butterfly," mm. 19–22; (b) Puccini, *Madama Butterfly*, act 1, rehearsal number 81

(a)

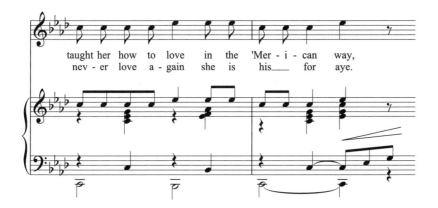

Example 5.2 (*continued*)

(b)

sophisticated harmony—begins with two phrases in which ninths resolve downward by step to the root before the next phrase begins.[50] My own unsystematic search has turned up only one other example from before 1920 of phrases ending on unresolved ninths: Jean Schwartz's tune for "Rock-a-bye Your Baby with a Dixie Melody" (1918) has a chorus whose first phrase ends on the ninth of a dominant chord (on the last syllable of the title phrase).[51]

Such unresolved dissonances (or dissonances that are resolved only in the next phrase, after the singer has taken a breath) become increasingly frequent in the 1920s and are the norm in the later songs of Tin Pan Alley's "golden era." An example far removed in mood from either "Poor Butterfly" or "Rock-a-bye Your Baby" is Rodgers and Hart's "Manhattan" (1925), whose first three measures include three such dissonances, all approached by ascending leap. Measure 1 has a leap to the major seventh of the tonic chord ("We'll have *Man-hat-tan*"), measure 2 a leap to the thirteenth of the dominant ("the Bronx and *Stat-en*"), and measure 3 concludes the phrase on the ninth of the tonic ("*Island too*")—the same sonority that ends the first phrase of "Poor Butterfly." By the end of the golden era, melodies that stress the upper notes of "tall" chords are the norm, as,

Example 5.3. "Poor Butterfly," chorus, with sustained notes labeled

* spelled enharmonically

for example, in Erroll Garner's "Misty" (1954), where the opening downbeat (after two pickup notes) emphasizes the seventh of the tonic harmony, approached and left by leap, and the next measure features a large
leap up to the ninth of a minor dominant harmony (actually the beginning of a ii^9–V^{13}–I progression in the key of the subdominant). This treatment of melodic dissonance contributes much to the tone of sophisticated
urbanity that is a unifying characteristic of the golden-era American pop
song. It would be an overstatement to assert that all of these later songs
are directly indebted to Raymond Hubbell's sole hit. Yet "Poor Butterfly"
undeniably bears important features of the harmonic sophistication that
characterizes the best songs of the decades after 1920, and its harmonic
language is certainly atypical of 1916, the year it appeared.

As the remainder of this chapter demonstrates, "Poor Butterfly" was an
enormously popular, influential, and long-lived song. Especially significant
here is the operatic provenance of the song's model. An unexamined commonplace of jazz history holds that the introduction into American popular music of "advanced" musical devices—chords of the ninth and higher,
whole-tone scales, harmonic progressions that transcend the tight circle-
of-fifths barbershop harmonies of ragtime—is the result of jazz musicians'
exposure to the French impressionism of Debussy and Ravel. True,
Debussy's earlier songs and piano pieces were familiar to Americans
before 1920.[52] And it would be a mistake to overlook the preponderance
of ninth chords in parlor songs such as Ethelbert Nevin's hugely successful "The Rosary" (1898).[53] But I would suggest that scholars have over-
looked another, more likely source for these devices. Puccini's operas
Manon Lescaut, Tosca, La bohème, and *Madama Butterfly* enjoyed tremendous popularity in the United States, whether in full productions or in
excerpts sung in recital—even in vaudeville—and disseminated in the
form of sheet music and phonograph records.[54] Far more than the music
of Debussy or Ravel, Puccini's operas had a strong foothold in American
culture, from which their influence could be felt not only by jazz musicians but also by songwriters. In drawing a line that connects French
impressionism to jazz, historians should not overlook a similar line that
connects Puccini to Tin Pan Alley.

If music scholars tend not to be cognizant of the similarity between
Puccini's style and that of Tin Pan Alley, the connection was not lost on
Puccini's publisher. "In 1921," writes Holly Gardinier, "G. Ricordi, the
publisher of Puccini's operas, sued all parties associated with the song
'Avalon.' The publisher argued that the melody was lifted from Puccini's
opera *Tosca,* specifically from the aria 'E lucevan le stella.' Puccini and his
publisher prevailed in the case and were awarded $25,000 in damages
and all future royalties to 'Avalon.'" Although the dispute concerned the
melody of the song's chorus, which begins with a dozen notes apparently
lifted straight out of "E lucevan le stella," the chorus also displays a little
of the Pucciniesque harmony I detect in "Poor Butterfly," namely, the
augmented dominant ninths at the midpoint (where the ninth resolves

Example 5.4. (a) Puccini, *Tosca,* "E lucevan le stella"; (b) Jolson and Rose, "Avalon," chorus

(a)

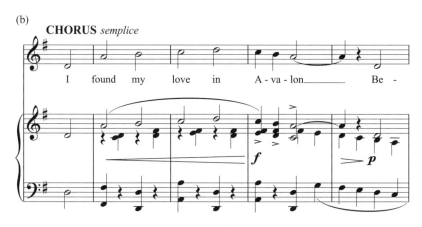

Oh!dol-ce ba ci,o   languideca - rez-ze,   mentr'iofre-ment-te

(b)

CHORUS *semplice*

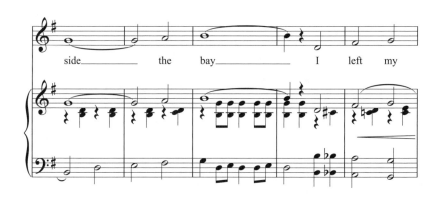

I   found   my   love   in   A - va - lon_____   Be -

side_____   the   bay_____   I   left   my

love   in   A - va - lon_____   and   sail'd_____   a -

Example 5.4 (*continued*)

Example 5.4 (*continued*)

melodically by leaping up a fifth), and the melody's climax on the ninth of an applied dominant (ex. 5.4).[55]

Only further research can answer the question of whether "Poor Butterfly" is a historical fluke or the most prominent example of a hitherto unrecognized line of musical influence. What can be answered here is the question of the song's influence on other songs that take Madame Butterfly as their subject matter.

AFTER "POOR BUTTERFLY"

In the five years following the publication of "Poor Butterfly," at least two dozen songs appeared that either continued the pre-1916 Butterfly themes, made reference to Puccini's opera, or simply "answered" "Poor Butterfly" in the time-honored tradition of riding on a hit song's coattails. The remainder of this chapter examines some of those songs, beginning with those that testify to the popularity of "Poor Butterfly" and continuing with songs that, in one way or another, retell the Butterfly narrative, transforming the characters or incidents in ways that reveal how powerfully Long's story, like Belasco's and Puccini's dramatizations, mirrored Americans' sense of themselves and of their relationship to exotic Others.

Within a year of its 1916 publication, "Poor Butterfly" had become ubiquitous, judging by Arthur Green and William Jerome's "If I Catch the Guy Who Wrote Poor Butterfly."[56] The cover depicts the song's persona, in white tie and tails and surrounded by butterflies, sitting atop a globe while in the foreground instrumentalists and singers perform "Poor Butterfly" for masses of people stretching from the Bering Strait to the Middle East (fig. 5.4). The lyrics suggest that the reason for the original song's popularity lay in the melody, not the words, since the original lyrics are either misquoted or replaced by "da-de-dum" vocables. For example, the original chorus's opening line, "Poor Butterfly! 'neath the blossoms waiting," becomes in the answer song "Poor Butterfly for you I'm falling," not only changing the

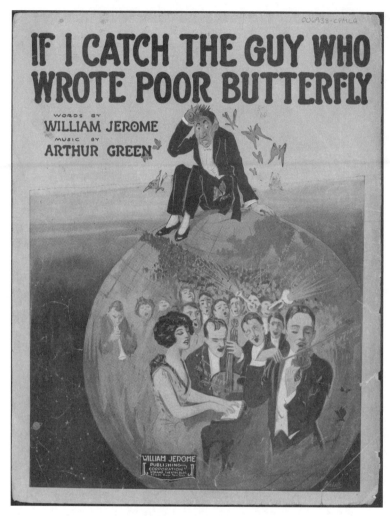

Figure 5.4. "If I Catch the Guy Who Wrote Poor Butterfly," cover

sentiment to that of a conventional love song but also introducing the voice of the Pinkerton figure, notably absent in the original.[57]

Also from 1917 is a novelty sung by Willie and Eugene Howard in a Shubert revue at the Winter Garden Theatre, Joseph A. Burke and Al Dubin's "My Yiddisha Butterfly."[58] Instead of pseudo-Japanese oriental-isms we find what Hamm identifies as typical markers of the Jewish dia-lect song: minor-key verse and "melodic figuration [that] often invokes the Yiddish theater, or even the synagogue," here displayed as raised-fourth chromaticism.[59] Also typical of Jewish dialect songs is the lyrics' conflation of aesthetic value and market value; the protagonist expresses his attraction to the song "Poor Butterfly" as a wish to own it, but his desire is checked by the sheet music's price tag:

> A fancy clothing cutter, Abie Perlmutter,
> Heard a song called "Butterfly";
> It was such a riot Abie thought he'd buy it,
> He cared for a dime as much as his right eye.
> He tried to buy a copy in the Ten Cent Store,
> He found that "Butterfly" would cost him twenty more;
> He said I don't need a Japanese Poor Butterfly,
> I know such a rich one and to her I can sigh:

To a fluttering melody he sings the chorus:

> Flutter, flutter, flutter 'round your Abie Perlmutter,
> Oi, my Yiddisha Butterfly!

Obsessed with money, Abie won't have a poor butterfly when a rich one can be had. He tells his sweetheart that dressed in a kimono she would "look like Geraldine Farrar and that's no lie, / Just like she looks when she plays 'Madame Butterfly.'" But even this comparison with America's most glamorous opera singer, who sang Cio-Cio-San in the Metropolitan premiere, is financially motivated, as the closing lines reveal:

> You're a beautiful girl and if I thought you're not
> I would love you the same, I would love you a lot,
> 'Cause I know how much your Fadder's got,
> My Yiddisha Butterfly.

Abie Perlmutter is a mirror inversion of Lieutenant Pinkerton, who, though flawed, is not stingy—when he departs, he leaves Cho-Cho-San enough money to support herself, their child, and a servant for three years. He is willing to spend freely to indulge his physical lust for Butterfly. Perlmutter, in contrast, is inspired less by sexual attraction to his nameless sweetheart than by lust for her father's money. And to his avarice must be added his cowardice, on the eve of the United States' entry into World War I:

> They are calling for soldiers, I should go I guess,
> But they don't want the married men, come on, say "Yes,"
> Would they miss one soldier more or less,
> My Yiddisha Butterfly.

Compared with Abie Perlmutter's, B. F. Pinkerton's shortcomings begin to seem minor.[60]

If these two songs pay scant attention to the lyrics of "Poor Butterfly," the same is not true of other songs, which alter the Butterfly narrative's meaning by changing the details or adding commentary and drawing new comparisons. Common to all of them is an impulse to retell and revise the Butterfly "text," whose fascination was inseparable from Americans' discomfort with its personification of the United States as an imperialist bully. Long's story, Belasco's play, and Puccini's opera, despite their differences in emphasis, all feature an American victimizer and a Japanese victim and thus cast the United States in an uncomfortably negative light. One way in which popular music attempted to revise that message was to "freeze" the story in a song that focuses on a single moment, thereby ignoring the tragic ending. Another was to revise the principal characters, downplaying their roles as victim and victimizer.

For example, Harry Tierney and Alfred Bryan's "My Yokohama Girl" (1917) "freezes" at the moment of early courtship, by focusing on a Yankee sailor's seduction of Fuji Kamo, who does nothing but sip tea and murmur "Hickey hoi." The sailor, in contrast, has the entire chorus in which to clarify, in the first person, the commercial basis of their relationship, concluding with "I will give some simolian to some Mongolian / Yokohama girl like you."[61] Similarly, the first verse of Edah Delbridge and A. Robert King's "Ko-Ko-San" (1919) describes a "tiny Japanee" sitting under a cherry tree; the chorus abruptly shifts to a first-person entreaty for Ko-Ko-San to "say you'll take me for your lover man."[62] The song ends with this entreaty, thus keeping the action frozen in the moment of courtship, with no concern for Butterfly's fate.

A song that freezes the story at a later stage is Richard A. Whiting and Raymond B. Egan's "The Japanese Sandman" (1920), after "Poor Butterfly," the most popular and long-lived pseudo-Japanese Tin Pan Alley song.[63] Though the lyrics tell us only that "there's a baby with a lady of Japan singing lullabies," the high incidence of Madame Butterfly imagery in popular culture would encourage buyers to read the cover (fig. 5.5) as a representation of Cho-Cho-San with her baby, Trouble. And perhaps it is not too far-fetched to read a Puccini reference in the song's introductory parallel ninth chords, which slide down first chromatically and then by whole step.[64] Likewise, the unusual wording of the cover and title page— "Told by Raymond B. Egan" and "Set to music by Richard A. Whiting"— positions the song as something preexisting this manifestation, as if the songwriters were arranging traditional material, such as a folk song. Since both words and music are indeed original, what is presumably not original is the subject of Japanese mother and child; for the American public circa 1920, by far the most familiar representation of that subject was Madame Butterfly. By focusing exclusively on the interaction between Cho-Cho-San and Trouble, "The Japanese Sandman" simultaneously makes reference to the Butterfly narrative and ignores its tragic ending and anti-American overtones.

In contrast, Joe Meyer and Bobbie Tremaine's "Happy Butterfly" (1920) acknowledges Cho-Cho-San's tragic fate only to negate it.[65] To droning fifths and exotic-sounding chords on the lowered submediant, the verse begins with a reference to Butterfly's vigil (no doubt by way of "Poor Butterfly") but goes on to argue that her case is exceptional:

> You have heard of Butterfly
> Waiting as the years pass by,
> Do not think that in old Japan

Figure 5.5. "The Japanese Sandman," cover

> Ev'ry maiden waits for a man,
> …
> Most girls have a lover gay to sing this way
> [Chorus] My star 'neath the willow tree,
> You are, little Japanee,
> not like poor Butterfly.

Seizing on Butterfly's refusal of Yamadori's marriage offer, a minor incident in the Long-Belasco-Puccini narrative, "Happy Butterfly" says that most Japanese women are not so foolish. The implication shifts the blame from Pinkerton to Cho-Cho-San.

Whereas this song effaces Pinkerton's culpability by slandering Cho-Cho-San, others achieve the same end by revising her character in ways that allow her to escape her tragic fate. At the same time, they invest in her an air of liberation associated with the first historical wave of feminism. The geisha heroine of Leo Edwards and Ballard MacDonald's "Mister Butterfly" (1917) knows of Cho-Cho-San's destiny but has no wish to share it.[66] To a pentatonic tune in ballad style she compares the sailor, not herself, to a butterfly that sips the honey and "pass[es] the faded flowers by," then gives him his walking papers:

> Ah! Sailor man you'll love today
> And then tomorrow sail away,
> Good-bye, Mister Butterfly.

Wise to the dangers of East-West love affairs, this savvy geisha rejects the sailor's advances. Just as the cover depicts her gaily waving good-bye to the departing battleship (fig. 5.6), so may the singer portraying her, by taking the optional notes in the sheet music, send off her sailor man with an operatic flourish on high A.

Education also leads to a happy ending in "Poor Little Butterfly Is a Fly Girl Now" (1919).[67] Here, though, the female protagonist learns not about the dangers of rapacious sailors but about decidedly Western techniques for keeping a man in her power.[68] The song opens with Butterfly's vigil, the part of the story that is the focus of "Poor Butterfly":

> All alone in her pagoda,
> Waiting for her sailor man,
> Poor Butterfly,
> Would sit and cry.

By the time Pinkerton makes his brief return, however, education has given Butterfly power over his decision making:

> Someone came along and showed her,
> How to keep him in Japan;
> He just came back for a day,
> [B]ut she said, "I guess you'll stay."

What has she learned? The latest dance steps, of course:

> Poor little Butterfly, has learned to roll her eye,
> And when she shimmies she's as cute as she can be;
> Say, when this baby shakes,
> She's got just what it takes,
> To keep her sailor boy from going out to sea.

Introduced to white audiences in 1918 by Gilda Gray and Mae West, the shimmy is an African-derived dance motion that involves shaking the shoulders so that the straps of the dancer's dress (chemise) slide down. Bee Palmer's shimmy was a highlight of the *Ziegfeld Follies* of 1919, and in

Figure 5.6. "Mister Butterfly," cover

the 1920s many jazz dancers learned to "shake their shimmy."[69] Cho-Cho-San also knows that "the 'Ballin' Jack,' / Was bound to bring him back," a reference to Chris Smith and Jim Burris's 1913 hit song "Ballin' the Jack," whose lyrics describe the steps for an African American solo dance featuring "a sensual, gyration…with bumps and grinds."[70] This Cho-Cho-San's repertoire extends beyond African-derived dance; she also has "learned to do an Oriental dance and how; wow! wow!"—a reference to belly dancing. Adding Middle Eastern to African dance gives Madame Butterfly strong seductive powers: "She knows that her sailor boy, / Will never say 'Ship ahoy.'" She has remade herself as a modern woman who is both clever and fashionable; in turn-of-the-century British and American slang, she is "fly." As perhaps the first "fly girl," in 1919 she anticipated the World War II–era Women's Air Force Service Pilots (WASPs) by two decades and the hip-hop expression by three quarters of a century.[71]

"Poor Little Butterfly Is a Fly Girl Now" makes clear its status as an answer song near the beginning. The verbal reference to "Poor Butterfly" at measures 9–10 coincides with a musical reference: three pickup notes leading to a sustained note on the fourth scale degree. To this expected musical reference M. K. Jerome adds a rather subtle and surprising one to "Un bel dì," the most frequently excerpted number from Puccini's opera. Each half of the verse begins with that aria's characteristic texture, in which the melody is stated in octaves with rather static harmony notes filling in. Jerome's melody resembles Puccini's: the first three measures of both begin on scale degrees $\hat{8}$–$\hat{7}$–$\hat{6}$. But Jerome disguises the allusion by using the stalest pseudo-Japanese rhythmic clichés (ex. 5.5). Still, the reference to "Un bel dì," the aria in which Butterfly anticipates what will happen when Pinkerton returns, is especially apt. Even the cover resembles the 1908 U.S. imprint of "Un bel dì" as a separate number (fig. 5.7).[72] This evidence of the connection between "Poor Butterfly" and Puccini's opera testifies to how closely intertwined operatic and popular cultures remained in the United States two decades into the twentieth century.

Not every song that focuses on Cho-Cho-San changes her character so radically. "Yan-Kee" (1920), George Gershwin and Irving Caesar's less successful follow-up to their 1919 hit "Swanee," adds only one new detail: this Madame Butterfly entertains the notion of pursuing her missing Pinkerton to the United States.[73] As recorded by the "coon shouter" Marion Harris for Columbia in the same year, "Yan-Kee" indulges in crude orientalisms: choppy repeated notes, drones, Chinese cymbals and woodblock, whining oboe and bassoon solos, and references to the opening of *The Mikado*.[74] Slightly modifying her stage Negro dialect for the song's pseudo-Japanese pidgin, Harris pronounces her *r*s as *l*s even for words not thus misspelled in the sheet music. The third-person verse establishes the now-familiar story, giving way in the chorus to the geisha's first-person lament (ex. 5.6).[75]

Just as "My Japanese Cherry Blossom," back in 1901, used ragtime patterns to link Japanese and African American ethnicities as objects of scorn, here Gershwin gives the chorus, in the Butterfly figure's first-person voice, a touch of the blues. The opening phrase, over an orientalist tonic-dominant drone (not shown in ex. 5.6), includes the lowered "blue" seventh; the published accompaniment doubles the melody in "Japanese-sounding" parallel fourths. After a literal repeat, the phrase is transposed up a fourth over a subdominant harmony, thereby alluding to the twelve-bar blues pattern and simultaneously introducing a melodic "blue" third.[76] But what ensues—a quotation not from Puccini but from Gilbert and Sullivan's *Mikado*—undermines the poignancy of this geisha's blues lament.[77]

If revising Cho-Cho-San's character is one way to reduce the harshness of the Butterfly narrative, an even more effective way is to revise Pinkerton.

Example 5.5. (a) Puccini, *Madama Butterfly*, "Un bel dì," opening; (b) "Poor Little Butterfly Is a Fly Girl Now," mm. 5–12

(a)

Example 5.5 (*continued*)

(b)

All a-lone in her pa - go - da,   Wait-ing for her sail-or man, Poor But-ter-

fly,_____Would sit and   cry;_____

One method for weakening the sense of Western culpability was to make both protagonists Asian, the strategy of "In Old Japan" (1917), "In China" (1919), and "So Long! Oo-long (How Long You Gonna Be Gone?)" (1920).[78] Another was to portray the sailor, back home in the West, nostalgically reviewing the events of the Butterfly narrative. This kinder, gentler Pinkerton sees the error of his ways and begs forgiveness in Raymond Hubbell's answer song to his own hit, "I'm Coming Back to You Poor Butterfly" (1917), whose music reworks the motives of "Poor Butterfly" so feebly that it confirms the impression of Hubbell as a one-hit wonder.[79] The unreality of this scenario is underlined in "Garden of My Dreams," written to accompany the Ziegfeld chorus girls as they paraded before Joseph Urban's "gigantic re-creation of a miniature bonsai with cherry tree and bridge" in the *Ziegfeld Follies of* 1918 (the image of a gigantic miniature is quintessentially Ziegfeldian).[80] After the song's persona buys a "Japanee" bowl ("Truly I admired it / And I soon acquired it"), it grows larger in his imagination, and soon he is pledging his undying love. The Butterfly figures are not one but many; they are not real persons but

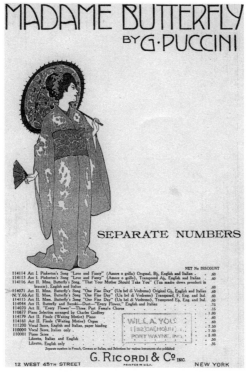

Figure 5.7. (a) "Poor Little Butterfly Is a Fly Girl Now," (b) "Un bel dì," 1908 U.S. edition, covers

painted images, objects; the persona only imagines he has visited Tokyo, and his fantasizing is enacted onstage as a Ziegfeld leg show. In this context his pledge of fidelity cannot be taken seriously.

The mood of nostalgia need not be connected with any promise, however feeble, to return. The persona in Walter Donaldson and J. Kiern Brennan's "Suki San (Where the Cherry Blossoms Fall)" (1917) pictures a present-tense Suki San as she "hums a lonesome lovesick tune" that closely resembles "Un bel di."[81] Although he apostrophizes, "Suki San, I hear you call," the persona does no more than idly wish he were back at that earlier meeting: "How I'd love once more to stray, / As we used to hand in hand." No promise to return, no realization that he truly loves her—for this Pinkerton, the thought of Butterfly's vigil conjures up only the mildest melancholy.

The most commercially successful of the "Poor Butterfly" answer songs simply applies the Madame Butterfly motif to another popular genre, the Hawaiian song. In "Hawaiian Butterfly" (1917) the persona sends a wire to his "beautiful Hulu" promising that "sometime in the bright Hawaiian

Example 5.6. Gershwin and Caesar, "Yan-Kee," chorus (voice only)

sunshine, / Dear, I'm going to make you all mine."[82] But his plans are groundless fantasies, as the closing lines reveal: "When I come back some day, we'll fly away, / Hawaiian Butterfly." The music bears no resemblance to either Puccini or "Poor Butterfly"; rather, it is a typical example of the *hapa-haole* (half white) Hawaiian song, with lazy triplets and dotted rhythms in a slow fox trot tempo.[83] In its lyrics, if not in its music, this song is descended from the Negro dialect songs about dalliances with dark-skinned Islanders that entered the popular music repertoire in significant numbers in 1898, the year the United States annexed Hawaii. In the following years, as the song persona lost obvious African American identifiers, nostalgic reminiscence became the dominant mood, allowing white audiences to indulge in fantasies of interracial romances that would bear no inconvenient consequences. Simply by coining its title phrase, "Hawaiian Butterfly" draws a parallel between those fantasies and the less romantic realities that formed the basis of Long's "Madame Butterfly" and its artistic successors.[84]

The last important Butterfly song is also the one most explicitly linked to Puccini's opera. "Cho-Cho-San" was issued in 1921 by Puccini's publisher, Ricordi, with a cover that borrowed artwork from the house's own 1908 series of *Madama Butterfly* offprints and billed the number as a "song fox-trot on melodies by G. Puccini arranged by Hugo Frey" (fig. 5.8; compare fig. 5.7). The verse, to the tune of the Humming Chorus that in the opera accompanies Butterfly's vigil, describes Cho-Cho-San in the third person; the nonrhyming second line and the awkward setting of the word "sailor" to three melody notes (resulting in a melisma on the word's weak syllable) do not inspire admiration for the lyricist Jesse Winne's versification (ex. 5.7). The chorus shifts to the first person and we hear the voice not of Cho-Cho-San, whose aria "Un bel di" is the basis of the tune, but of the absent Pinkerton. Ferde Grofé's arrangement of "Cho-Cho-San," as recorded by Paul Whiteman's orchestra, includes a more extended quotation of the aria than found in the sheet music and ends with a literal quotation of the stern octaves and unresolved harmony that conclude the opera, with a sock cymbal now providing the closing punctuation.[85]

Here is a summation of the processes we have observed in Butterfly songs throughout this chapter. Puccini's music is assimilated into an American popular style so thoroughly that it no longer sounds like a foreign element. Cho-Cho-San is not portrayed as a person with some control over her fate but is frozen into an emblem of self-sacrifice, patience, and passivity. Most radical is the revision of Pinkerton from the "inexpressible cad" of the Long-Belasco-Puccini narrative into a distant but still ardent lover who promises to return "some fine day." Moreover, by setting Pinkerton's promises to music originally meant for Butterfly, "Cho-Cho-San" makes clear the focus of American fascination with the Butterfly narrative: not with the Japanese "Other" but with the mirror that Pinkerton holds up to his compatriots. If Long's readers and Belasco's and Puccini's audiences were displeased with what they saw in that mirror, then the

Figure 5.8. "Cho-Cho-San," cover

majority of Butterfly songs set about to change that image into something more reassuring.

World War I had drawn the U.S. public's attention away from Asia and toward Europe, and exhaustion with the war led to a postwar period of indifference to nondomestic issues. In this context, the mere fact that the fashion for Butterfly songs lasted as late as 1921 speaks to the potency of the Butterfly myth. Although that fashion came to an end with "Cho-Cho-San," the process of retelling Cho-Cho-San's story certainly had not reached its conclusion. Whether treating that story lightly, as in the 1938 cartoon "Poor Little Butterfly," which makes Cho-Cho-San literally a but-

Example 5.7. "Cho-Cho-San," voice only

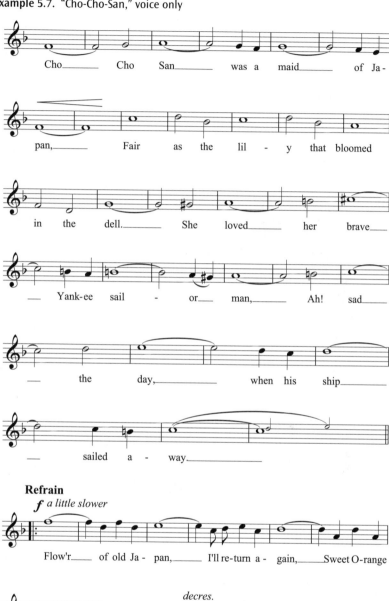

Example 5.7 (*continued*)

terfly, or taking it oh-so-seriously, as in the 1989 musical *Miss Saigon,*
which makes Pinkerton a sensitive New Age guy, popular culture throughout the twentieth century continued to rework the Butterfly myth, hoping to find an image in its mirror that was at once true to life and not too
painful to behold.[86]

Part III

EPHRAHAM AND HIS EQUALS

Chapter 6

National Identity in "That Opera Rag"

A strong vein of self-deprecation has run through American humor from Revolutionary times nearly into our own. Born of the contrast between the early Yankee settlers and their more refined British fore-bears, the American self-portrait in humorous songs, plays, and journal-ism has both celebrated and deplored the same shortcomings in American manners that so offended British tourists from Mrs. Trollope to Charles Dickens. Beginning with Brother Jonathan, the simple Vermont farmer who was the model for Uncle Sam, and extending through Mark Twain's innocents and Henry James's not-so-innocents abroad, comic personifi-cations of the national character have paradoxically derided Americans' homespun simplicity of manner while simultaneously equating it with sincerity, virtue, and a natural nobility that has nothing to do with aristocracy.[1]

The contradictions in these national self-portraits are compounded when the emblematic comic figure is African American. Recent critical thinking about the nineteenth-century minstrel show has begun to delve deeply into those contradictions.[2] My purpose here is to extend the inves-tigation begun by scholars of minstrelsy into the early twentieth century by examining a representative of that repertory of popular song called by its practitioners and their audiences the "coon song"—songs whose lyrics use a stereotyped Negro dialect based on actual African American speech but modified into a conventionalized stage patois through use in min-strelsy.[3] Few musical genres are today held in lower esteem; Sam Dennison has written that "if it were possible to measure vulgarity in music, the coon song would certainly represent the nadir."[4] Dennison's dissection of the racism in these songs counters (but has not entirely displaced) the prevailing scholarly view of the Negro dialect song as a "deservedly forgot-ten" genre.[5] As Dennison argues, we cannot afford to forget this cultural product of a crucial episode in American history, no matter how unpleas-ant some aspects of it may now appear. Keeping these songs in our mem-ory, though, means not only coming to terms with their racist content but also reaching beyond the concealing curtain of that racism to uncover other meanings they may have held for their public.

By combining the African American stereotypes of the Negro dialect song with allusions to European opera, Ted Snyder and Irving Berlin's "That Opera Rag" (1910) also documents how opera served as a point of reference and widely understood symbol with which Americans could address a complex nexus of emotions and attitudes toward class distinctions, racial difference, national identity, and changing gender roles. To apprehend the multiple levels of meaning in "That Opera Rag," including but not limited to the obviously racist, this chapter asks three questions in turn. First, how do music and text interact in this song? (Answering this question raises a related question: How did songwriter and lyricist collaborate in the creation of the song?) Second, how did the song function in the stage comedy in which it was first introduced? And third, how did the singer's stage persona influence the audience's response? At each of these three focal points—song, dramatic work, and stage persona—racial stereotypes and operatic quotations play a new expressive role. Only when all of these levels of expressive function are considered together may we begin to fully grasp the song as a cultural artifact that takes its place among the ambivalent representations of the American character.

COLLABORATIVE CREATORS: TED SNYDER AND IRVING BERLIN

"That Opera Rag" is the product of a collaboration between the songwriter and publisher Ted Snyder and his staff lyricist, the twenty-one-year-old Irving Berlin, whom Snyder had hired the previous year.[6] Like most of their forty-two songs published between 1909 and 1912, "That Opera Rag" credits the words to Berlin and the music to Snyder on the first page of the sheet music.[7] As Charles Hamm explains, however, that attribution

> is probably more a function of the respective positions and statuses of the two men in the publishing house, and of royalty distribution, than of their respective contributions to the song in question. Berlin probably drafted the lyrics for most of these pieces and Snyder came up with the first musical ideas, but distinctions between composer and lyricist almost certainly broke down in the throes of creation, and both words and music of the completed songs must represent some degree of collaboration....Occasional disagreements between the attributions on the first page of a song and those on its cover, or between either of these and the information submitted for copyright entries, support the notion that the division of labor in writing a song was not strictly maintained.[8]

To this description of the pair's working methods should be added the case of "Wild Cherries (Coony, Spoony Rag)," a song that Snyder first wrote as an instrumental rag and to which Berlin later added words.[9] Moreover, the songs of Snyder and Berlin, like virtually all Tin Pan Alley products, involved an uncredited collaborator: the staff arranger who prepared the piano-vocal score for publication.[10]

In short, rarely if ever did Berlin submit finished lyrics for which Snyder then devised a musical setting complete in all its details—a relationship between poet and composer that is the norm in the creation of art song.

The creative circumstance in which music may precede words, or in which two or more writers may craft words and music simultaneously, suggests that methods of song analysis developed for the interpretation of art song may need revision before being successfully applied to Tin Pan Alley products. David Brackett notes that "one difficulty in transferring [art song] approaches to the analysis of popular song is that they tend to rely on a strict dichotomy between the 'poet' and the 'composer,'" as well as the assumption of a creative process in which words precede music. Endorsing Kofi Agawu's proposal to work from "a music-to-text rather than the more familiar text-to-music approach," or better yet, to treat the two simultaneously and thus "avoid a taxonomy of inputs," Brackett reminds us that "it is not as if we first hear the words, then the music, and then put the whole thing together."[11] For reasons that will become clear, "That Opera Rag" shows evidence that the composition of the music preceded, at least in part, the crafting of the lyrics. The song can thus be apprehended not as a musical setting of words but as a mutual interaction between words and music.

THE MUSIC OF "THAT OPERA RAG"

In its broad structural outlines, the music of "That Opera Rag" conforms to Tin Pan Alley conventions of its era: a piano introduction, a short vamp before the voice enters, then verse and chorus (fig. 6.1).[12] Three features, however, defy stylistic expectations: (1) the tonal scheme of both verse and chorus is highly unusual, (2) the presence of operatic quotations is a departure from the norm, and (3) partially as a result of the second feature, irregular phrase lengths disrupt the foursquare phrasing typical of the genre. These features are represented schematically in table 6.1.

Most unusual is the tonal scheme, an oscillation between A minor and F major. The majority of Tin Pan Alley songs are in a single key, with a sizable minority in two keys. Within that minority, two schemes predominate: either the verse is in a minor key with the chorus in the relative major, or the verse is in a major key with the chorus in the key of the subdominant, a pattern reminiscent of the march or piano rag.[13] "That Opera Rag" stands apart from either double-key scheme for two reasons: first, the two keys form a mediant relationship, and second, the alternation of keys occurs twice, once in the verse and again in the chorus, rather than centering the verse in A minor and the chorus in F major. As we will see, however, each key change acts on a local level much like one or the other of the two standard double-key schemes.

The first alternation of keys underscores the verse's division into two contrasting sections or strains. The first, in A minor, is built on a two-measure melodic unit, a syncopated version of the Miserere from act 4 of Giuseppe Verdi's *Il trovatore* (ex. 6.1). The melodic unit has a strong rhythmic profile: the first measure has a rest on the downbeat, and the

(a)

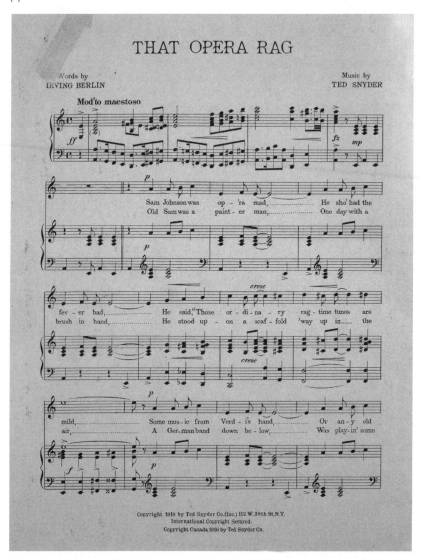

Figure 6.1. "That Opera Rag"

(b)

Figure 6.1 (*continued*)

(c)

Figure 6.1 (*continued*)

(d)

Figure 6.1 *(continued)*

Table 6.1. "That Opera Rag": Structural Divisions, Quotations, and Tonal Plan

Section:	Introduction		Verse			
Subsection:	Intro	Vamp	A^1	A^2	B^1	B^2
Phrasing (mm.):	4	1	2 + 2 + 4	2 + 2 + 5	2 + 2 + 4	2 + 2 + 4
Quotation:			*Trovatore*, Miserere			
Harmony:	a:	i	i → V	i → III	F: V–I–V–I	V → V/iii
Measures:	1–4	5	6–13	14–22	23–30	31–38

Section:	Chorus			
Subsection:	A	B	C	D
Phrasing:	2 + 2 + 2 +2	4 + 4	5	4
Quotation:	*Carmen*, Toreador Song		*Lucia*, Sextet	"Home, Sweet Home!"
Harmony:	a: i → iv	F: I → vi → V	I → ii	→ I
Measures:	39–46	47–54	55–59	60–63

second measure contains a long-short-long ragtime pattern. The second strain, in F major, varies the two-measure unit (see ex. 6.2): the first measure is simplified, and the second measure's ragtime rhythm is altered to short-long-long. More significantly, the first measure serves now as anacrusis, and the syncopated measure falls on the strong structural downbeat.

The verse's seventeen-measure first strain divides into two nearly equal phrases: an antecedent, ending in a half cadence on the dominant (m. 13), and a consequent, ending in a full cadence on the mediant, C (m. 21), which is then reharmonized as the dominant of F in preparation for the second strain. The movement from C to F is thus experienced locally as a drop from tonic to subdominant, as at the trio of a march or piano rag—or at the transition from verse to chorus in "Alexander's Ragtime Band" (1911). What makes this modulation unusual is its occurrence not between verse and chorus but between the two strains of the verse. The drop to the subdominant is associated with a musical relaxation, and the music of the second strain is simpler, lacking the asymmetry of section A. Its first half ends in a full cadence on the tonic (m. 29), the second in a half cadence in the key of the mediant, A minor (m. 37), as preparation for the chorus, which begins in that key.

Choruses in earlier Tin Pan Alley songs display a variety of formal patterns—mostly ABAC and AABC, and only rarely AABA, the predominant pattern during the "golden era" of the 1920s through the 1950s. Not only does the chorus of "That Opera Rag" use a pattern uncommon in any period—four distinct musical ideas, ABCD, none of which recurs—but the four sections are also of unequal lengths: eight, eight, five, and four measures respectively. Moreover, each section of the chorus is based on

Example 6.1. Verdi, *Il trovatore,* act 4, Miserere, mm. 10–12

Example 6.2. "That Opera Rag," (a) mm. 6–7; (b) mm. 22–23

quoted material. Section A stretches the first four measures of the Toreador Song from Georges Bizet's *Carmen* (ex. 6.3) over eight measures by syncopating and extending the basic figure. Following Bizet's original, the melody descends a ninth by sequence, ending on the subdominant, D minor (m. 45). Section B moves to F major for a quotation of the second theme from the Toreador Song, unsyncopated apart from the Scotch snap

Example. 6.3. Bizet, *Carmen*, act 2, Toreador Song, (a) mm. 9–12; (b) mm. 37–38

in measure 49. Whereas Bizet presents these two themes in parallel minor and major, Snyder and Berlin, by eliding the intervening material, arrive at the same mediant relationship found in the verse, between A minor and F major. Significantly, the approach to F major is from D minor, creating the local effect of a relative minor–major relationship—the other of the two double-key schemes mentioned earlier.

Section C, also in F major, emphasizes the supertonic, as does the source of its quotation, the Sextet from Gaetano Donizetti's *Lucia di Lammermoor* (ex. 6.4). In the Sextet the quoted phrase is followed by diminished seventh and cadential six-four chords; in "That Opera Rag" those same harmonies begin section D, a quotation of the familiar "Home, Sweet Home!"

The chorus, then, is almost entirely patchwork. Ironically, the only phrase not derived from preexistent material, the second half of section B (mm. 51–54), recurs nearly verbatim in the verse of Berlin's 1912 song "When the Midnight Choo-Choo Leaves for Alabam'" (ex. 6.5). In other words, the only new material in the chorus is a formulaic turn to the

Example 6.4. Donizetti, *Lucia di Lammermoor*, act 1, Sextet, mm. 39–42

dominant. The chorus's pastiche quality, combined with the verse's quasi-rag structure, suggests that Snyder, with or without Berlin's help, devised at least some of the music independently of a lyric; in other words, "That Opera Rag" probably began life as an example of the "ragging the classics" instrumental genre, which was common early in the century.[14] Like all

Example 6.5. (a) "That Opera Rag," mm. 48–52; (b) "When the Midnight Choo-Choo Leaves for Alabam,'" mm. 18–22

Example 6.5 (*continued*)

such instrumental pieces, its humor would lie in the juxtaposition of high-brow operatic melodies with the syncopated rhythms and sectional construction of lowbrow ragtime.

In that light, the introduction can be heard as a spoof of operatic gran-diloquence. Thundering octaves and rapidly changing diminished harmonies begin *fortissimo* and crescendo to a *forzato* cadence in measure 4, whereupon the dynamic drops suddenly to *mezzo piano*, the texture radically thins, the rhythm slows to an augmentation of the opening bass pattern, and the harmonic activity freezes on the tonic—altogether, a hyperdramatic contrast more typical of opera than of popular music. Moreover, if the introduction suggests opera in a generalized way, then the vamp, with its habanera rhythm and minor key, specifically evokes *Carmen*. Yet the ensuing melody comes from Verdi, and when the Bizet quotation finally arrives in the chorus, it is not the Habanera but the Toreador Song. One bit of opera is as good as another, the music implies. Here, "ragging the classics" reduces the classics to rags.

THE LYRICS OF "THAT OPERA RAG"

In devising words for Snyder's music, Berlin created a scenario that matches the music's comic confusion. The song's persona is Sam Johnson, a black housepainter afflicted with a love of opera. The lyric reflects the music's phrase structure, most evidently in the verses, where the 2 + 2 + 4 musical phrasing parallels the number of feet per poetic line, 3 + 3 + 6, and the rhyme scheme, *aabccb* (see table 6.2). Verse 1 even contains a narrative analogue of the music's two-key structure: the first strain, in A minor, describes the song's persona, whereas the second strain, in F major, narrates an event. The change of key now functions like a raising of the curtain separating the prologue from the first act of a drama.

The regular rhyme and meter of the verse act as a foil for the chaos that is unleashed at the chorus. Making a virtue of the need to fit words to

Table 6.2. "That Opera Rag," Lyrics: Meter and Rhyme Schemes

[Verse 1]	Feet	Rhyme[a]
Sam Johnson was op'ra mad,	3	A
He sho' had the fever bad,	3	A
He said, "Those ordinary ragtime tunes are mild,"	6	B
Some music from Verdi's hand,	3	C
Or any old op'ra grand,	3	C
Would never fail to set this op'ra darkie wild."	6	B
One ev'ning at a ball,	3	D
They heard Sam Johnson call,	3	D
Unto the leader man to play some "William Tell";	6	E
The leader swelled his chest,	3	F
[A]nd said, "I'll do my best."	3	F
So when he played they heard Sam Johnson yell.	5	E
[Chorus]		
Hear dat strain,	2	A
Mister Verdi come to life again,	5	A
Oh that operatic sweet refrain,	5	A
Sho' would drive a crazy man insane,	5	A
Just let me die and meet those brainy men,	5	B
Who manufactured notes of opera grand,	5	B′
Oh! Verdi where, where oh art thou?	4	C
Let me shake you by the hand, man, you know what's grand,	7	B′
Good Lord, it's over, they're playin' "Home Sweet Home."	5	D
[Verse 2]		
Old Sam was a painter man,	3	A
One day with a brush in hand,	3	A′
He stood upon a scaffold 'way up in the air,	6	B
A German band down below,	3	C
Was playin' some "Rig'letto,"	3	C
Sam said, "I know that's op'ra, be it here or there."	6	B
While he daubed up the wall	3	D
He tried hard not to fall,	3	D
But in the street the band kept right on playin' fair,	6	B
They played some "Faust" below,	3	F
[J]ust then old Sam let go,	3	F
He tumbled down below a-shouting in the air.	6	B
[Chorus] Hear dat strain, [etc.]		

[a] A prime indicates a near-rhyme; e.g., "man/hand" is marked B/B′.

preexistent music, Berlin furnishes the patchwork of quotations with a jumble of metrical and rhyme schemes that, in contrast to the orderly poetry of the verse's third-person narration, give voice in first person to Sam Johnson's increasingly confused state of mind. The opening melodic sequences generate four lines of close rhyme, "strain/again/refrain/insane." To the second section, with a 4 + 4 phrase structure, Berlin sets a couplet in iambic pentameter with the false rhyme "men/grand." The *Lucia* quotation, five measures long, generates a nonrhyming line and a line of interior near-rhymes, "hand/man/grand." The final quotation is as much of a shock to the song's persona as to its listeners; all Sam Johnson can do is mark its appearance in a nonrhyming line. Just as the music fails to resolve the tonal oscillations between A minor and F major, Johnson's efforts to articulate his response to that music ultimately collapse in defeat, as the final line fails to rhyme with any preceding line. Words and music do not find closure so much as they simply come to an incongruous stop.

At the end of verse 1 Johnson requests Gioacchino Rossini's *William Tell;* then, to the tune of Bizet's Toreador Song, he identifies the music as Verdi. Here is the nub of the joke: this housepainter can't tell one opera from another; his response is the same whether he hears "Some music from Verdi's hand / Or any old opera grand." His inadequate knowledge of opera parallels his overreaching language, with its Shakespearean misquotation ("Where, where oh art thou?"). Sam Johnson's crime is his cultural ambition—he values elite music over the "ordinary ragtime tunes" appropriate to his race and class—and in verse 2 his punishment is meted out by Gounod's *Faust.* Instead of ending with Marguerite's ascent to heaven, here the music of that opera precipitates a descent, as the would-be connoisseur falls from his scaffold and is put back in his rightful social place.[15]

The lyrics, then, give a new and surprising meaning to the music's crazy quilt of operatic quotation, which now can be heard to represent Sam Johnson's uneducated and disorderly response to high culture. This reading contradicts our inclination today to hear music that "rags the classics" as a spoof of elite culture; instead, the satire here targets the cultural aspirations of society's lowest members. The mix of high and low styles is not some sort of Bakhtinian carnivalesque to celebrate the toppling of hegemonic discourse, but quite the opposite: its humor attempts to defuse, however momentarily, the anxiety some Americans felt at the prospect of the social disorder that might ensue if black housepainters really were to develop a passion for opera.

IN SEARCH OF SAM JOHNSON

Does "That Opera Rag" truly express a fear of opera-loving African Americans? Or are we to read the song as metaphoric; that is, does it use racist imagery to address concerns that are other than racial?[16] Before considering any metaphoric interpretations of "That Opera Rag," we must ask whether the song is describing a situation that might have any factual basis.

By no coincidence, "That Opera Rag" dates from a period when many African Americans were indeed asserting their cultural aspirations, aspirations that included an appreciation of opera. That appreciation is evident, for example, in music reviews in the black press, which imply an informed readership.[17] Those readers in turn made up the audience for such performers as the Black Patti Troubadours, an African American organization whose musical revues typically concluded with an "operatic kaleidoscope" of excerpted scenes and arias.[18] Sam Johnson probably knows his opera from this type of performance; he recognizes the standard encore "Home, Sweet Home!" as a signal that the show is over.[19]

Like Sam Johnson, Scott Joplin probably learned the operatic repertoire otherwise than in full stagings. A similarly limited access to opera may account for the dramatic and structural weaknesses of *Treemonisha*, the operatic obsession whose failure marred the last years of Joplin's life.[20] That work's stiff dramaturgy and piecemeal musical construction suggest that Joplin knew many operatic excerpts and few complete operas. When the failure of *Treemonisha* hastened the final decline in its composer's fragile health, Joplin learned firsthand that African Americans who professed a love for opera yet lacked a complete mastery of the repertoire ventured into operatic culture at their own personal risk.

The operatic symbolism in "That Opera Rag" finds a further parallel in W. E. B. Du Bois's short story "Of the Coming of John," part of *The Souls of Black Folk* (1903). The story describes a visit to New York City by John Jones, a small-town southern black. At a matinee concert, where he is seated next to a white couple, Jones is entranced by the

> high and clear…music of Lohengrin's swan. The infinite beauty of the wail lingered and swept through every muscle of his frame, and put it all a-tune.…
> A deep longing swelled in all his heart to rise with that clear music out of the dirt and dust of that low life that held him prisoned and befouled. If he could only live up in the free air where birds sang and setting suns had no touch of blood! Who had called him to be the slave and butt of all? And if he had called, what right had he to call when a world like this lay open before men?

Absorbed in the music, Jones grasps the arms of his chair and, unaware, brushes the arm of the white woman next to him, who recoils at his touch. An usher directs him to the manager's office, where he is politely but firmly told to leave. Soon "John was gone, walking hurriedly across the square and down the broad streets, and as he passed the park he buttoned his coat and said, 'John Jones, you're a natural-born fool.'"[21]

Despite their differences in perspective, "That Opera Rag" and "Of the Coming of John" are fundamentally in agreement: when whites feel they must protect their heritage from black usurpation, any contact between

African Americans and European high culture is fraught with danger. At the sound of operatic music, Sam Johnson loses self-control and suffers physical injury; John Jones gains self-awareness and suffers social indignity. Just as Sam Johnson is ruined by his taste for opera and falls from his scaffold, so too is John Jones ruined by hearing Wagner's music; returning to the South, he refuses to bow to arbitrary white authority, and ultimately he is lynched.[22] For both Sam Johnson and John Jones, contact with white culture is a dangerous business. The emblem of that white culture is opera.

FROM *MRS. JIM* TO *GETTING A POLISH*

A concern for racial difference is indisputably at the core of "That Opera Rag." Yet a consideration of the song's original theatrical context reveals a new level of meaning, in which racial discourse is used to address a topic that extends beyond the boundaries of race: namely, the question of an American national identity.

The original sheet music cover for "That Opera Rag," issued in April 1910, refers to "Booth Tarkington & Harry Leon Wilson's Comedy 'Mrs. Jim'" (fig. 6.2). Tarkington, who would later win the Pulitzer Prize for his novel *The Magnificent Ambersons* (1918), was familiar to audiences in 1910 for a series of more-or-less successful stage comedies written in collaboration with Wilson. These plays imitated, with ever diminishing results, the first in the series, a moneymaker called *The Man from Home* (1907). That play established the formula from which Tarkington and Wilson never strayed, consisting of "characters and situations that [the playwrights] had observed during their foreign residence [in Paris]: unmarried American heiresses traveling abroad with more dollars than sense; unprincipled European aristocrats preying on American naïveté; homespun tourists from the Midwest aping the irreverence of Mark Twain's innocents." Ironically, the playwrights miscalculated the effect on their audience of Daniel Voorhies Pike, the title character of the first play: "Tarkington and Wilson expected their audiences indulgently to forgive Pike his nonsense when he complained of Europe and bragged of America, but the reaction was a complete surprise: 'When our young man announced from the stage that he wouldn't "trade our State Insane Asylum for the worst ruined ruin in Europe" they didn't laugh at him forgivingly, they applauded him thunderously. In all such matters they felt as he did.'" Moreover, "the critics were as surprised at the applause as the authors."[23] In short, Tarkington and Wilson had created a comedy that, like the very first American play to receive a professional production, Royall Tyler's *The Contrast* (1787), struck some viewers as a lampoon of American provinciality and others as a satire on European pretension.[24] Either way, the play was a hit.

Among the plays that tried to reproduce the success of *The Man from Home* was one that

Figure 6.2. "That Opera Rag," cover

was first written as "Mrs. Jim's Romance," then produced unsuccessfully [in 1909] as *If I Had Money*, and finally overhauled by Tarkington alone and given its last title [*Getting a Polish*].[25] It is a burlesque comedy of manners somewhat in the vein of *The Man from Home*, though the contrast is between the Far West and New York rather than between America and Europe. Mrs. Jim, keeper of a boardinghouse in Yellow Dog, Montana, and her deceased husband's partner, John Blake, strike it rich, then go off to New York to get a polish. After many adventures in New York society, most of them concerned with the rapacity of various Easterners for the riches of the Yellow Dog gold mine, Mrs. Jim and Blake find that they are really meant for each other and go back to Montana.[26]

This summary fits the adaptation of the play published as a short story, "Mrs. Jim," in *The World Today* in August 1910, while the play was still out of town.[27] But three months later, when the show reached Wallack's Theatre in New York, *Mrs. Jim* had become *Getting a Polish*, and the play's locus of decadence had crossed the Atlantic. In a preview of five shows opening on Monday, 7 November, the Sunday *New York Times* reported that *Getting a Polish* "is about a Montana widow who gets rich enough to go to Paris and acquire refinement," and Paris remains the locale in the review that appeared three days later.[28]

Was the setting changed because anti–New York humor was unlikely to play well on Broadway? Or had *Mrs. Jim*'s short-lived substitutions of New York for Paris, and Wall Street financiers for "dukes and earls and vassals and valets," been a temporary variation on the playwrights' standard formula, tailored to out-of-town audiences?[29] In either setting, the play's class humor, as in *The Man from Home*, cuts in both directions. Whether one applauds or sneers at Mrs. Jim's preference for homespun over crepe de chine, the play's meaning is unchanged: it doesn't pay to upset the social order. Sudden wealth cannot transform a commoner into an aristocrat, and Mrs. Jim, after her taste of empyrean culture, recognizes her proper place as the rough-hewn West.

But before she heads home, she sings a song to entertain the Old World sophisticates gathered in her Parisian apartment. The song is "That Opera Rag," whose operatic quotations are now a stand-in for "the worst ruined ruin in Europe." They represent a European culture that, although more developed than that of the United States, is also degenerate. And the syncopations carry a defiant barb: Mrs. Jim's performance is a gesture of resistance to a decadent, depleted Europe that seeks an infusion of vitality from a naïve, energetic America, now personified by Sam Johnson, who no longer represents just African Americans but all Americans, taking his place alongside the Yankee peddler Sam Slick and the Pawtucket spinner Sam Patch.[30] This Sam's brush with European culture, like Mrs. Jim's, is hazardous, but whereas Mrs. Jim has the good sense to ease herself back down the social ladder voluntarily, Sam Johnson falls precipitously. As a cautionary fable, the song thus reinforces the play's moral: stay in your place. And if you're an American, pretending to be a suave European is just asking for trouble.

MAY IRWIN: A BLUE-EYED COON SHOUTER

The thematic parallels between *Getting a Polish* and "That Opera Rag" contradict the widespread assumption that theatrical song interpolations early in the twentieth century were invariably arbitrary and irrelevant to the dramatic situation. One possible reason for this misapprehension was the weak control that playwrights and songwriters could exercise over how songs were interpolated. To the present-day historian, song interpolation is all too easily understood to be symptomatic of the commercial music world's failure to uphold a paradigm of the art music world: "the notion of a single artist controlling all aspects of a work's creation."[31] Although the mongrel stage entertainments of early twentieth-century New York seem to inhabit the opposite end of the aesthetic spectrum from Wagner's music dramas, in fact the interpolation of "That Opera Rag" into *Getting a Polish* turns out to be a confirmation of the self-same paradigm. Here, however, the controlling artistic personality is not a librettist-composer but a quintessential figure in popular music, the star performer—whose concern, moreover, is not only with how the song functions within the play but also with how it enhances a carefully crafted public persona. Only when we consider "That Opera Rag" as the artistic product not only of Ted Snyder and Irving Berlin but also of May Irwin, who sang it onstage, does yet another level of meaning become apparent.

Though her name is unfamiliar today, May Irwin (1862–1938) was one of the most popular entertainers of her day. After her first successful starring role, in *The Widow Jones* (1895), she formed her own theatrical company, with which she appeared in comedies written especially for her and for which she selected, and sometimes wrote, the music.[32] A journalist, cookbook author, political activist, and canny businesswoman who carefully controlled every aspect of her career, Irwin anticipated such late twentieth-century pop star/entrepreneurs as Madonna and Michael Jackson, whose primary artistic creation is their own public persona.[33]

In *The Widow Jones* Irwin arrived at the theatrical genre, stage persona, and singing style that would serve her throughout a long career. The play was a farce-comedy, that is, a spoken play in which a few songs were interpolated.[34] Over the next two decades, in more than a dozen such farce-comedies, Irwin played essentially the same character: a woman of a certain age, wealthy by either inheritance or her own business acumen, who dodges the obstacles that wealth places in her path. Sorting out the sincere suitors from the fortune hunters allowed Irwin to play romantic scenes despite her age and her large size. In fact, her size was a crucial part of her romantic comedy, a connection not lost on her audiences. Reviewers "focused on the fact that she was larger, more forceful, and funnier than the average female performer. As one critic explained, May Irwin's 'gladiator shoulders…tread of a goliath and…nervous energy of a locomotive' contrasted with the characteristics of the 'slim, sweet maid.'"[35]

It was in the interpolated songs that Irwin made her reputation as a "coon shouter," a white woman who mimicked African American performance styles and sang songs depicting, often in the most viciously derogatory terms, the African American experience. The protagonists in these songs were typically "aggressive and overly sexual black men who carried razors as weapons and had many volatile, short-lived romantic liaisons, thus linking black men to violent, sexual threats to the social order."[36] That description fits the song persona with which Irwin was associated throughout her career, one she herself brought to *The Widow Jones*. "May Irwin's 'Bully' Song," adapted for her by Charles Trevathan from a song he reportedly picked up at a St. Louis sporting house, gave Irwin the opportunity to take on the persona of a violent predator who hunts down and kills a rival bully.[37]

M. Alison Kibler makes a direct connection between the song's "physically threatening black male body" and Irwin's appearance. "Racial masquerade," she writes, "was one route to success and celebrity for women who were not conventionally attractive (particularly women who were fat)." Assuming a black persona enabled Irwin to make comic use of what reviewers called her "grotesque gait" and "funny, bulky substitute for a dance."[38] Unlike some of her sister "coon shouters," however—women such as Fay Templeton, Marie Cahill, Stella Mayhew, and "the last of the red hot mamas," Sophie Tucker—May Irwin never performed in blackface. Indeed, part of her appeal lay in the comic contrast between her sweet appearance—a typical review described her as "innocent looking...pink and white and...blue-eyed"—and the virulent racism and raucous energy of her dancing and singing.[39] But like those other singers, and unlike Lillian Russell, Anna Held, and other contemporaneous female performers known for their uninhibited and sometimes risqué stage demeanor, Irwin was fat. Conventionally beautiful women had no need of racial masquerade to explore the early twentieth century's more open portrayal of female sexuality onstage. In order to create a stage persona of a woman who is sexually attractive and powerful though not a conventional beauty, Irwin appropriated the mannerisms not only of African Americans but also of white men, who were free to incorporate racial masquerade as part of their stage demeanor—that is, in mimicking African Americans, she was behaving like a white man. Turning the minstrel mask to a new use, she appropriated a masculine behavior, minstrelsy, for a new model of stage femininity.[40]

Irwin exhibited that new stage behavior not only visually, in her comic dancing, but audibly as well, in her singing. On a handful of 1907 phonograph records that document her energetic singing style, she generally restricts her voice, a rather light soprano in timbre, to the chest register, where it takes on a huskiness that caused one reviewer to describe it as her "customary 'semi-mezzo' voice."[41] Using the conventionalized stage dialect that signified African American speech, she delivers some lines in a manner closer to speaking than singing, and her nonvibrato sustained notes are somewhat nasal, plangent, and powerful. Comparison of her records with published sheet music shows that she took liberties with notated lyrics, pitches, and rhythms. In short, her vocal style anticipates many elements of jazz singing and stands in sharp contrast to the cultivated, semi-operatic voices commonly heard onstage early in the century.[42]

Irwin's renditions of Negro dialect songs were generally received as the high points of her shows—and reviews make it clear that they were *her* shows.[43] The *New York Times* review of *Getting a Polish* is typical in this respect: the reviewer found the play itself a tired retread of Tarkington and Wilson's earlier work, with plot complications that were "elementary in the extreme," though "Miss Irwin...makes the most of them" with interpolated songs that were "generally out of place. However, to lose them would be to lose [Irwin's] 'coon songs,' and that would be a pity."[44] In other words, *Getting a Polish* had few artistic ambitions beyond that of providing a forum for May Irwin's clowning and singing.[45]

What the playgoers at Wallack's Theatre witnessed, then, was not just any performance of "That Opera Rag"—as the sheet music cover asserts, they were witnessing one of "May Irwin's song successes."[46] And her rendition added its own layer of meaning. Just as Irwin used her stage persona and made-to-order farce-comedies to advance an image of a strong, independent woman who was sexually attractive despite her unconventional looks, and just as she used Negro dialect songs to explore an uninhibited, hitherto masculine stage demeanor, here she used this song's operatic quotations to link her star image with nineteenth-century Europe's iconic female performer, the prima donna. As Judith Tick writes, "So great was the adulation of the 19th-century singer that writers like George Sand, George Eliot and Willa Cather made her the symbol of the 'femme libre'—the emancipated woman—whose voice represented power, freedom and a moral authority that transcended convention."[47] Mary Garden was one example of this new *femme libre:* "I believed in myself and I never permitted anything or anybody to destroy that belief. My eye never wavered from the goal, and my whole life went into the operas I sang. I wanted liberty and I went my own way."[48] Compare Irwin's explanation for her own success (by 1898 she was worth $200,000): "I made up my mind years ago that I would be a star someday. I knew my turn would come, and I was always preparing for it. And I made up my mind, too, that I should not work all my life. I know exactly when I shall retire from the stage and spend the rest of my life enjoying the fruit of my labor. And I mean to live in luxury."[49] Though she sang in the untutored style of a "coon shouter" and was more at home on the lowbrow vaudeville stage than in the highbrow opera house, and though she expressed her ambitions in terms more materialistic than idealistic, May Irwin embodied in her own way the new century's emancipated woman.

"That Opera Rag" reveals three distinct—and contradictory—levels of meaning. First, when viewed as an autonomous artwork, it offers a racist commentary on the heightened cultural aspirations of the first post–Civil War generation of African Americans: the housepainter Sam Johnson foolishly abandons his own culture ("ordinary ragtime tunes") for a white culture that he can only imperfectly assimilate, a point emphasized by the mismatch between verbal and musical allusions. At this level, the song emphasizes the cultural gulf separating blacks and whites. Second, when taken as a not-so-irrelevant interpolation into *Getting a Polish*, the song cautions Americans against an idolatry of European culture: Mrs. Jim, who sings "That Opera

Rag," voluntarily gives up her ambition to acquire a European "polish" and returns to Montana. At this level, the song unites black and white Americans against a foreign and hostile Europe. Finally, when seen in the context of May Irwin's career, the song becomes an opportunity to assimilate at least one positive aspect of European culture, the operatic prima donna as *femme libre*, into the lowbrow vernacular of American music and theater. At this third level, the song draws together American popular culture and European high culture in their comparable adulation of the diva.

None of these interpretations cancels out the others. Rather, they coexist in a cultural space where the contradictory forces that propelled America into the modern age can find expression in a Negro dialect song built on operatic quotations.

Chapter 7

Opera, Ragtime, and the Musical Color Line

Many Americans early in the twentieth century would not have questioned the propositions that opera is for white people, for blacks there is ragtime, and interactions between the two groups (and between the two musics) are to be avoided. This dichotomy between white and black, opera and ragtime, was naturally much more complicated in fact than in theory. For one thing, the racial division and the musical division were never perfectly congruent. Ragtime had one clear, overriding characteristic that identified it for contemporaneous audiences—it was music that "has to do with the Negro."[1] Yet Americans in huge numbers, both black and white, found the music intoxicatingly attractive, and that attraction challenged the racial status quo. Twentieth-century whites were, as Eric Lott writes about their nineteenth-century forebears, neither "unenthusiastic about black cultural practices [nor] untroubled by them."[2] For that matter, the very concept of whiteness was in flux, as the song portraits of Italian immigrants have already suggested.

Moreover, ragtime songs, like their earlier minstrel counterparts, came to function as, again in Lott's words, "acknowledged, if unlikely, representatives of a peculiarly American culture." As we have already seen in "That Opera Rag," black characters in ragtime songs can act as "popular oracles," representing not only African Americans but all Americans. Songs that portray black opera lovers as ridiculous, for instance, may thus carry the implication that all Americans, by aping the cultural preferences of an essentially foreign Europe, are falsifying their true natures and opening themselves to ridicule. In short, songs that on the surface deal with racial difference often deal on a metaphorical level with class difference; like nineteenth-century minstrel acts, their "racial meanings [are] inextricable from [their] class argument."[3] Ragtime songs that reference opera thus draw parallels between the racial hierarchy that kept blacks beneath whites in the United States, the musical hierarchy that rated lowbrow popular idioms as inferior to highbrow opera, and the cultural hierarchy that placed the United States beneath Europe.

This chapter explores the implications of these racial, social, and cultural parallels as they manifest themselves in operatic novelties that either feature African American characters or overtly pit ragtime against opera.

Example 7.1. Connolly and Craven, "We'll Have No More Coon Rag-time Songs To-night," chorus, mm. 1–4

These novelties continue a line of development begun at the turn of the century by songs that probe the musical "color line," to borrow Frederick Douglass's fine phrase.[4] For example, "We'll Have No More Coon Rag-time Songs To-night" (1900) contrasts Irish American and African American musical tastes in the person of Mike Clancy, who complains that his daughter, Annie, is continually playing "nigger ragtime songs" on the piano.[5] Yet he sings his complaint to the very cakewalk rhythms he denounces (ex. 7.1). Though his words uphold a color line, the music subverts it.

On the other side of the color line is Frank Orth's "Give Me Rag, Rag, Rag" (1901), whose African American persona is "always happy when I'm singin' ragtime."[6] When he claims that the audience at a society ball prefers his music to another performer's rendition of "The Holy City," we are left to wonder whether to believe him or whether this "ragged coon" mistook his listeners' catcalls for cheers. Either way, the inference is that ragtime, not any "higher" musical form, suits this uneducated African American.

A similar sentiment underlies Negro dialect songs in which opera makes a cameo appearance. When Sousa's band is scheduled to march through an African American neighborhood in "When Sousa Comes to Coon-town" (1902), "they aint going to play no overtures from William Tell"; instead they will play a ragtime march by Jasper Green, the implication being that the proper music for black audiences uses black idioms and is written by black composers, even if performed by a white ensemble. In William Tracey's "I'm Crazy'bout a Ragtime Minstrel Band" (1908), Nicodemus Washington has "no use for opera grand"; he expresses his preferences in the title phrase. Likewise, in Ted Snyder and Irving Berlin's "Piano Man" (1910), the song's persona compares the title character favorably to Verdi and Beethoven; the dialect lyrics leave no doubt that the persona, the piano man, and the music he plays are all thoroughly African American.[7] Implicit in all these song is the notion that white music occupies a higher cultural position, one to which African Americans must not aspire.

This last idea underscores the songs to be examined in the first part of this chapter, songs in which African American characters make the social blunder of aspiring to an appreciation of the fine arts in general and opera in particular. The remainder of the chapter then exposes the other side of the coin: songs that express the tensions felt by white Americans between, on the one hand, a love for European opera undermined by a sense that it is essentially alien, and on the other hand, an attraction to ragtime that carries the unwelcome implication that black music may be emblematic of American society as a whole. For these Americans, replacing a borrowed European culture with a native vernacular culture was complicated by issues of race and class.

Considered as a whole, the songs in this chapter reveal a picture of the United States on the verge of declaring its cultural independence from Europe, yet hesitant to recognize its native culture's non-European face.

AFRICAN AMERICAN OPERA LOVERS

Many African Americans born in the years just after the Civil War rose to the challenge of taking part in American society as educated free men and women.[8] Among this new educated class in black society were opera singers and opera lovers, who risked being denounced by whites as social climbers and artistic pretenders. Moreover, it was hinted, African Americans responded to music in overly sexualized ways that confirmed their cultural and racial inferiority.

Yet these racial arguments mask class arguments in which black versus white metaphorically represents lowbrow white Americans versus their highbrow European heritage. On this level, the crossing of racial boundaries stands in for the crossing of class boundaries, the black opera lover for the white parvenu, and a sexualized response for the physicalized response of the dancer. Each of these themes—social climbing, artistic pretension, and inappropriate response—manifests itself in ragtime novelty songs.

Black Opera Lovers as Social Climbers

When African American song personae imitate the behavior of the mon-eyed classes and make dubious claims of educational accomplishment, they overstep racial, social, and educational boundaries. In this context, opera functions as a symbol of cultural property that is off limits to African Americans. One such persona is pictured with lorgnette on the cover of Tom Lemonier and Alex Rogers's "I'd Like to Be a Real Lady."[9] She longs to treat her friends to ostentatious displays of wealth but betrays no real interest in high culture; she would like to hire the oper-atic soprano Emma Calvé "to sing while we all played ping pong." Likewise, "out at my French country home I'd have my social set, / Watch Bernhardt playing Romeo while I play Juliet"; she can name a famous theatrical personality and allude to Shakespeare but seems unaware that Sarah Bernhardt would be oddly cast in the role of Romeo.[10] The chorus makes use of a cakewalk rhythm in augmentation, lending the music a fitting comic grandiloquence.[11]

A theme related to social climbing is that of an ignorant person who poses as one who is knowledgeable, or who considers his ignorance a positive attribute, or who denigrates book learning in favor of a prag-matic slyness. This theme and its variations constitute a stock subject in Negro dialect songs that originates in the antebellum minstrel figure of Zip Coon, the "larned skolar" who dresses as a dandy and carries his spectacles on a string about his neck.[12] An early twentieth-century example is "An Ignoramus Coon" (1902), whose persona admits that "Chemistry and history to me is a mystery" but boasts that "I can make it come a seven, and I never miss eleven, / I've studied mighty hard at craps."[13]

A similarly self-educated persona is given voice in Chris Smith's "I Want to Know Where Tosti Went (When He Said 'Good-bye')" (1920), a vehicle for Bert Williams in his last Broadway show, the revue *Broadway Brevities of 1920*.[14] At the outset the song's persona boasts, "I has no education but I'm blessed with Mother Wit / On any kind of subject can converse a little bit." In verse 2 his knowledge extends to opera: "I ain't no music master I can't even read a note / But I can 'member ev'ry thing that Mister Wagner wrote." The chorus is a litany of things he knows:

> I know just where Columbus went
> When he sailed from sunny Spain
> I know what causes thunder and
> I know what makes it rain
> My great granddaddy left for me
> A book on ancient history
> I know 'bout Adam and Eve
> In the garden of Eden
> 'Cause I've been readin'.

But his extensive self-education fails him when he needs to interpret a then-famous art song:

> I can solve most any kind of mystery
> But here's one thing that puzzles me
> I want to know where Tosti went when he said
> "Good-Bye" forever.

Of the many songs of Sir Francesco Paolo Tosti (1846–1916), perhaps the most popular in his lifetime and for some years afterward was "Good-bye," a setting of John Whyte-Melville's lugubrious poem. As a recital and recording favorite with opera singers—among those who recorded it were Nellie Melba, John McCormack, Enrico Caruso (in Italian), and Rosa Ponselle (four times between 1918 and 1934)—"Good-bye" was a nonoperatic piece with operatic associations, much like "Home, Sweet Home!" or "Ciribiribin." The humor in "I Want to Know Where Tosti Went" resides in the persona's too-literal interpretation; he cannot apprehend the sentiment as a universalized expression of parting. At the same time, the song may be read as a send-up of a more genteel audience's willingness to accept metaphorical language unquestioningly, that is, to accede complacently to anything that sounds poetic. This persona, if nothing else, brings a commonsensical critical intelligence to his listening.[15]

Black Opera Lovers as Artistic Pretenders

Related to songs of educational pretense are songs of artistic pretense. In one operatic novelty the protagonist lays claim to a European cultural heritage that, the song implies, is not his own. In another, the protagonist's efforts to organize the performance of an operatic ensemble lead to catastrophe. Both songs brand as illegitimate an African American's attempt to position himself within a European musical tradition.

The title character in Ben M. Jerome and John Gilroy's "Mozart Lincoln" (1903) is a "colored bard" who, with great effort, writes "a ballad in cakewalk time," but his composition is a failure: "On a shelf his song was laid, / With a bunch of junk it stayed." One night, upon hearing an organ play, he knows that the music is familiar, and before long he identifies the tune: "Why! it am the one I wrote."[16] At an all-Wagner concert at Steinway Hall and again when Sousa's band plays at Brighton Beach, the same thing happens: he hears familiar music and concludes that it is his own melody. The song's instrumental introduction quotes the Prelude to act 3 of *Lohengrin*, and the Pilgrim's Chorus from *Tannhäuser* serves as an interlude between verses. This, presumably, is the music Mozart Lincoln claims as literally his own (a claim he makes in cakewalk rhythm). Predating "That Opera Rag" by seven years, this song pushes a similar joke even further; whereas Sam Johnson cannot tell one opera from another, Mozart Lincoln thinks that everything familiar-sounding is something he himself wrote. His ignorance of the classical repertory overwhelms his claims to legitimacy as a composer, which are based on a single unsuccessful cakewalk.

Like Mozart Lincoln, many Negro dialect song personae seem to confuse classical and popular music. The male persona in Irving Berlin's "Alexander's Ragtime Band" (1911) calls Alexander's organization "a classical band what's peaches," even though its repertoire, as far as we can tell, consists of bugle calls and "the Swanee River played in ragtime." Likewise, Joe Hollander and Jeff Branen's "Hear That Orchestra Rag" (1912), one of many "Alexander" imitations, praises a "classical crew" that plays "soulful syncopations," that is, ragtime. And the female persona in Ernest Breuer and Herman Kahn's "He's the World's Best Music Man" (1912), thinks herself highbrow because she has a taste for "dreamy rag[s]" and dance music. But perhaps these personae are not confused and the soulful syncopations are in fact ragtime versions of classics: in Seymour Furth and William J. Vandeveer's "Hear the Pickaninny Band" (1911), an African American band marches in parade to the music of "that Schubert serenade." Schubert also figures in W. C. Handy's "Shoeboot's Serenade" (1915), in which the trombonist Shoeboot Reeder serenades his Melinda with a song that combines the melody of "Ständchen" with traditional blues figures and lyrics ("I woke up this morning with the blues all 'round my bed").[17]

Among the many implications of these songs is the idea that black musicians either cannot or choose not to play classical music without ragging it. Either way, the songs imply, blacks are not eligible to participate in the European performance tradition. Whereas Handy portrays his musician in a positive light—Shoeboot Reeder assimilates Schubert into his own expressive musical language—white songwriters see them as falling short of accepted musical standards. That perspective is even more pronounced in Irving Berlin's "Opera Burlesque on the Sextette from Lucia di Lammermoor," which was featured in two revues in 1912. In the first, *A Night with the Pierrots*, a curtain raiser for *The Whirl of Society*, it was sung by an ensemble featuring the show's headliner, Al Jolson; in the second, Lew Fields's *Hanky-Panky*, it was one of two Berlin interpolations that livened up a dull score by the prolific but pedestrian A. Baldwin Sloane.[18]

Berlin's "Opera Burlesque" is an extended travesty of a single piece, the celebrated Sextet from Donizetti's *Lucia di Lammermoor*, a long-lived operatic excerpt that carried new cultural significance in twentieth-century America. J. Peter Burkholder cites nineteenth-century American instrumental arrangements of the Sextet, such as that in Stephen Foster's *Social Orchestra* (1854), as models for Charles Ives's Polonaise in C, an early work modeled on Donizetti.[19] Such arrangements were common; the Library of Congress's "Music for the Nation" database contains more than sixty such transcriptions of music from *Lucia* for piano, harp, guitar, and organ, as well as vocal publications, sometimes with English words bearing no relation to the original text.[20]

This process of divorcing the music of the *Lucia* Sextet from its original dramatic context—and, through instrumental arrangements, from any verbal meaning at all—allowed the Sextet melody in the twentieth century to act as a free-floating signifier. A new context might seem at first to depart little from its point of origin but in fact may carry an entirely different meaning. One example is the successful 1908 Victor recording of the Sextet with Marcella Sembrich, Enrico Caruso, and others, which was the basis for a 1911 silent film of actors (not singers) pantomiming a rather dull stand-and-sing operatic performance; the intent was to exhibit the film and the record in synchronization. Victor's in-house promotion of that record, which sold for the then-unheard-of price of seven dollars, recast the Sextet in the role of advertiser's bait: "Do not underestimate the value of the Sextet as an advertising medium. This feature of the record is very much more valuable to the average dealer than the actual profit he may make on its sales. Not all of your customers can afford to purchase a $7.00 record, but the mere announcement of it will bring them to your store as a magnet attracts steel."[21] In Donizetti's opera the Sextet conveys the conflicting emotions of Sir Walter Scott's antagonistic Ashtons and Ravenswoods; as an attraction to lure customers into a store, it conveys merely the generalized sheen of high-status music.

Ironically, cultural appropriation of the Sextet that distorts its intended meaning is perhaps an inevitable result of the music's reception among non-Italian-speaking audiences. Much of the dramatic tension in bel canto opera is generated by the emotional pressure that comes of forcing strong passions into rigid poetic and musical forms, a musical and textual analogue for the social strictures that limit the characters' actions. These operas can be dramatically powerful when characters express volcanic emotion in music that on the surface is placid. Unfortunately, the emotive dissonance between word and music is meaningful only to a listener who understands Italian or has made an effort to comprehend the opera's scenario. Without that understanding, listeners are left with pretty tunes and insipid harmonies. When Lucia's acquiescence to an arranged political marriage drives her to insanity, she sings a mad scene so formalized (despite the coloratura excrescences) that its climax could be published in a version for young nineteenth-century American harpists as the "popular rondo" from *Lucia*, or for ballroom dancers as one strain of "The Ravenswood Waltzes."[22]

Even divorced from its dramatic context, the Sextet held such sway on American musical tastes that it continued to symbolize refined singing well into the twentieth century. As with the soprano cadenza with flute obbligato traditionally inserted into *Lucia*'s mad scene, popular reference to the Sextet perhaps reached its nadir in a midcentury Three Stooges short. *Squareheads of the Round Table* (1948) features a sequence in which Larry, Moe, and Shemp, as medieval troubadours playing violin, mandolin, and concertina respectively, serenade the fair Elaine to the tune of the *Lucia* Sextet. When Elaine (Christine McIntyre, who sang "Voices of Spring" in *Micro-Phonies*) appears on her balcony and adds her coloratura, the texture, with one soprano sailing high over the male ensemble, is remarkably close to Donizetti's original. The humor comes not from the contrast between the old and new dramatic contexts—the old context by this point is irrelevant—but from the contrast between the highbrow music and the Stooges' ungainly voices and lowbrow slang. As a guard approaches, their words turn to gibberish, and Larry gives an imitation of Caruso's *Pagliacci* laugh; now the music signifies "opera" in the most generic sense. When Elaine's high voice enters, its cultivated tone matches the music, but her slangy promise to raise the window shade "when the coast is clear" lowers her utterance to the level of her serenaders.[23] Unmoored from its original meaning, the Sextet is simply a ready target for the lampooning of refined music.

This trend away from considering the Sextet as a dramatic moment from a familiar opera and toward regarding it as a generalized signifier of cultured music may be observed in popular songs of the first two decades of the century. We have already seen the Sextet quoted in "Rosa Rigoletto" and in "That Opera Rag," neither song hinting in the least at the dramatic import of the original. Berlin's full-blown "Opera Burlesque," in contrast, does lampoon the Sextet's dramatization of two warring parties locked in frozen tableau. At the same time, however, the burlesque mocks the very process of trivialization of which it is a part, portraying that process as a descent into an inappropriate racial context.

The beginning is exactly the same as Donizetti's original, apart from its transposition to B-flat (ex. 7.2). When the first voice enters at the pickup to measure 3, however, Berlin switches to cut time, and from here to the end the music proceeds in a jaunty march tempo that contemporary audiences would have construed as ragtime.[24] Donizetti's melody is divided between a lead voice and a vocal quartet that always sings either in unison or in homophony; in other words, the texture is in effect more a duet than a true quintet (much less the sextet on which it is based). The second part in the duet (i.e., the accompanying voices) either shares the melody in alternation with the lead part or, more often, fills in rests in the lead's melody with echoes or with contrasting commentary. In this respect the "Opera Burlesque" resembles a once-common practice in the performance of popular songs on stage and on phonograph records: the transformation of a solo song into a duet or "double version." As Charles Hamm points out, double versions of songs published only as solos were regularly prepared by Tin Pan Alley publishers and distributed to professional entertainers, but very little of this material has survived; almost all evidence of the practice today exists on phonograph records.[25] Like the "burlesque opera" on the Quartet from *Rigoletto* that fills the back page of "Nighttime in Little Italy," this *Lucia* travesty is a rare printed document of a standard early twentieth-century performance practice. By changing the longer notes in Donizetti's melody to short notes followed by rests, Berlin creates "holes" that the accompanying voices fill with words that either echo or comment on the soloist's.

The lyrics begin self-referentially by defining this "Opera Burlesque" as "some ragtime op'ra"; in other words, the music itself is "ragtime opera," an important point in light of what follows. Its subject is a man named

Example 7.2. Berlin, "Opera Burlesque," mm. 1–10

Ephraham, a stock character name in Negro dialect songs, the first syllable typically pronounced as a long vowel: "Ee-phra-ham."[26] In the opera house's gallery (i.e., in the cheapest seats) Ephraham would sit as "quiet as a mouse," in contrast to the boisterous immigrants of the Italian dialect songs. Yet at a climactic moment he loses his restraint; when Caruso hits a high note "Ephraham would begin to holler, / That note alone is worth a dollar"—a materialistic sentiment common in Berlin's Jewish dialect songs but out of place in his Negro dialect numbers. Unlike the Italian American opera lovers, who stereotypically have little use for learning, Ephraham seeks out the score to the *Lucia* Sextet; and unlike Abie Perlmutter in "My Yiddisha Butterfly," who balks at paying thirty cents for music from *Madama Butterfly*, Ephraham purchases the music, then hunts for "colored men who could sing that sextet he heard so beautiful." The scoring for five singers, instead of the requisite six, may be a musical joke indicating that he cannot find enough musically literate African Americans to perform the sextet as written.[27]

Though Ephraham objects to their out-of-tune singing, his ensemble ignores his injunctions to stop. Oddly, he does not object to their ragging the music: "But they kept on goin,' blowin,' showin' / How they could sing that Ragtime Op'ra." Now that term describes not Berlin's travesty but the Sextet itself as sung by Ephraham's ensemble. After one more line, the lyrics' third-person narration gives way to pure dialogue; the performers no longer describe the story but enact it, the solo singer as Ephraham and the vocal quartet as his band of singers. The "ragtime opera" does not merely tell the story of a disastrous performance but also recreates it. This intensification occurs as the music reaches the precadential harmonies that were the basis for the *Lucia* quotation in "That Opera Rag" and that form the climactic moment in the original Sextet.[28] From here to the end, Ephraham's threats ("Where's my gun, where's my gun?") and entreaties ("I'd be willing to pay / If you stop right away") alternate with the quartet's self-encouragement to "Keep it up, keep it up!" The travesty closes with a cadenza in which, in operatic fashion, two different lyrics are sung simultaneously ("Don't you intend to ever stop?" and "We don't intend to ever stop!"); after one last injunction ("Please stop!"), the quartet races heedlessly to the finish ("Keep it up, keep it up, keep it up, keep it up!").

"Opera Burlesque" is not Ephraham's sole appearance in an Irving Berlin song. As Charles Hamm notes, Berlin himself frequently performed "Ephraham Played upon the Piano" (1911), whose second verse begins with praise for Ephraham's self-taught musicianship: "Any kind of music he could understand / Still he didn't play by ear, he played by hand."[29] Whether or not one accepts Hamm's speculation that Ephraham was not only an alter ego for Berlin (whose musical literacy was marginal) but also possibly the protagonist of Berlin's never-written ragtime opera, it certainly makes sense to avoid a too-literal reading of "Opera Burlesque" as a put-down of African Americans.[30] At a time when no American composer and few American performers in the classical tradition were recognized as equal to their European counterparts, the cacophony of Ephraham's vocal ensemble, like Mozart Lincoln's crude cakewalk, might be interpreted as a commentary on the futility of all efforts to claim classical music as part of an American cultural heritage. Like Sam Johnson in "That Opera Rag," Ephraham and Mozart Lincoln resemble all Americans, black or white, who by expressing their love for European high culture open themselves to ridicule as artistic arrivistes.

The Dangers of Inappropriate Responses to Opera

In "That Opera Rag," Sam Johnson loses control when he hears opera and falls from his scaffold. The female characters in the following songs likewise lose control, but in a different way. Here, their response is inappropriately sexualized, a condition that makes them vulnerable to sexual predation and dishonor. It is possible to read these songs as warnings, expressed metaphorically in terms of race and gender, about the dangers inherent in attempting to overstep social boundaries. Moreover, as will become clear later in this chapter, their anxiety about physicalized responses to music resonate with white concerns about the stimulating effects of the contemporaneous ragtime dance craze.

Florenz Ziegfeld's *Follies of 1910*, which introduced Fannie Brice singing "Sadie Salome (Go Home)," also marked the first time an important African American entertainer appeared in an otherwise white revue. Bert Williams's hit in this, his first *Follies*, was likewise an operatic novelty, "That Minor Strain," by the black songwriters Ford Dabney and Cecil Mack.[31] The music, in the suave style Dabney used in his dance numbers for Vernon and Irene Castle, makes no operatic quotations. Mack's lyrics, however, describe a woman's response to hearing Caruso:

> Miss Janie Shadd was music mad,
> She'd sing ragtime in her sleep
> And at Wagner she'd weep,
> Said his music was deep.[32]
> One night she went with her beau, heard Caruso,
> The way she acted nearly broke up the show,
> When he made high C in minor key,
> She shouted loud with glee:
>
> [chorus] O that minor strain,
> Lawdy how that music creeps into my brain,
> Oh that sweet refrain,
> Rag it honey drag it for your lovin' Jane,
> Don't you stop it dear don't you chop it dear
> If you do I'll go insane
> There it is again that tantalizing minor strain.

In verse 2 Miss Jane is "in shame" but unable to explain why "that sweet minor stuff" gives her "a feeling divine, near lost her mind." She is aware that her response is out of place, and her awareness brings shame; nevertheless, she ends by asking, "Now just once again to ease my pain, / Sing me that minor strain." The music's effect is hypnotic, addicting, and she must have it whatever the consequences.

Several contemporaneous Negro dialect songs depict a similar female response to music. Three songs by Irving Berlin, for example—"Wild Cherries (Coony, Spoony Rag)" (1909), "Stop That Rag (Keep on Playing, Honey)" (1909), and "When I Hear You Play That Piano, Bill!" (1910)—are all sung by female personae in whom ragtime arouses amorous feelings.[33] What makes Janie Shadd different is the type of music that engenders her response—not ragtime but opera. Her sexualized response to Caruso—"Rag it honey drag it for your lovin' Jane"—brings operatic music down to the low social level of ragtime. Unlike the women in those other songs, she feels shame, indicating that a response that would be normal in a ragtime setting is abnormal in the more refined opera house.

But if Miss Shadd experiences nothing more than shame, then she gets off more easily than Miss Amanda Snow, the protagonist of "That Dreamy Barcarole Tune" (1910). Miss Snow has no use for ragtime; instead,

> Grand op'ra's got hold of me,
> once more I want to see,
> That "Tales of Hoffman," take me there today.
> The talk I don't understand,
> but when they strike up the band,
> A tune they play in such a winning way.[34]

At this point the music changes from common-meter ragtime to $\frac{6}{8}$ for an allusion to Offenbach's Barcarolle ("Belle nuit, ô nuit d'amour"). After four measures a more complete statement of the melody begins, but now with ragtime syncopations (ex. 7.3).

To this raggy barcarolle Amanda Snow describes her reactions to the music:

> That dreamy, dreamy Barcarole tune,
> Just carries me right away,
> Just want to close my eyes and spoon,
> Oh, kiss me long and while they play oh, please, don't take your lips away.
> That melody, goes chasing through me,
> Fear something will happen soon,
> If they don't stop that dreamy like, honey-like, creamy-like,
> Cuddlin,' lovin, Barcarole Tune.

She finds the music sexually arousing; with closed eyes she wants to spoon and to taste long kisses. In verse 2 she thinks she's "going to swoon.... [I] lose my mind and don't know what I'm doin'." She is quite right to "fear something will happen soon"; in such a state she is open to sexual predation and, in the moral climate of the time, dishonor.

In "That Dreamy Barcarole Tune" such a danger is implicit, but in other songs it is explicit. For instance, in Ted Snyder and Irving Berlin's "Colored

Romeo" (1910), Liza Snow's superficial reading of *Romeo and Juliet* inspires her to find her own Romeo, who takes her for a ride in his car (a metaphor for sexual activity); when the car strikes a tree, Liza is left sitting on the ground alone, duped and deserted.[35] Liza Snow differs from Amanda Snow only in the specific sort of European high culture that triggers her loss of control; for one it is Shakespeare, for the other it is opera.

Example 7.3. Goetz, Grossman, and Shiers, "That Dreamy Barcarole Tune," mm. 14–26

Example 7.3 (continued)

Likewise, in Irving Berlin's "That Mesmerizing Mendelssohn Tune" (1909), undoubtedly the model for "That Dreamy Barcarole Tune," the persona hears Mendelssohn's "Spring Song" and importunes, "Love me to that ever lovin' Spring song melody, / Please me, honey, squeeze me to that Mendelssohn strain." The persona's gender is made explicit retroactively in a Snyder and Berlin song of the next year, "Herman, Let's Dance That Beautiful Waltz," in which Lena Kraussmeyer says:

> I heard that a coon who heard Mendelssohn's tune,
> kissed the first man she saw, if it's true;
> That very same feeling I feel on me stealing
> And Herman I'm looking at you.

In other words, the African American who is sexually aroused by hearing Mendelssohn is female; moreover, when a German American woman has the same feeling while dancing, she identifies it as a characteristically black response to music.[36]

Altogether, the songs in which black women respond to music in a sexualized way appear to participate in the racist stereotyping documented by Patricia Morton in *Disfigured Images*.[37] Yet the same response is found in the indisputably white "Yip-I-Addy-I-Ay!"—a huge hit for Blanche Ring, whose energetic 1910 Victor recording displays a clipped, rather British diction and trained semioperatic vocal technique with no hint of African American performance styles. Here a German cellist so excites Sally from Spring Valley that she loses her self-control and declares, "I don't care what becomes of me, / When you play me that sweet melody." They get married that very night, and Herman Von Bellow finds that his troubles have just begun:

> But even before break of day,
> Poor Von Bellow, heard his new wife yell-oh,
> "For goodness sake, wake up and play!"[38]

Surely it is not only his new wife's insatiable appetite for music that keeps him up at night.

Even if "Yip-I-Addy-I-Ay!" and "Herman, Let's Dance That Beautiful Waltz" show that African American women had no monopoly on the sexualized response to music, a female susceptibility to music's aphrodisiac powers was nonetheless more often depicted circa 1910 as a black trait than as a white one. After 1920 that would no longer be true; as Irving Berlin would write in a 1921 song with no clear ethnic markers:

> Say it with music,
> Beautiful music,
> Somehow they'd rather be kissed
> To the strains of Chopin or Liszt.
> A melody mellow played on a cello,
> Helps mister Cupid along
> So say it with a beautiful song.[39]

Just as this mildly risqué topic was first associated in popular songs with low-status African American characters and later extended to the general population, so too with topics of musical preference. In the songs discussed thus far, African American characters display either a natural preference for ragtime or an unnatural and thus comic preference for high-status European music, often specifically for opera. Common to all of these songs is an assumption that black music—and only black music—is appropriate for black audiences. Nevertheless, much as the depiction of music as an aphrodisiac was at first closely associated with African Americans and only later became generalized to both black and white Americans, the expression of a preference for black music originates with black personae and then is taken up by white personae. Once this topic had become established in Negro dialect songs, it became possible to present a preference for ragtime as a generalized American taste and, as a corollary, to present a distaste for opera as a defensible posture for any American, regardless of color.

Such a shift in meaning would signal a corresponding alteration in the fundamental assumption that music, like other aspects of American society, should be segregated by a color line. If ragtime (and later, jazz) were to become the marker of a uniquely American musical culture, by analogy with the way opera was emblematic of European culture, then its corollary would be the recognition that African American musicians speak for all Americans regardless of race. Central to this development would be the debate about ragtime that took place not only in the musical press but also in the music itself.

"THAT COMPLICATED MUSIC": JUXTAPOSING OPERA AND RAGTIME

No sooner had ragtime emerged upon the national scene than a critical discourse about the new music began to take shape in print. As early as 1899, a critic in the *Boston Musical Record* praised ragtime as "young and unhackneyed and throbbing with life. And it is racial...I feel safe in predicting that ragtime...will be taken up and developed into a great dance-form to be handled with respect, not only by a learning body of Negro creators, but by the scholarly musicians of the whole world." The main hindrance to this development would be resistance from ragtime's enemies, which the same writer grouped into "two classes": one "sees in all popular music a diminution of the attention due to Bach's works"; the other "thinks he has dismissed the whole musical activity of the Negro by a single contemptuous word."[40] Typical of the first kind of "enemy" were assertions that ragtime was merely a passing fad, as in this comment from the *Metronome* dated 20 May 1901: "Ragtime's days are numbered. We are sorry to think that anyone should imagine that ragtime was of the least musical importance."[41] The second kind tended to dismiss ragtime as derivative of European music, as evident in the comments of A. J. Goodrich in the *Musician* in November 1901: "Unusual rhythmic combinations and syncopations have been used so extensively by high-class composers that it is not possible for coon song composers to invent anything along these lines."[42]

By the second decade of the twentieth century, however, criticism of ragtime, both positive and negative, had developed some new themes. One was the argument that, as an urban, commercial music, ragtime could not be accorded the dignity of folk music, which *Musical America* in 1913 described as a "product of the idyllic village atmosphere, mirroring the joys and sorrows, hopes and passions of the country people." Ragtime, in contrast, "exalts noise, rush and street vulgarity."[43] Similarly, Charles Buchanan argued in *Opera Magazine* in 1916 that "there is an irreconcilable difference between a people's song which has grown out of an unsophisticated soil, and a people's song which has grown out of pavements, vaudevilles and cabarets."[44] Controversy over ragtime's folk status was one manifestation of a concern over ragtime's suitability as a representative art of the American people as a whole, as later arguments make clear.

Buchanan's effort to distinguish ragtime from folk music was at least partly a response to an impassioned defense of ragtime by the *New Republic's* broad-minded classical music critic Hiram K. Moderwell. Moderwell had argued in 1915 that ragtime, after two decades of existence, was "the one type of American popular music that has persisted and undergone consistent evolution," and that as "a type of music substantially new in music history" (*pace* Goodrich), ragtime could act as the foundation for "an American school of composition," much as folk song had in nineteenth-century Russia. Ragtime's suitability resides not only in the "purely technical elements of interest" that lend it "its adaptability to the expression of many distinct moods" but also, and especially, in its vulgarity, "the generous warmth of everydayness" with which it expresses "the uninspired but tireless high spirits of the American people." To the argument that a true folk music must be rural in origin, Moderwell responds that in the "jerk and rattle" of the nation's city streets may be sensed a personality that "helps to form our characters and conditions our mode of action. It should have an expression in art, simply because any people must express itself if it is to know itself."[45]

Criticizing Moderwell's assessment of ragtime as "this folk-music of the American city," James Cloyd Bowman countered that "if you can pervert the tastes of ten million persons in these United States—no matter how inferior they are as a class—into liking a thing...you may then...call the thing American and...the fullest expression of the life of the people....The concrete product of such reasoning is found in men of the type of William Hearst, Harold Bell Wright, Billy Sunday, and George M. Cohan." To this Moderwell responded: "Ragtime is American, exactly as skyscrapers are American....On that point there is no dispute. How much you like it is another matter." Dissecting the snobbery in Bowman's class argument, Moderwell concludes: "The important point is that ragtime, whether it be adjudged good or bad, is original with Americans—it is their own creation. And a people must do its own art-creation, for the same reasons that an individual must do his own lovemaking."[46]

Evident in all of these arguments is the search for an innately American music, a music that expresses something profound about the American character and that can carve out a place for the nation among the world's other musical cultures. In this respect the debate over ragtime extends the controversy over local color sparked by Antonín Dvořák's praise of American Indian and African American music as resources for symphonic composers.[47] Even musicians as sympathetic to Dvořák's position as Daniel Gregory Mason were chary of ragtime, which Mason viewed as a "debased form" of "the genuine old plantation tunes, the 'spirituals' and 'shouts' of the slaves."[48] That the latter, but not the former, might be suitable for an American art music rests on the assumption that folk music must be rural, not urban, in origin—a reassuring notion for musicians of the time who, in MacDonald Moore's words, "viewed the Negro as an interesting character from a separate section of the country, comfortably far away."[49] The temporal and geographical proximity of ragtime meant that it could not be so easily romanticized. Moreover, the presence of ragtime musicians in the here and now raised the discomfiting possibility that ragtime—and by implication, popular music in all its forms, especially its black forms—might not merely provide the raw materials for a distinctive American music but in fact already constitute that music.

The debate about ragtime took place not only in the popular press but also in the products of Tin Pan Alley, and nowhere more overtly than in novelty songs that juxtapose ragtime and opera. Thus far we have encountered songs in which operatic topics, whether verbal allusions or musical quotations or both, are introduced into a ragtime idiom. The characters in these songs sometimes love the blending of styles, sometimes hate it. Here I explore some of the broader social meanings that underlie this juxtaposition by considering songs whose music and lyrics make the contrast explicit. These songs touch on issues of race, class, and gender, but ultimately those issues are absorbed into the larger question of an American musical identity. From a twenty-first-century vantage point, it seems obvious that the African-inflected popular music of the United States—everything from blues to hip-hop—has exerted a greater worldwide influence than its classical music. A century ago, however, such an outcome was only beginning to be apprehended. These songs illuminate the processes by which Americans in that era were coming to terms with the notion that, in the words of Ira Gershwin, "the real American folk song"—or symphony, for that matter—"is a rag."[50]

Novelties with European Characters

As Jack Sullivan has shown in *New World Symphonies*, European interest in the United States as a locus of exotic color grew throughout the 1800s and by the turn of the century had developed into a significant influence on European artists.[51] Predating the fascination with jazz of French composers such as Ravel and Milhaud in the 1920s was the interest in ragtime of the somewhat older generation of Debussy and Satie. Ragtime marches figured prominently in the music played by Sousa's band on its highly successful European tours of 1900, 1901, and 1905. In those years the London *Times* could praise ragtime with a wholeheartedness in striking contrast to some of the American critics quoted earlier: "Ragtime is absolutely characteristic of its inventors—from nowhere but the United States could such music have sprung....Here for those who have ears to hear are the seeds from which a national art may ultimately spring."[52] The enthusiasm for ragtime shown by European audiences apparently came as a surprise to many Americans who hitherto had considered such lowbrow music to be a guilty pleasure. As the songs discussed here demonstrate, Americans found in the European ragtime craze first a source of humor and later a source of national pride. Songs that place the contrast between ragtime and opera in a European setting allowed U.S. audiences to savor a reversal of direction in transatlantic cultural exchange.

Irving Berlin's "International Rag" (1913) celebrates the enthusiasm overseas for American popular music and dance. Although the lyrics make

the global claim that "the world is ragtime crazy," the only countries mentioned by name are European: England, France, Germany, Spain, Russia,
and Italy. The last-named arrives eight measures from the end—a position
that frequently carries strong emphasis—for a direct confrontation
between ragtime and opera. The minor subdominant harmony creates a
mock serious tone as the lyrics claim that "Italian opera singers have
learned to snap their fingers" to ragtime. In the 1913 Victor record by the
popular duo of Arthur Collins and Byron G. Harlan, this moment offers
the occasion for some interpolated gibberish sung to a snippet of "Vesti la
giubba" from *Pagliacci*, complete with an imitation of Caruso's laugh, as
heard on his famous 1907 recording of Leoncavallo's aria. Unlike earlier
ragtime songs, "The International Rag" makes no use of Negro dialect; the
implication is that white Americans can poke gentle fun at European
opera and exult in ragtime's world supremacy.[53]

That rise to supremacy can already be detected a decade earlier, in
the short-lived musical comedy *The Blonde in Black* (1903), which had
depicted an American woman traveling to Paris to teach the cakewalk to
high society, much as Aida Overton Walker had in London that summer
during the tour of *In Dahomey*. Revived two years later with a better
score, a new title—*The Sambo Girl*—and a new leading lady, Eva Tanguay,
the 1905 version included a Harry O. Sutton and Jean Lenox song titled
simply "Ragtime," in which Tanguay exhorts Parisians to follow the latest American fashions. In both versions, the show's title signals racial
masquerade; as in *Getting a Polish*, the cultural contrast that fuels the
"Yankee fable" is heightened by Africanizing the American character.
The ethnic neutrality of "The International Rag" was still some years
away.[54]

The European reaction to American ragtime proselytizers is depicted
in Melville J. Gideon and E. Ray Goetz's "Oh! That Yankiana Rag" (1908),
a song interpolated into the musical comedy *Miss Innocence*, Florenz
Ziegfeld's vehicle for his wife, the popular French actress Anna Held.
(The same show also introduced "My Cousin Caruso.") After a verse
whose music quotes Charles Borel-Clerc's "La Mattchiche" (1905) to
describe how ragtime has eclipsed the previous dance craze for the maxixe (a Brazilian tango), a Joplinesque dance interlude leads into a refrain
in which Held must have imbued stock Negro dialect phrases—"lovin'
peach," "my own baby," "honeybug"—with her Gallic accent. Unlike with
Sutton and Lenox's "Ragtime," there is no indication that the juxtaposition of French refinement and American vernacular is being played for
laughs.[55] Again, this earlier song differs from "The International Rag" not
only in its use of snippets of Negro dialect but also in its allusions to
European dance music rather than opera.

Another song from the second decade of the century juxtaposes rag-
time and opera not in present-day Europe but in antiquity. Sigmund
Romberg and Harold Atteridge's "Ragtime Pipe of Pan," written for the
Winter Garden revue *A World of Pleasure* (1915), places the Greek god in

Arcady, where he plays ragtime on his reed pipe, whose five-note runs, in imitation of Papageno's panpipes, make a musical pun by invoking Viennese classicism in a song set in classical Greece.[56] The ragtime-playing Greek god inverts chronology and makes American vernacular music antecedent to European music—an illogical image, to be sure, but one that humorously lends ragtime, and by extension American popular culture, a legitimacy that many Americans were now willing to entertain.[57]

Novelties with American Characters

The European enthusiasm for ragtime placed an imprimatur on African American vernacular music that Americans themselves were hesitant to bestow. That hesitancy may be traced in the songs examined here, which bring to an American setting the polemical juxtaposition of highbrow opera and lowbrow ragtime. Ranging from 1906 to 1918, these songs trace the American public's emerging acceptance of ragtime as an American counterpart to the European musical tradition as emblematized in opera. Three overlapping but successive stages may be discerned: a guilty admission that Americans prefer simple melodies to elaborate music; an anti-intellectual, jingoistic rejection of "fancy" music in favor of red-blooded American tunes; and finally, a reconciliation and recognition that an enjoyment of one kind of music does not preclude enjoyment of another. In essence, these songs cover a period that begins with a general sense of cultural inferiority and ends with a growing confidence in the United States as an equal if junior partner in the world's nations.

Raymond Hubbell and Robert B. Smith's "Whistle When You Walk Out," from *Mam'selle Sallie* (1906), was sung by "Professor Marrow and Chorus" and no doubt was set in Madame Woodbury's Seminary, where the musical comedy's heroine is a student.[58] The three verses describe a long-haired composer whose "appetite was greater than his income" but who adamantly disavows light music and aims above mere commercial success. Each verse ends by mentioning an opera he aspires to match: *Il trovatore*, *Cavalleria rusticana*, and *Tannhäuser*. A new interlude after each verse quotes a fragment of the opera in question, sung with the original text: Manrico's melody from the Miserere, the Intermezzo (hummed), and the Pilgrim's Chorus, respectively. The chorus then breaks away from the narrative to draw a generalizing moral:

> Oh, you can try to be a Mozart, you can please the classic few,
> You can write like Mister Wagner, and you can starve like Verdi too.[59]
> But the people like to whistle and they know what they're about,
> Now the critics may roast, but what you like most
> Is to whistle when you walk out.

An artistic manifesto for commercial hacks, "Whistle When You Walk Out" acknowledges the superiority of operatic music over popular music but argues the financial necessity of giving the public what it wants—and, more importantly, what it is willing to pay for. (Ten years later, Hubbell would mitigate somewhat the opposing forces of art and commerce in "Poor Butterfly.")

Far less apologetic in tone is "The American Rag Time," from George M. Cohan's *The American Idea*, his tenth original musical comedy in less than eight years. By the time *The American Idea* opened at the New York Theatre on 5 October 1908, Cohan had fallen into a comfortable routine that had begun to wear thin, if not with his public, then with his critics, one of whom judged the show to be "just like all the other Cohan pieces."[60] That is, it combined snappy, slang-filled dialogue with unabashed flag waving and transatlantic animosity. This time around, two American millionaires' daughters, scouting in Paris for aristocratic husbands, settle on two nobles who eventually turn out to be Brooklyn boys in disguise. Somewhere along the way one of the characters leads the chorus in "The American Rag Time," a lively march with hardly any syncopation and lyrics that start off with a lowbrow sneer:

> I never fell for William Tell,
> I never liked that complicated music;
> No, not for mine,
> [chorus:] No not for mine!
> [solo:] Grand Opera stuff is all a bluff,
> Give me that good old syncopated music,
> I think its fine,
> [chorus:] Superfine![61]

The second verse similarly dismisses *Lohengrin* and *Faust* in favor of ragtime and Sousa marches. The chorus praises ragtime for its "patriotic swing."

The put-down of highbrow European culture was part of Cohan's stock in trade. What makes this song unusual is its elevation not of traditional patriotic tunes (as in "The Yankee Doodle Boy" of 1904), nor of Irish American ethnic pride (as in 1907's "Harrigan"), but of African American music as emblematic of all Americans. In case there should be any doubt about ragtime's ethnic origins, both verses reiterate the phrase "Now honey," and verse 2 adds "Listen baby, ain't it simply grand?"— vocabulary unmistakably associated with the Negro dialect song. Cohan is free of the qualms that beset "nine out of ten musicians," who, according to Moderwell, "if caught unawares, will like this music until they remember that they shouldn't."[62]

The frontal attack on opera, a staple of American comedy in the middle and later parts of the century, was an anomaly in the years before World War I, with the exception of Cohan and his direct imitators. One of the few songs to take a similar stance is Kerry Mills and S. M. Lewis's "The Ragtime College Girl," from *The Fascinating Widow* (1911), a vehicle for the female impersonator Julian Eltinge. A plot contrivance causes Eltinge's male character to disguise himself as "Mrs. Monte" and hide in a women's dormitory, where he sings this song to the residents. Its object is to persuade college girls to "always be at ease, act how you please," and disregard the dictates of polite society—in effect, to be an "I Don't Care" girl. And just as Eva Tanguay in 1908's *The Sambo Girl* had associated her carefree stage persona with ragtime, here too Eltinge urged his charges to admit that syncopated dance music has more appeal for them than the salon music and operatic singing they feel they ought to prefer:

> Now you can't compare the "Maiden's Prayer"
> To something really smart;
> You'll hear Melba sing some mournful thing
> And still you'll call it art.
> When a lively strain gets on your brain
> You'll hum it all day long;
> Your feet keep time to every rhyme
> Of a catchy ragtime song.[63]

The opposition of opera (here personified by Nellie Melba) to lighter music is essentially the same as in 1906's "Whistle When You Walk Out," with the important difference that the earlier song made no argument that popular music was better, simply that it was more profitable for composers. Here ragtime, not opera, is "really smart," and the open rejection of cultivated music is seen as fashionable and up to date.[64] Fortunately, the anti-intellectualism and chauvinism of Cohan's and Mills's songs represented a passing moment in an ongoing debate—though their attitude was one that would recur with greater strength later in the century.

As the 1910s continued, however, other songs sought a rapprochement between ragtime and opera by demonstrating how much the former owed to the latter. Although the "well-known music master" in "Everything Is Ragtime Now" (1913), for instance, complains that "the classics are forgotten," in fact the classical repertory has shaped the language of the new popular music: verse 2 acknowledges that "grand opera is ragtime" (i.e., some rags are based on operatic melodies).[65] The advertising pages in the sheet music for this song attest to opera's pervading influence. The inside front cover offers complete materials for amateur minstrel shows, including a series of "minstrel overtures," medleys of popular tunes in which are scattered bits of *Il trovatore*, *Carmen*, and *Faust*. The back pages tout pedagogical materials, piano rags, and "The Artistic Series," a collection of recital albums for voice, piano, and violin with full-cover photos of, among others, Enrico Caruso. Even more than the song itself, its attendant advertisements demonstrate how an inherited European tradition existed side by side with lively but crude native products.

Though published a year later, in 1914, "That Bohemian Rag" is an example of the sort of operatic rag that irked the music master of "Everything Is Ragtime Now." Introduced in Gus Edwards's vaudeville act, the song rags tunes from *La bohème* in a process described by the self-referential lyrics: "Oh, Puccini, I have stolen your sweet melody" is sung to the melody of Rodolfo's act 4 "O Mimì, tu più non torni," and a melody derived from act 1's "Mi chiamano Mimì" fits these lines:

> Since I "copped" Bohemé [sic]
> Other tunes are tame,
> They are all the same;
> That sweet melody
> Makes a dandy rag,
> Makes a dandy drag.
> Syncopated time makes the classics fine
> Makes the music shine
> They used to call it "La Bohemé,"
> But now, although the tune's the same,
> The title page reads "That Bohemian Rag."

Just as Americans may modify the pronunciation of the opera's title, so too may they adapt the music to fit the newly popular animal dances, since "turkey trotting's lovely to a classical tune."[66]

Around the time that "That Bohemian Rag" was reaching the vaudeville stage, a few magazine and newspaper articles reported that Irving Berlin was planning to write a ragtime opera, and Berlin told one interviewer that he already had "snatches—here and there—of the score completed."[67] Although nothing ever came of this project, traces of it may have found their way into his first complete musical comedy score, *Watch Your Step* (1914). Written for the dance team of Vernon and Irene Castle, *Watch Your Step* was regarded at the time, not quite accurately, as the first musical comedy with music entirely in a syncopated dance idiom, that is, in ragtime.[68] Moreover, the show emphasized the contrast between its own syncopated music and opera by setting the second act at the Metropolitan Opera House. The act opens with "Metropolitan Nights," in which the chorus sings, to march music in $\frac{6}{8}$, about the parade of fashion and wealth in the audience. Like the Arnoldian critics of the Gilded Age, such as George William Curtis, Berlin lampoons not opera but rather an unmusical elite, for whom ostentatious display, not music, is the reason to go to the Met:

> If you want to see Metropolitan sights, Metropolitan sights,
> You'll have to stand to be bored a bit
> By some classical song 'mid the suffering throng
> Fashion demands it on Metropolitan Nights.[69]

If act 2 opens with the conflict between opera as art and operagoing as fashion statement, then the end of the act escalates into open warfare between opera and ragtime. The finale, "Ragtime Opera Medley," strings together six operatic excerpts in a travesty dance suite that runs for twenty-three pages of vocal score, making it the most ambitious number in an ambitious score. Berlin must have thought highly of it, since he published it as a separate number, even though it had no chance of selling as well as a conventional verse-and-chorus pop song; issued with a text-only cover such as was the norm for classical music scores, it evidently was offered as a prestige publication.[70]

The lyrics call attention to the operatic quotations and to the dance types into which they are transformed. After a pompous introduction whose chromatic descending sequence is probably Berlin's untutored attempt to sound operatic, the first section casts the Triumphal March from *Aida* as a rag (ex. 7.4), with lyrics that address Verdi's music directly, arrogantly claiming to correct the faults in the original:

Example 7.4. Berlin, "Ragtime Opera Medley," mm. 1–15

Example 7.4 (*continued*)

But you'll be sweet-er when we be - gin___

turn-ing you in - to a rag___

Op'ra
You always sound like an uproar
And that's the reason it's not a sin turning you into a rag.
You'll soon be placed with the popular taste
For we're going to rearrange you, change you into a rag.

Changing to ¾ meter, the second section transforms Musetta's Waltz from *La bohème* into a hesitation waltz (ex. 7.5), bringing the accompanimental arpeggios into the vocal melody, as in Gus Edwards's 1909 novelty "I'm After Madame Tetrazzini's Job." The chorus insists on dancing to Puccini's music despite any objections the composer may make, in a couplet that implies another Americanized pronunciation of the opera's title: "He may roar and scream / Nevertheless we will hesitate to La Boheme."

Reverting to cut time, the third section is a maxixe based on the Flower Song from Gounod's *Faust* (ex. 7.6). Now it is music connoisseurs whose objections will be disregarded: "Op'ra lovers if you do not approve of what we remove of Faust / Just 'roust' and occupy the back seats while we maxixe to the Flower song from Faust."

A reference to Berlin's 1911 dance hit "Everybody's Doing It Now" leads into the fourth section, a tango burlesque of the Toreador Song from *Carmen* (ex. 7.7). The Habanera would seem a more logical choice, since it and the tango are based on the same rhythm, but Berlin's use of the

Example 7.5. "Ragtime Opera Medley," mm. 45–56

Toreador Song is in better keeping with the medley's modus operandi, namely, grotesque distortion.

For the same reason, the most tragic music quoted is transformed into the fastest and most boisterous of the entire medley: "Vesti la guibba" from *Pagliacci*, here made into a one-step (ex. 7.8). With brash music thoroughly subverting the meaning of the original aria, the lyrics can afford to take a tone less adversarial though no less aggressive than in the earlier sections:

Example 7.6. "Ragtime Opera Medley," mm. 84–96

Example 7.7. "Ragtime Opera Medley," mm. 109–15

We like you Pagliacci
Because you melody mellow, by Leon Cavallow
affords us something new
And so we'll one-step to you.

With a dramatic fortissimo half-diminished chord the tempo changes from the fastest to the slowest tempo, *largo*, in a four-measure transition to the sixth section, a burlesque of the Quartet from *Rigoletto* (ex. 7.9). Here the ghost of Verdi (sung in *Watch Your Step* by Harry Ellis, whose name appears in the score) begs the chorus not to subject his music to

Example 7.8. "Ragtime Opera Medley," mm. 133–41

such rough treatment. As in the earlier "Opera Burlesque on the Sextette from Lucia di Lammermoor," Berlin creates a "double version" in which a soloist sings Verdi's melody while the rest of the vocal ensemble, in unison or homophonic harmony, fills in the long notes or rests at the ends of phrases with rapid-patter responses. And also as in that earlier burlesque, a dialogue between Verdi and the singers leads to his demand that they stop and their refusal to do so:

> VERDI: you know it's wrong
> CHORUS: what's wrong, what's wrong?
> VERDI: To change my song
> CHORUS: your song is wrong
> VERDI: 'Twill drive me mad
> CHORUS: Too bad, too bad,
> VERDI: you'll have to stop!
> CHORUS: No! No! No! No!

The chorus becomes progressively bolder in its disdain for Verdi: "We're growing weary of your dreary little melody / That's why we play it the way it ought to be." Echoing the commercialism of "Whistle When You

Walk Out," the ensemble admits that "we hate to pay admission for your dreary composition." And evoking both music and lyrics of Berlin's "International Rag" of the previous year, a self-described "raggedy melody, full of originality," the singers tell Verdi's ghost why they rag his *Rigoletto:* "Oh, you know, it's slow, and so we'll sprinkle on your melody a bit of originality." This section ends, again much like the "Opera Burlesque," with Verdi's final words, "Stop! Stop! Stop! Stop! No! No!" falling on deaf

Example 7.9. "Ragtime Opera Medley," mm. 171–78

Example 7.9 (*continued*)

ears as the chorus enthusiastically concludes, "We're goin' to rag it, / Rag, rag, rag, rag your Rigoletto."

A reprise of the *Pagliacci* travesty brings the medley to a close. The coda consists of four measures of broad, operatic-sounding tremolos, followed by a brisk tag with alternating raised and lowered thirds suggesting the blues (ex. 7.10).

Although its largest section, the *Rigoletto* travesty, uses the same techniques Berlin had used two years earlier in the "Opera Burlesque," the dramatic effect is entirely different. In the *Lucia* burlesque the characters are African American, and their ragging of the Sextet is something they cannot help doing. They unwittingly perform Donizetti's music in the only musical style that comes "naturally" to them, and the humor lies in the perceived distance between Ephraham's benighted singers and the more knowledgeable listener, who may enjoy a joke at the characters' expense. In contrast, the characters in the medley are white, and their revisions of operatic music are conscious and at least partially hostile. The would-be master who loses control of the ensemble is not a black opera lover but the iconic opera composer Giuseppe Verdi, and the medley seems to invite us to participate in the chorus's roasting of him, much as Julian Eltinge had invited his ragtime college girls to admit that they secretly preferred catchy tunes to highbrow music. Disdain for opera, which in the first decade of the century could be expressed in popular song only by African American characters, could now, in the century's second decade, be openly expressed by fashionable whites.

Turning outside the world of musical comedy for a moment, we can find a similar sentiment expressed in an early poem by the playwright

Example 7.10. "Ragtime Opera Medley," mm. 301–8

Eugene O'Neill. His "Ballard [sic] of the Modern Music Lover" (1912) opens with this stanza:

> I have tried to fall for the stuff of Mozart
> Handel, Haydn—a dozen more
> But I guess my ear isn't framed for "beaux arts"
> For I found them all a terrible bore.
> I suffered through concerts by the score
> Orgies of music that shook the room
> Till my brain was sick and my head was sore
> But the joy of my heart is a rag time tune.

and closes with this "Envoy":

> High-brows, whom classic music quickeneth
> Heed well the burden of my vulgar rune,
> Your lofty tumbling wearies me to death.
> The joy of my heart is a rag time tune.[71]

O'Neill's use of high-flown poetic diction in an encomium to lowly ragtime may be seen as a literary equivalent of the operatic quotations found in popular songs in the same period. The implication is that the preference for lowbrow music is a deliberate aesthetic choice made by a discriminating listener, not merely the shortcomings of someone inferior by nature or through inadequate education. What is new here in the second decade of the century is the notion that an educated listener may be initiated into operatic culture but still prefer a less elevated music.

Another number in *Watch Your Step* reinforces the same message. As published in the show's vocal score, "Simple Melody" begins with a verse sung by Ernesta Hardacre, a female lead "too good to be true," that compares modern "spoony rags and coony drags" unfavorably with the sentimental songs of an earlier generation; in the following chorus she asks to hear "a simple melody / Like my mother sang to me," words sung to music with the chromatic passing tones common to 1890s tearjerkers. Algy Cuffs, "a matinee idol," then sings his verse to new music, which compares ragtime favorably not with sentimental songs but with "long-haired" music:

I don't care for long haired musicians with their classy melodies
They're all full of high-toned ambitions but their music doesn't please
Give me something snappy and popular the kind that darkies play
Lots of rhythm and I go with 'em and that's why I say,
[chorus] Musical Demon, set your honey a dreamin' won't you play me some rag
Just change that classical nag to some sweet beautiful drag.[72]

The opposition is asymmetrical: Ernesta prefers sentimental parlor songs to ragtime, while Algy prefers ragtime (here described explicitly as African American) to classical music. While one character expresses conservative tastes and the other is more up to date, they are not really talking about the same thing. Yet the music adds a layer of meaning that reconciles their opposing viewpoints: Algy's syncopated chorus is sung simultaneously with Ernesta's flowing melody, demonstrating their common harmonic foundation. Although the lyrics describe irreconcilable differences, the music says that those differences are merely surface features of an underlying unity. Berlin the lyricist portrays Americans whose tastes are divided along class and racial lines; Berlin the composer paints a picture of inclusive musical pluralism.

Here in a nutshell is the paradoxical condition of America's musical life early in the twentieth century. Ragtime was a homegrown music that inspired both pride and shame: pride in its demonstrated appeal across a wide cultural spectrum, which suggested at least a potential claim for artistic value, and shame in its origins among a despised caste, which complicated white Americans' ability to claim it as a marker of national identity. Opera, on the other hand, inspired similarly conflicted feelings: a genuine affection for the music had become increasingly hard to sustain against a growing resentment of what opera emblematized—the dead hand of Europe's cultural superiority over a young and unformed nation. A sign of America's coming of age would be the creation of a music both distinctive and distinguished; ragtime, and soon jazz, would be the beginnings of that music. The challenge for Americans of the ragtime era, and for their descendants, would be how to foster their own music without losing their ability to appreciate the music of the opera house.

Conclusion

One last song summarizes the ragtime era's tension between imported highbrow culture and native lowbrow entertainment. Among Sigmund Romberg and Harold Atteridge's songs for the summer revue *The Passing Show of 1918* is a number for Willie and Eugene Howard called "The Galli-Curci Rag."[1] A topical novelty, it commemorates the New York debut in January 1918 of the coloratura soprano Amelita Galli-Curci, who appeared with the touring Chicago Opera Association at the Lexington Theatre, singing the title role in Meyerbeer's *Dinorah*. The public response was the greatest received by any soprano in New York since Tetrazzini's debut ten years earlier; the highlight of act 2, the "Shadow Song" ("Ombra leggiera"), generated an enormous outburst of applause.[2] Much as with Tetrazzini and Caruso a decade earlier, the public adulation for Galli-Curci was newsworthy enough to be joked about in a topical revue.[3] Romberg and Atteridge accordingly supplied *The Passing Show* with this song, which humorously enacts a lowbrow form of diva worship.

Fittingly, "The Galli-Curci Rag" begins with a quotation from the "Shadow Song" (ex. 8.1).[4] The song's (male?) persona must attend the opera whenever Galli-Curci sings. He sits in the balcony, where "she can get a look at me"; this turn of phrase puts the emphasis on the listener, not the performer or composer, and is the first hint of a popular, not classical, music aesthetic, in which the customer is always right—and this customer is up in the balcony, not in the more expensive seats patronized by the elite. The *Dinorah* quotation continues as the persona speculates on how exciting it would be to hear Galli-Curci "rag a little"; the quotation gives way to syncopation as the lyrics, using the latest slang, asks for "a little jazz in her wonderful trill."

For the chorus the music drops down to the subdominant, trio-like, for an extended quotation of the Triumphal March from *Aida* (ex. 8.2). By citing an opera not associated with Galli-Curci, the music implies that all opera, not just the specific singer in the title, is fair game for the popular musician's reworking. At the same time, the lyrics address Galli-Curci directly, asking her to sing a rag even "though it's wrong," that is, contrary to her status as a serious performing artist; still, it would be a treat to hear her sing "a melody sweet with the blues." This recognition that African American music (specifically ragtime, blues, and jazz) is foreign to opera is, on the one hand, an admission of popular music's inferior status and, on the other hand, an argument that such lower-status music has attractive qualities nonetheless: "Altho no opera sung ever has it / Ragtime is great when you jazz it."

"The Galli-Curci Rag" comments not only on the diva's recent New York premiere but also on a critical debate that had appeared the year before in the little magazine *Seven Arts*. In July 1917 Hiram Moderwell, the most prominent highbrow defender of ragtime, had put forth a "modest proposal" to win ragtime the esteem of America's cultural elite by means of a formal recital of ragtime songs by a classically trained vocalist. Such a program, Moderwell argued, might bring to these shores the acclaim ragtime had won elsewhere: "Such distinguished visitors as Ernest Bloch and Percy Grainger are delighted and impressed by American ragtime; foreign peoples accord it a jolly respect. Only the native-born, foreign-educated musician scorns and deplores it."[5] Anticipating the argument from trained singers that "ragtime must be sung with the 'vaudeville technique,'" Moderwell counters: "No particular technique is needed. There are only two kinds of singing: good and bad. Ragtime must be well sung, that is all."[6] In a subsequent letter to the editor, Carl Van Vechten called this assertion "an absolute misstatement of fact." Like other specialized repertoires, ragtime requires a "special technique" for its "proper interpretation." For a successful ragtime song recital Van Vechten "would trust Al Jolson or Nora Bayes or Fannie Brice farther in the matter than Emma Eames, Alma Gluck, or Amelita Galli-Curci."[7]

The persona in "The Galli-Curci Rag" clearly sides with Moderwell: if Galli-Curci were to jazz up her act, he asserts, "what a wonderful rag it would be." But the song's humorous tone suggests that the

Example 8.1. (a) Meyerbeer, *Dinorah,* Shadow Song, mm. 7–15; (b) Romberg and Atteridge, "The Galli-Curci Rag," mm. 1–9

(a)

Example 8.1 (*continued*)

(b)

songwriters—a native-born American lyricist and a Hungarian-born, Vienna-trained, naturalized American composer—know their business well enough to agree with Van Vechten. Ragtime, though it draws on opera among other European and non-European sources, is a thoroughly American art form not only in the "music itself" but also in its attendant performance practices.

As it must have been performed in *The Passing Show of 1918* by Willie and Eugene Howard, the song blends the various ethnic strains of the era's popular music. The Howard Brothers foregrounded their Jewish identity onstage; contemporary reviews and later reminiscences regularly describe them as Jewish or Hebrew comedians.[8] Although there is no indication of Yiddish dialect humor in the score, they probably would not have sup-

Example 8.2. "The Galli-Curci Rag," chorus, mm. 1–16

Example 8.2 (*continued*)

pressed that element of their act for this one song. Also, even though the song was issued as a vocal solo, in typical publishing practice, the sheet music retains a trace of the duet or "double" version in the italicized catch lines that appear over the piano part during the held notes in the vocal line. Whereas the lyrics proper have no obvious ethnic markers, the catch lines begin with Negro dialect ("Razz it up jazz it up / Start to mooch Galli Cooch"), then switch to Italian dialect ("makes the wop start to hop / raise the deuce with Caruse"). Thus in performance the song accessed the subgenres of Jewish, Italian, and African American dialect humor.

In this way "The Galli-Curci Rag" speaks for everyone in the balcony regardless of ethnicity. And what it has to say is a call for musical pluralism. A performance by Galli-Curci is not to be missed; her "Shadow Song" is so memorable that its quotation six months after the fact is likely to spark nods of recognition from the diva worshipers in attendance at a Broadway summer revue. At the same time, ragtime, blues, and jazz have an appeal that cannot be denied, and even opera lovers are not immune to their intoxicating effect. Neither European art music nor American popular music is the property of a single social group, and conversely, the individual music lover does not have to make a choice between one or the other.[9]

At the dawn of the Jazz Age, many Americans were beginning to realize that their own vernacular musical traditions were worthy of celebration and, moreover, that celebrating them did not demand either jingoism or boorish disdain for imported culture. Emerging from World War I a global military power, the United States was poised to assert itself as a cultural force as well. As the subsequent decades would confirm, that exported culture would be the product not of America's elite but of its common people—movies, comic books, chewing gum, and above all, popular music rooted in African American idioms. American anti-intellectualism and xenophobia would never entirely go away, to be sure, nor would animosity toward such elitist institutions as opera. And the racial reconciliation implied in music that combines opera and ragtime would remain a dream throughout the Civil Rights era and beyond. Nevertheless, here at the beginning of the American century was an awareness that American music, for all its uniqueness, was nourished by its roots in both African and European musical traditions.

Notes

Library Sigla

The following abbreviations denote sheet music collections that house songs discussed herein. When note references cite box and item numbers, they are presented as three-digit numerals separated by a decimal; for example, "Johns Hopkins University, Milton S. Eisenhower Library, Lester S. Levy Sheet Music Collection, box 148, item 111" is abbreviated "Levy 148.111." URLs are included here for collections that have made digitized images available on the Internet.

CPM	Middle Tennessee State University, Center for Popular Music
Duke	Duke University, Rare Book, Manuscript, and Special Collections Library, Historic American Sheet Music Project, http://scriptorium.lib.duke.edu/sheetmusic/
Hay	Brown University, John Hay Library, Sheet Music Collection, http://memory.loc.gov/ammem/award97/rpbhtml/aasmhome.html
Levy	Johns Hopkins University, Milton S. Eisenhower Library, Lester S. Levy Sheet Music Collection, http://levysheetmusic.mse.jhu.edu/
Lilly	Indiana University, Lilly Library, Sam De Vincent Collection of American Sheet Music, http://www.letrs.indiana.edu/s/sheetmusic/
NYPL	New York Public Library, Digital Library Collection, *Performing Arts in America, 1875–1923*, http://digital.nypl.org/lpa/nypl/lpa_home4.html
Templeton	Mississippi State University, Mitchell Memorial Library, Charles H. Templeton Sheet Music Collection, http://library.msstate.edu/ragtime/main.html
UCB	University of Colorado, Boulder, Music Library, Digital Sheet Music Collection, http://www-libraries.colorado.edu/mus/smp/index.html
UCLA	University of California at Los Angeles, Music Library, Special Collections, Archive of Popular American Music, including the Digital Archive of Popular American Music, http://digital.library.ucla.edu/apam/

Introduction

1. John Dizikes, *Opera in America: A Cultural History* (New Haven, Conn.: Yale University Press, 1993).

2. Bountiful examples of nineteenth-century U.S. publications of operatic music may be found at online sheet music archives, most notably the Library of Congress's *American Memory* project at http://memory.loc.gov/ammem. The classic study of Italian influences on American song is Charles Hamm, *Yesterdays: Popular Song in America* (New York: Norton, 1979), 62–88.

3. Katherine K. Preston, *Opera on the Road: Traveling Opera Troupes in the United States, 1825–60* (Urbana: University of Illinois Press, 1993), xi.

4. Renee Lapp Norris, "Opera and the Mainstreaming of Blackface Minstrelsy," *Journal of the Society for American Music* 1 (2007): 341–65; see also Norris, "Two Parodies of French Opera Performed by Blackface Minstrels," *Sonneck Society for American Music Bulletin* 225, no. 1 (Spring 1999): 9–11, and Preston, *Opera on the Road*, 312.

5. Van Wyck Brooks, "'Highbrow' and 'Lowbrow,'" in *America's Coming-of-Age* (1915), reprinted in *Three Essays on America* (New York: Dutton, 1934), 15–35.

6. Lawrence W. Levine, *Highbrow/Lowbrow: The Emergence of Cultural Hierarchy in America* (Cambridge, Mass.: Harvard University Press, 1988), 102.

7. Joseph Horowitz, *Wagner Nights: An American History* (Berkeley: University of California Press, 1994), 324. This mid-twentieth-century "midculture" is the subject of Horowitz's earlier *Understanding Toscanini: A Social History of American Concert Life* (New York: Knopf, 1987; rev. ed., Berkeley: University of California Press, 1994).

8. Karen Ahlquist, *Democracy at the Opera: Music, Theater, and Culture in New York City, 1815–60* (Urbana: University of Illinois Press, 1997).

9. Karen Ahlquist, "Mrs. Potiphar at the Opera: Satire, Idealism, and Cultural Authority in Post–Civil War New York," in *Music and Culture in America, 1861–1918*, ed. Michael Saffle, Essays in American Music (New York: Garland, 1998), 39.

10. Ahlquist, "Mrs. Potiphar at the Opera," 44.

11. Ahlquist, "Mrs. Potiphar at the Opera," 45.

12. On the rise of the popular music industry, see Craig H. Roell, "The Development of Tin Pan Alley," in *America's Musical Pulse: Popular Music in Twentieth-Century Society*, ed. Kenneth J. Bindas (Westport, Conn.: Greenwood Press, 1992), 113–21, and Russell Sanjek, *American Popular Music and Its Business: The First Four Hundred Years*, vol. 3, *From 1900 to 1984* (New York: Oxford University Press, 1988).

13. William Spengemann, introduction to *The American*, by Henry James (New York: Penguin Books, 1981), 9.

14. Constance Rourke, *American Humor: A Study of the National Character* (New York: Harcourt Brace Jovanovich, 1931), 141–42, 288, 295–96. Rourke's recognition that the role of the emblematic American was not assigned solely to Anglo-American characters was slow to take root in cultural criticism, but the notion that the African American characters in blackface minstrelsy represented not only black but also white Americans is now a commonplace in minstrel scholarship; see esp. Eric Lott, *Love and Theft: Blackface Minstrelsy and the American Working Class* (New York: Oxford University Press, 1993), and William J. Mahar, *Behind the Burnt Cork Mask: Early Blackface Minstrelsy and Antebellum American Popular Culture* (Urbana: University of Illinois Press, 1999).

15. Spengemann, introduction, 11.

16. Anatol Friedland and Edward Madden, "My Sist' Tetrazin'" (New York: Trebuhs, 1909), copy in CPM.

17. Both musicians' use of classical music is discussed in Larry Hamberlin, "Red Hot Verdi: European Allusions in the Music of Jelly Roll Morton and Louis Armstrong," paper presented at the seventeenth congress of the International Musicological Society, Leuven, Belgium, August 2002. See also Joshua Berrett, "Louis Armstrong and Opera," *Musical Quarterly* 76 (1992): 216–41. On the role of the phonograph in propagating opera, see William Howland Kenney, *Recorded Music in American Life: The Phonograph and Popular Memory, 1890–1945* (New York: Oxford University Press, 1999).

18. Ted Snyder and Irving Berlin, "That Opera Rag," no. 37 in Irving Berlin, *Early Songs, 1907–1914*, ed. Charles Hamm, Recent Researches in American Music, vols. 20–22, Music of the United States of America, vol. 2, parts 1–3 (Madison, Wisc.: A-R Editions, 1994), 1:136–39; Charles Hamm, *Irving Berlin: Songs from the Melting Pot: The Formative Years, 1907–1914* (New York: Oxford University Press, 1997), 75–76, 193. My attempt to answer the questions raised by "That Opera Rag" forms the substance of chapter 6.

19. Especially useful bibliographies include Barbara Cohen-Stratyner, ed., *Popular Music, 1900–1919* (Detroit: Gale Research, 1988), Ken Bloom, *American Song*, 2 parts in 4 vols. (New York: Schirmer Books, 1996, 2001), and Donald J. Stubblebine, *Early Broadway Sheet Music: A Comprehensive Listing of Published Music from Broadway and Other Stage Shows, 1843–1918* (Jefferson, N.C.: McFarland, 2002). Websites for the most valuable archives are included in the list of library sigla at the beginning of the notes.

20. Hamm, critical commentary, in Berlin, *Early Songs* 1:230–41, 2:336–51, 3:278–83.

21. J. Peter Burkholder, *All Made of Tunes: Charles Ives and the Uses of Musical Borrowing* (New Haven, Conn.: Yale University Press, 1995), 322–27, 365–68.

22. Burkholder, *All Made of Tunes*, 325.

23. For example, two nineteenth-century satirical songs about opera are Carl Hess, arr., "After the Opera's Over" (San Francisco: Gray, 1872), Levy 054.001, and W. H. C. West, "The Jenny Lind Mania" (New York: Hall & Son, n.d.), Levy 187.073.

24. See Gerald Bordman, *American Musical Revue: From "The Passing Show" to "Sugar Babies"* (New York: Oxford University Press, 1985).

25. Several LP recordings containing opera parodies are listed at the Durbeck Archive's website, http://www.durbeckarchive.com/parody.htm. On "What's Opera, Doc?" see Daniel Goldmark, *Tunes for 'Toons: Music and the Hollywood Cartoon* (Berkeley and Los Angeles: University of California Press, 2005), 132–60.

Chapter 1

1. The key work on the sacralization of high culture in the United States is Lawrence W. Levine, *Highbrow/Lowbrow: The Emergence of Cultural Hierarchy in America* (Cambridge, Mass.: Harvard University Press, 1988). Apropos classical music and opera in particular, see Joseph Horowitz, *Wagner Nights: An American History* (Berkeley: University of California Press, 1994), and Horowitz, *Classical Music in America: A History of Its Rise and Fall* (New York: Norton, 2005).

2. On the rise of commercial entertainment, see David Nasaw, *Going Out: The Rise and Fall of Public Amusements* (New York: Basic Books, 1993). On the birth of Tin Pan Alley, see Russell Sanjek, *Pennies from Heaven: The American*

Popular Music Business in the Twentieth Century (New York: Da Capo Press, 1996).

3. Alan M. Kraut, *The Huddled Masses: The Immigrant in American Society, 1880–1921* (Arlington Heights, Ill.: Harlan Davidson, 1982), 20. According to Leonard Dinnerstein and David M. Reimers, the 5 million Italians who immigrated between 1876 and 1930 constitute the largest immigrant group in those years, followed, in order, by Jews and Poles (*Ethnic Americans: A History of Immigration*, 4th ed. [New York: Columbia University Press, 1999], 50).

4. John F. Kasson, *Amusing the Million: Coney Island at the Turn of the Century* (New York: Hill and Wang, 1978), 39; Dinnerstein and Reimers, *Ethnic Americans*, 54; Humbert S. Nelli, "Italians," in *Harvard Encyclopedia of American Ethnic Groups,* ed. Stephan Thernstrom (Cambridge, Mass.: Belknap Press, 1980), 548.

5. George Pozzetta, "Italian Americans," in *Gale Encyclopedia of Multicultural America*, ed. Rudolph J. Vecoli (New York: Gale Research, 1995), 767–69; see also the website of the Little Italy Neighbors Association, http://www.thing.net/~lina/littleitaly.html.

6. It is likely that operagoing was more prevalent among the relatively prosperous Italians in the United States than among their poorer relations in Italy. As both Pozzetta and Nelli point out, the foods common to what most Americans think of as Italian cuisine represent not what Italians customarily ate in the old country but what they could now afford to eat in the New World ("Italian Americans," 772; "Italians," 556). As newly urbanized immigrants, Italian Americans in New York took advantage of the city's entertainment offerings, naturally gravitating toward those that favored the Italian language. Of these, almost all would have been centered in Little Italy, with one notable exception—performances of Italian opera.

7. Paola A. Sensi-Isolani, "Italians," in *A Nation of Peoples: A Sourcebook on America's Multicultural Heritage*, ed. Elliot Robert Barkan (Westport, Conn.: Greenwood Press, 1999), 301.

8. Matthew Frye Jacobson, *Whiteness of a Different Color: European Immigrants and the Alchemy of Race* (Cambridge, Mass.: Harvard University Press, 1998), 7–8, 56.

9. Neil Moret [Charles Daniels] and James O'Dea, "Niccolini: Waltz Song" (New York: Remick, 1905), copy in CPM. Anna Boyd, the performer depicted in the cover's photographic inset, was not among the cast for either show and presumably sang the song in vaudeville. In citations of song publications throughout the notes and bibliography, I have listed composer first and lyricist second; where a third collaborator is present, or where both music and words are attributed to both songwriters, I have added the parenthetical annotations "(m)" and "(w)" to clarify attribution. Quotations of lyrics, here and throughout, preserve the originals' spelling and punctuation with minimal intervention.

10. *Dwight's Journal of Music*, 6 July 1878, 263, quoted in Levine, *Highbrow/Lowbrow*, 100; the editorial insertion is Levine's. This association appears obliquely in a song whose title promises more than it delivers, "When Verdi Plays the Hurdy Gurdy," by Walter Donaldson and Charles McCarron (New York: Broadway Music, 1916), Duke A-66.

11. Irving Kolodin, *The Story of the Metropolitan Opera, 1883–1950: A Candid History* (New York: Knopf, 1953), 123, 598.

12. One was Pietro Mascagni, "Ave Maria," arr. Leopold Kessler (Boston: Ditson, 1893), Duke 527. An entirely different "Ave Maria," adapted from the same piece,

with Italian words by P. Mazzoni and English words by F. E. Weatherly, was published around the same time by National Music Co. (Chicago, n.d.), Levy 140.024.

13. Pietro Mascagni, "Intermezzo from Cavalleria Rusticana" (Philadelphia: Eclipse, n.d.), Duke 676. The back cover advertises a piano piece with a copyright date of 1914; the featured music, which carries no copyright information, reproduces the Intermezzo exactly as it appears in G. Schirmer's piano vocal score of the complete opera.

14. Tom Lemonier and Alex Rogers, "I'd Like to Be a Real Lady" (New York: Shapiro, Bernstein, 1902), in Hay; this song, from Bert Williams and George Walker's *In Dahomey*, is discussed in chapter 7.

15. Jacobson, *Whiteness of a Different Color*, 4.

16. Thomas S. Allen, "Any Rags?" (Boston: Krey, 1902), Levy 145.036 (the title page includes the question mark, missing on the cover); Allen, "Scissors to Grind" (Boston: Jacobs, 1904), Duke B-426.

17. A countervailing piece of evidence is an answer song to "Any Rags?": Bert Potter's "Any Ice?" (Boston: Krey, 1904), Levy 145.032. This song, whose lyrics allude to both "Any Rags?" and "Scissors to Grind," makes no use of Negro dialect, and the cover portrays an Anglo-American iceman; yet the music uses ragtime syncopations, an unusually early association of ragtime with white ethnicity. This point is taken up at length in chapter 7.

18. Thomas S. Allen, "Strawberries (Here Comes the Strawberry Man)" (Boston: Daly, 1909), Levy 149.125.

19. Collins's recording of "Strawberries," Columbia 1195 (1909), is reproduced in *Phonograph Pioneers*, audio cassette (St. Johnsbury, Vt.: Vintage Recording, n.d.); the accent is particularly heavy in an interpolated spoken comic bit before the second chorus.

20. *Weber and Fields' Funny Sayings: Comprising Funny Things Said by Weber and Fields, and Other Noted Humorists* [cover: *Weber and Fields Stage Whispers*] (New York: Ogilvie, 1904), 36–37. Only a few jokes in this small book resemble Weber and Fields's stage act; this story is not one of them.

21. A color engraving depicting Mascagni's arrest, first published in the *Corriere illustrato della domenica*, 23 November 1902, may be viewed online at http://www.mascagni.org/framed-images/504430.

22. Alan Mallach, *Pietro Mascagni and His Operas* (Boston: Northeastern University Press, 2002), 157–58.

23. Al Piantadosi and Thomas J. Gray, "Rusty-Can-O Rag," (New York: Feist, 1910), Levy 154.101a. The cover offers "apologies to Pietro Mascagni" and tells us that the song was "successfully sung by Ben Welch," though it must have been a departure from his specialty, "humorous stories that had a tear behind them" (George Jessel, eulogy for Al Jolson, 26 October 1950, http://www.geocities.com/Broadway/4195/news4.html).

24. Ted Snyder and Irving Berlin, "Wild Cherries (Coony, Spoony Rag)" (New York: Snyder, 1909), Levy 077.198.

25. This line may refer to Caruso's somewhat erratic performances during his rocky 1908–9 season; see chapter 2's discussion of "My Cousin Caruso," a song clearly alluded to here.

26. Gus Edwards, "I'm After Madame Tetrazzini's Job" (New York: Edwards, 1909), copy in NYPL; Lester S. Levy reproduces part of this song in *Give Me Yesterday: American History in Song, 1890–1920* (Norman: University of Oklahoma Press, 1975), 30–33.

27. *New York Telegraph*, 15 April 1909, cited in Charles Neilson Gattey, *Luisa Tetrazzini: The Florentine Nightingale* (Portland, Ore.: Amadeus Press, 1995), 112–13.

28. Peter G. Davis, *The American Opera Singer: The Lives and Adventures of America's Great Singers in Opera and Concert, from 1825 to the Present* (New York: Doubleday, 1997), 264–83.

29. Gus Edwards and Edward Madden, "Rosa Rigoletto" (New York: Edwards, 1910), copy in Lilly.

30. Gus Edwards, "Italian Romeo" (New York: Song Review, 1911), copy in CPM.

31. John Stromberg and Robert B. Smith, "Come Down Ma Evenin' Star" (New York: Witmark, 1902), Levy 145.149. The song, which had become something of a signature song for Russell, had not faded in popularity by 1911; on the contrary, she recorded it for Victor in March 1912. Edwards, with the lyricist Will Cobb, had written "If a Girl Like You Loved a Boy Like Me" for Russell (New York: Edwards, 1905); a copy is at Levy 147.058.

32. A. Pestalozza, "Ciribiribin: Waltz," arr. Charles J. Roberts (New York: Carl Fischer, 1909), Lilly 241.096; Pestalozza and Frank Sheridan, "If You Only Will: Ciribiribin" (New York: John Franklin Music, 1909), Levy 147.067;Pestalozza and Henry S. Sawyer, "Ciribiribin: Waltz Song" (New York: McKinley Music, 1909), Levy 145.140.

33. See the discussion of May Irwin in chapter 6.

34. Caruso went beyond popularizing songs to try his hand at composing at least two. "Dreams of Long Ago" (1912), the cover asserts, was "especially composed by Enrico Caruso for Henry W. Savage's production 'The Million'"—the same Henry W. Savage who in 1906 staged the first U.S. production of *Madama Butterfly*. Caruso's melody (the title page credits him with nothing more) is an undistinguished waltz song, a pallid genre piece (Enrico Caruso and Earl Carroll, "Dreams of Long Ago" [New York: Feist, 1912], Levy 189.070). Caruso's other published composition, "Liberty Forever!" (printed in the *Chicago Herald Examiner* for Sunday, 23 June 1918), is a thirty-two-measure World War I song, written in collaboration with Vincenzo Bellezzi, in the style of a red-blooded American football march, complete with cakewalk syncopations and oom-pah accompaniment (Levy 096.095b; the cover of the newspaper section in which the two-page song appears may be viewed at Levy 096.095a; a 1918 recording by the Victor Military Band has been reissued on Enrico Caruso, *Complete Recordings*, vol. 12, *1902–1920*, Naxos 8.110753 [2004]).

35. A. F. Frankenstein and F. B. Silverwood, "I Love You California" (n.p.: n.p., 1913), Levy 189.082.

36. Gitz Rice and Harold Robe, "Dear Old Pal of Mine" (New York: Ricordi, 1918), Levy 096.051.

37. Al Piantadosi (m), Jack Glogau (m), Joe McCarthy (w), "That Italian Serenade" (New York: Feist, 1911), Lilly 122.008.

38. Lewis F. Muir, "Chilly-Billy-Bee Rag" (New York: Helf, 1910), Lilly 201.029.

39. Lewis F. Muir and Ed Moran, "When My Marie Sings Chilly Billy Bee" (New York: Helf, 1910), Levy 154a.117a. On the publication sequence of the two numbers, see David Jasen, *Tin Pan Alley: The Composers, the Songs, the Performers, and Their Times: The Golden Age of American Popular Music from 1886 to 1956* (New York: Fine, 1988), 82.

40. The "cheesecloth gowns" refer to Mary Garden's revealing costumes in Manhattan Opera Company performances of such operas as *Thaïs*, in which "every motion of her sinuous body was visible through the thin, rose-colored drapery, which clung to limbs and torso with studied persistency" (*New York Press*, 26 November 1907, quoted in John Frederick Cone, *Oscar Hammerstein's Manhattan Opera Company* [Norman: University of Oklahoma Press, 1966], 132).

41. The year 1910 also saw the publication of an extremely similar song, Melville J. Gideon and E. Ray Goetz's "When Rosalie Sings 'Ciribiribi'" (New York: Shapiro, 1910; Levy 154a.119b)—even the covers share a strong resemblance. Ironically, the music, though the work of a generally inferior composer, is better, while the lyrics, the work of a more accomplished writer, are worse. Once again, the song's persona is a bragging boyfriend, in this case one whose inamorata has not yet left Italy and thus seems unlikely to appear soon on a New York operatic stage. See Larry Hamberlin, "American Popular Songs on Operatic Topics" (Ph.D. diss., Brandeis University, 2004), 119–23.

42. Fred Fisher and Joe McCarthy, "Night Time in Little Italy" (New York: McCarthy & Fisher, 1917), Duke 20. The title page reads "When It's Night Time in Little Italy," the cover reads "Night-time in Little Italy," and the back page reads "Night Time in Little Italy."

43. Charles Hamm, *Irving Berlin: Songs from the Melting Pot: The Formative Years, 1907–1914* (New York: Oxford University Press, 1997), 15–18, 20. An instrumental version of this song on a 1919 Edison Diamond Disc recording by the Frisco Jazz Band inserts an entirely different interpolation between the second and third choruses: a jazz version of "O Sole Mio"; the record may be heard at the Library of Congress website "Inventing Entertainment: The Motion Pictures and Sound Recordings of the Edison Companies" (http://memory.loc.gov/ammem/edhtml/edhome.html, accessed 5 May 2003).

44. I expand on this point in "Red Hot Verdi: European Allusions in the Music of Jelly Roll Morton and Louis Armstrong," paper presented at the seventeenth congress of the International Musicological Society, Leuven, Belgium, August 2002.

45. Adam Geibel and Richard Henry Buck, "Kentucky Babe: A Plantation Lullaby" (Boston: White-Smith, 1896), Levy 141.152.

Chapter 2

1. Lawrence W. Levine, *Highbrow/Lowbrow: The Emergence of Cultural Hierarchy in America* (Cambridge, Mass.: Harvard University Press, 1988), 102.

2. Peter G. Davis, *The American Opera Singer: The Lives and Adventures of America's Great Singers in Opera and Concert, from 1825 to the Present* (New York: Doubleday, 1997), 240.

3. *New York Telegraph*, quoted in Howard Greenfeld, *Caruso* (New York: Putnam, 1983), 83–84.

4. Reviews quoted in Greenfeld, *Caruso*, 86.

5. Reviews quoted in Greenfeld, *Caruso*, 86.

6. *New York Post*, quoted in Greenfeld, *Caruso*, 86.

7. Reviews quoted in Greenfeld, *Caruso*, 88–89.

8. Reviews quoted in Greenfeld, *Caruso*, 89.

9. Quoted in Greenfeld, *Caruso*, 90.

10. Quoted in Greenfeld, *Caruso*, 91.

11. Quoted in Greenfeld, *Caruso*, 91–92.

12. "Seen on the Stage," a preview of the next week's openings, *New York Times*, 7 July 1907; Gerald Bordman, *American Musical Revue: From "The Passing Show" to "Sugar Babies"* (New York: Oxford University Press, 1985), 32. Bordman includes a photo of this scene, which receives no mention in the short review of opening night, "'Follies of 1907': New Jardin de Paris Review Has the Anna Held Chorus," *New York Times*, 9 July 1907, which merely describes the thirteen parts as "vaudeville acts."

13. Gus Edwards and Edward Madden, "My Cousin Caruso" (New York: Edwards, 1909), Levy 148.111.

14. Fred Fischer and Jesse Lasky, "My Brudda Sylvest'" (New York: Fischer, 1908), Levy 148.108. The apostrophe in Sylvest' appears on the title page but not the cover; such discrepancies are common in this repertoire. Like Marx, most writers and performers of "Italian" material were not Italian at all: Fischer and Lasky were Jewish, and the inset photo on the cover of "My Brudda Sylvest'" shows an Irish dance team, Mabel Hite and Mike Dowlin, who presumably sang the song in vaudeville. The cover art is by the lyricist Gene Buck, whose song "Garden of My Dreams" is discussed in chapter 5.

15. Website of the Little Italy Neighbors Association, http://www.thing.net/~lina/littleitaly.html.

16. David A. J. Richards, *Italian American: The Racializing of an Ethnic Identity* (New York: New York University Press, 1999), 113.

17. George Pozzetta, "Italian Americans," in *Gale Encyclopedia of Multicultural America*, ed. Rudolph J. Vecoli (New York: Gale Research, 1995), 773.

18. Alan M. Kraut, *The Huddled Masses: The Immigrant in American Society, 1880–1921* (Arlington Heights, Ill.: Harlan Davidson, 1982), 138–39; Pozzetta, "Italian Americans," 774.

19. Greenfeld, *Caruso*, 135–36.

20. Harry Von Tilzer and Andrew B. Sterling, "Mariutch (Make-a the Hootch-a ma Kootch) Down at Coney Isle" (New York: Von Tilzer, 1907), Levy 148.005; the same team also wrote "I Want a Girl Just Like the Girl That Married Dear Old Dad" and "Rufus Rastus Johnson Brown."

21. The return to Italy is a common trope in Italian dialect songs, reflecting the truth that many Italian Americans crossed the ocean more than once before deciding to remain in the United States (Richards, *Italian American*, 112–13). Von Tilzer's song is an answer to a specific predecessor, Al Piantadosi and George Ronklyn's "My Mariuccia (Take a Steamboat)" (New York: Barron & Thompson, 1906; Lilly 099.043), in which Mariuccia runs away with Tony, a worker in the Department of Street Cleaning. Another answer song is James Brockman's "My Marianina" (New York: Hitland/Helf & Hager, 1907; copy in CPM), in which Marianina "fly da coop" not to Italy but to a burlesque show, where she takes up with an Irish comedian and becomes a singer of Irish songs. Answering both Piantadosi's original and Von Tilzer's response is Halsey K. Mohr and Edgar Leslie's "The Police Won't Let Mariuch-a Dance (Unless She Move da Feet)" (New York: Rose & Snyder, 1907), Lilly 195.045.

22. James Huneker, *New Cosmopolis* (New York: Scribners, 1915), 154, 162, 164, quoted in Kasson, *Amusing the Million*, 96.

23. John F. Kasson, *Amusing the Million: Coney Island at the Turn of the Century* (New York: Hill and Wang, 1978), 97, citing Bruce Bliven, "Coney Island for Battered Souls," *New Republic* 28 (23 November 1921): 374.

24. Significantly, the cover depicts the song's persona, not the titular Mariutch, thus emphasizing Coney Island's working-class audience, not its alluring performers. The cover's insert photo of Sadie Fields is a reminder of how easily female performers could represent male song personae onstage.

25. Charles Hamm summarizes Irving Berlin's Italian novelty songs in *Irving Berlin: Songs from the Melting Pot: The Formative Years, 1907–1914* (New York: Oxford University Press, 1997), 33–40.

26. Indeed, Lester S. Levy makes no mention of it, though he mentions the following *Pagliacci* quotation, in his description of this song in *Give Me Yesterday: American History in Song, 1890–1920* (Norman: University of Oklahoma Press, 1975), 40.

27. Caruso had sung *Carmen* earlier that season.

28. It is unlikely, of course, that in 1908 Edwards had heard any of Ives's music. Rather, the influence probably ran in the opposite direction. J. Peter Burkholder suggests that Ives's "patchwork" technique was at least partially inspired by the work of Tin Pan Alley tunesmiths; see J. Peter Burkholder, *All Made of Tunes: Charles Ives and the Uses of Musical Borrowing* (New Haven, Conn.: Yale University Press, 1995), 322–27.

29. The record has been reissued on Enrico Caruso, *Complete Recordings*, vol. 12, *1902–1920*, Naxos 8.110753 (2004). I have been unable to locate a copy of the June 1909 recording of the same song by Byron G. Harlan for Columbia (Magic Notes A-714).

30. On Louis Armstrong's quotations of this operatic melody, for example, see Joshua Berrett, "Louis Armstrong and Opera," *Musical Quarterly* 76 (1992): 216–41.

31. William R. Moran, "Discography of Original Recordings," in *Enrico Caruso: My Father and My Family*, by Enrico Caruso Jr. and Andrew Farkas (Portland, Ore.: Amadeus Press, 1990), 621. In 1902 Caruso had recorded the same aria for the Gramophone and Typewriter Company in Milan (608).

32. The association of this particular Caruso record with Italian ethnicity is evident in Irving Berlin's "My Sweet Italian Man" (New York: Waterson, Berlin & Snyder, 1913), no. 144 in Irving Berlin, *Early Songs, 1907–1914*, ed. Charles Hamm, Recent Researches in American Music, vols. 20–22, Music of the United States of America, vol. 2, parts 1–3 (Madison, Wisc.: A-R Editions, 1994), where Hamm adds the designation "II" to distinguish this song from an unrelated song with the same title. The song's persona expresses his love for his "gal" back in Italy in stereotypical terms—"Just for her, I'd go and put my pick and shove' in hock, / I'd climb into the river, and I swim-a like a rock"—culminating in the final statement, "That's how much I love my Italian gal." Berlin sets the last line to the "Ridi, pagliacco" tune from "Vesti la giubba." Here continues that tune's process of dissociation from its original context, a process that begins with "My Cousin Caruso" and that would allow the phrase later in the century to become a generic signifier of opera in the most undifferentiated sense. In *Pagliacci* this music expresses Canio's complex mixture of self-pity and self-loathing, but here it is used to express an uncomplicated romantic sentiment. This reallocation of affect resonates with Groucho Marx's absentminded singing two decades later, in *A Night at the Opera* (1935), of "Ridi, pagliacci, I love you very much-ee."

33. See William Howland Kenney, *Recorded Music in American Life: The Phonograph and Popular Memory, 1890–1945* (New York: Oxford University Press,

1999), especially chapter 3, "'His Master's Voice': The Victor Talking Machine Company and the Social Reconstruction of the Phonograph," 44–64.

34. Even here, however, Victor willingly pursued the immigrant market for records, hawking records to, in the words of a 1917 house publication, "people who find music as essential to life as goulash and spaghetti" (quoted in Kenney, *Recorded Music in American Life*, 76).

35. Billy Murray does just this in the Victor recording cited in note 29. Not all Caruso impersonators were male; Cecilia Loftus offered a "startling Caruso imitation" (Bernard Sobel, *A Pictorial History of Vaudeville* [New York: Citadel Press, 1961], 217).

36. Burkholder, *All Made of Tunes*, 326.

37. The Vitaphone Project, *Vitaphone News*, http://www.geocities. com/~ppicking/vitaphone13.html.

38. Georgie Price, "Memoirs" [1950s], posted by his son, Marshall Price, at http://www.afn.org/~afn49304/bio.txt.

39. Greenfeld, *Caruso*, 209. Brief excerpts from *My Cousin* are included in two video documentaries: *The Art of Singing: Golden Voices of the Century*, VHS cassette (NVC Arts 0630–15898–3, 1996), and *Bel Canto: The Tenors of the 78 Era*, vol. 1, *Caruso, Gigli, Schipa*, VHS cassette (West Long Branch, N.J.: Kultur, 1997). Caruso and Farkas, *Enrico Caruso*, report that both films were released in England, where at least one showing accompanied Caruso/Caroli's onscreen performance of "Vesti la giubba" with one of the tenor's recordings, the *Daily Express* reporting that "the synchronization between sound and picture was practically perfect" (261). Yet the makers of *The Art of Singing* assert that none of Caruso's recordings of the arioso can be synchronized with the film rendition. Even without sound, the film is a fascinating document of Caruso's performance in a signature role.

40. Gus Edwards and Edward Madden, "Mister Pagliatch" (New York: Remick, 1912), copy in CPM. This is probably the same song as the "Mr. Pagliacci" listed in a program for *The Passing Show of 1912*, described in Ken Bloom, *American Song*, part 1, *The Complete Musical Theatre Companion: Second Edition, 1877–1995* (New York: Schirmer Books, 1996), 3395.

41. On subversive uses of ethnic humor, see Joseph Boskin and Joseph Dorinson, "Ethnic Humor: Subversion and Survival," in *American Humor*, ed. Arthur Power Dudden (New York: Oxford University Press, 1987), 97–117.

42. Al Piantadosi and Billy Dunham, "Good-bye Mister Caruso" (New York: Cooper, 1909), Levy 146.110.

43. Greenfeld, *Caruso*, 147–48, citing the *New York Telegraph*, 8 April 1909, and the *New York Times*, 14 April 1909.

44. Thomas S. Allen, "My Irish Caruso" (Boston: Daly, 1909), Lilly 121.073. Allen is also the author of "Strawberries," discussed in chapter 1.

45. Other instances of Caruso name-checking occur in Edgar A. Guest's extra verses to Fred B. Sheer, "Kitty the Whistling Girl" (Detroit: Grinnell Bros., 1909), Levy 021.046b, and Jean Schwartz and Irving Berlin, "The Ki-i-youdleing Dog" (New York: Jerome & Schwartz, 1913), critical edition in Berlin, *Early Songs*, no. 151; for commentary on both songs, see Hamberlin, "American Popular Songs on Operatic Topics," 55–56, 59.

46. Irving Kolodin, *The Story of the Metropolitan Opera, 1883–1950: A Candid History* (New York: Knopf, 1953), 331; Kolodin, quoted in Greenfeld, *Caruso*, 231.

47. Abner Silver, "When Caruso Comes to Town" (New York: Witmark, 1920), copy in UCLA.

48. Jean Schwartz (m), William Jerome (w), and E. Ray Goetz (w), "When John McCormack Sings a Song" (New York: Waterson, Berlin & Snyder, 1915), copy in CPM. The cover features a large photo of Bayes and a small drawing of McCormack, contrary to what one might expect in a tribute song. Bayes recorded the song for Victor (45105) in 1916; my thanks to Paul Charosh for bringing that recording to my attention. Another recording, by Sam Ash, was issued on Columbia Little Wonder 167 (1915) and may be heard at the *Antique Phonograph Music Program* website, http://www.wfmu.org/playlists/shows/7259.

49. A reference to Yosef (Yossele) Rosenblatt (1882–1933), a Ukrainian American cantor whose Victor and Columbia recordings, beginning in 1913, were widely popular among Jewish listeners.

50. She was, however, capable of making playful reference to the professional effacement of her Jewishness. In the 1920 play *Her Family Tree*, in which Bayes played herself, she and her party guests use a Ouija board and crystal ball to find out if in an earlier life she "might have been a goldfish or a bluebird, or a bluefish or a Goldberg" (Gerald Bordman, *American Musical Theatre: A Chronicle*, 2nd ed. [New York: Oxford University Press, 1992], 357). Bayes's real first name is variously given as Eleanor, Leonora, or Dora in different sources; the star of a suffragist musical, *Ladies First* (1918), and a coauthor of the perennial "Shine On, Harvest Moon" (1908), Bayes is a figure worthy of more focused scholarly research.

51. This slang usage, which I have not been able to locate elsewhere, appears to be a form of syndoche in which an article of clothing represents the person who wears it, like calling a woman a "skirt."

52. Anthony Slide, *The Vaudevillians: A Dictionary of Vaudeville Performers* (Westport, Conn.: Arlington House, 1981), 75–77. Willie Howard's operatic humor was captured on film, in the silent short *Between the Acts at the Opera* (1926) and as an amateur opera singer in the feature *Millions in the Air* (1935).

53. Bordman, *American Musical Theatre*, 357. This song's inclusion in the show is mentioned on the sheet music cover.

54. Jack Stanley and George A. Little, "They Needed a Song Bird in Heaven (So God Took Caruso Away)" (New York: Mills, 1921), Levy 157.046.

55. I have been unable to consult Robert A. Keiser and Ballard MacDonald, "When Patti Sang 'Home Sweet Home'" (New York: Shapiro, Bernstein, 1917), cited in Barbara Cohen-Stratyner, ed. *Popular Music, 1900–1919* (Detroit: Gale Research, 1988), 385. The two Galli-Curci songs and three Tetrazzini songs are discussed herein. I have been unable to locate copies of the other three Tetrazzini novelties: Jean Schwartz and William Jerome, "When Sist' Tetrazin' Met Cousin Carus," from the 1910 revue *Up and Down Broadway* (Bloom, *American Song*, 4521); Jerome Kern and Paul West, "Sing, Sing, You Tetrazzini," from the 1912 musical comedy *The Red Petticoat* (Bloom, *American Song*, 3679); and Silvio Hein and George V. Hobart, "The Tetrazzini Family," from the 1908 musical comedy *The Boys and Betty* (Bloom, *American Song*, 511).

56. Anatol Friedland and Edward Madden, "My Sist' Tetrazin'" (New York: Trebuhs, 1909), copy in CPM.

57. The name Verdi is invariably rhymed with "birdie" or "hurdy gurdy" in these songs, indicating an Americanized pronunciation of the composer's name. Similarly, Madden and other lyricists rhyme the name Hammerstein with "green," "scene," etc., rather than "wine," "shine," etc. Lyric quotations here and elsewhere

preserve, with no further comment, the various misspellings of Tetrazzini's name found in the sources.

58. A chronology of Tetrazzini's performances is in Charles Neilson Gattey, *Luisa Tetrazzini: The Florentine Nightingale* (Portland, Ore.: Amadeus Press, 1995), 280–326.

59. Jason Rubin, "Lew Fields and the Development of the Broadway Musical" (Ph.D. diss., New York University, 1991), 197–209. The song, however, was not issued with the composite cover used for Raymond Hubbell and Glen MacDonough's songs in the show (e.g., "The Soubrette's Secret," cited in chapter 3).

60. Rubin, "Lew Fields," 206, 209. Still, opera parody must have appealed to the *Midnight Sons* audience: according to Bloom, *American Song*, 2858, another song on the bill was "Carmen the Second," by Raymond Hubbell and Glen MacDonough, a song I have been unable to locate.

61. Irving Berlin, "Yiddisha Nightingale" (New York: Snyder, 1911), Levy 078.235. See Charles Hamm, *Irving Berlin: Songs from the Melting Pot: The Formative Years, 1907–1914* (New York: Oxford University Press, 1997), 40–46, on characteristics of Berlin's Jewish novelty songs.

62. "Tettrazini" [*sic*] is set to three notes, implying that the final vowel is to be dropped, as in the Italian dialect songs; doing so, of course, also improves the rhyme. This lyric appears in the sheet music, but Maurice Burkhardt sings a different one on his Victor recording (17028-B, ca. December 1911).

63. Irving Berlin, "Ragtime Mocking Bird" (New York: Snyder, 1912), Levy 078.120; George Gershwin and Irving Caesar, "Nashville Nightingale," from *Nifties of 1923*, reprinted in *The Music and Lyrics of George Gershwin*, ed. Peter Foss, rev. ed. (London: Chappell, 1991), 2:64–67.

Chapter 3

1. Jacques Barzun, *Music in American Life* (Garden City, N.Y.: Doubleday, 1956), 15–16. Barzun describes this thin book as "not a sociological survey" but rather "a piece of testimony, which might conceivably be of use to the future musicologist" (13)—and it has been.

2. On similar responses to the "New Woman" in Victorian England, see Elaine Showalter, *Sexual Anarchy: Gender and Culture at the Fin de Siècle* (New York: Viking, 1990), 38–43.

3. The jokes, at http://www.mit.edu/~jcb/jokes/#vocal, are available by following the link "Web Sites of Interest to Musicologists" at http://www.ams-net. org/. Sixteen jokes are about sopranos (seventeen, if we include the tenor joke that asks the question "What do you see if you look up a soprano's skirt?"), whereas only thirteen jokes are about other voice types.

4. Michel Poizat, "'The Blue Note' and 'The Objectified Voice and the Vocal Object," *Cambridge Opera Journal* 3 (1991): 199. This article is derived from Poizat, *The Angel's Cry: Beyond the Pleasure Principle in Opera*, trans. Arthur Denner (Ithaca, N.Y.: Cornell University Press, 1992); originally published as *L'Opéra, ou Le Cri del'ange: Essai surla jouissance de l'amateur de l'opéra* (Paris: Métaillié, 1986).

5. See Edward Baron Turk, "Deriding the Voice of Jeanette MacDonald: Notes on Psychoanalysis and the American Film Musical," in *Embodied Voices: Representing Female Vocality in Western Culture*, ed. Leslie C. Dunn and Nancy A. Jones (Cambridge: Cambridge University Press, 1994), 103–19.

6. Lawrence Kramer, "Opera: Two or Three Things I Know about Her," in *Siren Songs: Representations of Gender and Sexuality in Opera*, ed. Mary Ann Smart (Princeton, N.J.: Princeton University Press, 2000), 193.

7. Carolyn Abbate, "Opera, or The Envoicing of Women," in *Musicology and Difference: Gender and Sexuality in Music Scholarship*, ed. Ruth Solie (Berkeley: University of California Press, 1993), 228–29. See also her *Unsung Voices: Opera and Musical Narrative in the Nineteenth Century* (Princeton, N.J.: Princeton University Press, 1991).

8. George W. Meyer and Sam M. Lewis, "My Music Teacher" (New York: Meyer, 1912), Levy 153.167.

9. The comma in this line appears one word later in the source.

10. Susan McClary, *Feminine Endings: Music, Gender, and Sexuality* (Minneapolis: University of Minnesota Press, 1991), 93. The quotation appears in the context of her discussion of *Lucia di Lammermoor*.

11. For example, the sheet music collection at Duke includes George Rosey (apparently a pseudonym for G. M. Rosenberg, the copyright holder), "Gounod's Opera *Faust* Arranged in Simplified Form" (New York: Stern, 1902), part of Stern's series Selections from Standard Operas. Piano arrangements of *Il trovatore* in the Duke collection range from the elementary medley arranged by Friedrich August Kummer and published (as "Trovatore no. 1") as part of the series *Operatic Leaves: Beautiful Melodies, Selected from Favorite Operas, Carefully Fingered, and without Octaves* (Boston: Ditson, 1869) to Louis Moreau Gottschalk's knuckle-busting "Miserere du *Trovatore*: Paraphrase de concert" (Boston: Ditson, 1888).

12. Jean Schwartz and William Jerome, "Since Sister Nell Heard Paderewski Play" (New York: Shapiro, Bernstein, 1902), from the show *The Wild Rose* (1902), as sung by Dan W. Quinn on a 1902 Edison cylinder. My thanks to Paul Charosh for providing a tape recording of the cylinder. Schwartz, incidentally, received his early musical training from his sister, a pupil of Liszt (Gerald Bordman, *American Musical Theatre: A Chronicle*, 2nd ed. [New York: Oxford University Press, 1992], 200).

13. A similar ambiguity—whether the protagonist is a singer or a pianist—marks Francis C. Westphal's "When Lucy Sings That Lucia Tune" (Chicago: Rossiter, 1911; copy in CPM), in which an African American persona expresses his love for the melody of the Sextet from Donizetti's *Lucia di Lammermoor* because "my Lucy gal used to play it for me," presumably on the piano. Only in the last line of the chorus does Lucy sing the tune, and then only in an ungrammatical patch that suggests a later hand (the publisher's?). See Larry Hamberlin, "American Popular Songs on Operatic Topics" (Ph.D. diss., Brandeis University, 2004), 160–67.

14. Irving Berlin, "Tra-La, La, La!" (New York: Waterson, Berlin & Snyder, 1913), Levy 087.189; no. 168 in Irving Berlin, *Early Songs*, ed. Charles Hamm, 3 vols., Recent Researches in American Music, vols. 20–22, Music of the United States of America, vol. 2, parts 1–3 (Madison, Wisc.: A-R Editions, 1994).

15. For a discussion of Berlin's songs about "normal" Americans, i.e., characters lacking non-Anglo ethnic markers, see Charles Hamm, *Irving Berlin: Songs from the Melting Pot: The Formative Years, 1907–1914* (New York: Oxford University Press, 1997), 55–56.

16. Quotations of Offenbach's Barcarolle at the beginning of a chorus can also be found in Edwards, "I'm After Madame Tetrazzini's Job," and Goetz, Grossmann, and Shiers, "That Dreamy Barcarolle Tune" (see chapter 7, n. 34).

17. Edison 2136 (1913), reissued on *Comic Songs by Billy Murray and Company*, vol. 6, *The Ragtime Era, 1913–1916*, audio cassette (West Palm Beach, Fla.: Vintage Recordings, n.d.).

18. Charles Segal, "The Gorgon and the Nightingale: The Voice of Female Lament and Pindar's Twelfth *Pythian Ode*," in *Embodied Voices: Representing Female Vocality in Western Culture*, ed. Leslie C. Dunn and Nancy A. Jones (Cambridge: Cambridge University Press, 1994), 30.

19. Leslie C. Dunn and Nancy A. Jones, introduction to *Embodied Voices: Representing Female Vocality in Western Culture*, ed. Leslie C. Dunn and Nancy A. Jones (Cambridge: Cambridge University Press, 1994), 1–2; their reference is to Roland Barthes, "The Grain of the Voice," in *Image, Music, Text*, trans. Stephen Heath (New York: Noonday Press/Farrar, Straus & Giroux, 1977), 181–83.

20. Bram Dijkstra, *Idols of Perversity: Fantasies of Feminine Evil in Fin-de-Siècle Culture* (New York: Oxford University Press, 1986), 258.

21. Raymond Hubbell and Glen MacDonough, "The Soubrette's Secret" (New York: Harris, 1909), Lilly 241.035. See also Hamberlin, "American Popular Songs," 196–99.

22. Harry Von Tilzer and Jack Mahoney, "When Priscilla Tries to Reach High C" (New York: Von Tilzer, 1916), copy in CPM. This song is an improvement over an earlier effort by Von Tilzer alone, "When Susan Thompson Tries to Reach High C" (New York: Dunn, 1899), copy in Indiana Historical Society. This song, about an African American who sings "opera selections" at a "colored show," was also published as a newspaper supplement on 22 October 1899; see John Graziano, "Music in William Randolph Hearst's *New York Journal*," *Notes*, 2nd ser., 48 (1991): 406–7.

23. One record, an Edison Diamond Disc, carries the catalog number EdDE 50363; my thanks to Paul Charosh for making available a tape recording of this disc. The second record, an Edison Blue Amberol cylinder, may be heard online at *The Antique Phonograph Music Program* website, http://www.wfmu.org/Playlists/Mac/mac.011124.html. Although some Blue Amberol cylinders were simply re-pressings of Diamond Discs (see "Edison Blue Amberol," in *Menlo Park in Edison, New Jersey: The Birthplace of Recorded Sound*, http://www.edisonnj.org/menlopark/vintage/blueamberol.asp), in this case the performers recorded a different, and longer, rendition of the song.

24. The libretto may be viewed at http://math.boisestate.edu/gas/ruddigore/libretto.txt.

25. Columbia A1962, reissued on *Ragtime Showcase*, vol. 1, *Anna Chandler, Marguerite Farrell, Elsie Janis*, audio cassette (West Palm Beach, Fla.: Vintage Recordings, n.d.). Farrell, whose career spanned vaudeville to operetta (she was in the cast of John Philip Sousa's 1913 operetta *The American Maid*), displays considerable vocal skill on this record, singing the vocalises legato (in contrast to Jones's staccato rendition) and making the most of the cadenza with flute obbligato. Multiple recordings of other popular songs of this era often rely on the same stock arrangements; in Farrell's record, however, the arrangement is altogether different from that used in both of the Jones and Murray records, making more significant the interpolation of a *Lucia-* style cadenza in all three.

26. Billy Merson, "The Spaniard That Blighted My Life" (New York: Harms/Francis, Day & Hunter, 1911). Merson, a music hall performer, had recorded this song in 1911; Jolson made his Victor recording in March 1913, a month after *The Honeymoon Express*, into which he interpolated the song, had opened at the Winter Garden.

27. *Micro-Phonies*, VHS reissue on *The Three Stooges*, vol. 2 (Columbia, 1987).

28. A kiyoodle is a mangy dog; the use of the term here extends even further the animal imagery mentioned above. Jean Schwartz and Irving Berlin, "The Ki-i-youdleing Dog" (New York: Jerome & Schwartz, 1913; critical edition in Berlin, *Early Songs*, no. 151), describes a musical dog thus: "Morning, noon and night he's around running loose, / Singing like a four-legged Mister Carouse"; see Hamberlin, "American Popular Songs," 37.

29. Either a reference to her high notes, or more likely, an implication that the sound of her voice was mistaken for that of a cat stuck in a tree.

30. Felix Arndt and Louis Weslyn, "My Gal's Another Gal like Galli-Curci" (New York: Stern, 1919), copy in UCLA. The bragging-boyfriend persona is familiar from "Rosa Rigoletto," in chapter 1.

31. On "Home, Sweet Home!" as a standard operatic encore, see chapter 6, note 19.

32. Lane later appeared in a 1928 musical comedy, *The Madcap*, and a 1929 revue, *Broadway Nights*, according to the *Internet Broadway Database* (http://www.ibdb.com/default.asp); see also Bordman, *American Musical Theatre*, 436, 453. In addition to the three large photographs, the cover includes five small drawings of "my gal" in costume, probably representing Eurydice (either Gluck's or Offenbach's), Carmen, Leonora *(Il trovatore)*, Cho-Cho-San, and Nedda *(Pagliacci)*.

33. Hughie Cannon, "Bill Bailey, Won't You Please Come Home?" (New York: Howley, Haviland & Dresser, 1902), Levy 145.079.

34. Irving Berlin, "I Love a Piano" (New York: Berlin, 1915), Levy 077.117. Later editions emend the first edition's dated reference to Paderewski and simultaneously broaden the persona's musical tastes to include "music from Broadway." Tellingly, the lyrical patch is not quite grammatical.

35. Bert Williams and George Walker, "She's Getting Mo' like the White Folks Every Day" (New York: Shapiro, Bernstein & Von Tilzer, 1901), Levy 149.088.

36. Ironically, Verdi stands in opposition not to an indisputably African American song but to a white appropriation—"The Swanee River." By invoking Stephen Foster's "Old Folks at Home," Williams and Walker align themselves with W. E. B. Du Bois, who praised Foster's sentimental plantation songs for incorporating "whole phrases of Negro melody," in contrast to "the debasements and imitations—the Negro 'minstrel' songs, many of the 'gospel' hymns, and some of the contemporary 'coon' songs,—a mass of music in which the novice may easily lose himself and never find the real Negro melodies" (*The Souls of Black Folk* [1903; reprint, New York: Signet, 1985], 270). And here is a further irony: Williams and Walker express their solidarity with Du Bois in the very "coon song" genre he despised.

37. Bert Grant and Joe Young, "Serenade Me Sadie with a Rag-time Song" (New York: Remick, 1912), copy in Lilly.

38. Lewis F. Muir and Fred Watson, "Oh, You Bear Cat Rag" (New York: Helf, 1910), copy in CPM; Gene Green, "Stop That Bearcat Sadie" (Chicago: Rossiter, 1912), Levy 154.161.

39. A period dance manual describes the basic step of the grizzly bear as follows: "The gentleman advances, swaying in rhythm to the right and left, as much as possible on his toes, in order to give his movement more moderation and suppleness. The lady makes the same movements, extending the left foot back when the gentleman

advances the right foot and vice versa. The gentleman and the lady advance and go backwards in turn. It is understood that the legs are bent slightly, in order to imitate as much as possible the gait of Master Brown. Nothing is uglier, however, than to bend the knees exaggeratedly" (Max Rivera, *Le Tango et les danses nouvelles* [Paris, 1913], 52–53, translation at "Mixed Pickles' Vintage Dance Timeline: Early 20th Century Dance," http://www.mixedpickles.org/20cdance.html).

40. Victor Herbert and Harry B. Smith, "Art Is Calling for Me (I Want to Be a Prima Donna)" (New York: Witmark, 1911), Levy 075.007. The cover is not visible in the digital images at Levy (http://levysheetmusic.mse.jhu.edu/otcgi/llscgi60); a copy in the Library of Congress carries the subtitle "The Prima Donna Song." Although the title page carries the rubric "Stellina and Chorus," the vocal line in the first system is illogically marked "Mina," the name of Stellina's maid. Edward N. Waters discusses the composition of *The Enchantress* and gives a synopsis in Edward N. Waters, *Victor Herbert: A Life in Music.* New York: Macmillan, 1955), 405–10.

41. Herbert did, however, attempt a Negro dialect song, "Hannah" (New York: Harris, 1907; Levy 074.047), in his 1906 musical comedy *Dream City.* With mild cakewalk rhythms and sophisticated harmonies, it is an example of what one reviewer called the new fashion of "neat coon songs," sung by more refined singers such as Lillian Russell, in contrast to the more "raucous" songs of 1890s coon shouters such as May Irwin and Fay Templeton (quoted in M. Alison Kibler, *Rank Ladies: Gender and Cultural Hierarchy in American Vaudeville* [Chapel Hill: University of North Carolina Press, 1999], 129). Another "neat coon song" is "Come Down Ma Evenin' Star," discussed in chapter 1.

42. Victor Herbert and Edgar Smith, *Dream City and The Magic Knight*, vocal score (New York: Harris, 1907), copy in Library of Congress. Several numbers from the vocal score were issued as offprints in the same year, among them "An Operatic Maiden," copy in Levy 074.126.

43. Bordman, *American Musical Theatre*, 223–24; Gerald Bordman, *American Musical Revue: From "The Passing Show" to "Sugar Babies,"* New York: Oxford University Press, 1985), 23–24. The work's origins and a synopsis are in Waters, *Victor Herbert*, 304–9.

44. Smith's Weber-and-Fields credits include *Whirligig* (1899), *Fiddle-Dee-Dee* (1900), *Hoity-Toity* (1901), *Twirly-Whirly* (1902), and *Whoop-Dee-Do* (1903); for Weber he wrote *Higgledy-Piggledy* (1904) and *Twiddle-Twaddle* (1906).

45. A press preview was given the preceding night, hence the opening date of 24 December 1906 in some sources.

46. On the Weber-and-Fields format, see Jason Rubin, "Lew Fields and the Development of the Broadway Musical" (Ph.D. diss., New York University, 1991), 65–95. A number from *Hoity-Toity*, "My Japanese Cherry Blossom," is discussed in chapter 5.

47. A monthly supplement to the Victor record catalog for June 1905 lists Blauvelt's recordings of Verdi and Gounod arias, as well as Scottish songs and "Home, Sweet Home!" ("Record Catalogs and Other Issues of the Victor Talking Machine Company," http://home.att.net/~dbro/vicpap.html).

48. Lydia Thompson, for instance, whose British Blondes were the premier burlesque company in nineteenth-century America, appeared early in her career in the fairy extravaganza *Chrystabelle, or The Rose without a Thorn;* see Kurt Gänzl, "Thompson, Lydia," in *The Encyclopedia of the Musical Theatre*, 2nd ed. (New York: Schirmer Books, 2001), 2045.

49. Bram Dijkstra connects such imagery in fin-de-siècle painting both to male fantasies of compliant and thus childlike women and to longings, shared by both sexes, for prelapsarian innocence (*Idols of Perversity*, 185–98). The association of fairies with a blend of the innocent and the risqué may be seen in the title of a short 1905 film intended for peep show exhibition, "Airy Fairy Lilian Tries On Her New Corsets," reproduced in *"The Great Train Robbery" and Other Primary Works*, vol. 1 of *The Movies Begin: A Treasury of Early Cinema, 1894–1913*, 5 DVDs (Kino International, 2002).

50. Robert C. Allen, *Horrible Prettiness: Burlesque and American Culture* (Chapel Hill: University of North Carolina Press, 1991).

51. Seymour Furth and Addison Burkhardt, "When Tetrazzini Sings" (New York: Trebuhs, 1908), copy in UCLA; Ken Bloom incorrectly gives the title as "When Tetrazzini Sings High F" (*American Song*, part 1, *The Complete Musical Theatre Companion: Second Edition, 1877–1995* [New York: Schirmer Books, 1996], 2869), possibly reflecting a variant reading in the playbill of *The Mimic World*, a revue described as a mixture of burlesque and vaudeville (Bordman, *American Musical Theatre*, 242).

52. Theodore F. Morse and Vincent P. Bryan, "Henrietta, Dainty Henrietta" (New York: Howley, Haviland & Dresser, 1901), Levy 146.159.

53. The first-person songs about female singers are "I'm After Madame Tetrazzini's Job," "My Music Teacher," "Art Is Calling for Me," "An Operatic Maiden," and "The Soubrette's Secret." Songs about male singers discussed elsewhere in these pages are "Strawberries," "Italian Romeo," and "My Irish Caruso."

54. Waters, *Victor Herbert*, 307; Victor Herbert and Edgar Smith, "Ta! Ta! My Dainty Little Darling" (New York: Harris, 1907), Levy 074.144.

55. In addition to several musical comedies, Farkoa sang in a 1911 London production of Johann Strauss's *Nightbirds;* he also made several records, including the very popular "Laughing Song," sung in French (Berliner 1302, 1896, reproduced in *Music from the New York Stage, 1890–1920*, vol. 1, *1890–1908*, 3 CDs [Wadhurst, U.K.: Pavilion Records, 1993]).

56. John Gilroy and Harry Linton, "I Sing a Little Tenor" (New York: Howley, Haviland & Dresser, 1902), Levy 147.028. The *Internet Broadway Database* (http://www.ibdb.com) lists seventeen productions in which Hart appeared in the space of fourteen years, 1900–1914. The 1902 *Wild Rose* should not be confused with Rudolf Friml's 1926 operetta of the same name.

57. Levy has several editions of "Rocked in the Cradle of the Deep"; the earliest is dated 1840. A copy of "The Palms" in Duke is dated 1889; it is still sung on Palm Sunday in at least one rural Vermont church.

58. Worton David (m, w) and George Arthurs (m, w), "I Want to Sing in Opera" (Sydney: Albert, 1910), copy in National Library of Australia accessible at http://nla.gov.au/nla.mus-an10717316. Wilkie Bard, "I Want to Sing in Opera," Jumbo 563 LXO-1146, recorded ca. November 1910, reissued on Wilkie Bard, *She Sells Seashells*, (Windyridge CDR 13, 2002). On the same CD anthology is "The Cleaner," a song whose persona is that of a cleaning woman who sings, "I want to be a principal girl in a new revue."

59. Bordman, *American Musical Theatre*, 269; Anthony Slide, "Julian Eltinge," in *The Vaudevillians: A Dictionary of Vaudeville Performers* (Westport, Conn.: Arlington House, 1981), 46–47.

60. Worton David (m, w), George Arthurs (m, w), and Jerome Kern (m, w), "I Want to Sing in Opera" (New York: Harms/Francis, Day & Hunter, 1910), copy in CPM; note the copyright date of 1910, although the publication has a composite cover for a production of *The Siren* that did not open until 28 August 1911.

Chapter 4

1. The skimpy Gospel narrative of the "daughter of Herodias" (Matt. 14: 1–12, Mark 17–29) is fleshed out somewhat by Flavius Josephus's *Antiquities of the Jews* (book 18, chapter 5.4), in which Salome is named but no dance is mentioned. On the fragmentary nature of the story's source materials, see Megan Becker-Leckrone, "Salome©: The Fetishization of a Textual Corpus," *New Literary History* 26, no 2 (1995): 242–47. For overviews of the Salome theme in literature and art respectively, see Mario Praz, "Salome in Literary Tradition," in Derrick Puffet, *Richard Strauss: Salome* (Cambridge: Cambridge University Press, 1989), 11–20, and Nanette B. Rodney, "Salome," *Metropolitan Museum of Art Bulletin* 11, no. 7 (1953): 190–200. Anthony Pym, "The Importance of Salomé: Approaches to a *fin de siècle* Theme," *French Forum* 14 (1989): 312–13, documents the heightened interest in Salome at the turn of the century; of 388 artistic, literary, theatrical, and musical representations of Salome created between 1840 and 1940, 82 percent date from the years 1880–1920.

2. Edward Said, *Orientalism* (New York: Vintage Books, 1979), 3; Lawrence Kramer, "Culture and Musical Hermeneutics: The Salome Complex," *Cambridge Opera Journal* 2 (1990): 270, 271; Gilles de Van, "Fin de Siècle Exoticism and the Meaning of the Far Away," trans. William Ashbrook, *Opera Quarterly* 11, no. 3 (1995): 78. As Becker-Leckrone elucidates in "Salome©," 240, it is devilishly difficult to maintain clear distinctions between various aspects of the Salome "text": the historical figure of Salome, her character as depicted artistically, her narrative, and her dance, which since Oscar Wilde is typically called the Dance of the Seven Veils. Like other writers, I tend to conflate all of these constituent parts, separating one element or another when needed or indeed possible.

3. Sander L. Gilman, "Strauss and the Pervert," in *Reading Opera*, ed. Arthur Groos and Roger Parker (Princeton, N.J.: Princeton University Press, 1988), 306–27; Gilman, "Salome, Syphilis, Sarah Bernhardt and the 'Modern Jewess,'" *German Quarterly* 66 (1993): 195–211; Davinia Caddy, "Variations on the Dance of the Seven Veils," *Cambridge Opera Journal* 17 (2005): 37–58; Bhabha quoted in Amy Koritz, "Dancing the Orient for England: Maud Allan's 'The Vision of Salome,'" *Theatre Journal* 46 (1994): 63–78. For a persuasive refinement of Gilman's interpretation, see Anne L. Seshadri, "The Taste of Love: Salome's Transfiguration," *Women and Music* 10 (2006): 24–44.

4. Similar to this chapter in subject matter, if not interpretation, is Charles A. Kennedy, "When Cairo Met Main Street: Little Egypt, Salome Dancers, and the World's Fairs of 1893 and 1904," in *Music and Culture in America, 1861–1918*, ed. Michael Saffle (New York: Garland, 1998), 271–98. Mary Simonson, "'The Call of Salome': American Adaptations and Recreations of the Female Body in the Early Twentieth Century." *Women and Music* 11 (2007): 1–16, offers an intriguing interpretation of the American performers of "Salome-as-New-Woman." An important work on a related topic, representations of the Far East in early twentieth-century American popular song, is Charles Hiroshi Garrett, "Chinatown, Whose Chinatown? Defining America's Border with Musical Orientalism," in *Struggling to*

Define a Nation: American Music and the Twentieth Century (Berkeley and Los Angeles: University of California Press, 2008), 121–64. On representations of the Middle East in French music of the late nineteenth century, see Ralph Locke, "Cutthroats and Casbah Dancers, Muezzins and Timeless Sands: Musical Images of the Middle East," in *The Exotic in Western Music*, ed. Jonathan Bellman (Boston: Northeastern University Press, 1998), 104–36. For nonmusicological work on American representations of Islamic cultures, focusing on the post–World War II era, see Douglas Little, *American Orientalism: The United States and the Middle East since 1945* (Chapel Hill: University of North Carolina Press, 2002), and Brian T. Edwards, *Morocco Bound: Disorienting America's Maghreb, from Casablanca to the Marrakech Express* (Durham, N.C.: Duke University Press, 2005).

5. On Chadwick, see Steven Ledbetter, "Two Seductresses: Saint-Saëns's Delilah and Chadwick's Judith," in *A Celebration of American Music: Words and Music in Honor of H. Wiley Hitchcock*, ed. Richard Crawford, R. Allen Lott, and Carol J. Oja (Ann Arbor: University of Michigan Press, 1990), 281–301; on Hadley, see Nicholas E. Tawa, *Mainstream Music of Early Twentieth-Century America: The Composers, Their Times, and Their Works* (Westport, Conn.: Greenwood Press, 1992), 80–81.

6. This study of the popular songs concerning Salome confirms Rachel Shteir's comment, apropos the vaudeville Salome dancers, that "if in France Salome stood as a symbol of women's inexpressible, raging desire, in America she crashed into puritanism and became both funny and obscene" (*Striptease: The Untold History of the Girlie Show* [New York: Oxford University Press, 2004], 46).

7. See Irving Kolodin, *The Story of the Metropolitan Opera, 1883–1950: A Candid History* (New York: Knopf, 1953); John Frederick Cone, *Oscar Hammerstein's Manhattan Opera Company* (Norman: University of Oklahoma Press, 1966); John Dizikes, *Opera in America: A Cultural History* (New Haven, Conn.: Yale University Press, 1993); and Peter G. Davis, *The American Opera Singer: The Lives and Adventures of America's Great Singers in Opera and Concert, from 1825 to the Present* (New York: Doubleday, 1997).

8. Details on expenses come from a recounting of the opening-night story in a newspaper piece previewing the 1909 Manhattan Opera production: "What It Means to Present 'Salome': An Eloquent Description of Difficult Problems by Those Who Ought to Know: Rehearsals before This Week's Final Battle," *New York Times*, 24 January 1909.

9. On the late disclosure of Morgan's role, see Cone, *Oscar Hammerstein's Manhattan Opera Company*, 210–11.

10. The strenuousness of this rehearsal may account for the moving of the opera's opening night from the traditional Monday night to Tuesday. Filling the Monday night spot was *Aida;* see "At the Metropolitan," *New York Times*, 20 January 1907.

11. Kolodin, *Story of the Metropolitan Opera*, 212.

12. "Strauss's 'Salome' the First Time Here: A Remarkable Performance at the Metropolitan," *New York Times*, 23 January 1907.

13. "Strauss's 'Salome' the First Time Here."

14. "What It Means to Present 'Salome.'"

15. "How the Audience Took It: Many Disgusted by the Dance and the Kissing of the Head," *New York Times*, 23 January 1907.

16. On Salome as a subversion of the gaze—"the traditional privilege of men to scrutinize women's bodies"—see Kramer, "Culture and Musical Hermeneutics," 272–75.

17. "What It Means to Present 'Salome.'" On the Hippodrome, see "Opening of Hippodrome," *New York Tribune*, 13 April 1905, and Gerald Bordman, *American Musical Theatre: A Chronicle*, 2nd ed. (New York: Oxford University Press, 1992), 210.

18. Kolodin relates that "Morgan personally offered to reimburse Conried" but was refused; Kolodin, *Story of the Metropolitan Opera*, 213.

19. In addition to the rather sensationalistic journalism cited here, at least two remarkably perceptive critical essays appeared in response to the Met *Salome;* see Henry Krehbiel's *New York Tribune* review of the following day, 23 January 1907, reprinted as "The *Salome* of Wilde and Strauss" in *The Attentive Listener: Three Centuries of Music Criticism*, ed. Harry Haskell (London: Faber & Faber, 1995), 223–28, and Lawrence Gilman's essay "Strauss' 'Salome': Its Art and Its Morals," in *Aspects of Modern Opera: Estimates and Inquiries* (New York: Lane, 1909), 65–105.

20. *New York Times*, 13 January 1907. To my knowledge, this was the first U.S. performance of Sudermann's *Johannes* (1898).

21. "Sothern and Marlowe in 'John the Baptist': Sudermann's Uninspired Play of Many Pictorial Scenes: Salome and Her Dance: Miss Marlowe in a Role of Oriental Seductiveness and Mr. Sothern in a Figure of Drab Monotone," *New York Times*, 22 January 1907. The quotation about the play's importance is from "Plays New and Old That Invite," *New York Times*, 20 January 1907, a "preview" that disregards the Saturday opening and reports that the following Monday would be the opening night.

22. The photo accompanies the preview "Looking Forward to a Week of Serious Drama," *New York Times*, 20 January 1907; Percival Pollard, "The Regnant Wave of the Sensational Dance: 'Salome' Craze Raged in Europe Long before It Came Here," *New York Times*, 23 August 1908.

23. All quotations are from Bret Harte, "Salomy Jane's Kiss," reprinted at *The Project Gutenberg Etext of "Stories in Light and Shadow,"* http://www.gutenberg.org/files/15192/15192-8.txt. I have been unable to locate a script of Armstrong's adaptation, but the synopsis cited below makes possible a limited comparison of short story and play.

24. If she had found him to be "white and spirit-like" at their first meeting, there is no other evidence of it in the story. Perhaps the spooky moonlit night has retroactively altered her recollection of his sunburn.

25. Oscar Wilde, *Salome: A Tragedy in One Act* (London: Elkin Mathews & John Lane, 1894), electronic reprint, Electronic Text Center, University of Virginia Library, March 2000, http://etext.lib.virginia.edu/toc/modeng/public/WilSalo.html.

26. For a synopsis and review of the play, see "'Salome Jane's Kiss' with Eleanor Robson: Harte's Story Basis for Paul Armstrong's Play: Some Capital Acting: But the Last Two Acts of the Play Not Up to the Standard of the Others," *New York Times*, 20 January 1907. Note that the anonymous reviewer applies the title of Harte's story to the play, whose proper title drops the last word, thereby softening the reference to what was the most shocking aspect of Wilde's version of the traditional Salome story. (The kiss arises late in the Salome tradition, in the American poet J. C. Heywood's dramatic poem *Salome, the Daughter of Herodias* [New York: Putnam, 1862], which was reviewed by Wilde—and there the kiss is bestowed not by Salome but by Herodias. The scene of Salome's kissing the head thus is original to Wilde.) Harte's posthumous novel *Salomy Jane* (Boston: Houghton Mifflin,

1910), incidentally, appears to be a "novelization" of the play and may not even be Harte's work at all.

27. Salomy Jane generated her own popular songs. One I have examined expands on the Western themes of the source but not on the Salome theme; see Helen Scott Barnes and Carlton Russell Foster, "Salomy Jane" (Los Angeles: Foster, 1916), copy in CPM.

28. See Gerald Bordman, *American Musical Revue: From "The Passing Show" to "Sugar Babies"* (New York: Oxford University Press, 1985), chapter 1.

29. "'Follies of 1907': New Jardin de Paris Review Has the Anna Held Chorus," *New York Times*, 9 July 1907, describes the thirteen scenes as "vaudeville acts." A valuable selection of contemporaneous writings about the exposition, a tercentenary celebration of the founding of Jamestown, may be found at "Jamestown Exposition," in Jim Zwick, ed., *World's Fairs and Expositions: Defining America and the World, 1876–1916*, http://www.boondocksnet.com/expos/jamestown.html.

30. Harry B. Smith, *First Nights and First Editions* (Boston: Little, Brown, 1931), 242.

31. Quoted in Bordman, *American Musical Revue*, 35. No music for Mlle. Dazie's dance survives. Bordman adds, "The reviewer also reported something no other paper seems to have noticed—that the police raided the theatre as soon as the dance was finished and arrested the dancer." I have found no other evidence to support this story of a police raid on the 1907 *Follies*, and subsequent events described later seem unlikely in the wake of a raid. In the same revue Mlle. Dazie also performed a "Jiu Jitsu Waltz," possibly a reference to *Madama Butterfly*'s premiere earlier that season; a photograph of her and her partner, Prince Tokio (unidentified in the photo), in this dance may be seen at NYPL.

32. Harry Von Tilzer and Vincent Bryan, "When Miss Patricia Salome Did Her Funny Little Oo La Palome" (New York: Von Tilzer, 1907), Levy 150a.031; my rendering of the title follows the sheet music title page and the lyrics on p. 5; the cover has the variant spelling "Oo-la-pa-lome." This song is no doubt identical to the "Bridget Salome" that was listed in the program, according to Ken Bloom, *American Song*, part 1, *The Complete Musical Theatre Companion: Second Edition, 1877–1995* (New York: Schirmer Books, 1996), 1236. Bordman calls Bayes "the most famous name in the cast" of the *Follies of 1907*; Bordman, *American Musical Theatre*, 231.

33. The association of the Cuban "La Paloma" with this ethnic stew is fitting, since the tune had become virtually an international folk song by the early 1900s, a favorite with Mexican mariachi bands and Hawaiian guitarists; see the discussion of James Thornton's "The Midway Paloma" in Hamberlin, "American Popular Songs on Operatic Topics," 343–44. In recent years a German record company, Trikont, has released a series of six CDs containing more than one hundred versions of "La Paloma," played and sung by country-and-western singers, Italian crooners, German brass bands, and many others (Trikont US-0220, 0227, 0241, 0272, 0327, 0328, 1995–2008).

34. My survey of Salome songs does not support William Kennedy's suggestion, based on a smaller sampling, that the variation in pronunciation "depend[ed] on the intention of the lyricist to convey a sense of culture or the lack of it" (Kennedy, "When Cairo Met Main Street," 283). "Suh-LOH-mee" is the accepted pronunciation in English, though not the one generally used by musicians and musicologists familiar with Strauss's opera.

35. Kennedy also notes the use of habanera rhythms "to create an exotic mood" (Kennedy, "When Cairo Met Main Street," 290). On the various devices of musical

exoticism, see Derek B. Scott, "Orientalism and Musical Style," *Musical Quarterly* 82 (1998): 309–35.

36. The revue, with music by Ludwig Englander and lyrics by Sydney Rosenfeld, opened at the Casino Theatre on 7 October 1907 and ran for 105 performances; a list of songs appearing on the program is in Bloom, *American Song*, 1461.

37. The former is the case in Donna Carlton, *Looking for Little Egypt* (Bloomington, Ind.: IDD Books, 1994), and Kennedy, "When Cairo Met Main Street." The latter is the case in Toni Bentley, *Sisters of Salome* (New Haven, Conn.: Yale University Press, 2002), and Derrick Puffett, ed., *Richard Strauss: Salome*, Cambridge Opera Handbook (Cambridge: Cambridge University Press, 1989).

38. I treat the dancers at the Chicago fair and the songs inspired by them at greater length in "Cairo on the Midway: Orientalism, Popular Song, and the Chicago Fair of 1893," paper presented at annual meetings of the International Association for the Study of Popular Music, U.S. branch, Murfreesboro, Tenn., 16–19 February 2006, and the Society for American Music, Chicago, Ill., 15–19 March 2006. A standard work on the racist underpinnings of the turn-of-the-century world's fairs is Robert W. Rydell, *All the World's a Fair: Visions of Empire at American International Expositions, 1876–1916* (Chicago: University of Chicago Press, 1984); see esp. 50, 66.

39. Carlton, *Looking for Little Egypt*, 43.

40. Quoted in Carlton, *Looking for Little Egypt*, 23, 46.

41. Carlton, *Looking for Little Egypt*, 62. In some prints, black bars cover the dancer's bosom and hips (though she is fully dressed), making this one of the earliest censored films.

42. Carlton, *Looking for Little Egypt*, 65–71.

43. James Thornton, "The Streets of Cairo, or The Poor Little Country Maid" (New York: Hardings, 1895), Levy 144.023a. On the tune's probably Algerian origins, see James Fuld, *The Book of World-Famous Music*, 3rd ed. (New York: Dover Books, 1985), 276–77.

44. Quoted in "What It Means to Present 'Salome.'"

45. Kennedy, "When Cairo Met Main Street," 297n33. Bentley gives the Lincoln Square Theatre as the location of Froelich's initial vaudeville performance (Bentley, *Sisters of Salome*, 38). In addition to Bentley's excellent summary, the Salomania of 1908 is documented in Elizabeth Kendall, *Where She Danced* (New York: Knopf, 1979), 74–90; Elaine Showalter, *Sexual Anarchy: Gender and Culture at the Fin de Siècle* (New York: Viking, 1990), 144–68; and Richard Bizot, "The Turn-of-the-Century Salome Era: High- and Pop-Culture Variations on the Dance of the Seven Veils," *Choreography and Dance* 2, no. 3 (1992): 71–87.

46. Bentley, *Sisters of Salome*, 39.

47. For biographical information on Allan, see Felix Cherniavsky, *The Salome Dancer* (Toronto: McClelland & Stewart, 1991), and Bentley, *Sisters of Salome*, 47–84. Koritz offers an insightful interpretation of Allan's career in "Dancing the Orient for England."

48. Compare, for example, the paintings by Moreau and Georges Rochegrosse reproduced in Rodney, "Salome," 198.

49. See the synopsis in Koritz, "Dancing the Orient for England," 66–67.

50. Abel Green and Joe Laurie Jr., *Show Biz from Vaude to Video* (New York: Holt, 1951), 9, 17–20.

51. Bentley, *Sisters of Salome*, 39.

52. J. Bodewalt Lampe, "A Vision of Salome" (New York: Remick, 1908), copy in Lilly 094.017; the subtitle on the cover reads "Fantasie [*sic*] Characteristique for Piano," that on the title page "Descriptive Fantasie [*sic*]." Unlike songs, instrumental compositions rarely carried photo insets of performers on the cover; moreover, at the time of publication Hoffmann had not yet gained the notoriety that soon would be hers. Thus the cover's failure to cite her does not weaken the likelihood that this was the music she used. Bentley's assertion that Hoffmann used Strauss's "Dance of the Seven Veils" (Bentley, *Sisters of Salome*, 39, 59) seems doubtful, and Bentley gets at least one other detail of the story wrong, confusing Oscar and Willie Hammerstein. Surely neither Oscar nor Willie Hammerstein would have been willing to pay the exorbitant royalties Strauss was able to demand for the *Salome* music, even if they or Hoffmann had preferred it to Lampe's. The Strauss attribution occurs again in Barbara Naomi Cohen, *The Borrowed Art of Gertrude Hoffmann* (Brooklyn: Dance Horizons, 1977), 11n13, with the additional comment that "new music by Max Hoffmann [Gertrude's husband and director of the Victoria Theatre orchestra] was added in September." No trace of Max Hoffmann's music has turned up; my thanks to Mary Simonson for alerting me to this information.

53. The minor key and tonic drone also appear in a middle section of a late-nineteenth-century American instrumental piece on the same theme; see William Loraine, "Salome: Intermezzo for the Pianoforte" (New York: Mills, 1898), copy at University of Maine, Maine Music Box, accessible online at the Sheet Music Consortium, http://digital.library.ucla.edu/sheetmusic/. This is, to my knowledge, the earliest American sheet music on the Salome theme.

54. A band arrangement (New York: Remick, 1908) is in the John Held Band Collection, Utah State Historical Society, and may be heard on the South Shore Concert Band's CD *Sounds of the Circus*, vol. 18 (Whitmarsh Recordings, n.d.). A quotation of the tune opens a 1931 recording of Walter Doyle's "Egyptian Ella" by the Ted Lewis Orchestra (Columbia 2427 D), reissued on *From Avenue A to the Great White Way: Yiddish and American Popular Songs* (Columbia Legacy, 2002). One of many cartoon references is in MGM's 1939 *Jitterbug Follies*, where a hint of the tune accompanies a visual reference to a severed head on a salver (reissued as an extra on *The Marx Brothers Collection* [Warner Home Video, 2004]). According to an online memoir, as late as 1951 contestants on *Stop That Tune*, a radio quiz show, were expected to recognize "a little-known belly dance number called 'The [*sic*] Vision of Salome'"; see Sam Ewing, "Fun, Games and Jackpots," http://home.no.net/ewing/p13.htm.

55. "The Vulgarization of Salome," *Current Literature* 45, no. 4 (October 1908): 437, cited in David Krasner, "Black *Salome*: Exoticism, Dance, and Racial Myths," in *African American Performance and Theater History*, ed. Harry J. Elam Jr. and David Krasner (New York: Oxford University Press, 2001), 200.

56. Lucinda Jarrett, *Stripping in Time: A History of Erotic Dancing* (London: Pandora, 1997), 94.

57. Tanguay's venue is identified in Jarrett, *Stripping in Time*, 94. A description of *The Sambo Girl* is in Bordman, *American Musical Theatre*, 753. Bentley confuses this drinking song with Tanguay's Salome dance (Bentley, *Sisters of Salome*, 39); it is hard to imagine Tanguay pouring champagne over the Allanesque costume she wears in a photo reproduced in Anthony Slide, *The Vaudevillians: A Dictionary of Vaudeville Performers* (Westport, Conn.: Arlington House, 1981), 148.

58. "The Call of Salome: Rumors That Salomania Will Have a Free Hand This Season," *New York Times*, 16 August 1908. Bentley apparently misjudges the tone of this article when she asserts that the Salome craze was debated in the 1908 presidential election (Bentley, *Sisters of Salome*, 40); the article merely pokes fun at William Jennings Bryan's knee-jerk adoption of any position that was the opposite of William Howard Taft's.

59. Caddy, "Variations on the Dance of the Seven Veils," 38.

60. Bentley, *Sisters of Salome*, 40.

61. Bloom, *American Song*, 2869; Jason Rubin, "Lew Fields and the Development of the Broadway Musical" (Ph.D. diss., New York University, 1991), 185–88. An illustration of Lotta Faust in her *Wizard of Oz* costume and a Billy Murray recording of "Sammy" may be seen and heard at David Maxine, "Tiger Tunes: Sammy," http://www.hungrytigerpress.com/tigertunes/sammy.shtml.

62. W. T. Francis and John E. Hazzard, "Salome" (New York: Harms, 1908); copy in UCLA, item SY105866. The title page lists as copyright holder Jerome Kern, who composed other numbers for the show. This song, which shows no evidence of his talent, is listed in the New York program book, where it was sung by Jack Gardner in the role of Herbert Henshaw, but evidently was dropped when the production went on tour (Bloom, *American Song*, 1318).

63. Gus Edwards and Will D. Cobb, "My Sunburned Salome" (New York: Edwards, 1908), copy in Lilly. The cover carries the variant title "Sunburnt Salome" and the subtitle "An Egyptian Deity"; the spelling in the lyrics is "sunburned," and I have chosen to refer to the song by the version of the title that uses that spelling. Kennedy, "When Cairo Met Main Street," uses the cover variant.

64. Ed Wynn and Stanley Murphy, "I'm Going to Get Myself a Black Salome" (New York: Shapiro, 1908), Levy 147.082. Wynn, born Isaiah Edwin Leopold, had been in vaudeville since 1902 and would land his first Broadway role in 1910; he later wrote, directed, composed for, and starred in a number of revues, including 1921's *The Perfect Fool*. My thanks to Wayne Shirley for pointing me toward information about Wynn.

65. When Jerome Kern and Oscar Hammerstein II gave the title "In Dahomey" to a production number set at the Chicago fair in *Show Boat* (1927), they may have been evoking Cook and Dunbar's musical as much as the fair's Dahomey Village.

66. Ben M. Jerome and Edward Madden, "The Dusky Salome" (New York: Trebuhs, 1908), Levy 146.030. Maude Raymond's recording of "The Dusky Salome" is included on *Music from the New York Stage*, vol. 2, *1908–1913* (Wadhurst, England: Pearl, 1993).

67. Eugene Black (pseudonym for Jean Schwartz) and William Jerome, "When Mister Shakespeare Comes to Town, or I Don't Like Them Minstrel Folks" (New York: Howley, Haviland & Dresser, 1901), copy in Hay. Other examples are Robert Adams and James O'Dea, "I Wants a Man Like Romeo" (Detroit: Whitney Warner, 1902), Levy 147.040, and Ted Snyder and Irving Berlin, "Colored Romeo" (New York: Snyder, 1910), Levy 077.039.

68. Thomas L. Riis gives a fascinating account of this period in African American theater in *Just before Jazz: Black Musical Theater in New York, 1890–1915* (Washington, D.C.: Smithsonian Institution Press, 1989).

69. *The Royal Magazine* (London, September 1903, 387), quoted in John Culme, *Footlight Notes*, 15 February 2003, http://www.gabrielleray.150m.com/ArchivePressText2003/20030215.html.

70. Tom Lemonier and Alex Rogers, "I'd Like to Be a Real Lady" (New York: Shapiro, Bernstein, 1902), copy in Hay. Harry Von Tilzer and Vincent Bryan, "I Wants to Be a Actor Lady," modern edition in Will Marion Cook et al., *The Music and Scripts of "In Dahomey,"* ed. Thomas L. Riis, Music of the United States of America 5:68–70 (Madison, Wisc.: A-R Editions, 1997). A modern performance of the latter is included in *"I Wants to Be a Actor Lady" and Other Hits from Early Musical Comedies,* NW221 (New World Records, 1978; CD reissue, 1993). The main character in John W. Bratton and Paul West's "I Want to Play Hamlet" (New York: Witmark, 1903), copy in Hay, is an African American actor whose attempt to stage an all-black *Hamlet* is ridiculed by the audience; one couplet brings Aida Walker to mind: "An' when de black Ophelia tried to do her bug house act / Dey made her do a cakewalk till the stage she bent and cracked."

71. Krasner, "Black *Salome,*" 198, 197, 199–200.

72. *Boston Globe,* 6 September 1908, and undated clipping, both quoted in Krasner, "Black *Salome,*" 201.

73. Melissa Peck astutely points out that overtones of miscegination may have made Walker reluctant to handle the (white) head of John the Baptist ("Performing the Erotic: Aida Overton Walker's Interpretation of Salome," paper presented at the Reception Study Society [RSS] Conference on Reception Study, Kansas City, Mo., 27–29 September 2007).

74. The earliest of the reviews of Walker's Salome cited in Krasner, "Black *Salome,*" dates from 27 August 1908, implying that she added the dance shortly before that date.

75. Robert Speare, "Victoria's Show Pleases Crowds," *New York Telegraph,* 6 August 1912, cited in Krasner, "Black *Salome,*" 206.

76. Cone, *Oscar Hammerstein's Manhattan Opera Company,* 185–86.

77. Cone, *Oscar Hammerstein's Manhattan Opera Company,* 211.

78. *New York Sun,* 29 January 1909, cited in Cone, *Oscar Hammerstein's Manhattan Opera Company,* 214; *New-York Daily Tribune,* 29 January 1909, cited in Davis, *American Opera Singer,* 231.

79. Davis, *American Opera Singer,* mentions twelve New York performances, but Cone, *Oscar Hammerstein's Manhattan Opera Company,* appendix 1, lists only ten.

80. Steward and Hammerstein quoted in Davis, *American Opera Singer,* 234.

81. Pollard, "The Regnant Wave of the Sensational Dance."

82. Orlando Powell and John P. Harrington, "Salome" (New York: Remick, 1909), copy in CPM. The spelling "Harrinton" on the title page is evidently a typographical error. This is not the song with the same title in *Fluffy Ruffles* (1908).

83. This topic is explored at length in M. Alison Kibler, *Rank Ladies: Gender and Cultural Hierarchy in American Vaudeville* (Chapel Hill: University of North Carolina Press, 1999). The composite cover for "That Opera Rag" (see chapter 6) features a similar large portrait of Irwin and the legend "May Irwin's Song Successes," thereby giving the performer top billing over the songwriters, much as the cover of "Salome" gives priority to Vance.

84. *Hippodrome News,* 25 March 1908, quoted in Sterling Morris, "Clarice Vance, 'The Southern Singer,'" http://www.tinfoil.com/Cv-bio.htm. As described in chapter 6, May Irwin, faced with similar career choices, did play romantic scenes for comic effect, an avenue that Vance rejected; Irwin played them not as a supporting character actress, however, but as the lead.

85. Morris, "Clarice Vance."

86. Orlando Powell's musical comedy *The Bicycle Girl* had crossed the Atlantic in 1895 for a brief run at New York's Grand Theatre (Bordman, *American Musical Theatre*, 140), and in 1910 Ada Jones would record for Edison his song "Put on Your Slippers, You're In for the Night," with lyrics by the American Seymour J. Furth (Christian Zwarg, "Truesound Transfers TT-1825," 2001, http://www. truesoundtransfers.de/Titellisten/TT1825.htm). Little is known about John P. Harrington; his song "Little Shepherdess of Devon," with music by Alec Hemley, was recorded in London by the baritone Robert Carr in 1912 (Christian Zwarg, "Truesound Online Discography Project," 2000, http://www.jabw.demon.co.uk/ zwarg.htm).

87. Morris, "Clarice Vance."

88. A 9 August 1908 *New York Times* article, published at the height of Salomania and headlined "Isadora Duncan Raps Maud Allan," was clearly intended to promote Duncan's New York performance of her Greek-inspired dances on 20 August, but it ran with a photo not of Duncan but of Allan in her notorious Salome costume. It is easy to understand why Duncan had little good to say about Allan.

89. Bentley, *Sisters of Salome*, 58. Also written in 1909 was Irving Berlin's ragtime burlesque "That Mesmerizing Mendelssohn Tune" (New York: Snyder, 1909), copy in NYPL. An unpublished and undated lyric sheet in the Library of Congress's Irving Berlin Collection preserves Berlin's "Spring Song Melody," whose chorus begins "Poor old 'Spring Song' melody, / Everyone has stolen thee. / Everyone who writes a song / Puts you where you don't belong," and adds, "Seems to me that everyone / Picks on poor old Mendelssohn"; Irving Berlin, *The Complete Lyrics of Irving Berlin*, ed. Robert Kimball and Linda Emmet (New York: Knopf, 2001), 14.

90. Bentley, *Sisters of Salome*, 67–68, 69.

91. Ted Snyder and Irving Berlin, "No One Could Do It Like My Father!" (New York: Snyder, 1909), Levy 077.188.

92. Edgar Leslie (w, m) and Irving Berlin (w, m), "Sadie Salome (Go Home)" (New York: Snyder, 1909), Levy 077.190.

93. Charles Hamm, *Irving Berlin: Songs from the Melting Pot: The Formative Years, 1907–1914* (New York: Oxford University Press, 1997), 12.

94. *Sic;* in 1909 this was still the Ted Snyder Company.

95. Bernard Sobel, *Burleycue: An Underground History of Burlesque Days* (New York: Farrar & Rinehart, 1931), 149–50. Brice would later use the spelling "Fanny" for her first name; because I discuss here only her early career, I have retained the earlier spelling "Fannie."

96. Archibald Joyce, "Vision of Salome" (New York: Francis, Day & Hunter, 1909), Levy 173.043. The presence of a 1909 arrangement by Emil Ascher in UCLA, Louis B. Schnauber/Film Music Society Collection, folder 1936, attests to the waltz's use as film music. Phonograph recordings of the waltz extend at least as late as 1933, when the Isham Jones Orchestra recorded it for Victor (24348).

97. "Musicians," *Encyclopedia Titanica*, http://www.encyclopedia-titanica.org. Both "Songe d'Automne" and "Vision of Salome" were in the White Star Line's orchestra books; a fleeting snippet of the latter may be heard in James Cameron's feature film *Titanic*.

98. Richard Strauss, "Salomes Tanz" (Berlin: Fürstner, 1905), Levy 172.093.

99. W. Anthony Sheppard, in "An Exotic Enemy: Anti-Japanese Musical Propaganda in World War II Hollywood," *Journal of the American Musicological*

Society 54 (2001), 329–30, points out the difficulty this lack of discrimination caused World War II–era Hollywood composers who were faced with the challenge of portraying the Japanese as enemies and the Chinese as allies.

100. See Robin Holloway, "*Salome:* Art or Kitsch?" in Puffett, ed., *Richard Strauss: Salome,* 145–60.

101. On a period recording by Vessala's Italian Band (Victor 31825), the "vah"s appear to be shouted, somewhat half-heartedly, by members of the band.

102. Quoted in Bentley, *Sisters of Salome,* 71.

103. David Z. Kushner, "Bloch, Ernest," in *The New Grove Dictionary of Music and Musicians,* 2nd ed., ed. Stanley Sadie (New York: Grove, 2001), 3:705.

104. Quoted in Hamm, *Irving Berlin,* 26.

105. S. G. Rhodes, "That Pipe Organ Rag" (St. Louis: Stark, 1912), copy in NYPL.

106. "A Salome of Color," *Stage Pictorial,* 1912, quoted in Krasner, "Black *Salome,*" 206. Even sympathetic reviewers, however, brought to Walker's performances biases influenced by lowbrow Salomes; the *New York Herald* called her dance a "ragtime Salome" (quoted in Krasner, "Black *Salome*").

107. Archibald Joyce, "The Passing of Salome: Valse Orientale" (London: Ascherberg, Hopwood & Crew; New York: Feist, 1912), copy in Lilly.

108. Jimmie V. Monaco and Joe McCarthy, "Fatima Brown" (New York: Feist, 1915), Levy 152.004.

109. Abner Silver and Alex Gerber, "Becky from Babylon" (New York: Witmark, 1920), copy in Lilly. The song was recorded by Fred Hager's Novelty Orchestra on Okeh 4280, 5 February 1921, according to Steve Abrams, *The Online Discographical Project,* http://settlet.fateback.com. A somewhat similar but less developed song about an oriental dancer from Cairo, Illinois, was in the 1918 Al Jolson vehicle *Sinbad;* see Sigmund Romberg and Harold Atteridge, "I Hail from Cairo" (New York: Schirmer, 1918), copy in NYPL.

110. Becky, a stock name in Jewish dialect songs, became an almost proprietary character for Fannie Brice, who sang "Becky Is Back in the Ballet" and other numbers in which she lampooned both ballet and popular dancing. A song in which Becky is an oriental dancer would surely have reminded audiences of Brice and may have been originally intended for her.

111. Robert Stolz and Bartley Costello, "Sal-O-May (Salome): Song of the Orient and Fox-Trot" (Vienna: Boheme; New York: Marks, 1920), copy in UCLA. A period recording by Yerkes Musical Bellhops, Banner 1020, was recorded August or September 1921; see Abrams, *Online Discographical Project.* A different English-language version titled "Step by Step (Salomé)" was recorded by the Ray Charles Singers, according to the cover of sheet music published in 1957 (copy in CPM); in 1961 Petula Clark topped the U.K. charts with a version called "Romeo."

112. Felix Bernard (m), Johnny S. Black (m), and Fred Fisher (w), "Dardanella" (New York: McCarthy & Fisher, 1919), Levy 151.135; A. Fred Phillips and Jack Caddigan, "Egyptian Moonlight: An Oriental Love Song" (New York: Garton, 1919), Levy 151.171; Rudy Wiedoeft (m, w) and Abe Olman (m, w), "Karavan" (Chicago: Forster, 1919), Levy 153.045.

113. Richard Howard, "When They Play That Old 'Salomy' Melody" (New York: Haviland, 1920), copy in CPM.

114. This common nostalgic trope of returning to an oriental sweetheart "some fine day" has its origins in the many popular songs that retell the story of *Madama Butterfly* from Pinkerton's perspective; see chapter 5.

115. Julius Lenzberg (m), Gus Kahn (w), and Bud De Sylva (w), "Moonlight on the Nile" (New York: Remick, 1919), Levy 153.144.

116. Ted Lewis (m, w) and Frank Ross (m, w), "Queen of Sheba" (New York: Berlin, 1921), Levy 156.177. The February 1921 Columbia recording by Ted Lewis and His Band can be heard at Scott Alexander, "Ted Lewis and His Band," in *The Red Hot Jazz Archive: A History of Jazz before 1930*, http://www.redhotjazz. com/tlband.html. On the fate motive, see Susan McClary, "The Musical Languages of *Carmen*," in *Georges Bizet: Carmen* (Cambridge: Cambridge University Press, 1992), 44–61. Lewis was apparently fond of "In the Hall of the Mountain King"; it forms the coda of "Egyptian Ella" (see n. 54).

117. Sigmund Romberg and Ballard MacDonald, "Fat, Fat, Fatima" (New York: Witmark, 1921), copy in UCLA. On *Love Birds* and its "jazz rags," see Bordman, *American Musical Theatre*, 298, 358.

118. Mary Simonson, "Performance, Multimedia, and Creativity in Early Twentieth-Century American Musical Life" (Ph.D. diss., University of Virginia, 2008), treats the film Salomes in greater depth.

119. Waxman's quotations of Strauss have been widely recognized by film scholars; the complete score has been recorded by the Scottish National Orchestra conducted by Joel McNeely (Varese Sarabande 302 066 316 2, 2002).

120. "All about 'Salome,'" *Variety*, 1 August 1908, cited in Andrew L. Erdman, *Blue Vaudeville: Sex, Morals, and the Mass Marketing of Amusement, 1895–1915* (Jefferson, N.C.: McFarland, 2004), 111.

Chapter 5

1. A somewhat distant third is Carmen. Although Ken Bloom's *American Song* (New York: Schirmer Books, 1996, 2001), which draws heavily from printed programs, lists several songs whose titles allude to Bizet's opera, I have been able to locate sheet music for only a few. Throughout this chapter I use the spelling Cho-Cho-San, found both in Puccini's American sources and in the Butterfly-inspired songs, except when referring specifically to the operatic role.

2. On film treatments of the Butterfly narrative, see Nick Browne, "The Undoing of the *Other* Woman: Madame Butterfly in the Discourse of American Orientalism," in *The Birth of Whiteness: Race and the Emergence of U.S. Cinema*, ed. Daniel Bernardi (New Brunswick, N.J.: Rutgers University Press, 1996), 227–56, and W. Anthony Sheppard, "Cinematic Realism, Reflexivity, and the American 'Madame Butterfly' Narratives," *Cambridge Opera Journal* 17 (2005): 59–93. Other versions of the "Butterfly narrative" (a term I have adopted from Sheppard) include James Michener's 1954 novel *Sayonara* (and the 1957 film adaptation starring Marlon Brando) and the rock group Weezer's 1996 album *Pinkerton*.

3. After its first appearance in *Century* 55, no. 33: 274–92, Long's story was included later that year in that magazine's special issue devoted to Japan; besides "Madame Butterfly," the issue included two other Long stories set in Japan, "Purple Eyes" and "A Gentleman of Japan," which had appeared in the July and October issues respectively. A reprint, apparently issued in anticipation of Puccini's opera, was issued by Grosset and Dunlap in 1903; the text of that edition may be viewed at http://xroads.virginia.edu/~HYPER/LONG/abstract.html. The development of the Butterfly narrative through French precedents, Long, and Belasco to Puccini's librettists is ably traced in Arthur Groos, "Lieutenant F. B. Pinkerton: Problems in the Genesis and Performance of *Madama Butterfly*," in *The Puccini*

Companion, ed. William Weaver and Simonetta Puccini (New York: Norton, 1994), 169–201. Also useful is Mosco Carner, *"Madam Butterfly": A Guide to the Opera* (London: Barrie & Jenkins, 1979), 22–31.

4. Frederick Douglass, *Narrative of the Life of Frederick Douglass, an American Slave* (1845), online edition at http://sunsite.berkeley.edu/Literature/Douglass/, chapter 6.

5. The later revisions of Pinkerton are explored in W. Anthony Sheppard, "Pinkerton's Lament," paper presented at the sixty-ninth annual meeting of the American Musicological Society, Houston, Texas, 14 November 2003.

6. *New York Times*, 1 November 1927, quoted in "John Luther Long, 1861–1927: Biographical Sketch," website for the John Luther Long Papers at the Harry Ransom Humanities Research Center, University of Texas, Austin, http://www.hrc.utexas.edu/research/fa/long.bio.html.

7. David Belasco, *Madame Butterfly: A Tragedy of Japan*, in *Six Plays* (Boston: Little, Brown, 1928), 32.

8. *Sunday New York Times*, 4 March 1900.

9. "Dramatic and Musical: 'Mme. Butterfly' Gives Blanche Bates an Opportunity," *New York Times*, 6 March 1900.

10. In the three-act version, act 2 closes with the Humming Chorus and act 3 begins with the dawn interlude; on the early forms of the opera and their various problems, see Groos, "Lieutenant F. B. Pinkerton."

11. The evil Duke of Mantua in *Rigoletto* is another example of a tenor role that fails to match the villainy of a Verdian baritone or bass. It seems to have been impossible to create, within the conventions of Italian opera, a truly villainous tenor role.

12. Richard Aldrich, "Puccini's Madame Butterfly," *New York Times*, 11 November 1906. Savage's troupe had opened in Washington, D.C., on 14 October 1906 and continued to Boston before playing New York's Garden Theatre.

13. [Richard Aldrich], "'Madam Butterfly' at the Garden Theatre: Puccini's Latest Opera in English by Col. Savage's Company: A Work of Great Charm," *New York Times*, 13 November 1906.

14. [Richard Aldrich], "'Mme. Butterfly' Sung in Italian: Puccini's Latest Opera Given at the Metropolitan for the First Time: A Fine Performance," *New York Times*, 12 February 1907.

15. Jason Rubin, "Lew Fields and the Development of the Broadway Musical" (Ph.D. diss., New York University, 1991), 105.

16. "Weber and Fields: A New Hotch-Potch of Music and Nonsense Produced," *New York Times*, 6 September 1901.

17. Unlike its predecessor, Gilbert and Sullivan's *The Mikado* (1885), *The Geisha* had introduced the East-West theme in the person of an English naval officer, Reggie Fairfax, who is smitten with O Mimosa San, a teahouse girl, only to end up rightfully paired with the virtuous (and English) Molly Seamore, who spends much of the play in Japanese disguise. No miscegenous pairing of the leads in this production—though two comic characters, the Marquis Imari and the teahouse's French translator, Juliette, end in a clinch. Enormously popular in the United States and throughout Europe, *The Geisha* would have been an obvious model on which to draw in any spoof of *Madame Butterfly*—and in fact had already been the subject of an earlier Weber and Fields burlesque, *The Geezer*, which had opened on 8 October 1896, just under a month after the U.S. production of *The Geisha* had opened. *The Geezer*, typically treating China and Japan

interchangeably, had reversed the East-West direction, with its story of a Chinese diplomat who comes to America in search of a bride for his emperor; see Rubin, "Lew Fields," 57–58, and Gerald Bordman, *American Musical Theatre: A Chronicle*, 2nd ed. (New York: Oxford University Press, 1992), 145. One sign of *The Geisha's* widespread dissemination is Anton Chekhov's story "Lady with Lapdog," part of which takes place during a provincial Russian performance of that comedy (translation by Ivy Litvinov in Anton Chekhov, *Short Stories*, ed. Ralph E. Matlaw, Norton Critical Edition [New York: Norton, 1979], 221–35).

18. John Stromberg and Edgar Smith, "My Japanese Cherry Blossom" (New York: Witmark, 1901), copy in CPM. According to Rubin, the song was replaced with "Ma Blushin' Rosie" and "Ma Poppy Belle," performed "in coon costume" (Rubin, "Lew Fields," 57–58). Templeton's use of Negro dialect songs is discussed in M. Alison Kibler, *Rank Ladies: Gender and Cultural Hierarchy in American Vaudeville* (Chapel Hill: University of North Carolina Press, 1999), 129.

19. Reginald de Koven and Eugene Field, "Japanese Lullaby" (New York: Schirmer, 1890), copy in Duke; Clayton Thomas and anon., "Japanese Love Song" (New York: Boosey, 1900), Levy 147.147. On orientalist tropes in nineteenth-century American popular music, see Krystyn R. Moon, *Yellowface: Creating the Chinese in American Popular Music and Performance, 1850s–1920s* (New Brunswick, N.J.: Rutgers University Press, 2005), 94–107.

20. Note that the song preserves Long's and Belasco's spelling of the heroine's name, as does the cast list in the *Times* review cited above; Rubin, referring to Edgar Smith's libretto in the Billy Rose Theatre Division at NYPL, gives the spelling "Choo Choo San" (Rubin, "Lew Fields," 105).

21. Belasco, *Madame Butterfly*, 16. Negro dialect songs were staples of the Weber and Fields burlesques; *The Geezer*, with no provocation from its source, had included "Miss Lucy" (Bordman, *American Musical Theatre*, 145).

22. Belasco, *Madame Butterfly*, 27. The lullaby further dehumanizes her by objectifying her as a picture on a fan—a strategy dating back to *The Mikado* and observed as well in "Japanese Love Song."

23. The earliest successor to "My Japanese Cherry Blossom" is Max Hoffmann's "My Little Japaneesee" (New York: Shapiro, Bernstein, 1903), listed in Barbara Cohen-Stratyner, ed., *Popular Music, 1900–1919* (Detroit: Gale Research, 1988), 258; I have been unable to locate a copy of this song, which was "sung in vaudeville by Mary Marble and used in Ned Wayburn's feature act *Daisy Dancers*," according to Cohen. Her description of the song as a "comic version of *Madama Butterfly*" must be incorrect, since Puccini's opera had not yet been premiered; the object of parody was no doubt Belasco's play.

24. Bob Cole and James Weldon Johnson, "My Lu Lu San: Japanese Love Song" (New York: Stern, 1905), Levy 148.143. This song was sung in *Mr. Hamlet of Denmark*, produced in 1905 by the University of Pennsylvania's all-male Mask and Wig Club. Although amateur theatricals fall outside the range of materials I have considered in this study, this song, written by two veteran commercial song-writers and published by a major Tin Pan Alley firm, is an exception. As a song of interracial romance it expands on the theme of love between two Zulus "down in the jungles" in Cole and Johnson's major hit "Under the Bamboo Tree" (New York: Stern, 1902), Levy 150.089.

25. Dolly Jardon and Edward Madden, "Lotus San: A Japanese Romance" (New York: Remick, 1908), Levy 148.019. Though published not long after

Madama Butterfly's U.S. premiere, this song draws not on Puccini but on *The Mikado*.

26. Harry O. Sutton and Jean Lenox, "Kokomo: A Japanese Love Song" (New York: Sutton, 1904), Levy 147.187. The title, obviously derived from the name of the Michigan city, might be a joking reference to the then-popular Indian intermezzo "Hiawatha" (1903), which had begun life as an instrumental named after a town in Kansas and was only later fitted with Indianist lyrics.

27. A similar use of first and third persons is found in another song from the same year, W. T. Francis and Vernon Roy's "Sweet Sana-oo" (New York: Harris, 1904), Levy 150.007, which tells of a Japanese woman who waits in vain for her lover, a "Japanese soldier man," simultaneously focusing on the female character while submerging her voice in that of the male character.

28. Although the sheet music cover has no performer photo (rather, it has a small inset of Sutton), the cover of the same team's 1908 song "I'd Rather Be Like Paw" (New York: Witmark), Levy 146.056, carries a prominent photo of Lenox and the caption "Sung by Jean Lenox in all the leading vaudeville houses." In 1905 the prolific Sutton and Lenox would write "I Don't Care" (New York: Shapiro, Remick), which became Eva Tanguay's signature song; Judy Garland sang it memorably in the 1949 MGM film *In the Good Old Summertime* and again in 1963 on her television program. That a songwriter was female was no guarantee of a more sympathetic treatment of the Butterfly figure; see the discussion herein of songs by Fleta Jan Brown, Dolly Jardon, and Anita Owen.

29. Fred Fisher and Joe McCarthy, "I Want to Go to Tokio" (New York: Feist, 1914), copy in Duke. A couplet in the chorus also introduces a pun that will be overworked in later songs: "Soon you're going to be / Sitting on my Japa(k)nee."

30. Anita Owen, "In Japan with Mi-Mo-San" (New York: Remick, 1915), copy in CPM.

31. Gilles de Van, "Fin de Siècle Exoticism and the Meaning of the Far Away," trans. William Ashbrook, *Opera Quarterly* 11, no. 3 (1995): 78, 90.

32. Will E. Dulmage and E. J. Meyers, "Poppy Time in Old Japan" (Chicago: Forster, 1915), copy in Duke.

33. Egbert Van Alstyne and Gus Kahn, "My Dreamy China Lady" (New York: Remick, 1916), Levy 153.155. Van Alstyne is remembered for "In the Shade of the Old Apple Tree," while Kahn also wrote "Ain't We Got Fun?" "My Buddy," "Carolina in the Morning," "Makin' Whoopee," and many others. Sam Ash recorded "My Dreamy China Lady" on a Columbia Little Wonder (a five-inch disc that played for about a minute and a half, catalog number LW 372) in April 1916, the same month in which Victor issued a conventional ten-inch disc (18034) with a performance by Henry Burr (a pseudonym for Harry McClaskey). On the conflation of Japanese and Chinese signifiers, see W. Anthony Sheppard, "An Exotic Enemy: Anti-Japanese Musical Propaganda in World War II Hollywood," *Journal of the American Musicological Society* 54 (2001), 329.

34. Irving Berlin, "Hurry Back to My Bamboo Shack" (New York: Waterson, Berlin & Snyder, 1916), Levy 077.108. The copy in Levy is missing pp. 3–4; the full lyric is in Irving Berlin, *The Complete Lyrics of Irving Berlin*, ed. Robert Kimball and Linda Emmet (New York: Knopf, 2001), 145.

35. By comparison, of the four songs Berlin wrote in the summer of 1916, one, "I've Got a Sweet Tooth Bothering Me," was interpolated into a musical comedy, *Step This Way*; another, "In Florida among the Palms," was interpolated in the *Ziegfeld Follies of 1916* after the revue's opening; and two, "Hurry Back to My

Bamboo Shack" and the rube song "He's Getting Too Darn Big for a One-Horse Town" were not placed in a show and were published with covers lacking performer insets (see Berlin, *Complete Lyrics*, 144–45, and copy of "He's Getting Too Darn Big" in Levy 077.098).

36. An advertisement in the *New York Times* on Sunday, 7 November 1915, indicates that the film was playing "today and all this week" at the Strand, a movie palace at Broadway and Forty-seventh Street, i.e., that the film opened one day earlier than the 8 November release date listed in Carl Bennett, *The Progressive Silent Film List* (2000), http://www.silentera.com/PSFL/data/M/MadameButterfly1915.html. The location of the filming is described in chapter 7 of Robert Mandatta Ponzio's online memoir, *St. Mary's Avenue*, http://sundog-stories.net/stmary/07.htm. "Theatrical Notes," *New York Times*, 3 November 1915, reports, "The picture version of 'Madama Butterfly' [*sic*; note the Italian form of the name], to be released shortly by the Famous Players Company, with Mary Pickford in the title role, is not taken from David Belasco's arrangement of the story, the manager announced yesterday." And the *Times* advertisement on 7 November 1915 bills the movie as a version of "John Luther Long's immortal classic." A Pickford film of *Madame Butterfly* might easily have been assumed to be associated with (and thus financially obligated to) Belasco, who had been instrumental in launching Pickford's career; see David Belasco, "When Mary Pickford Came to Me: The Story of the Man Who First Wrote Her Name in Light on Broadway," *Photoplay* 9, no. 1 (December 1915): 27–34, electronic reprint at *Silent Era Archive*, http://www.silentera.com/archive/photoplay/1915/1215/1215-27.html. This article, which appeared during the theatrical release of Pickford's *Madame Butterfly*, makes no mention of that film.

37. Biographical information on Miura (1884–1946) may be found in Mari Yoshihara, "The Flight of the Japanese Butterfly: Orientalism, Nationalism, and Performances of Japanese Womanhood," *American Quarterly* 56 (2004): 975–1001.

38. A program for the San Carlo company's Midwest tour, with a repertoire of *Madama Butterfly* and *Salome*, of all operas, is in the Redpath Chautauqua Collection at the University of Iowa and may be viewed at http://sdrcdata.lib.uiowa.edu/libsdrc/details.jsp?id=/sancarlo/12. The Redpath collection also holds two undated brochures that give a sense of how this performer, with "her gentle, quaint personality" and "all the exotic charm and simplicity of the Orient," was presented to midwestern audiences (quotations from "Tamaki Miura: Japanese Soprano," http://sdrcdata.lib.uiowa.edu/libsdrc/details.jsp?id=/miura/1; see also "Tamaki Miura: The World's Greatest Madam Butterfly," http://sdrcdata.lib.uiowa.edu/libsdrc/details.jsp?id=/).

39. "Boston Opera Repertoire," *New York Times*, 31 October 1915. Wednesday's *Times* carried no review; instead, it announced the forthcoming film version starring Mary Pickford, which opened a week later.

40. "Opening of Hippodrome," *New York Tribune*, 13 April 1905, quoted in Kees Gajentaan, *Times²: Recreation at the Crossroads of the World*, http://home.luna.nl/~xino/times2/ts06.htm.

41. Bordman, *American Musical Theatre*, 210.

42. Bordman, *American Musical Theatre*, 496.

43. Bordman, *American Musical Theatre*, 309. Newspaper advertisements for band concerts at the Hippodrome turn up with frequency in these years.

44. Bordman, *American Musical Theatre*, 316. A key sheet of photographs of Pavlova in rehearsal for *The Big Show*, part of the Billy Rose Theatre Division at NYPL, may be viewed at the library's website *Performing Arts in America, 1875–1923*, http://digilib.nypl.org. The replacement for that nameless vaudevillian was apparently Haru Onuki, about whom little is known. Bloom, *American Song*, includes Onuki in the cast list but makes no mention of a performer with a Chinese name (100). The *Internet Broadway Database*, www.idbd.com, includes neither Onuki nor a Chinese performer in its opening-night cast list (unless the single-named Toto is the latter); the *IBDB* listing is unreliable, however, in that it also fails to list Charlotte and Pavlova, who are included in Bloom's list. The sheet music has a composite cover used for all the published songs from *The Big Show*, with no mention of any performers; see Raymond Hubbell and John L. Golden, "Poor Butterfly" (New York: Harms/Francis, Day & Hunter, 1916), Levy 154.069.

45. Tom Lord, *The Jazz Discography*, version 3.3, CD-ROM (n.p.: Lord Music Reference, 2002), includes only those recordings that the compiler considers to be jazz; thus his listing of 326 recordings (323 under the heading "Poor butterfly" and 3 under the typos "Poor butterlfy" and "Poor butterly") includes only one before 1921, described in the next note. *Myrt and Marge* ran from 1931 to 1942; a clip of the show's opening music may be heard at *The Great Radio Soap Operas*, http://www.old-time.com/soaps/index.html.

46. Four instrumental versions of "Poor Butterfly" were recorded in early 1917, three within a few days of one another: Joseph C. Smith and His Orchestra made a Victor ten-inch record (18246) on 19 February 1917 (audible at Scott Alexander, "Joseph C. Smith and His Orchestra," in *The Red Hot Jazz Archive: A History of Jazz before 1930*, http://www.redhotjazz.com/jcso.html); Jaudas' Society Orchestra made an Edison Diamond Disc (50428-R) on 20 February 1917 (audible at Library of Congress, *Inventing Entertainment: The Motion Pictures and Sound Recordings of the Edison Companies*, http://memory.loc.gov/ammem/edhtml/edhome.html); and the Victor Military Band made a recording on 24 February 1917. In March 1917 a Columbia recording was made in London by Ciro's Club Coon Orchestra, an African American string band active in England (Lord, *Jazz Discography*). Other Victor artists who recorded the song include Fritz Kreisler and the operatic singers Frances Alda and Elsie Baker, the latter under the pseudonym of "Edna Brown" (Tim Gracyk, "Joseph C. Smith and His Orchestra," in *Popular American Recording Pioneers: 1895–1925*, http://www.garlic.com/~tgracyk/smith.htm). The recording by Elsie Baker (Victor 18211) demonstrates how an operatic contralto treated the song; my thanks to Paul Charosh for making a copy of Baker's recording available to me. Three brochures detailing Baker's career may be viewed at Library of Congress, *Traveling Culture: Circuit Chautauqua in the Twentieth Century*, http://memory.loc.gov/ammem/award98/iauhtml/.

47. The phrase, important as the song's title and often repeated in the answer songs to come, is a translation of Suzuki's twice-sung "povera Butterfly" in act 2 (at rehearsal numbers 15 and 16). Significantly, the singing translation for Suzuki's words, "poor little Butterfly," is a phrase also used in the answer songs, pointing perhaps to a familiarity with English-language performances of the opera.

48. The word *hack* comes up regularly in discussions of Hubbell's career; see, e.g., David Jasen, *Tin Pan Alley: The Composers, the Songs, the Performers, and Their Times: The Golden Age of American Popular Music from 1886 to 1956* (New York: Fine, 1988), 110, and Bordman, *American Musical Theatre*, 309.

49. Alec Wilder, *American Popular Song: The Great Innovators, 1900–1950*, ed. James T. Maher, 2nd ed. (New York: Oxford University Press, 1990), 22. The weakness of the subdominant scale degree is a recurring theme throughout the book.

50. Art Hickman and Harry Williams, "Rose Room (In Sunny Roseland)" (San Francisco: Sherman & Clay, 1917), copy in UCLA.

51. The same sonority is placed in rising sequence in the B section of this ABAC structure ("Just hang my cradle, Mammy mine, / Right on that Mason-Dixon Line"); see Jean Schwartz (m), Sam M. Lewis (w), and Joe Young (w), "Rock-a-bye Your Baby with a Dixie Melody" (New York: Waterson, Berlin & Snyder, 1918), Levy 154.093. Al Jolson introduced the song in the musical *Sinbad*.

52. In 1918 Daniel Gregory Mason remarked upon their "extraordinary popularity…during the last decade or so" (*Contemporary Composers* [New York: Macmillan, 1918], 135).

53. The influence of nineteenth-century parlor music on the melodic and harmonic language of turn-of-the-century popular song is persuasively argued by Peter van der Merwe in *Origins of the Popular Style: The Antecedents of Twentieth-Century Popular Music* (Oxford: Clarendon Press, 1989), 223–66. Van der Merwe locates in the Viennese waltz the beginning of parlor music's looser relationship between melody and harmony, the result of folk-derived modal practices, in which melodic logic need not be a result of harmonic logic. To take a very familiar example: the third phrase of Strauss's famous "Blue Danube" melody ends on the sixth scale degree, harmonized as the (unresolved) ninth of the dominant chord, and the fourth phrase ends on the same note, reharmonized as the (unresolved) added sixth of the tonic chord (231). The melody is shapely and clear, and the V–I harmony could not be simpler—but the two do not quite mesh.

54. Before her operatic career, Rosa Ponselle sang in a vaudeville act with her sister, Carmela, that included the Flower Duet from *Madama Butterfly* (Peter G. Davis, *The American Opera Singer: The Lives and Adventures of America's Great Singers in Opera and Concert, from 1825 to the Present* [New York: Doubleday, 1997], 268). In the case of *Madama Butterfly*, at least, Ricordi issued separate numbers with decorative covers resembling popular sheet music, with the result that "Un bel di" is included in Lilly. As a small sample of early phonograph records of Puccini's music, consider just three artists who recorded in the United States for the Victor Talking Machine Company: Enrico Caruso recorded twenty Puccini selections between 1904 and 1916 (Enrico Caruso Jr. and Andrew Farkas, *Enrico Caruso: My Father and My Family* [Portland, Ore.: Amadeus Press, 1990], 610–27), Geraldine Farrar recorded fifteen between 1909 and 1913 (Farrar discography at http://matsumo-web.hp.infoseek.co.jp/player/e-page6pa2.htm), and Frances Alda recorded seven between 1909 and 1915 (Frances Alda, *The Complete Victor Recordings, 1909–1915*, CD, Romophone 81034, 1999).

55. Holly Gardinier, *California Croonin': An Exhibit from the Special Collections of the Libraries of the Claremont Colleges*, http://voxlibris.claremont.edu/sc/events/cacroonin/cacroonin.html). According to David Jasen, the dispute was settled out of court (Jasen, *Tin Pan Alley*, 183–84). The title page of "Avalon" attributes music and lyrics to Al Jolson and Vincent Rose, with the line "arr. by J. Bodewalt Lampe" (New York: Remick, 1920; Levy 155.023). Rose was a classically trained West Coast bandleader, Lampe was a veteran composer ("A Vision of Salome," "Creole Belles"), and popular performers sometimes agreed to promote a song in exchange for a partial composer credit and thus a share of royalties.

56. Arthur Green and William Jerome, "If I Catch the Guy Who Wrote Poor Butterfly" (New York: Jerome, 1917); the copy in CPM has trimmed edges, nearly obscuring the dedication "to Raymond Hubbell and John L. Golden[,] writers of Poor Butterfly." A recording by Ada Jones on Starr/Gennett 7603 was issued in August 1917; Tim Gracyk, "Ada Jones (1 June 1873–22 May 1922)," in *Popular American Recording Pioneers*, http://www.garlic.com/~tgracyk/ada.htm.

57. If John Golden's statement quoted earlier is to be believed, then the lyrics as sung in *The Big Show* were lost in the cavernous acoustics of the Hippodrome. Moreover, for many listeners "Poor Butterfly" was primarily a tune for dancing— witness the four instrumental versions in fox trot rhythm recorded in February and March 1917; see note 46.

58. Joseph A. Burke and Al Dubin, "My Yiddisha Butterfly" (New York: Witmark, 1917), copy in Lilly. On the Howard brothers' Yiddish specialties and operatic burlesques, see Anthony Slide, *The Vaudevillians: A Dictionary of Vaudeville Performers* (Westport, Conn.: Arlington House, 1981), 75–76.

59. Charles Hamm, *Irving Berlin: Songs from the Melting Pot: The Formative Years, 1907–1914* (New York: Oxford University Press, 1997), 43.

60. Another 1917 song that testifies to the popularity of "Poor Butterfly" is Charles P. Shisler (m), Billy James (m), and Bobby Heath (w), "When It's Moonlight in Tokio" (New York: Witmark, 1917), electronic edition at *ParlorSongs*, http://parlorsongs.com/content/m/moonltok.htm; the sheet music cover and an inaccurate transcription of the lyrics may be viewed at *Halcyon Days Music*, August 2000, http://www.halcyondaysmusic.com/august/august2000.htm. A musical quotation occurs at measures 51–52, at the words "My butterfly," where a three-note pickup leads to a sustained downbeat dissonance: the (enharmonically spelled) augmented fifth that opens the second phrase in the chorus of "Poor Butterfly."

61. Harry Tierney and Alfred Bryan, "My Yokohama Girl" (New York: Remick, 1917), copy in Duke. Arthur Fields recorded the song on Edison Blue Amberol cylinder 3266 (1917), audible at *Antique Phonograph Music Program*, 20 January 2004, http://www.wfmu.org/playlists/AP. The tune is introduced as a contrasting theme in the Joseph C. Smith Orchestra's Victor recording of "For You a Rose" made on 25 June 1917; see Alexander, "Joseph C. Smith's Orchestra."

62. Edah Delbridge (m, w) and A. Robert King (m, w), "Ko-Ko-San" (New York: Shapiro, Bernstein, 1919), copy in CPM. I have found nothing that verifies the cover's statement "This number on all phonograph records and music rolls."

63. Richard A. Whiting and Raymond B. Egan, "The Japanese Sandman" (New York: Remick, 1920), Levy 156.017. Lord, *Jazz Discography*, lists 109 jazz recordings, to which many nonjazz renditions could be added. The recording by Nora Bayes with the Charles A. Prince Orchestra (25 August 1920), perhaps the first, adds Pucciniesque orchestral color to the list of stylistic traits outlined here; it has been reissued on *Hits of 1920: Whispering*, Naxos CD 8.120635 (2004).

64. The orientalizing tonic-dominant fifths are present, however, as a vamp before the verse in the Paul Whiteman Orchestra's very first recording, on which "The Japanese Sandman" backed "Whispering" (1920); the record may be heard at Scott Alexander, "Paul Whiteman, 'The King of Jazz' (1890–1967)," in *The Red Hot Jazz Archives: A History of Jazz before 1930*, http://www.redhotjazz.com/whiteman.html.

65. Joe Meyer and Bobbie Tremaine, "Happy Butterfly" (New York: Remick, 1920), copy in CPM. A recording of "Happy Butterfly" by the tenor Charles

Harrison, Victor 5646, was at one time listed on the now-defunct auction website for Arcane Records, www.arcanerecords.com.

66. Leo Edwards and Ballard MacDonald, "Mister Butterfly" (New York: Shapiro, Bernstein, 1917), copy in CPM.

67. M. K. Jerome (m), Sam M. Lewis (w), and Joe Young (w), "Poor Little Butterfly Is a Fly Girl Now" (New York: Waterson, Berlin & Snyder, 1919), copy in CPM. Lewis and Young, with various composers, wrote many hits, including "Rock-a-bye Your Baby with a Dixie Melody" (1918), "How Ya Gonna Keep 'Em Down on the Farm (After They've Seen Paree?)" (1919), "My Mammy" (1921), "Dinah" (1925), "I'm Sitting on Top of the World" (1925), "Five Foot Two, Eyes of Blue" (1925), "Laugh Clown Laugh" (1928), and "Lawd, You Made the Night Too Long" (1932).

68. In this respect the song resembles Arthur M. Fournier (m), Michael Corper (w), and Waldo C. Twitchell (w), "Yokohama" (San Francisco: Sherman, Clay, 1918), Levy 060.184, in which the Butterfly figure gains a heightened sensuality from contact with the West.

69. Rebecca A. Bryant, "Shaking Things Up: Popularizing the Shimmy in America," *American Music* 20, no. 2 (Summer 2002): 171–72.

70. Sonny Watson, "Ballin' the Jack," in *Dance History Archives*, http://www.streetswing.com/histmain/z3balin.htm. Chris Smith and Jim Burris, "Ballin' the Jack" (New York: Stern, 1913), Levy 151.060. The title phrase describes driving a locomotive (a "jack," i.e., male mule) at high speed ("high-balling").

71. Another instance of the adjective "fly" in the title of an American song is A. Baldwin Sloane and R. A. Barnet's "I'm a Very Fly Conductor," from the 1895 comedy *Excelsior, Jr.* (Bloom, *American Song*, 1213). Carl H. Scheele's misstatement that "Poor Little Butterfly Is a Fly Girl Now" is an "aviation tune" is apparently based on an incorrect association of the term with the WASPs; see his liner notes to *Come Josephine in My Flying Machine: Inventions and Topics in Popular Song, 1910–1929* (New York: New World Records, 1977). The term "fly girl" was repopularized by the Boogie Boys' 1985 hit "A Fly Girl" (no. 6 R&B); as the name of the dancers on the early 1990s television series *In Living Color* the term was associated particularly with the most successful of those dancers, Jennifer Lopez.

72. Giacomo Puccini, "Madame Butterfly's Song 'One Fine Day'" (New York: Ricordi, 1908), copy in Lilly.

73. George Gershwin and Irving Caesar, "Yan-Kee" (New York: Harms, 1920), copy in Smithsonian Institution, Archives Center, Sam DeVincent Collection of Illustrated American Sheet Music, ca. 1790–1987, series 4.13, box 41, folder A. "Yan-Kee" is one of the most obscure songs in the Gershwin canon. It is included in neither the nearly complete *Music and Lyrics of George Gershwin*, ed. Peter Foss, 2 vols., rev. ed. (London: Chappell, 1991), nor *Rediscovered Gershwin* (n.p.: Warner Brothers, 1991). This song is not Gershwin's only foray into orientalism; in 1921 he wrote "In the Heart of a Geisha" (lyric by Fred Fisher, author of the 1914 "I Want to Go to Tokio"), which I have not seen, and in 1929 he and Ira Gershwin worked on the unproduced musical comedy *East Is West*, also called *Ming Toy*, from which the one published number is "In the Mandarin's Orchard Garden" (reprinted in *Rediscovered Gershwin*, 211–15, lyrics in Ira Gershwin, *The Complete Lyrics of Ira Gershwin*, ed. Robert Kimball, rev. ed. [New York: Da Capo Press, 1998], 138). Intended as "a vocal accompaniment to a Chinese ballet on full stage", the latter is a pretentious pseudo-art song about a plain-looking flower that cannot attract the "love" of the bees among the gaudier orchids and eventually dies of loneliness. What kind of flower is it? A "poor little buttercup."

74. Columbia A3353, reproduced on *Vintage George Gershwin*, audiocassette (St. Johnsbury, Vt.: Vintage Recording, n.d.). The instrumentation recalls the indications for oboe, cymbal, and timpani in "Sweet Sana-oo" (1904).

75. Harris omits the published second verse, which compares Nankee with "poor Butterfly," but reprises the chorus with new nonsense lyrics:

> Yankee since you go away
> Nankee sit all day and pray
> Pray you please leave 'Melican shore
> Yankee come back for
> So cow pokey monga lay loo poo
> You multiply that by three
> Which only means you still the beans
> Since you go 'way from me
> If you say no come back to me
> Then I go fly to my Yankee

76. On this "truncated blues chord progression" and its use as a "black topic" in popular song, see Jeff Magee, "'Everybody Step': Irving Berlin, Jazz, and Broadway in the 1920s," *Journal of the American Musicological Society* 59 (2006): 700.

77. Another blues-influenced song, published two years before "Yan-Kee," takes a more compassionate look at the Butterfly narrative and comments on Cho-Cho-San's fate by drawing an analogy between her and Western women; see Clarence M. Jones and Walter Hirsch, "Am I a Butterfly? (To Whom You Say Good-bye)" (Chicago: Root, 1918), copy in CPM. The connection to Madame Butterfly, though not made explicit (there is no musical quotation), is unmistakable; in non–Madame Butterfly songs the butterfly symbolizes the one who abandons, not the one who is abandoned. Compare, e.g., Sigmund Romberg (m), Jean Schwartz (m), and Harold Atteridge (w), "Flutter on By My Broadway Butterfly" (New York: Remick, 1919), Levy 152.007, in which the song's persona admonishes the title character: "You give your honey sips / To O so many lips." Likewise, Walter Donaldson and Billy Rose's "Swanee Butterfly" (New York: Remick, 1925), copy in CPM, warns the title character not to become one of "those 'I don't care' kind of girls" (a reference to the notoriously risqué performer Eva Tanguay) because "Your arms weren't meant to roam / So save your charms for the one back home." A song similar to "Am I a Butterfly?" is W. C. Polla and Louis Seifert, "Why Do They Call Mama Poor Butterfly" (Hartford, Conn.: Church, 1919), copy in CPM, which makes the same comparison in a maudlin waltz song that, apart from an oblique musical reference to "Poor Butterfly," could have been written twenty years earlier.

78. Walter Smith, "In Old Japan" (San Francisco: Sherman, Clay, 1917), copy in CPM; Otto Motzan and A. J. Stasny, "In China" (New York: Stasny, 1919), Levy 152.183. Bert Kalmar (m, w) and Harry Ruby (m, w), "So Long! Oo-long (How Long You Gonna Be Gone?)" (New York: Waterson, Berlin & Snyder, 1920), Levy 156.221. Although songs about Japanese lovers at this time often had Butterfly references of one sort or another, some songs did not; an example is Joseph Kiefer (m, w) and Billy James (m, w), "My Rose of Old Japan" (New York: Waterson, Berlin & Snyder, 1919), copy in Duke.

79. Raymond Hubbell and Andrew Donnelly, "I'm Coming Back to You Poor Butterfly" (New York: Harms/ Francis, Day & Hunter, 1917), copy in Lilly. No performer is mentioned on the cover, and no phonograph recording seems to have been made, though the song is the first item in a Wurlitzer mechanical-instrument

roll medley (WMPO 872), described in a January 1918 Wurlitzer bulletin; see Hathaway, *Mandolin PianOrchestra Music Roll Database Project*. The same lyrical theme appears in a song with no musical resemblance: Frank Glick, "I'm Coming, Butterfly" (n.p.: Glick, 1919), copy in CPM. This song, written by an army captain for *I'll Say So*, a "musical extravaganza produced by the officers of Camp Lee, Va.," according to the cover, has Butterfly's captain returning "o'er the water [in] a vision...sweeter than a golden carol"; i.e., the song hints that the returning Pinkerton may be a hallucination.

80. Bordman, *American Musical Theatre*, 333; Louis A. Hirsch (m), Dave Stamper (m), and Gene Buck (w), "Garden of My Dreams" (New York: Harms/ Francis, Day & Hunter, 1918), copy in NYPL. The song is part of a medley on the Wurlitzer mechanical-instrument roll WCPO 507, described in an October 1918 Wurlitzer bulletin; see Terry Hathaway, *Mandolin PianOrchestra Music Roll Database Project* (2008), at http://www.mechanicalmusicpress.com/history/roll-proj/pdf_data/MPO_2008-09-07.pdf.

81. Walter Donaldson and J. Kiern Brennan, "Suki San (Where the Cherry Blossoms Fall)" (New York: Witmark, 1917), copy in CPM.

82. Billy Baskette (m), Joseph Santley (m), and George A. Little (w), "Hawaiian Butterfly" (New York: Feist, 1917), Levy 152.060. The song's success is indicated by the large number of copies in sheet music archives and its frequent appearance in sheet music auction catalogs. Successful songs often were issued in multiple imprints with changing performer insets, but the ten insets on extant copies of this song constitute an unusually large number and indicate a high consumer demand (the performers are Monte Austin, Brice and King, Emma Carus, Earl Fuller, Frances Kennedy, Dorothy Meuther, Moore and Gerald, Scarpioff, Bobbie Smith, and Florence Timponi). In addition to two piano rolls, at least five phonograph recordings were issued, by Ciro's Club Coon Orchestra (Columbia, September 1917), Hawaiian Guitars (Everlasting Cylinder), Jaudas' Society Orchestra (Edison Blue Amberol 3223), the Sterling Trio (Victor), and the Victor Military Band (Victor 35634). Joseph Santley was a popular dancer on stage and in film; his shared credit here (I know of no other song on which he has composer credit) may be related to his creation of a social dance also called the Hawaiian Butterfly (see Sonny Watson, "Joseph Santley," in *Dance History Archives*, http://www.streetswing.com/histmai2/d2santley.htm).

83. An impressive amount of information about Hawaiian-themed popular music is available at Keith Emmons, *Hawaiian and Tropical Vintage Sheet Music Image Archive*, http://www.hulapages.com/. Although almost all *hapa-haole* songs are about dark-skinned women, at least one is emphatically about "a maid of Americano shade," i.e., a white woman: Charles N. Daniels and Earle C. Jones, "I'll Come Back to You, My Honolulu Lou" (New York: Remick, 1912), copy in Lilly. Ironically, the song's cover depicts, from the back, a dark woman with large, "exotic" earrings watching a departing ship—a Butterflyesque scene.

84. Fantasies of returning to an exotic former lover also occur in songs set in other locations; typical is the persona's wish to "soon...return to Turkestan" to woo his "lonesome maid Armenian" in Felix Bernard (m), Johnny S. Black (m), and Fred Fisher (w), "Dardanella" (New York: McCarthy & Fisher, 1919), Levy 151.135. Harold Shaw, "There's a Little Butterfly in Normandy" (Los Angeles: Hatch, 1918), copy in CPM, while shifting the scene to France, sustains a nostalgic mood, complete with a quotation of "Un bel di."

85. G. Puccini and Jessie Winne, arr. Hugo Frey, "Cho-Cho-San" (New York: Ricordi, 1921), copy in CPM. The two Whiteman recordings (Victor 18777, 18

May 1921, and Victor 20200, 25 August 1926) may be heard at Scott Alexander, "Paul Whiteman and His Orchestra," in *The Red Hot Jazz Archives: A History of Jazz before 1930*, http://www.redhotjazz.com/pwo.html. Grofé's manuscript score and parts, housed in the Paul Whiteman Collection, Chapin Library, Williams College, do not include the extended quotation of "Un bel dì" heard in both recordings. In addition to the two Whiteman records, Eddie Elkins and His Orchestra recorded "Cho-Cho-San" on Columbia A3509 (17 October 1921). The Wurlitzer company included the song in three medleys on rolls for mechanical instruments, Wurlitzer 6609 for the Military Band Organ, WMPO 1071 for the Wurlitzer Mandolin PianOrchestra, and WCPO 9556 for the Concert PianOrchestra; see Gary Watkins, rev. Matthew O. Caulfield, *A Catalog of Music Rolls for the Wurlitzer Military Band Organ Style 165*, 17 January 2003, http://wurlitzer-rolls.com/index2.html, and Hathaway, "List of Currently Catalogued PianOrchestra Tunes," in *Mandolin PianOrchestra Music Roll Database Project*, 7 July 2001, http://www.hathaworld.com/music/PDF_data/Tunes07July01.pdf.

86. *Poor Little Butterfly*, dir. Ben Harrison, Color Rhapsody series (Columbia, 1938), may be viewed in low resolution at YouTube. The librettist of *Miss Saigon*, Alain Boublil, has written: "We didn't want a Pinkerton type (sexiest [*sic*] middle-aged officer); instead we wanted a young man whose life would be instantly transformed by meeting a young girl during the crucial last three weeks before the fall of Saigon." The locus of villainy is shifted from the Pinkerton figure to a character derived from *Butterfly's* Goro and called the Engineer, "the half-French, half-Vietnamese wheeler-dealer, an actual Vietnamese type that many French and English journalists have encountered, who became a pivotal character in our story" (Alain Boublil, "From Madame Chrysanthemum to Miss Saigon," at the *Miss Saigon* website, http://fade.to/miss-saigon). For the Engineer, as for the mercenary Madame Chrysanthème in Pierre Loti's nineteenth-century progenitor of the Butterfly narrative, "love is merely a commodity," according to Nicholas Hynter, who directed the first production; Hynter calls the Engineer "a slithering pimp who is as foreign to everybody he fleeces as the idea of morality is foreign to him" (Nicholas Hynter, "Miss Saigon in America," at *Miss Saigon* website). Now the bad guy is part Western, part Asian, but in essence conveniently neither.

Chapter 6

1. The standard, and still relevant, work on this topic is Constance Rourke, *American Humor: A Study of the National Character* (New York: Harcourt Brace Jovanovich, 1931).

2. Two especially valuable works among many are Eric Lott, *Love and Theft: Blackface Minstrelsy and the American Working Class* (New York: Oxford University Press, 1993), and William J. Mahar, *Behind the Burnt Cork Mask: Early Blackface Minstrelsy and Antebellum American Popular Culture* (Urbana: University of Illinois Press, 1999). Charles Hamm's useful review essay on three studies of minstrelsy appeared in the *Journal of the American Musicological Society* 53, no. 1 (Spring 2000): 165–82.

3. The characteristics of the Negro dialect song are summarized in Charles Hamm, *Irving Berlin: Songs from the Melting Pot: The Formative Years, 1907–1914* (New York: Oxford University Press, 1997), 70–71.

4. Sam Dennison, *Scandalize My Name: Black Imagery in American Popular Music* (New York: Garland, 1982), 351.

5. A view expressed by Linda Austern ("Cultural Migration, Appropriation, and Image in Twentieth-Century Anglo-American Popular Musics," paper presented at the seventeenth congress of the International Musicological Society, Leuven, Belgium, 5 August 2002).

6. Hamm, *Irving Berlin*, 6.

7. Other songs read "words and music by Irving Berlin and Ted Snyder"; some indicate one division of labor on the cover and another on the first page of music.

8. Hamm, *Irving Berlin*, 6.

9. Hamm, *Irving Berlin*, 81–84; another instance of Berlin's adding words to an instrumental piece is "Grizzly Bear" (music by George Botsford), a song registered for copyright on 19 April 1910, just nine days earlier than "That Opera Rag."

10. Although some songwriters no doubt left many small decisions to their arrangers, Berlin apparently was not one of these; anecdotal evidence suggests that, even though he could not read music, he knew what he wanted and maintained a tight control over the finished product; see, for instance, Robert Russell Bennett's recollection of working for Berlin, in Laurence Bergreen, *As Thousands Cheer: The Life of Irving Berlin* (New York: Viking Press, 1990), 365–66. On the widespread practice of dictating songs to arrangers, see Hamm, *Irving Berlin*, 8.

11. David Brackett, *Interpreting Popular Music* (Cambridge: Cambridge University Press, 1995), 30; his reference is to Kofi Agawu, "Theory and Practice in the Analysis of the Nineteenth-Century *Lied*," *Music Analysis* 11, no. 1 (March 1992): 25.

12. Ted Snyder and Irving Berlin, "That Opera Rag" (New York: Snyder, 1910), Levy 078.172. For a critical edition, see Irving Berlin, *Early Songs, 1907–1914*, ed. Charles Hamm, Recent Researches in American Music, vols. 20–22, Music of the United States of America, vol. 2, parts 1–3 (Madison, Wisc.: A-R Editions, 1994), 1:136–39. A notational oddity is the absence of repeat signs, but performers knew what to do with such conventionalized music: m. 5 could be repeated until the singer was "ready," that is, had concluded any of the stage business or patter that was often a part of popular song performance; after the chorus, the music would return to the vamp for the second verse, with its new lyric. Another convention, the reiteration of the chorus, usually marked with repeat signs and first and second endings, would be problematic here because of the unusual key scheme, though a spoken monologue interpolated between choruses, a common performance practice, would offer one solution. Finally, the last four measures could be repeated instrumentally as a coda, often in a faster tempo that reflected the vaudevillian's practice of "running off" after a number. On performance conventions see Hamm, *Irving Berlin*, 15–18; on "running off" see Caroline Caffin, "Vaudeville Music" (1914), reprinted in *American Vaudeville as Seen by Its Contemporaries*, ed. Charles W. Stein (New York: Knopf, 1984), 211. According to the discographer Paul Charosh, the singer Bob Roberts recorded "That Opera Rag" no less than three times between 1910 and 1912 (Hamm, *Irving Berlin*, 263); my efforts to locate any of these recordings have been unsuccessful.

13. "Shine On, Harvest Moon" is an example of the former, "Alexander's Ragtime Band" an example of the latter.

14. Instances of "ragging the classics," however, typically involve the syncopated transformation of a single classical selection, not several, as here. A similar medley approach characterizes two piano novelties: Felix Arndt, "An Operatic Nightmare: Desecration no. 2" (Cleveland: Fox, 1916), copy in CPM, and Julius

Lenzberg, "Operatic Rag" (New York: Remick, 1914), copy in Templeton. And although most pieces in this genre are instrumental, vocal examples are not unknown, e.g., "Shoeboot's Serenade" by W. C. Handy (New York: Handy, 1915; rev. ed., New York: Handy Brothers, 1945), copy in CPM.

15. A somewhat similar scenario is found in Berlin's "Samuel Brown (The Operatic Waiter)," a song that survives only as a typed lyric sheet in the Irving Berlin Collection at the Library of Congress. Charles Hamm summarizes: "Samuel Brown, a waiter in a fancy restaurant, likes the operatic music played by the house orchestra but neglects his duties, is fired, and is then 'pounded' by the other staff (to the music of the Anvil Chorus) until he 'just laid down and died'" (Hamm, *Irving Berlin*, 64–65). The full lyrics are reproduced in Irving Berlin, *The Complete Lyrics of Irving Berlin*, ed. Robert Kimball and Linda Emmet (New York: Knopf, 2001), 105.

16. A preference for the latter mode of interpretation runs through much of the minstrel-show scholarship of recent two decades, which is marked, as Charles Hamm notes, by the "privileging of class, sexuality, and gender over race, a result of the gradual assimilation into American scholarship of the writings of sundry neo-Marxist European theorists and philosophers" (review essay, 178). Although Hamm is referring to work on nineteenth-century blackface minstrelsy, his challenge to writers who would discount taking racist imagery at face value applies equally well to scholars of minstrelsy's artistic descendants.

17. A thorough bibliography of the literature on early African American opera singers may be found in John Graziano, "The Early Life and Career of the 'Black Patti': The Odyssey of an African American Singer in the Late Nineteenth Century," *Journal of the American Musicological Society* 53 (2000): 343–96. For a sampling of black newspaper criticism, see Eileen Southern, "In Retrospect: Black Prima Donnas of the Nineteenth Century," *Black Perspective in Music* 7 (1979): 95–106.

18. John Dizikes, *Opera in America: A Cultural History* (New Haven, Conn.: Yale University Press, 1993), 384–85.

19. By the early twentieth century only a faint trace remained of the operatic origin of "Home, Sweet Home!" which first appeared in Henry Bishop's opera *Clari* (1823). Since at least the time of Jenny Lind it was best known as a recital encore—a favorite of Adelina Patti's, for instance, a fact documented in the popular song "When Patti Sang 'Home Sweet Home,'" by Robert A. Keiser and Ballard MacDonald (New York: Shapiro, Bernstein, 1917).

20. Edward A. Berlin, *King of Ragtime: Scott Joplin and His Era* (New York: Oxford University Press, 1994), 210–12; Hamm, *Irving Berlin*, 107–9.

21. W. E. B. Du Bois, *The Souls of Black Folk* (1903; reprint, New York: Signet, 1985), 252–54.

22. Although Du Bois would become a founder of the NAACP in 1909, less than a year before the publication of "That Opera Rag," already this early story betrays his complex attitude toward integration, memorably articulated as the concept of double consciousness; see David Levering Lewis, *W. E. B. Du Bois, 1868–1919: Biography of a Race* (New York: Holt, 1993), 281–82.

23. James Woodress, *Booth Tarkington: Gentleman from Indiana* (New York: Greenwood Press, 1954), 146–48. The same story, rephrased, appears also in the introduction to the reprint of *The Man from Home* in *The Best Plays of 1899–1909*, ed. Burns Mantle and Garrison P. Sherwood (New York: Dodd, Mead, 1947), 303–4.

24. On Tyler, see Rourke, *American Humor*, 15–16.

25. It was during this final overhaul that *Mrs. Jim* served as a working title.

26. Woodress, *Booth Tarkington*, 155–56.

27. "Mrs. Jim, by Booth Tarkington and Harry Leon Wilson: A Comedy of American Life, Dealing in a Satirical Vein with the Prevailing Pursuit of Love and Money, with Its Attendant Embarrassments and Evils: Condensed by Lucy France Pierce," *The World Today* 19, no. 2 (August 1910): 897–904; copy in Indiana University, Lilly Library.

28. "Many New Plays Bid for Favor," *New York Times*, 6 November 1910; "New Farces and Players in Them," *New York Times*, 9 November, 1910. The change of title must have taken place at the last moment; as late as 3 November 1910 the *Cleveland Leader* was still referring to the play as *Mrs. Jim*, not *Getting a Polish*; see citation in Hamm, *Irving Berlin*, 193.

29. The quotation is from "New Farces and Players in Them." The reviewer found the Paris setting to be a reversion to formula: Tarkington and Wilson, "evidently believing that one good turn deserves another, have gone about to make another play along practically the same lines as 'The Man From Home,' and with something very near the same sort of characters and complications."

30. See Rourke, *American Humor*, 72–74.

31. John Covach, "Popular Music, Unpopular Musicology," in *Rethinking Music*, ed. Nicholas Cook and Mark Everist, rev. ed. (Oxford: Oxford University Press, 2001), 469.

32. A newspaper description of Irwin's purchase of a song for *Getting a Polish* is reproduced in Hamm, *Irving Berlin*, 193.

33. Biographical information on Irwin is from Sharon Irene Ammen, "May Irwin's Strategies of Influence: A Look Back at America's 'Secretary of Laughter'" (Ph.D. diss., University of Maryland, 1997).

34. On farce-comedy as a genre see Stanley Applebaum, ed., *Show Songs from "The Black Crook" to "The Red Mill": Original Sheet Music for Sixty Songs from Fifty Shows, 1866–1906* (New York: Dover, 1974), xvi. A common error in the literature on Irwin is the description of her shows as musical comedies. Each of her stage vehicles, like other farce-comedies, contained only three to six musical numbers, as opposed to the more than a dozen numbers required for a musical comedy.

35. M. Alison Kibler, *Rank Ladies: Gender and Cultural Hierarchy in American Vaudeville* (Chapel Hill: University of North Carolina Press, 1999), 126, 128.

36. Kibler, *Rank Ladies*, 119. Kibler relates this violent figure to the archetypal Zip Coon, but the danger of conflating the various "dandy" figures of minstrelsy into the Zip Coon archetype is pointed out by Mahar in *Behind the Burnt Cork Mask*, 203–9.

37. Stanley Green, "Hits from Early Musical Comedies," in liner notes to *"I Wants to Be a Actor Lady" and Other Hits from Early Musical Comedies* (New World Records, 1978, reissued on CD, NW221, 1993), 20; the song is reprinted in Applebaum, *Show Songs*, 77–81. Irwin continued to sing "The Bully" into the 1920s (see Kibler, *Rank Ladies*, 126; Kibler's date of 1925 contradicts Douglas Gilbert's date of 1920 in *American Vaudeville: Its Life and Times* [New York: Whittlesey House, 1940], 96). Irwin's 1907 Victor recording of "The Bully" remained in catalog until 1919—a long dozen years of popularity; see Ammen, "May Irwin's Strategies of Influence," 339.

38. Kibler, *Rank Ladies*, 128, 112–13. Like Kibler's, most other analyses of "coon shouting" are the work of cultural critics and are poorly grounded in the

music. One work similar to Kibler's, this one focused on the 1920s, is Peter Antelyes, "Red Hot Mamas: Bessie Smith, Sophie Tucker, and the Ethnic Maternal Voice in American Popular Song," in *Embodied Voices: Representing Female Vocality in Western Culture*, ed. Leslie C. Dunn and Nancy A. Jones (Cambridge: Cambridge University Press, 1994), 212–29.

39. *New York Times*, 17 September 1895, quoted in Anthony Slide, *The Vaudevillians: A Dictionary of Vaudeville Performers* (Westport, Conn.: Arlington House, 1981), 77.

40. The label "coon shouter" was consistently applied to women, not men, and never to African Americans of either sex. Further research is necessary to determine the extent to which "coon shouting" represents the appropriation by women of a vocal style established by male minstrels.

41. Cited in Gerald Bordman, *American Musical Theatre: A Chronicle*, 2nd ed. (New York: Oxford University Press, 1992), 172, apropos Irwin's appearance in *The Belle of Bridgeport* in 1900. In addition to several Bettini cylinders recorded in the 1890s by a singer who may or may not be Irwin, six Victor 78-rpm recordings by Irwin are known to exist; see Ammen, "May Irwin's Strategies of Influence," 339–40. Five of the six have been reissued on *Music from the New York Stage, 1890–1920*, vol. 1, *1890–1908*, 3 CDs (Wadhurst, England: Pearl, 1993).

42. In the days before electrical amplification, a solid technique, especially in terms of breath support and diction, was required of popular as well as operatic singers in order to be heard and understood throughout a performance hall. Most recorded performances before 1920 display evidence of some degree of classical training.

43. "Most reviews of Irwin's vehicles included at least one remark about the inadequacy of the play [i.e., script]. Most of these same reviews, however, praised May Irwin's performance" (Ammen, "May Irwin's Strategies of Influence," 89).

44. "New Farces and Players in Them"; the subheading reads, "May Irwin Provides Most of the Polish in the One at Wallack's."

45. Indeed, Tarkington himself acknowledged the play to be no more than a May Irwin vehicle: "In writing this play, Mr. Wilson and I have merely played the part of jewellers endeavoring to furnish the setting in which a jewel of matchless luster would sparkle to the best advantage"; the context makes clear that Irwin was the jewel (quotation in "Actress Makes Free with Comedy Role," *Indianapolis Star*, 9 August 1911, cited in Ammen, "May Irwin's Strategies of Influence," 58). Exactly what songs were in the show remains a bit of a puzzle. The *Sunday Times* preview ("Many New Plays Bid for Favor") mentions three songs. Most likely these were "That Opera Rag" and "My Wife Bridget," the latter by Irving Berlin without Ted Snyder, and "Teaching Me Fadder to Waltz," by Michael Carey. Ken Bloom, *American Song: The Complete Musical Theatre Companion*, 2nd ed. (New York: Schirmer Books, 1996), 375, lists three other songs that apparently were cut before the show opened, including "He Sympathized with Me," the other Snyder and Berlin song listed on the cover of "That Opera Rag."

46. The cover design reinforces this view: Irwin's portrait dominates, and her name is in the largest lettering, larger than the show title and much larger than the tiny letters that lists the songs and songwriters. My hunch is that this emphasis was made at Irwin's direction at least as much as the Ted Snyder Company's. Almost all the covers of songs associated with Irwin (many are reproduced in Ammen, "May Irwin's Strategies of Influence") are dominated by her image, which is always larger than the small insets of performers seen on many sheet music covers.

47. Judith Tick, "Women in Music, §II, 4: Western Classical Traditions since 1800," *The New Grove Dictionary of Music and Musicians*, ed. S. Sadie and J. Tyrell (London: Macmillan, 2001), 27:529.

48. Quoted in Tick, "Women in Music," 27:529.

49. Quoted in Eve Golden, *Golden Images: Forty-one Essays on Silent Film Stars* (Jefferson, N.C.: McFarland, 2001), 59.

Chapter 7

1. The quotation is from E. M. Wickes, *Writing the Popular Song* (Springfield, Mass.: Home Correspondence School, 1916), as cited in Charles Hamm, *Irving Berlin: Songs from the Melting Pot: The Formative Years, 1907–1914* (New York: Oxford University Press, 1997), 104. Hamm argues convincingly that African American subject matter justifies the classification as ragtime of songs that have little or no syncopation, such as "Alexander's Ragtime Band"; such songs were perceived to be ragtime by their intended audiences.

2. Eric Lott, *Love and Theft: Blackface Minstrelsy and the American Working Class* (New York: Oxford University Press, 1993), 234.

3. Lott, *Love and Theft*, 234, 63.

4. Frederick Douglass, "The Color Line," *North American Review* 132 (June 1881): 567–77, electronic ed., University of Virginia (1999), at http://etext.lib. virginia.edu/.

5. Charles Connolly and Edward Craven, "We'll Have No More Coon Ragtime Songs To-night" (New York: Witmark, 1900), copy in Hay.

6. Frank Orth, "Give Me Rag, Rag, Rag" (Philadelphia: Wilsky, 1901), copy in UCB.

7. Jim Vaughn (m), Tom Lemonier (m), and Alex Rogers (w), "When Sousa Comes to Coon-town" (New York: Shapiro, Bernstein, 1902), copy in Duke, modern ed. in Will Marion Cook et al., *The Music and Scripts of "In Dahomey,"* ed. Thomas L. Riis, Music of the United States of America 5 (Madison, Wisc.: A-R Editions, 1997); William Tracey, "I'm Crazy 'bout a Ragtime Minstrel Band" (Chicago: Forster Music, 1908), copy in UCB; Ted Snyder (m, w) and Irving Berlin (m, w), "Piano Man" (New York: Snyder, 1910), Levy 078.108.

8. The remarkable achievements of the first post–Civil War generation are summarized in Juliet E. K. Walker, "African Americans," in *A Nation of Peoples: A Sourcebook on America's Multicultural Heritage*, ed. Elliot Robert Barkan (Westport, Conn.: Greenwood Press, 1999), 19–47. Perhaps the richest primary source is W. E. B. DuBois, *The Souls of Black Folk* (1903; reprint, New York: Signet, 1985).

9. Tom Lemonier and Alex Rogers, "I'd Like to Be a Real Lady" (New York: Shapiro, Bernstein, 1902), copy in Hay, modern edition in Cook et al., *Music and Scripts of "In Dahomey."*

10. The allusions to Shakespeare ally this song with "I Wants to Be a Actor Lady" and with the disdainful female protagonists in Eugene Black [pseudonym for Jean Schwartz] and William Jerome, "When Mister Shakespeare Comes to Town, or I Don't Like Them Minstrel Folks" (New York: Howley, Haviland & Dresser, 1901), copy in Hay, and in Robert Adams and James O'Dea, "I Wants a Man Like Romeo" (Detroit: Whitney Warner, 1902), Levy 147.040. The team of Schwartz and Jerome also wrote a song in which a white persona expresses boredom at a performance of *Hamlet*: "Hamlet Was a Melancholy Dane" (New York:

Shapiro, Bernstein, 1902), Levy 146.127. Unlike this persona, depicted on the sheet music cover with the chin whiskers of a "rube," or country dweller, African American characters in these songs and others described later in this chapter never express displeasure with Shakespeare unless his plays have cost them the affection of high-minded lady friends. Yet another of those ladies is the persona in John Golden's "Mister Othello," from his 1909 musical *The Candy Shop*; in an excerpt sung by Ada Jones in a *Candy Shop* medley on *Broadway through the Gramophone (1844–1929): New York in European Footsteps*, vol. 1, *1844–1909*, CD (Pearl: GMS 0082 Mono ADD, n.d.), the persona expresses to her beau an ill-placed admiration for Othello, concluding, "I'm sorry for you, Ephraham, but you'll never do." (Not included in the medley is another number from *The Candy Shop* that I have been unable to locate, one with the tantalizing title "Some Ragtime Opera.")

11. Similarly, in Jean Schwartz and William Jerome, "Good-bye Mr. Ragtime (Since the Merry Widow Waltz Has Come to Town)" (New York: Cohan & Harris, 1908), copy in UCB, the lyrics assert that blacks have abandoned ragtime for the "Merry Widow" Waltz, but the music, rather than quote *The Merry Widow*, is a thoroughly conventional ragtime tune. A dissenting opinion would come four years later, incidentally; Louis A. Hirsch's "How Do You Do, Miss Ragtime?" (New York: Shapiro, 1912), copy in UCB, a number for Blossom Seeley in the revue *The Whirl of Society*, would confirm that the waltz fad faded well before the enthusiasm for ragtime dances, *pace* "Good-bye Mr. Ragtime."

12. "Zip Coon" (New York: Birch, 1834), in Library of Congress, *American Memory*, http://memory.loc.gov; see also William J. Mahar, *Behind the Burnt Cork Mask: Early Blackface Minstrelsy and Antebellum American Popular Culture* (Urbana: University of Illinois Press, 1999), 203–9.

13. R. P. Lilly and Frank Dumont, "An Ignoramus Coon" (Philadelphia: Morris, 1902), copy in CPM.

14. Chris Smith, "I Want to Know Where Tosti Went (When He Said 'Good-bye')" (New York: Shapiro, Bernstein, 1920), copy in NYPL. On *Broadway Brevities*, see Gerald Bordman, *American Musical Theatre: A Chronicle*, 2nd ed. (New York: Oxford University Press, 1992), 354. Smith is best remembered for his 1913 hit "Ballin' the Jack."

15. For a period U.S. edition, see F. Paolo Tosti, "Good-bye" (New York: Van Loan, n.d.), Levy 174.118. Other popular songs that quote "Good-bye" include Irving Berlin, "Keep Away from the Fellow Who Owns an Automobile" (New York: Snyder, 1912), Levy 077.166, and F. Henri Klickmann and Cal de Voll, "Tosti's 'Good-bye' Melody" (Chicago: McKinley, 1921), copy in CPM. "Midnight Eyes," an unpublished Berlin song whose lyrics are preserved in a 1912 typescript in the Library of Congress's Irving Berlin Collection, probably quotes Tosti's music for the penultimate and antepenultimate lines: "Goodbye—they're calling, / Goodbye—I'm falling"; see Irving Berlin, *The Complete Lyrics of Irving Berlin*, ed. Robert Kimball and Linda Emmet (New York: Knopf, 2001), 65. An instrumental quotation occurs between verses in the song "She Says 'No'!" recorded by Bob Nelson on Columbia 81942 (20 August 1924), audible at *The Antique Phonograph Music Program*, 18 February 2003, http://www.wfmu.org/playlists/AP. Online auction catalogs list two songs I have not seen that no doubt quote "Good-bye": Jean Havez, "Mister Tosti, Why Did you Say 'Good-bye'?" (1916), and a British number, "Did Tosti Raise His Bowler Hat?" Literary references to "Good-bye" are too numerous to list and range from P. G. Wodehouse to D. H. Lawrence. In what may be the last popular-culture reference to "Good-bye," Groucho Marx sings a

snippet of it in *A Day at the Races* (1937), a reference perhaps to a theatrical superstition against singing this song in the dressing room.

16. Ben M. Jerome and John Gilroy, "Mozart Lincoln" (New York: Bloom, 1903). The song was part of *The Darling of the Gallery Gods* (opened 22 June 1903 at the Crystal Gardens), a burlesque of David Belasco's drama *The Darling of the Gods*, which had opened the preceding December.

17. Irving Berlin, "Alexander's Ragtime Band" (New York: Snyder, 1911; Irving Berlin, *Early Songs*, ed. Charles Hamm [Madison, Wisc.: A-R Editions, 1994], no. 60); Joe Hollander and Jeff Branen, "Hear That Orchestra Rag" (New York: Branen, 1912), copy in UCB; Ernest Breuer and Herman Kahn, "He's the World's Best Music Man" (Chicago: Rossiter, 1912), copy in UCB; Seymour Furth and William J. Vandeveer, "Hear the Pickaninny Band" (New York: Morris, 1911); W. C. Handy, "Shoeboot's Serenade" (New York: Handy, 1915; rev. ed., New York: Handy Brothers, 1945), copy in CPM. The cover of Handy's 1945 arrangement carries the subtitle "A Blues Song," yet the original cover, shown as an insert, calls it a "Rag Song with Trombone Obligato [*sic*]." Elliott Hurwitt catalogs this song in his "W. C. Handy as Music Publisher: Career and Reputation" (Ph.D. diss., City University of New York, 2000), but to my knowledge this and other references to "Ständchen" in popular music have otherwise gone unnoticed in the scholarly literature.

18. *A Night with the Pierrots*, whose program lists this song as "The Ragtime Sextette," was the first part of a three-part bill, of which *The Whirl of Society* was the second and main part of the evening; it opened 5 March 1912 (Bordman, *American Musical Theatre*, 275; Berlin, *Complete Lyrics*, 49). The program for *Hanky-Panky* gives the title as "Ragtime Opera"; that show opened on 5 August 1912 (Ken Bloom, *American Song* [New York: Schirmer Books, 1996, 2001], 442). I give the title as it appears in Berlin, *Early Songs*, no. 102, 2:166–79; Hamm's edition is based on the 1912 Waterson, Berlin & Snyder publication. The vocal parts are labeled with characters' names; these do not correspond to the characters in *Hanky-Panky* (listed in Berlin, *Complete Lyrics*, 49) and presumably are those in *A Night with the Pierrots*. There are two period recordings, issued under yet another title, "Lucia Sextette Burlesque": Billy Murray and mixed chorus, Edison 1107 (four-minute cylinder, September 1912), and Billy Murray and the Vaudeville Quartet, Victor 17119 (ten-inch disc, August 1912); my thanks to Prof. Hamm for providing a cassette copy of the latter record.

19. J. Peter Burkholder, *All Made of Tunes: Charles Ives and the Uses of Musical Borrowing* (New Haven, Conn.: Yale University Press, 1995), 17–18.

20. Ives's use of C major for his polonaise and his early experience as an organist suggest that he may have been familiar with W. A. Weber's organ arrangement of the Sextet in that key, published as "Chi ma frena [*sic*]," no. 2 in the "Combination Organ Series" (Boston: Automatic Music Paper, 1881), or possibly the arrangement by Candido Chianei for vocal trio and piano, also transposed to C, published with the English words "What Withholds My Angry Fury" (Boston: Reed, 1848); both pieces may be viewed at Library of Congress, *American Memory: Historical Collections for the National Digital Library*, http://memory.loc.gov.

21. Quoted at "The Seven-Dollar Sextet", http://bassocantante.com/opera/lucia.html. A clip from the silent film is included in the videotape *The Art of Singing: Golden Voices of the Century* (NVC Arts 0630–15898-3, 1996).

22. N. C. Bochsa, arr., "No. 2. Lucia: Four Melodies," in the series "Gems for Young Harpists" (New York: Browne, 1854), digital images at Library of Congress, *American Memory*, http://memory.loc.gov; Jullien, "The Ravenswood Waltzes:

Composed on Donizetti's Opera *Lucia De Lammermoor*" (New York: Firth, Pond, 1853), Levy 167.123. My reading of the mad scene is indebted to Susan McClary, *Feminine Endings*, 90–99.

23. Admittedly, her words, sung in a cultivated soprano, are harder to understand than the Stooges'—a circumstance that reinforces Poizat's notions of female vocality. *Squareheads of the Round Table* is included in the VHS anthology *The Three Stooges: I'm a Monkey's Uncle* (Columbia, 1993).

24. In this respect "Opera Burlesque" resembles the previous year's "Alexander's Ragtime Band"; on the debate over whether "Alexander" is true ragtime, see Hamm, *Irving Berlin*, 102–6.

25. Hamm, *Irving Berlin*, 17, 20.

26. Ada Jones, for example, sings this pronunciation in the "Mr. Othello" portion of the *Candy Shop* medley cited in n. 10.

27. Although the lyrics specify male singers, the Vaudeville Quartet, which accompanies Billy Murray in the Victor record cited in n. 18, consists of one woman and three men. Moreover, this was the combination that accompanied Jolson in *A Night with the Pierrots*, where the other singers were Violet Colby, Willie and Eugene Howard, and Ernest Hare. Robert Kimball and Linda Emmet, seemingly unaware that the music is scored for only five singers, surmise that either a sixth singer was unbilled or that "as a joke five singers sang six parts" (Berlin, *Complete Lyrics*, 49); the evidence of the score suggests that the effect of one woman and four men performing a self-described male sextet, a joke more visual than auditory, was Berlin's idea.

28. The same passage is also quoted in "Rosa Rigoletto"; see chapter 1.

29. Irving Berlin, "Ephraham Played upon the Piano" (New York: Snyder, 1911), Levy 077.066. In Irving Berlin, "The Funny Little Melody" (Berlin, *Early Songs*, appendix), a song Hamm transcribed from a 1912 phonograph record, Ephraham is "a fiddler full of harmony" who writes the titular tune. Other songwriters also contributed songs about an African American musician named Ephraham, e.g., George W. Meyer and Joe Goodwin, "Brass Band Ephraham Jones" (New York: Feist, 1911), Levy 151.083.

30. Hamm, *Irving Berlin*, 79–80, 109–12; see also Charles Hamm, "Irving Berlin's Early Songs as Biographical Documents," *Musical Quarterly* 77 (Spring 1993): 10–34. My approach to this repertory differs from Hamm's in that I consider popular songs as reflecting not so much the songwriter's psyche as the public's zeitgeist.

31. Ford Dabney and Cecil Mack [pseud. R. C. McPherson], "That Minor Strain" (New York: Gotham-Attucks, 1910), copy in NYPL.

32. Here is a comic version of not only the black response to Wagner we have seen in W. E. B. DuBois's "Of the Coming of John" (1903; see chapter 6) but also the female response of Aunt Georgiana, who weeps "quietly, but almost continuously" throughout an all-Wagner program in Willa Cather's short story "A Wagner Matinee," *Everybody's Magazine* 10 (February 1904): 325–28, reprinted in Willa Cather, *Collected Short Fiction, 1892–1912*, ed. Virginia Faulkner (Lincoln: University of Nebraska Press, 1970), 235–42. On the special reverence for Wagner among American women see Joseph Horowitz, *Wagner Nights: An American History* (Berkeley: University of California Press, 1994), chapter 12, "Protofeminism."

33. Lyrics in Berlin, *Complete Lyrics*, 10, 12, 18. As a counterexample to "That Minor Strain," in one song a black man prefers opera but his girlfriend prefers

sentimental songs and ragtime; see Henry Frantzen and Jack Drislane, "Sing a Good Old Ragtime Song" (New York: Haviland, 1909), copy in Hay.

34. E. Ray Goetz (m, w), Bernard Grossman (m, w), and Ralph Shiers (m, w), "That Dreamy Barcarole Tune" (New York: Shapiro, 1910), Levy 154a.002.

35. Ted Snyder and Irving Berlin, "Colored Romeo" (New York: Snyder, 1910), Levy 077.039. For a similar metaphorical use of the automobile see Berlin, "Keep Away from the Fellow Who Owns an Automobile" (New York: Snyder, 1912). In Gus Edwards and Vincent Bryan, "In My Merry Oldsmobile" (New York: Witmark, 1905), Levy 060.088, a young man tells his girlfriend, "You can go as far as you like with me / In my merry Oldsmobile." Here is a sampling of titles from automobile songs in the Levy Sheet Music Collection: "The Automobile Honeymoon" (1902), "In an Automobile Built for Two" (1906), "Will You Take a Ride in My Automobile" (1906), "Hold Me Tighter, Mr. Lighter" (1907), "Give Me a Spin in Your Mitchell, Bill" (1909), "Take Me Out for a Joy Ride" (1909), "On the Old Back Seat of the Henry Ford" (1916), "In Our Little Lovemobile" (1917), "Come On Papa" (1918), and "Don't Take Advantage (Of My Good Nature): The Great Automobile Song" (1919).

36. Irving Berlin, "That Mesmerizing Mendelssohn Tune" (New York: Snyder, 1909), copy in NYPL; Ted Snyder and Irving Berlin, "Herman, Let's Dance That Beautiful Waltz" (New York: Snyder, 1910), Levy 077.096. Other songs that attempted to capitalize on Berlin's "Mendelssohn Rag" (as its cover subtitles it) include Aubrey Stauffer, "That Lovin' Traumerei" (Chicago: Stauffer, 1910), copy in Duke, in which Phoebe Snow prefers the way Moses Johnson plays Schumann, *Il trovatore*, and *William Tell* to the sound of Caruso's voice (Al Jolson recorded this song for Victor in April 1912); and George W. Meyer and Sam M. Lewis, "That Mellow Melody" (New York: Meyer, 1912), copy in CPM, whose persona begs a cellist to "hug me like you do your cello."

37. Patricia Morton, *Disfigured Images: The Historical Assault on Afro-American Women* (New York: Greenwood Press, 1991). Not all African American women in popular songs share this response, however; in Irving Berlin's "Try It on Your Piano" (New York: Snyder, 1910), Levy 078.191, Lucy Brown, echoing a standard music publisher's advertising phrase, tells the pianist Benjamin Manner to "try it on your piano, / But you can't try it on me."

38. John H. Flynn and Will D. Cobb, "Yip-I-Addy-I-Ay!" (New York: Cobb, 1908), Levy 150a.095. Ring's recording is included on *Music from the New York Stage, 1890–1920*, vol. 1, *1890–1908*, 3 CDs (Wadhurst, England:Pearl, 1993).

39. Irving Berlin, "Say It with Music" (New York: Berlin, 1921), Levy 079.168.

40. Rupert Hughes, "A Eulogy of Ragtime," *Boston Musical Record*, 1 April 1899, quoted in Rudi Blesh and Harriet Janis, *They All Played Ragtime*, 4th ed. (New York: Oak, 1971), 131–32.

41. Quoted in Blesh and Janis, *They All Played Ragtime*, 134.

42. Quoted in Blesh and Janis, *They All Played Ragtime*, 133.

43. *Musical America*, 29 March 1913, quoted in Blesh and Janis, *They All Played Ragtime*, 132.

44. Charles L. Buchanan, "Ragtime and American Music," *Opera Magazine: Devoted to the Higher Forms of Musical Art*, February 1916, 18.

45. Hiram Kelly Moderwell, "Ragtime," *New Republic* 4, no. 50 (16 October 1915): 284–86.

46. James Cloyd Bowman, "Anti-Ragtime," letter, *New Republic* 5, no. 53 (6 November 1915): 19, and Moderwell's response in the same issue.

47. Antonín Dvořák, "Music in America," *Harper's New Monthly Magazine*, February 1895; reprinted in *Dvořák in America, 1892–1895*, ed. John C. Tibbetts (Portland, Ore.: Amadeus Press, 1993), 370–80. See also Barbara L. Tischler, *An American Music: The Search for an American Musical Identity* (New York: Oxford University Press, 1986), and MacDonald Smith Moore, *Yankee Blues: Musical Culture and American Identity* (Bloomington: Indiana University Press, 1985), esp. 73–82.

48. Daniel Gregory Mason, *Contemporary Composers* (New York: Macmillan, 1918), 256; though the bulk of Mason's book is devoted to essays on Strauss, Elgar, Debussy, and d'Indy, the opening and closing chapters tackle more general topics, the latter summarizing the ragtime debate from the contra position.

49. Moore, *Yankee Blues*, 82.

50. George Gershwin and Ira Gershwin, "The Real American Folk Song Is a Rag" (1918), reprinted in George Gershwin, *Rediscovered Gershwin* (n.p.: Warner Brothers, 1991). This first collaboration between the Gershwin brothers was introduced by Nora Bayes in *Ladies First*, 24 October 1918; see Ira Gershwin, *The Complete Lyrics of Ira Gershwin*, ed. Robert Kimball, rev. ed. (New York: Da Capo Press, 1998), 4–5.

51. Jack Sullivan, *New World Symphonies: How American Culture Changed European Music* (New Haven, Conn.: Yale University Press, 1999).

52. London *Times*, quoted in Blesh and Janis, *They All Played Ragtime*, 134.

53. Irving Berlin, "The International Rag" (New York: Waterson, Berlin & Snyder, 1913), Levy 078.166; the cover in Levy includes a photo of Sophie Tucker. Recorded by Arthur Collins and Byron G. Harlin, Victor 17431-A (1913); my thanks to Charles Hamm for making a tape of this record available. A similar triumphalism marks the claim that ragtime alone can defeat the Hun, made in a World War I answer song to another Berlin hit, Alfred Bryan (m, w), Cliff Hess (m, w), and Edgar Leslie (m, w), "When Alexander Takes His Ragtime Band to France" (New York: Waterson, Berlin & Snyder, 1918), Levy 097.152.

54. Harry O. Sutton and Jean Lenox, "Ragtime" (New York: Shapiro, Remick, 1904), Levy 149.047 (the copyright date was 1904 but the revised musical opened in 1905); in 1904 Sutton and Lenox depicted another strong-willed woman in the Butterfly song "Kokomo," discussed in chapter 5. On *The Blonde in Black* and *The Sambo Girl*, see Bordman, *American Musical Theatre*, 193, 753. The sequence of dates—*The Blonde in Black* in the summer of 1903, the copyright date of 1904 for "Ragtime," and *The Sambo Girl's* opening night on 16 October 1905—suggests that the reworking of the earlier show into the latter was quite slow and thorough. In *The Blonde in Black*, a black wig stands in for the blackface of minstrelsy. A sambo is a person of three-quarters African ancestry, according to the 1898 edition of *Brewer's Dictionary of Phrase and Fable*; thus Tanguay's exuberant stage behavior carried elements of racial masquerade as well. On Tanguay, see M. Alison Kibler, *Rank Ladies: Gender and Cultural Hierarchy in American Vaudeville* (Chapel Hill: University of North Carolina Press, 1999), 41, 219, and Anthony Slide, *The Vaudevillians: A Dictionary of Vaudeville Performers* (Westport, Conn.: Arlington House, 1981), 146–48. A 1906 recording of Tanguay's signature song, "I Don't Care," also introduced in *The Sambo Girl* (audible at Michigan State University, "An Inventory of Audio Recordings in the Vincent Voice Library," http://www.lib.msu.edu/digital/vincent/findaids/Music.html), hints at how she must have interacted with her audience with an attractive spontaneity; the effect is somewhat reminiscent of Carol Channing.

55. Melville J. Gideon and E. Ray Goetz, "Oh! That Yankiana Rag" (New York: Shapiro, 1908), Levy 148.184; Charles Borel-Clerc, "La Mattchiche (La Maxixe): Le Grand Succes Parisien de 1905" (Paris: Hachette, n.d.), Levy 185. 044. That Held is responding to ragtime as a dance and not merely as music for listening is not to be ignored.

56. Sigmund Romberg and Harold Atteridge, "The Ragtime Pipe of Pan" (New York:Schirmer, 1915), Levy 154.083. On *A World of Pleasure*, see Bordman, *American Musical Theatre*, 309–10.

57. Another song that situates ragtime in antiquity is Dave Stamper and Gene Buck, "There's Rag Time in the Air" (New York: Harms/Francis, Day & Hunter, 1916), copy in NYPL. Sung in the *Ziegfeld Follies of 1916*, probably as part of that edition's Anthony and Cleopatra skit, the song has a Roman persona who plays a lyre and sings about the ubiquity of the ragtime craze in a send-up of songs such as "Everything Is Ragtime Now" (see later).

58. Raymond Hubbell and Robert B. Smith, "Whistle When You Walk Out" (New York: Harris, 1906), Levy 150.059. The composite cover gives the show's title as *Mam'selle Sally*, but Bordman and other sources agree on the spelling *Sallie*; see Bordman, *American Musical Theatre*, 225.

59. Verdi, of course, enjoyed considerable financial success; by transforming him into a starving artist, the song situates him higher up the artistic ladder to emphasize its own embrace of the unabashedly commercial.

60. Quoted in Bordman, *American Musical Theatre*, 245.

61. George M. Cohan, "The American Rag Time" (New York: Cohan & Harris, 1908), Levy 076.005.

62. Moderwell, "Ragtime," 284. Likewise, John N. Burk wrote in the *Harvard Musical Review* in January 1914: "There are few of those above the ragtime sphere who will admit having caught its fascination. Most people seem to have a peculiar, highly sensitized faculty of closing their ears to what they are unwilling to recognize as music" (quoted in Blesh and Janis, *They All Played Ragtime*, 134–35).

63. Kerry Mills and S. M. Lewis, "The Ragtime College Girl" (New York: Mills, 1911), Levy 154.081. A synopsis of *The Fascinating Widow* is in Bordman, *American Musical Theatre*, 271–72. Another song that rejects opera, this time for partiotic music, is Arthur Campbell and Nellie Dunbar Ward, "The National Air of the U.S.A. Sounds Sweetest of All to Me" (New York: Remick, 1912; copy in CPM), whose persona declares, "I heard 'Faust' and 'Carmen,' but I said 'Goldarn'em / they don't make a hit with me.' " In contrast, a song about homesickness for the United States uses ragtime to stand for all things American but makes no comparison with other kinds of music: "When you're away from home across the foam you'll get mighty homesick when you hear some Ragtime music" (Melville J. Gideon and E. Ray Goetz, "Ragtime Land" [New York: Shapiro, 1909], Levy 149.048).

64. A similar sentiment is found in Raymond Hubbell and Harry B. Smith's "Give Us a Ragtime Tune" (New York: Remick, 1910), copy in UCB, from *The Bachelor Belles*, a musical comedy about "an organization dedicated to celibacy" (Bordman, *American Musical Theatre*, 261). The composite cover shows two women in cap and gown and another holding an artist's palette, and the performer's insert shows the ballerina Adelaide Genee en pointe, suggesting that the Bachelor Belles are also devoted to learning and the fine arts; yet the song extols the musical theater over boring old Shakespeare.

65. Charley Straight and J. Brandon Walsh, "Everything Is Ragtime Now" (New York: Witmark, 1913), copy in UCB.

66. Gus Edwards (m), Louis Silvers (m), and Jean C. Havez (w), "That Bohemian Rag" (New York: Remick, 1914), copy in UCB.

67. Quoted in Hamm, *Irving Berlin*, 212; the articles cited appeared in late 1913 and early 1914.

68. See Hamm, *Irving Berlin*, 222, which quotes a Boston reviewer who called *Watch Your Step* "an apotheosis of syncopation." This perception ignored not only the precedent set by the Williams and Walker musicals but also the presence of nonsyncopated music, notably Irene Castle's big waltz number, in Berlin's score.

69. Irving Berlin, *Watch Your Step* (New York: Berlin, 1915), 68 (the musical premiered in 1914; the vocal score was published in 1915); microfilm copy of vocal score provided by Charles Hamm.

70. See Irving Berlin, "Ragtime Opera Medley" (New York: Waterson, Berlin & Snyder, 1914), Levy 078.121.

71. Eugene O'Neill, "Ballard of the Modern Music Lover," in *A Bibliography of the Works of Eugene O'Neill: Together with the Collected Poems of Eugene O'Neill*, by Ralph Sanborn and Barrett H. Clark (1931; reprint, New York: Blom, 1968), 133–34; the poem is dated 17 September 1912.

72. Irving Berlin, "Simple Melody," in *Watch Your Step*, 106–10; the character descriptions are taken from the cast list following the title page. For the abbreviated sheet music version, see Irving Berlin, "(Won't You Play a) Simple Melody" (New York: Berlin, 1914), copy in NYPL.

Conclusion

1. Sigmund Romberg and Harold Atteridge, "The Galli-Curci Rag" (New York: Remick, 1918), copy in UCB. The composite cover mentions no performers; Anthony Slide connects the song with the Howard Brothers in *The Vaudevillians: A Dictionary of Vaudeville Performers* (Westport, Conn.: Arlington House, 1981), 76.

2. Irving Kolodin, *The Story of the Metropolitan Opera, 1883–1950: A Candid History* (New York: Knopf, 1953), 321. Although *Dinorah's* libretto is in French, this production was apparently sung in Italian, the language of Galli-Curci's two recordings of the Shadow Song (Victrola 6129 and 74532).

3. A related song, "My Gal's Another Gal like Galli-Curci," is discussed in chapter 3.

4. A nineteenth-century U.S. edition is G. Meyerbeer, "Shadow Air" (Philadelphia: Andre, n.d.), Levy 120.072; the first-page heading is the opera's subtitle, *Le Pardon de Ploërmel*.

5. H. K. Moderwell, "A Modest Proposal," in "Two Views of Ragtime," *Seven Arts* 2, no. 9 (July 1917): 369–76, quotation on 369. The opposing view was that of Charles L. Buchanan, whose article "Ragtime and American Music" (376–82) was similar, though not identical, in content to his article of the same title published in *Opera Magazine* in February 1916.

6. Moderwell, "A Modest Proposal," 371.

7. Carl Van Vechten, "Communication," letter, *Seven Arts* 2, no. 11 (September 1917): 669–70.

8. See, e.g., Slide, *The Vaudevillians*, 75.

9. On the relationship between social networks and musical categories, see Fabian Holt, *Genre in Popular Music* (Chicago: University of Chicago Press, 2007), esp. 20–29. A song that makes a similar point with no obvious ethnic markers was in the *Ziegfeld Follies of 1918:* Louis A. Hirsch and Gene Buck, "When I Hear a Syncopated Tune" (New York: Witmark, 1918), copy in CPM, which acknowledges that while "the great composers we all know are great,…when I hear a syncopated tune, I simply can't make my feelings behave!" (a reference to Anna Held's signature song of twelve years earlier, "I Just Can't Make My Eyes Behave," by Gus Edwards and Will D. Cobb).

Bibliography

Sheet Music

When two authors are listed, composer appears before lyricist; where a third collaborator is present, or where both music and words are attributed to both songwriters, the parenthetical annotations "(m)" and "(w)" clarify attribution.

Adams, Robert, and James O'Dea. "I Wants a Man Like Romeo." Detroit: Whitney Warner, 1902.

Allen, Thomas S. "Any Rags?" Boston: Krey, 1902.

———. "My Irish Caruso." Boston: Daly, 1909.

———. "Scissors to Grind." Boston: Jacobs, 1904.

———. "Strawberries (Here Comes the Strawberry Man)." Boston: Daly, 1909.

Arndt, Felix. "An Operatic Nightmare: Desecration no. 2." Cleveland: Fox, 1916.

Arndt, Felix, and Louis Weslyn. "My Gal's Another Gal like Galli-Curci." New York: Stern, 1919.

Barnes, Helen Scott, and Carlton Russell Foster. "Salomy Jane." Los Angeles: Foster, 1916.

Baskette, Billy (m), Joseph Santley (m), and George A. Little (w). "Hawaiian Butterfly." New York: Feist, 1917.

Berlin, Irving. "Alexander's Ragtime Band." New York: Snyder, 1911.

———. "Ephraham Played upon the Piano." New York: Snyder, 1911.

———. "He's Getting Too Darn Big for a One-Horse Town." New York: Waterson, Berlin & Snyder, 1916.

———. "Hurry Back to My Bamboo Shack." New York: Waterson, Berlin & Snyder, 1916.

———. "I Love a Piano." New York: Berlin, 1915.

———. "The International Rag." New York: Waterson, Berlin & Snyder, 1913.

———. "Keep Away from the Fellow Who Owns an Automobile." New York: Snyder, 1912.

———. "My Sweet Italian Man." New York: Waterson, Berlin & Snyder, 1913.

———. "Ragtime Mocking Bird." New York: Snyder, 1912.

———. "Ragtime Opera Medley." New York: Waterson, Berlin & Snyder, 1914.

———. "Say It with Music." New York: Berlin, 1921.

———. "That Mesmerizing Mendelssohn Tune." New York: Snyder, 1909.

———. "Tra-La, La, La!" New York: Waterson, Berlin & Snyder, 1913.

———. "Try It on Your Piano." New York: Snyder, 1910.

———. *Watch Your Step*. Vocal score. New York: Berlin, 1915.

———. "(Won't You Play a) Simple Melody." New York: Berlin, 1914.

———. "Yiddisha Nightingale." New York: Snyder, 1911.

Bernard, Felix (m), Johnny S. Black (m), and Fred Fisher (w). "Dardanella." New York: McCarthy & Fisher, 1919.

Black, Eugene [Jean Schwartz], and William Jerome. "When Mister Shakespeare Comes to Town, or I Don't Like Them Minstrel Folks." New York: Howley, Haviland & Dresser, 1901.

Bochsa, N. C., arr. "No. 2. Lucia: Four Melodies." Gems for Young Harpists. New York: Browne, 1854.

Borel-Clerc, Charles. "La Mattchiche (La Maxixe): Le Grand Succes Parisien de 1905." Paris: Hachette, n.d.

Botsford, George, and Irving Berlin. "Grizzly Bear." New York: Snyder, 1910.

Bratton, John W., and Paul West. "I Want to Play Hamlet." New York: Witmark, 1903.

Breuer, Ernest, and Herman Kahn. "He's the World's Best Music Man." Chicago: Rossiter, 1912.

Brockman, James. "My Marianina." New York: Hitland /Helf & Hager, 1907.

Bryan, Alfred (m, w), Cliff Hess (m, w), and Edgar Leslie (m, w). "When Alexander Takes His Ragtime Band to France." New York: Waterson, Berlin & Snyder, 1918.

Burke, Joseph A., and Al Dubin. "My Yiddisha Butterfly." New York: Witmark, 1917.

Campbell, Arthur, and Nellie Dunbar Ward. "The National Air of the U.S.A. Sounds Sweetest of All to Me." New York: Remick, 1912.

Cannon, Hughie. "Bill Bailey, Won't You Please Come Home?" New York: Howley, Haviland & Dresser, 1902.

Caruso, Enrico, and Vincenzo Bellezza. "Liberty Forever!" *Chicago Herald Examiner,* 23 June 1918.

Caruso, Enrico, and Earl Carroll. "Dreams of Long Ago." New York: Feist, 1912.

Castling, Harry. "The Pick-a-ninny." New York: Harms, 1902.

Cohan, George M. "The American Rag Time." New York: Cohan & Harris, 1908.

Cole, Bob, and James Weldon Johnson. "My Lu Lu San: Japanese Love Song." New York: Stern, 1905.

———. "Under the Bamboo Tree." New York: Stern, 1902.

Connolly, Charles, and Edward Craven. "We'll Have No More Coon Rag-time Songs To-night." New York: Witmark, 1900.

Dabney, Ford, and Cecil Mack [R. C. McPherson]. "That Minor Strain." New York: Gotham-Attucks, 1910.

Daniels, Charles N., and Earle C. Jones. "I'll Come Back to You, My Honolulu Lou." New York: Remick, 1912.

David, Worton (m, w), George Arthurs (m, w), and Jerome Kern (m, w). "I Want to Sing in Opera." New York: Harms/Francis, Day & Hunter, 1910.

Delbridge, Edah (m, w), and A. Robert King (m, w). "Ko-Ko-San." New York: Shapiro, Bernstein, 1919.

Donaldson, Walter, and J. Kiern Brennan. "Suki San (Where the Cherry Blossoms Fall)." New York: Witmark, 1917.

Donaldson, Walter, and Charles McCarron. "When Verdi Plays the Hurdy Gurdy." New York: Broadway, 1916.

Donaldson, Walter, and Billy Rose. "Swanee Butterfly." New York" Remick, 1925.

Donizetti, Gaetano. "Chi ma frena [sic]." Arranged by W. A. Weber. Combination Organ Series 2. Boston: Automatic Music Paper, 1881.

———. "What Withholds My Angry Fury." Arranged by Candido Chianei for vocal trio and piano. Boston: Reed, 1848.

Dulmage, Will E., and E. J. Meyers. "Poppy Time in Old Japan." Chicago: Forster, 1915.

Edwards, Gus. "I'm After Madame Tetrazzini's Job." New York: Edwards, 1909.
———. "Italian Romeo." New York: Song Review, 1911.
Edwards, Gus, and Vincent Bryan. "In My Merry Oldsmobile." New York: Witmark, 1905.
Edwards, Gus, and Will D. Cobb. "If a Girl Like You Loved a Boy Like Me." New York: Edwards, 1905.
———. "My Sunburned Salome." New York: Edwards, 1908.
Edwards, Gus, and Edward Madden. "Mister Pagliatch." New York: Remick, 1912.
———. "My Cousin Caruso." New York: Edwards, 1909.
———. "Rosa Rigoletto." New York: Edwards, 1910.
Edwards, Gus (m), Louis Silvers (m), and Jean C. Havez (w). "That Bohemian Rag." New York: Remick, 1914.
Edwards, Leo, and Ballard MacDonald. "Mister Butterfly." New York: Shapiro, Bernstein, 1917.
Fischer, Fred, and Jesse Lasky. "My Brudda Sylvest'." New York: Fischer, 1908.
Fischer, Fred, and Joe McCarthy. "I Want to Go to Tokio." New York: Feist, 1914.
———. "Night Time in Little Italy." New York: McCarthy & Fisher, 1917.
Flynn, John H., and Will D. Cobb. "Yip-I-Addy-I-Ay!" New York: Cobb, 1908.
Fournier, Arthur M. (m), Michael Corper (w), and Waldo C. Twitchell (w). "Yokohama." San Francisco: Sherman, Clay, 1918.
Francis, W. T., and John E. Hazzard. "Salome." New York: Harms, 1908.
Francis, W. T., and Vernon Roy. "Sweet Sana-oo." New York: Harris, 1904.
Frankenstein, A. F., and F. B. Silverwood. "I Love You California." N.p.: n.p., 1913.
Frantzen, Henry, and Jack Drislane. "Sing a Good Old Ragtime Song." New York: Haviland, 1909.
Friedland, Anatol, and Edward Madden. "My Sist' Tetrazin'." New York: Trebuhs, 1909.
Furth, Seymour, and Addison Burkhardt. "When Tetrazzini Sings." New York: Trebuhs, 1908.
Furth, Seymour, and William J. Vandeveer. "Hear the Pickaninny Band." New York: Morris, 1911.
Geibel, Adam, and Richard Henry Buck. "Kentucky Babe: A Plantation Lullaby." Boston: White-Smith, 1896.
Gershwin, George, and Irving Caesar. "Yan-Kee." New York: Harms, 1920.
Gideon, Melville J., and E. Ray Goetz. "Oh! That Yankiana Rag." New York: Shapiro, 1908.
———. "Ragtime Land." New York: Shapiro, 1909.
———. "When Rosalie Sings 'Ciribiribi.'" New York: Shapiro, 1910.
Gilroy, John, and Harry Linton. "I Sing a Little Tenor." New York: Howley, Haviland & Dresser, 1902.
Glick, Frank. "I'm Coming, Butterfly." N.p.: Glick, 1919.
Goetz, E. Ray (m, w), Bernard Grossman (m, w), and Ralph Shiers (m, w). "That Dreamy Barcarole Tune." New York: Shapiro, 1910.
Gottschalk, Louis Moreau. "Miserere du *Trovatore:* Paraphrase de concert." Boston: Ditson, 1888.
Grant, Bert, and Joe Young. "Serenade Me Sadie with a Rag-time Song." New York: Remick, 1912.
Green, Arthur, and William Jerome. "If I Catch the Guy Who Wrote Poor Butterfly." New York: Jerome, 1917.
Green, Gene. "Stop That Bearcat Sadie." Chicago: Rossiter, 1912.

Handy, W. C. "Shoeboot's Serenade." New York: Handy, 1915; rev. ed., New York: Handy Brothers, 1945.

Herbert, Victor, and Edgar Smith. *Dream City and The Magic Knight*. Vocal score. New York: Harris, 1907.

———. "Hannah." New York: Harris, 1907.

———. "An Operatic Maiden." New York: Harris, 1907.

———. "Ta! Ta! My Dainty Little Darling." New York: Harris, 1907.

Herbert, Victor, and Harry B. Smith. "Art Is Calling for Me (I Want to Be a Prima Donna)." New York: Witmark, 1911.

Hess, Carl, arr. "After the Opera's Over." San Francisco: Gray, 1872.

Hickman, Art, and Harry Williams. "Rose Room (In Sunny Roseland)." San Francisco: Sherman & Clay, 1917.

Hirsch, Louis A. "How Do You Do, Miss Ragtime?" New York: Shapiro, 1912.

Hirsch, Louis A., and Gene Buck. "When I Hear a Syncopated Tune." New York: Witmark, 1918.

Hirsch, Louis A. (m), Dave Stamper (m), and Gene Buck (w). "Garden of My Dreams." New York: Harms/Francis, Day & Hunter, 1918.

Hoffmann, Max. "My Little Japaneesee." New York: Shapiro, Bernstein, 1903.

Hollander, Joe, and Jeff Branen. "Hear That Orchestra Rag." New York: Branen, 1912.

Howard, Richard. "When They Play That Old 'Salomy' Melody." New York: Haviland, 1920.

Hubbell, Raymond, and Andrew Donnelly. "I'm Coming Back to You Poor Butterfly." New York: Harms/ Francis, Day & Hunter, 1917.

Hubbell, Raymond, and John L. Golden. "Poor Butterfly." New York: Harms/ Francis, Day & Hunter, 1916.

Hubbell, Raymond, and Glen MacDonough. "The Soubrette's Secret." New York: Harris, 1909.

Hubbell, Raymond, and Harry B. Smith. "Give Us a Ragtime Tune." New York: Remick, 1910.

Hubbell, Raymond, and Robert B. Smith. "Whistle When You Walk Out." New York: Harris, 1906.

Jardon, Dolly, and Edward Madden. "Lotus San: A Japanese Romance." New York: Remick, 1908.

Jerome, Ben M., and John Gilroy. "Mozart Lincoln." New York: Bloom, 1903.

Jerome, Ben M., and Edward Madden. "The Dusky Salome." New York: Trebuhs, 1908.

Jerome, M. K. (m), Sam M. Lewis (w), and Joe Young (w). "Poor Little Butterfly Is a Fly Girl Now." New York: Waterson, Berlin & Snyder, 1919.

Jolson, Al (m, w), and Vincent Rose (m, w). "Avalon." Arranged by J. Bodewalt Lampe. New York: Remick, 1920.

Jones, Clarence M., and Walter Hirsch. "Am I a Butterfly? (To Whom You Say Good-bye)." Chicago: Root, 1918.

Joyce, Archibald. "The Passing of Salome: Valse Orientale." London: Ascherberg, Hopwood & Crew; New York: Feist, 1912.

———. "Vision of Salome." New York: Francis, Day & Hunter, 1909.

Jullien. "The Ravenswood Waltzes: Composed on Donizetti's Opera *Lucia De Lammermoor*." New York: Firth, Pond, 1853.

Kalmar, Bert (m, w), and Harry Ruby (m, w). "So Long! Oo-long (How Long You Gonna Be Gone?)." New York: Waterson, Berlin & Snyder, 1920.

Keiser, Robert A., and Ballard MacDonald. "When Patti Sang 'Home Sweet Home.'" New York: Shapiro, Bernstein, 1917.

Kiefer, Joseph (m, w), and Billy James (m, w). "My Rose of Old Japan." New York: Waterson, Berlin & Snyder, 1919.

Klickmann, F. Henri, and Cal de Voll. "Tosti's 'Good-bye' Melody." Chicago: McKinley, 1921.

Koven, Reginald de, and Eugene Field. "Japanese Lullaby." New York: Schirmer, 1890.

Kummer, Friedrich August, arr. "Trovatore no. 1." In series *Operatic Leaves: Beautiful Melodies, Selected from Favorite Operas, Carefully Fingered, and without Octaves.* Boston: Ditson, 1869.

Lampe, J. Bodewalt. "A Vision of Salome: Descriptive Fantasie [*sic*]." New York: Remick, 1908.

Lemonier, Tom, and Alex Rogers. "I'd Like to Be a Real Lady." New York: Shapiro, Bernstein, 1902.

Lenzberg, Julius. "Operatic Rag." New York: Remick, 1914.

Lenzberg, Julius (m), Gus Kahn (w), and Bud De Sylva (w). "Moonlight on the Nile." New York: Remick, 1919.

Leslie, Edgar (w, m), and Irving Berlin (w, m). "Sadie Salome (Go Home)." New York: Snyder, 1909.

Lewis, Ted (m, w), and Frank Ross (m, w). "Queen of Sheba." New York: Berlin, 1921.

Lilly, R. P., and Frank Dumont. "An Ignoramus Coon." Philadelphia: Morris, 1902.

Loraine, William. "Salome: Intermezzo for the Pianoforte." New York: Mills, 1898.

Mascagni, Pietro. "Ave Maria." Arranged by Leopold Kessler. Boston: Ditson, 1893.

———. "Ave Maria." Italian words by P. Mazzoni, English words by F. E. Weatherly. Chicago: National, n.d.

———. "Intermezzo from Cavalleria Rusticana." Philadelphia: Eclipse, n.d.

Merson, Billy. "The Spaniard That Blighted My Life." New York: Harms/Francis, Day & Hunter, 1911.

Meyer, George W., and Joe Goodwin. "Brass Band Ephraham Jones." New York: Feist, 1911.

Meyer, George W., and Sam M. Lewis. "My Music Teacher." New York: Meyer, 1912.

———. "That Mellow Melody." New York: Meyer, 1912.

Meyer, Joe, and Bobbie Tremaine. "Happy Butterfly." New York: Remick, 1920.

Meyerbeer, G. "Shadow Air." Philadelphia: Andre, n.d.

Mills, Kerry, and S. M. Lewis. "The Ragtime College Girl." New York: Mills, 1911.

Mohr, Halsey K., and Edgar Leslie. "The Police Won't Let Mariuch-a Dance (Unless She Move da Feet)." New York: Rose & Snyder, 1907.

Monaco, Jimmie V., and Joe McCarthy. "Fatima Brown." New York: Feist, 1915.

Moret, Neil [Charles Daniels], and James O'Dea. "Niccolini: Waltz Song." New York: Remick, 1905.

Morse, Theodore F., and Vincent P. Bryan. "Henrietta, Dainty Henrietta." New York: Howley, Haviland & Dresser, 1901.

Motzan, Otto, and A. J. Stasny. "In China." New York: Stasny, 1919.

Muir, Lewis F. "Chilly-Billy-Bee Rag." New York: Helf, 1910.

Muir, Lewis F., and Ed Moran. "When My Marie Sings Chilly-Billy-Bee." New York: Helf, 1910.

Muir, Lewis F., and Fred Watson. "Oh, You Bear Cat Rag." New York: Helf, 1910.

Orth, Frank. "Give Me Rag, Rag, Rag." Philadelphia: Wilsky, 1901.

Owen, Anita. "In Japan with Mi-Mo-San." New York: Remick, 1915.

Pestalozza, A. "Ciribiribin: Waltz." Arranged by Charles J. Roberts. New York: Fischer, 1909.

Pestalozza, A., and Henry S. Sawyer. "Ciribiribin: Waltz Song." New York: McKinley, 1909.

Pestalozza, A., and Frank Sheridan. "If You Only Will: Ciribiribin." New York: Franklin, 1909.

Phillips, A. Fred, and Jack Caddigan. "Egyptian Moonlight: An Oriental Love Song." New York: Garton, 1919.

Piantadosi, Al, and Billy Dunham. "Good-bye Mister Caruso." New York: Cooper, 1909.

Piantadosi, Al (m), Jack Glogau (m), Joe McCarthy (w). "That Italian Serenade." New York: Feist, 1911.

Piantadosi, Al, and Thomas J. Gray. "Rusty-Can-O Rag." New York: Feist, 1910.

Piantadosi, Al, and George Ronklyn. "My Mariuccia (Take a Steamboat)." New York: Barron & Thompson, 1906.

Polla, W. C., and Louis Seifert. "Why Do They Call Mama Poor Butterfly." Hartford, Conn.: Church, 1919.

Potter, Bert. "Any Ice?" Boston: Krey, 1904.

Powell, Orlando, and John P. Harrington. "Salome." New York: Remick, 1909.

Puccini, Giacomo. "Madame Butterfly's Song 'One Fine Day.'" New York: Ricordi, 1908.

Puccini, G., and Jessie Winne. "Cho-Cho-San." Arranged by Hugo Frey. New York: Ricordi, 1921.

Rhodes, S. G. "That Pipe Organ Rag." St. Louis: Stark, 1912.

Rice, Gitz, and Harold Robe. "Dear Old Pal of Mine." New York: Ricordi, 1918.

Romberg, Sigmund, and Harold Atteridge. "The Galli-Curci Rag." New York: Remick, 1918.

———. "I Hail from Cairo." New York: Schirmer, 1918.

———. "The Ragtime Pipe of Pan." New York: Schirmer, 1915.

Romberg, Sigmund, and Ballard MacDonald. "Fat, Fat, Fatima." New York: Witmark, 1921.

Romberg, Sigmund (m), Jean Schwartz (m), and Harold Atteridge (w). "Flutter on By My Broadway Butterfly." New York: Remick, 1919.

Rosey, George [G. M. Rosenberg], arr. "Gounod's Opera *Faust* Arranged in Simplified Form." Selections from Standard Operas. New York: Stern, 1902.

Schwartz, Jean, and Irving Berlin. "The Ki-i-youdleing Dog." New York: Jerome & Schwartz, 1913.

Schwartz, Jean, and William Jerome. "Good-bye Mr. Ragtime (Since the Merry Widow Waltz Has Come to Town)." New York: Cohan & Harris, 1908.

———. "Hamlet Was a Melancholy Dane." New York: Shapiro, Bernstein, 1902.

———. "Since Sister Nell Heard Paderewski Play." New York: Shapiro, Bernstein, 1902.

Schwartz, Jean (m), William Jerome (w), and E. Ray Goetz (w). "When John McCormack Sings a Song." New York: Waterson, Berlin & Snyder, 1915.

Schwartz, Jean (m), Sam M. Lewis (w), and Joe Young (w), "Rock-a-bye Your Baby with a Dixie Melody." New York: Waterson, Berlin & Snyder, 1918.

Shaw, Harold. "There's a Little Butterfly in Normandy." Los Angeles: Hatch, 1918.

Sheer, Fred B. "Kitty the Whistling Girl." Detroit: Grinnell Bros., 1909.

Shisler, Charles P. (m), Billy James (m), and Bobby Heath (w). "When It's Moonlight in Tokio." New York: Witmark, 1917.

Silver, Abner. "When Caruso Comes to Town." New York: Witmark, 1920.

Silver, Abner, and Alex Gerber. "Becky from Babylon." New York: Witmark, 1920.

Smith, Chris. "I Want to Know Where Tosti Went (When He Said 'Good-bye')." New York: Shapiro, Bernstein, 1920.

Smith, Chris, and Jim Burris. "Ballin' the Jack." New York: Stern, 1913.

Smith, Walter. "In Old Japan." San Francisco: Sherman, Clay, 1917.

Snyder, Ted, and Irving Berlin. "Colored Romeo." New York: Snyder, 1910.

———. "Herman, Let's Dance That Beautiful Waltz." New York: Snyder, 1910.

———. "No One Could Do It Like My Father!" New York: Snyder, 1909.

———. "That Opera Rag." New York: Snyder, 1910.

———. "Wild Cherries (Coony, Spoony Rag)." New York: Snyder, 1909.

Snyder, Ted (m, w), and Irving Berlin (m, w). "Piano Man." New York: Snyder, 1910.

Stamper, Dave, and Gene Buck. "There's Rag Time in the Air." New York: Harms/ Francis, Day & Hunter, 1916.

Stanley, Jack, and George A. Little. "They Needed a Song Bird in Heaven (So God Took Caruso Away." New York: Mills, 1921.

Stauffer, Aubrey. "That Lovin' Traumerei." Chicago: Stauffer, 1910.

Stolz, Robert, and Bartley Costello. "Sal-O-May (Salome): Song of the Orient and Fox-Trot." Vienna: Boheme; New York: Marks, 1920.

Straight, Charley, and J. Brandon Walsh. "Everything Is Ragtime Now." New York: Witmark, 1913.

Strauss, Richard. "Salomes Tanz." Berlin: Fürstner, 1905.

Stromberg, John, and Edgar Smith. "My Japanese Cherry Blossom." New York: Witmark, 1901.

Stromberg, John, and Robert B. Smith. "Come Down Ma Evenin' Star." New York: Witmark, 1902.

Sutton, Harry O., and Jean Lenox. "I Don't Care." New York: Shapiro, Remick, 1905.

———. "I'd Rather Be Like Paw." New York: Witmark, 1908.

———. "Kokomo: A Japanese Love Song." New York: Sutton, 1904.

———. "Ragtime." New York: Shapiro, Remick, 1904.

Thomas, Clayton, and anon. "Japanese Love Song." New York: Boosey, 1900.

Thornton, James. "The Streets of Cairo, or The Poor Little Country Maid." New York: Hardings, 1895.

Tierney, Harry, and Alfred Bryan. "My Yokohama Girl." New York: Remick, 1917.

Tosti, F. Paolo. "Good-bye." New York: Van Loan, n.d.

Tracey, William. "I'm Crazy 'bout a Ragtime Minstrel Band." Chicago: Forster, 1908.

Van Alstyne, Egbert, and Gus Kahn. "My Dreamy China Lady." New York: Remick, 1916.

Van Alstyne, Egbert, and Harry Williams. "Cavalier' Rustican' Rag." New York: Remick, 1910.

Vaughn, Jim (m), Tom Lemonier (m), and Alex Rogers (w). "When Sousa Comes to Coon-town." New York: Shapiro, Bernstein, 1902.

Von Tilzer, Harry. "When Susan Thompson Tries to Reach High C." New York: Dunn, 1899.

Von Tilzer, Harry, and Vincent Bryan. "I Wants to Be a Actor Lady." Reprinted in Will Marion Cook et al., *The Music and Scripts of "In Dahomey,"* edited by Thomas L. Riis, Music of the United States of America 5:68–70. Madison, Wisc.: A-R Editions, 1997.

———. "When Miss Patricia Salome Did Her Funny Little Oo La Palome." New York: Von Tilzer, 1907.

Von Tilzer, Harry, and Jack Mahoney. "When Priscilla Tries to Reach High C." New York: Von Tilzer, 1916.

Von Tilzer, Harry, and Andrew B. Sterling. "Mariutch (Make-a the Hootch-a ma Kootch) Down at Coney Isle." New York: Von Tilzer, 1907.

West, W. H. C. "The Jenny Lind Mania." New York: Hall & Son, n.d.

Westphal, Francis C. "When Lucy Sings That Lucia Tune." Chicago: Rossiter, 1911.

Whiting, Richard A., and Raymond B. Egan. "The Japanese Sandman." New York: Remick, 1920.

Wiedoeft, Rudy (m, w), and Abe Olman (m, w). "Karavan." Chicago: Forster, 1919.

Williams, Bert, and George Walker. "She's Getting Mo' Like the White Folks Every Day." New York: Shapiro, Bernstein & Von Tilzer, 1901.

Wynn, Ed, and Stanley Murphy. "I'm Going to Get Myself a Black Salome." New York: Shapiro, 1908.

"Zip Coon." New York: Birch, 1834.

Modern Editions of Songs and Lyric Collections

Applebaum, Stanley, ed. *Show Songs from "The Black Crook" to "The Red Mill": Original Sheet Music for Sixty Songs from Fifty Shows, 1866–1906.* New York: Dover, 1974.

Berlin, Irving. *The Complete Lyrics of Irving Berlin.* Edited by Robert Kimball and Linda Emmet. New York: Knopf, 2001.

———. *Early Songs.* Edited by Charles Hamm. 3 vols. Recent Researches in American Music, vols. 20–22. Music of the United States of America 2, parts 1–3. Madison, Wisc.: A-R Editions, 1994.

Cook, Will Marion, et al. *The Music and Scripts of "In Dahomey."* Edited by Thomas L. Riis. Music of the United States of America 5. Madison, Wisc.: A-R Editions, 1997.

Gershwin, George. *The Music and Lyrics of George Gershwin.* 2 vols. Edited by Peter Foss. Rev. ed. London: Chappell, 1991.

———. *Rediscovered Gershwin.* N.p.: Warner Brothers, 1991.

Gershwin, Ira. *The Complete Lyrics of Ira Gershwin.* Edited by Robert Kimball. Rev. ed. New York: Da Capo Press, 1998.

Books, Journals, and Newspapers

Abbate, Carolyn. "Opera, or The Envoicing of Women." In *Musicology and Difference: Gender and Sexuality in Music Scholarship,* edited by Ruth Solie, 228–29. Berkeley: University of California Press, 1993.

———. *Unsung Voices: Opera and Musical Narrative in the Nineteenth Century.* Princeton, N.J.: Princeton University Press, 1991.

Ahlquist, Karen. *Democracy at the Opera: Music, Theater, and Culture in New York City, 1815–60.* Urbana: University of Illinois Press, 1997.

———. "Mrs. Potiphar at the Opera: Satire, Idealism, and Cultural Authority in Post–Civil War New York." In *Music and Culture in America, 1861–1918*, edited by Michael Saffle, 29–52. Essays in American Music. New York: Garland, 1998.

[Aldrich, Richard]. "'Madam Butterfly' at the Garden Theatre: Puccini's Latest Opera in English by Col. Savage's Company: A Work of Great Charm." *New York Times*, 13 November 1906.

———. "'Mme. Butterfly' Sung in Italian: Puccini's Latest Opera Given at the Metropolitan for the First Time: A Fine Performance." *New York Times*, 12 February 1907.

Aldrich, Richard. "Puccini's Madame Butterfly." *New York Times*, 11 November 1906.

Allen, Robert C. *Horrible Prettiness: Burlesque and American Culture.* Chapel Hill: University of North Carolina Press, 1991.

Ammen, Sharon Irene. "May Irwin's Strategies of Influence: A Look Back at America's 'Secretary of Laughter.'" Ph.D. diss., University of Maryland, 1997.

Antelyes, Peter. "Red Hot Mamas: Bessie, Smith, Sophie Tucker, and the Ethnic Maternal Voice in American Popular Song." In *Embodied Voices: Representing Female Vocality in Western Culture*, edited by Leslie C. Dunn and Nancy A. Jones, 212–29. Cambridge: Cambridge University Press, 1994.

"At the Metropolitan." *New York Times*, 20 January 1907.

Austern, Linda. "Cultural Migration, Appropriation, and Image in Twentieth-Century Anglo-American Popular Musics." Paper presented at the seventeenth congress of the International Musicological Society, Leuven, Belgium, 5 August 2002.

Barzun, Jacques. *Music in American Life.* Garden City, N.Y.: Doubleday, 1956.

Becker-Leckrone, Megan. "Salome©: The Fetishization of a Textual Corpus." *New Literary History* 26, no 2 (1995): 239–60.

Belasco, David. *Madame Butterfly: A Tragedy of Japan.* In *Six Plays*, 3–32. Boston: Little, Brown, 1928.

———. "When Mary Pickford Came to Me: The Story of the Man Who First Wrote Her Name in Light on Broadway." *Photoplay* 9, no. 1 (December 1915): 27–34; online edition at *Silent Era Archive*, http://www.silentera.com/archive/photoplay/1915/1215/1215–27.html.

Bentley, Toni. *Sisters of Salome.* New Haven, Conn.: Yale University Press, 2002.

Bergreen, Laurence. *As Thousands Cheer: The Life of Irving Berlin.* New York: Viking Press, 1990.

Berlin, Edward A. *King of Ragtime: Scott Joplin and His Era.* New York: Oxford University Press, 1994.

Berrett, Joshua. "Louis Armstrong and Opera." *Musical Quarterly* 76 (1992): 216–41.

Bizot, Richard. "The Turn-of-the-Century Salome Era: High- and Pop-Culture Variations on the Dance of the Seven Veils." *Choreography and Dance* 2, no. 3 (1992): 71–87.

Blesh, Rudi, and Harriet Janis. *They All Played Ragtime.* 4th ed. New York: Oak, 1971.

Bloom, Ken. *American Song.* 2 parts in 4 vols. Part 1. *The Complete Musical Theatre Companion: Second Edition, 1877–1995.* Vol. 1. *A-S.* Vol. 2. *T-Z and Indexes.* Part 2. *The Complete Companion to Tin Pan Alley Song.* Vol. 3. *Songwriters.* Vol. 4. *Indexes.* New York: Schirmer Books, 1996, 2001.

————. *American Musical Revue: From "The Passing Show" to "Sugar Babies."* New York: Oxford University Press, 1985.

————. *American Musical Theatre: A Chronicle.* 2nd ed. New York: Oxford University Press, 1992.

Boskin, Joseph, and Joseph Dorinson. "Ethnic Humor: Subversion and Survival." In *American Humor,* edited by Arthur Power Dudden, 97–117. New York: Oxford University Press, 1987.

"Boston Opera Repertoire." *New York Times,* 31 October 1915.

Bowman, James Cloyd. "Anti-Ragtime." Letter. *New Republic* 5, no. 53 (6 November 1915): 19.

Brackett, David. *Interpreting Popular Music.* Cambridge: Cambridge University Press, 1995.

Brooks, Van Wyck. "'Highbrow' and 'Lowbrow.'" In *America's Coming-of-Age* (1915); reprinted in *Three Essays on America,* 15–35. New York: Dutton, 1934.

Browne, Nick. "The Undoing of the *Other* Woman: Madame Butterfly in the Discourse of American Orientalism." In *The Birth of Whiteness: Race and the Emergence of U.S. Cinema,* edited by Daniel Bernardi, 227–56. New Brunswick, N.J.: Rutgers University Press, 1996.

Bryant, Rebecca A. "Shaking Things Up: Popularizing the Shimmy in America." *American Music* 20, no. 2 (Summer 2002):168–87.

Buchanan, Charles L. "Ragtime and American Music." *Opera Magazine: Devoted to the Higher Forms of Musical Art,* February 1916, 17–19, 25.

————. "Ragtime and American Music." In "Two Views of Ragtime." *Seven Arts* 2, no. 9 (July 1917): 376–82.

Burkholder, J. Peter. *All Made of Tunes: Charles Ives and the Uses of Musical Borrowing.* New Haven, Conn.: Yale University Press, 1995.

Caddy, Davinia. "Variations on the Dance of the Seven Veils." *Cambridge Opera Journal* 17 (2005): 37–58.

Caffin, Caroline. "Vaudeville Music." 1914; reprinted in *American Vaudeville as Seen by Its Contemporaries,* edited by Charles W. Stein, 209–13. New York: Knopf, 1984.

"The Call of Salome: Rumors That Salomania Will Have a Free Hand This Season." *New York Times,* 16 August 1908.

Carlton, Donna. *Looking for Little Egypt.* Bloomington, Ind.: IDD Books, 1994.

Carner, Mosco. *"Madam Butterfly": A Guide to the Opera.* London: Barrie & Jenkins, 1979.

Caruso, Enrico, Jr., and Andrew Farkas. *Enrico Caruso: My Father and My Family.* Portland, Ore.: Amadeus Press, 1990.

Cather, Willa. "A Wagner Matinee." *Everybody's Magazine* 10 (February 1904): 325–28; reprinted in Willa Cather, *Collected Short Fiction, 1892–1912,* edited by Virginia Faulkner, 235–42. Lincoln: University of Nebraska Press, 1970.

Chekhov, Anton. "Lady with Lapdog." Translated by Ivy Litvinov. In Anton Chekhov, *Short Stories,* edited by Ralph E. Matlaw, Norton Critical Edition, 221–35. New York: Norton, 1979.

Cherniavsky, Felix. *The Salome Dancer.* Toronto: McClelland & Stewart, 1991.

Cohen, Barbara Naomi. *The Borrowed Art of Gertrude Hoffmann.* Brooklyn: Dance Horizons, 1977.

Cohen-Stratyner, Barbara, ed. *Popular Music, 1900–1919.* Detroit: Gale Research, 1988.

Cone, John Frederick. *Oscar Hammerstein's Manhattan Opera Company.* Norman: University of Oklahoma Press, 1966.

Covach, John. "Popular Music, Unpopular Musicology." In *Rethinking Music,* edited by Nicholas Cook and Mark Everist, rev. ed., 452–70. Oxford: Oxford University Press, 2001.

Davis, Peter G. *The American Opera Singer: The Lives and Adventures of America's Great Singers in Opera and Concert, from 1825 to the Present.* New York: Doubleday, 1997.

Dennison, Sam. *Scandalize My Name: Black Imagery in American Popular Music.* New York: Garland, 1982.

Dijkstra, Bram. *Idols of Perversity: Fantasies of Feminine Evil in Fin-de-Siècle Culture.* New York: Oxford University Press, 1986.

Dinnerstein, Leonard, and David M. Reimers. *Ethnic Americans: A History of Immigration.* 4th ed. New York: Columbia University Press, 1999.

Dizikes, John. *Opera in America: A Cultural History.* New Haven, Conn.: Yale University Press, 1993.

Douglass, Frederick. "The Color Line." *North American Review* 132 (June 1881): 567–77; electronic ed., University of Virginia, 1999, at http://etext.lib.virginia.edu/.

———.*Narrative of the Life of Frederick Douglass, an American Slave.* 1845; electronic edition at Berkeley Digital Library, *SunSITE,* http://sunsite.berkeley.edu/Literature/Douglass/.

"Dramatic and Musical: 'Mme. Butterfly' Gives Blanche Bates an Opportunity." *New York Times,* 6 March 1900.

Du Bois, W. E. B. *The Souls of Black Folk.* 1903. Reprint, New York: Signet, 1985.

Dunn, Leslie C., and Nancy A. Jones. Introduction to *Embodied Voices: Representing Female Vocality in Western Culture,* edited by Leslie C. Dunn and Nancy A. Jones, 1–3. Cambridge: Cambridge University Press, 1994.

Dvořák, Antonín. "Music in America." *Harper's New Monthly Magazine,* February 1895. Reprinted in *Dvořák in America, 1892–1895,* edited by John C. Tibbetts, 370–80. Portland, Ore.: Amadeus Press, 1993.

Edwards, Brian T. *Morocco Bound: Disorienting America's Maghreb, from Casablanca to the Marrakech Express.* Durham, N.C.: Duke University Press, 2005.

Erdman, Andrew L. *Blue Vaudeville: Sex, Morals, and the Mass Marketing of Amusement, 1895–1915.* Jefferson, N.C.: McFarland, 2004.

"'Follies of 1907': New Jardin de Paris Review Has the Anna Held Chorus." *New York Times,* 9 July 1907.

Fuld, James. *The Book of World-Famous Music.* 3rd ed. New York: Dover Books, 1985.

Gänzl, Kurt. "Thompson, Lydia." In *The Encyclopedia of the Musical Theatre,* 2nd edition, 2044–46. New York: Schirmer Books, 2001.

Garrett, Charles Hiroshi. *Struggling to Define a Nation: American Music and the Twentieth Century.* Berkeley and Los Angeles: University of California Press, 2008.

Gattey, Charles Neilson. *Luisa Tetrazzini: The Florentine Nightingale.* Portland, Ore.: Amadeus Press, 1995.

Gilbert, Douglas. *American Vaudeville: Its Life and Times.* New York: Whittlesey House, 1940.

Gilman, Lawrence. "Strauss' 'Salome': Its Art and Its Morals." In *Aspects of Modern Opera: Estimates and Inquiries,* 65–105. New York: Lane, 1909.

Gilman, Sander L. "Salome, Syphilis, Sarah Bernhardt and the 'Modern Jewess,'" *German Quarterly* 66 (1993): 195–211.

———. "Strauss and the Pervert." In *Reading Opera*, edited by Arthur Groos and Roger Parker, 306–27. Princeton, N.J.: Princeton University Press, 1988.

Golden, Eve. *Golden Images: Forty-one Essays on Silent Film Stars.* Jefferson, N.C.: McFarland, 2001.

Goldmark, Daniel, *Tunes for 'Toons: Music and the Hollywood Cartoon.* Berkeley and Los Angeles: University of California Press, 2005.

Graziano, John. "The Early Life and Career of the 'Black Patti': The Odyssey of an African American Singer in the Late Nineteenth Century." *Journal of the American Musicological Society* 53 (2000): 343–96.

———. "Music in William Randolph Hearst's *New York Journal." Notes,* 2nd ser., 48 (1991): 383–424.

Green, Abel, and Joe Laurie Jr. *Show Biz from Vaude to Video.* New York: Holt, 1951.

Greenfeld, Howard. *Caruso.* New York: Putnam, 1983.

Groos, Arthur. "Lieutenant F. B. Pinkerton: Problems in the Genesis and Performance of *Madama Butterfly."* In *The Puccini Companion,* edited by William Weaver and Simonetta Puccini, 169–201. New York: Norton, 1994.

Hamberlin, Larry. "American Popular Songs on Operatic Topics." Ph.D. diss., Brandeis University, 2004.

———. "Cairo on the Midway: Orientalism, Popular Song, and the Chicago Fair of 1893." Paper presented at annual meetings of the International Association for the Study of Popular Music, U.S. branch, Murfreesboro, Tenn., 16–19 February 2006, and the Society for American Music, Chicago, Ill., 15–19 March 2006.

———. "Red Hot Verdi: European Allusions in the Music of Jelly Roll Morton and Louis Armstrong." Paper presented at the seventeenth congress of the International Musicological Society, Leuven, Belgium, August 2002.

Hamm, Charles. *Irving Berlin: Songs from the Melting Pot: The Formative Years, 1907–1914.* New York: Oxford University Press, 1997.

———. "Irving Berlin's Early Songs as Biographical Documents." *Musical Quarterly* 77 (Spring 1993): 10–34.

———. Review essay on studies of minstrelsy. *Journal of the American Musicological Society* 53, no. 1 (Spring 2000): 165–82.

———. *Yesterdays: Popular Song in America.* New York: Norton, 1979.

Harte, Bret. *Salomy Jane.* Boston: Houghton Mifflin, 1910.

———. "Salomy Jane's Kiss." Reprint at *The Project Gutenberg Etext of "Stories in Light and Shadow,"* http://www.gutenberg.org/files/15192/15192–8.txt.

Heywood, J. C. *Salome, the Daughter of Herodias.* New York: Putnam, 1862.

Holloway, Robin. "*Salome:* Art or Kitsch?" In *Richard Strauss: Salome,* edited by Derrick Puffett. Cambridge Opera Handbook, 145–60. Cambridge: Cambridge University Press, 1989.

Holt, Fabian. *Genre in Popular Music.* Chicago: University of Chicago Press, 2007.

Horowitz, Joseph. *Classical Music in America: A History of Its Rise and Fall.* New York: Norton, 2005.

———. *Understanding Toscanini: A Social History of American Concert Life.* New York: Knopf, 1987. Rev. ed. Berkeley: University of California Press, 1994.

———. *Wagner Nights: An American History.* Berkeley: University of California Press, 1994.

"How the Audience Took It: Many Disgusted by the Dance and the Kissing of the Head." *New York Times,* 23 January 1907.

Hurwitt, Elliott. "W. C. Handy as Music Publisher: Career and Reputation." Ph.D. diss., City University of New York, 2000.

"Isadora Duncan Raps Maud Allan." *New York Times,* 9 August 1908.

Jacobson, Matthew Frye. *Whiteness of a Different Color: European Immigrants and the Alchemy of Race.* Cambridge, Mass.: Harvard University Press, 1998.

Jarrett, Lucinda. *Stripping in Time: A History of Erotic Dancing.* London: Pandora, 1997.

Jasen, David. *Tin Pan Alley: The Composers, the Songs, the Performers, and Their Times: The Golden Age of American Popular Music from 1886 to 1956.* New York: Fine, 1988.

Kasson, John F. *Amusing the Million: Coney Island at the Turn of the Century.* New York: Hill and Wang, 1978.

Kaye, Joseph. *Victor Herbert: The Biography of America's Greatest Composer of Romantic Music.* 1931. Reprint, Freeport, N.Y.: Books for Libraries Press, 1970.

Kendall, Elizabeth. *Where She Danced.* New York: Knopf, 1979.

Kennedy, Charles A. "When Cairo Met Main Street: Little Egypt, Salome Dancers, and the World's Fairs of 1893 and 1904." In *Music and Culture in America, 1861–1918,* edited by Michael Saffle, 271–98. New York: Garland, 1998.

Kenney, William Howland. *Recorded Music in American Life: The Phonograph and Popular Memory, 1890–1945.* New York: Oxford University Press, 1999.

Kibler, M. Alison. *Rank Ladies: Gender and Cultural Hierarchy in American Vaudeville.* Chapel Hill: University of North Carolina Press, 1999.

Kolodin, Irving. *The Story of the Metropolitan Opera, 1883–1950: A Candid History.* New York: Knopf, 1953.

Koritz, Amy. "Dancing the Orient for England: Maud Allan's 'The Vision of Salome.'" *Theatre Journal* 46 (1994): 63–78.

Kramer, Lawrence. "Culture and Musical Hermeneutics: The Salome Complex." *Cambridge Opera Journal* 2 (1990): 269–94.

———. "Opera: Two or Three Things I Know about Her." In *Siren Songs: Representations of Gender and Sexuality in Opera,* edited by Mary Ann Smart, 186–203. Princeton, N.J.: Princeton University Press, 2000.

Krasner, David. "Black *Salome:* Exoticism, Dance, and Racial Myths." In *African American Performance and Theater History,* edited by Harry J. Elam Jr. and David Krasner, 192–211. New York: Oxford University Press, 2001.

Kraut, Alan M. *The Huddled Masses: The Immigrant in American Society, 1880–1921.* Arlington Heights, Ill.: Harlan Davidson, 1982.

Krehbiel, Henry. "The *Salome* of Wilde and Strauss." *New York Tribune,* 23 January 1907. Reprinted in *The Attentive Listener: Three Centuries of Music Criticism,* edited by Harry Haskell, 223–28. London: Faber & Faber, 1995.

Kushner, David Z. "Bloch, Ernest." In *The New Grove Dictionary of Music and Musicians,* 2nd ed., edited by Stanley Sadie, 3:705. New York: Grove, 2001.

Ledbetter, Steven. "Two Seductresses: Saint-Saëns's Delilah and Chadwick's Judith." In *A Celebration of American Music: Words and Music in Honor of H. Wiley Hitchcock,* edited by Richard Crawford, R. Allen Lott, and Carol J. Oja, 281–301. Ann Arbor: University of Michigan Press, 1990.

Levine, Lawrence W. *Highbrow/Lowbrow: The Emergence of Cultural Hierarchy in America.* Cambridge, Mass.: Harvard University Press, 1988.

Levy, Lester S. *Give Me Yesterday: American History in Song, 1890–1920.* Norman: University of Oklahoma Press, 1975.

Lewis, David Levering. *W. E. B. Du Bois, 1868–1919: Biography of a Race.* New York: Holt, 1993.

Little, Douglas. *American Orientalism: The United States and the Middle East since 1945.* Chapel Hill: University of North Carolina Press, 2002.

Locke, Ralph. "Cutthroats and Casbah Dancers, Muezzins and Timeless Sands: Musical Images of the Middle East." In *The Exotic in Western Music,* edited by Jonathan Bellman, 104–36. (Boston: Northeastern University Press, 1998).

Long, John Luther. "Madame Butterfly." *Century* 55, no. 33 (1898): 274–92; reprint, New York: Grosset and Dunlap, 1903; online edition at University of Virginia American Studies Programs, *Hypertexts,* http://xroads.virginia. edu/~HYPER/LONG/abstract.html.

"Looking Forward to a Week of Serious Drama." *New York Times,* 20 January 1907.

Lord, Tom. *The Jazz Discography.* Version 3.3. CD-ROM. N.p.: Lord Music Reference, 2002.

Lott, Eric. *Love and Theft: Blackface Minstrelsy and the American Working Class.* New York: Oxford University Press, 1993.

McClary, Susan. *Feminine Endings: Music, Gender, and Sexuality.* Minneapolis: University of Minnesota Press, 1991.

———."The Musical Languages of *Carmen.*" In *Georges Bizet: Carmen,* 44–61. Cambridge: Cambridge University Press, 1992.

Magee, Jeff. "'Everybody Step': Irving Berlin, Jazz, and Broadway in the 1920s." *Journal of the American Musicological Society* 59 (2006): 679–732.

Mahar, William J. *Behind the Burnt Cork Mask: Early Blackface Minstrelsy and Antebellum American Popular Culture.* Urbana: University of Illinois Press, 1999.

Mallach, Alan. *Pietro Mascagni and His Operas.* Boston: Northeastern University Press, 2002.

Mantle, Burns, and Garrison P. Sherwood, eds. Introduction to *The Man from Home.* In *The Best Plays of 1899–1909,* 303–4. New York: Dodd, Mead, 1947.

"Many New Plays Bid for Favor." *New York Times,* 6 November 1910.

Mason, Daniel Gregory. *Contemporary Composers.* New York: Macmillan, 1918.

Moderwell, Hiram Kelly. "A Modest Proposal." In "Two Views of Ragtime." *Seven Arts* 2, no. 9 (July 1917): 369–76.

———. "Ragtime." *New Republic* 4, no. 50 (16 October 1915): 284–86.

———. Response to James Cloyd Bowman, "Anti-Ragtime," letter. *New Republic* 5, no. 53 (6 November 1915): 19.

Moon, Krystyn R. *Yellowface: Creating the Chinese in American Popular Music and Performance, 1850s–1920s.* New Brunswick, N.J.: Rutgers University Press, 2005.

Moore, MacDonald Smith. *Yankee Blues: Musical Culture and American Identity.* Bloomington: Indiana University Press: 1985.

Moran, William R. "Discography of Original Recordings." In *Enrico Caruso: My Father and My Family,* by Enrico Caruso Jr. and Andrew Farkas. Portland, Ore.: Amadeus Press, 1990.

Morton, Patricia. *Disfigured Images: The Historical Assault on Afro-American Women.* New York: Greenwood Press, 1991.

Nasaw, David. *Going Out: The Rise and Fall of Public Amusements.* New York: Basic Books, 1993.

Nelli, Humbert S. "Italians." In *Harvard Encyclopedia of American Ethnic Groups*, edited by Stephan Thernstrom,545–60. Cambridge, Mass.: Belknap Press, 1980.

"New Farces and Players in Them: May Irwin Provides Most of the Polish in the One at Wallack's." *New York Times*, 9 November, 1910.

Norris, Renee Lapp. "Opera and the Mainstreaming of Blackface Minstrelsy." *Journal of the Society for American Music* 1 (2007): 341–65.

———. "Two Parodies of French Opera Performed by Blackface Minstrels." *Sonneck Society for American Music Bulletin* 225, no. 1 (Spring 1999): 9–11.

O'Neill, Eugene. "Ballard [*sic*] of the Modern Music Lover." In *A Bibliography of the Works of Eugene O'Neill: Together with the Collected Poems of Eugene O'Neill*, by Ralph Sanborn and Barrett H. Clark, 133–34. 1931. Reprint, New York: Blom, 1968.

"Opening of Hippodrome." *New York Tribune*, 13 April 1905.

Peck, Melissa. "Performing the Erotic: Aida Overton Walker's Interpretation of Salome." Paper presented at the Reception Study Society (RSS) Conference on Reception Study, Kansas City, Mo., 27–29 September 2007.

"Plays New and Old That Invite." *New York Times*, 20 January 1907.

Poizat, Michel. " 'The Blue Note' and 'The Objectified Voice and the Vocal Object." *Cambridge Opera Journal* 3 (1991): 199.

Pollard, Percival. "The Regnant Wave of the Sensational Dance: 'Salome' Craze Raged in Europe Long before It Came Here." *New York Times*, 23 August 1908.

Pozzetta, George. "Italian Americans." In *Gale Encyclopedia of Multicultural America*, edited by Rudolph J. Vecoli, 765–82 New York: Gale Research, 1995.

Praz, Mario. "Salome in Literary Tradition." In, *Richard Strauss: Salome*, edited by Derrick Puffet, 11–20. Cambridge Opera Handbook. Cambridge: Cambridge University Press, 1989.

Preston, Katherine K. *Opera on the Road: Traveling Opera Troupes in the United States, 1825–60*. Urbana: University of Illinois Press, 1993.

Puffett, Derrick, ed. *Richard Strauss: Salome*. Cambridge Opera Handbook. Cambridge: Cambridge University Press, 1989.

Pym, Anthony. "The Importance of Salomé: Approaches to a *fin de siècle* Theme." *French Forum* 14 (1989): 311–22.

Richards, David A. J. *Italian American: The Racializing of an Ethnic Identity*. New York: New York University Press, 1999.

Riis, Thomas L. "Concert Singers, Prima Donnas, and Entertainers: The Changing Status of Black Women Vocalists in Nineteenth-Century America." In *Music and Culture in America, 1861–1918*, edited by Michael Saffle, 53–78. New York: Garland, 1998.

———. *Just before Jazz: Black Musical Theater in New York, 1890–1915*. Washington, D.C.: Smithsonian Institution Press, 1989.

Rodney, Nanette B. "Salome." *Metropolitan Museum of Art Bulletin* 11, no. 7 (1953): 190–200.

Roell, Craig H. "The Development of Tin Pan Alley." In *America's Musical Pulse: Popular Music in Twentieth-Century Society*, edited by Kenneth J. Bindas, 113–21. Westport, Conn.: Greenwood Press, 1992.

Rourke, Constance. *American Humor: A Study of the National Character*. New York: Harcourt Brace Jovanovich, 1931.

Rubin, Jason. "Lew Fields and the Development of the Broadway Musical." Ph.D. diss., New York University, 1991.

Rydell, Robert W. *All the World's a Fair: Visions of Empire at American International Expositions, 1876–1916.* Chicago: University of Chicago Press, 1984.

Said, Edward. *Orientalism.* New York: Vintage Books, 1979.

"'Salome Jane's Kiss' with Eleanor Robson: Harte's Story Basis for Paul Armstrong's Play: Some Capital Acting: But the Last Two Acts of the Play Not Up to the Standard of the Others." *New York Times,* 20 January 1907.

Sanjek, Russell. *American Popular Music and Its Business: The First Four Hundred Years.* Vol. 3. *From 1900 to 1984.* New York: Oxford University Press, 1988.

———.*Pennies from Heaven: The American Popular Music Business in the Twentieth Century.* New York: Da Capo Press, 1996.

Scott, Derek B. "Orientalism and Musical Style." *Musical Quarterly* 82 (1998): 309–35.

"Seen on the Stage." *New York Times,* 7 July 1907.

Segal, Charles. "The Gorgon and the Nightingale: The Voice of Female Lament and Pindar's Twelfth *Pythian Ode.*" In *Embodied Voices: Representing Female Vocality in Western Culture,* edited by Leslie C. Dunn and Nancy A. Jones, 17–34. Cambridge: Cambridge University Press, 1994.

Seldes, Gilbert. *The Seven Lively Arts.* New York: Harper, 1924.

Sensi-Isolani, Paola A. "Italians." In *A Nation of Peoples: A Sourcebook on America's Multicultural Heritage,* edited by Elliot Robert Barkan, 294–310 Westport, Conn.: Greenwood Press, 1999.

Seshadri, Anne L. "The Taste of Love: Salome's Transfiguration." *Women and Music* 10 (2006): 24–44.

Shapiro, Nat, and Bruce Pollock, eds. *Popular Music, 1920–1979: An Annotated Index.* 3 vols. Detroit: Gale Research, 1985.

Sheppard, W. Anthony. "Cinematic Realism, Reflexivity, and the American 'Madame Butterfly' Narratives." *Cambridge Opera Journal* 17 (2005): 59–93.

———. "An Exotic Enemy: Anti-Japanese Musical Propaganda in World War II Hollywood." *Journal of the American Musicological Society* 54 (2001): 303–57.

———. "Pinkerton's Lament." Paper presented at the sixty-ninth annual meeting of the American Musicological Society, Houston, Texas, 14 November 2003.

Showalter, Elaine. *Sexual Anarchy: Gender and Culture at the Fin de Siècle.* New York: Viking, 1990.

Shteir, Rachel. *Striptease: The Untold History of the Girlie Show.* New York: Oxford University Press, 2004.

Simonson, Mary. "'The Call of Salome': American Adaptations and Recreations of the Female Body in the Early Twentieth Century." *Women and Music* 11 (2007): 1–16.

———. "Performance, Multimedia, and Creativity in Early Twentieth-Century American Musical Life." Ph.D. diss. University of Virginia, 2008.

Slide, Anthony. *The Vaudevillians: A Dictionary of Vaudeville Performers.* Westport, Conn.: Arlington House, 1981.

Smith, Harry B. *First Nights and First Editions.* Boston: Little, Brown, 1931.

Snyder, Robert W. *The Voice of the City: Vaudeville and Popular Culture in New York.* New York: Oxford University Press, 1989.

Sobel, Bernard. *Burleycue: An Underground History of Burlesque Days.* New York: Farrar & Rinehart, 1931.

———. *A Pictorial History of Vaudeville.* New York: Citadel Press, 1961.

"Sothern and Marlowe in 'John the Baptist': Sudermann's Uninspired Play of Many Pictorial Scenes: Salome and Her Dance: Miss Marlowe in a Role of Oriental Seductiveness and Mr. Sothern in a Figure of Drab Monotone." *New York Times*, 22 January 1907.

Southern, Eileen. "In Retrospect: Black Prima Donnas of the Nineteenth Century." *Black Perspective in Music* 7 (1979): 95–106.

Spaeth, Sigmund. *Read 'Em and Weep: The Songs You Forgot to Remember.* Garden City, N.Y.: Doubleday, Page, 1927.

———. *Weep Some More, My Lady.* Garden City, N.Y.: Doubleday, Page, 1927.

Spengemann, William. Introduction to Henry James, *The American* (1876–77), 7–25. New York: Penguin Books, 1981.

"Strauss's 'Salome' the First Time Here: A Remarkable Performance at the Metropolitan." *New York Times*, 23 January 1907.

Stubblebine, Donald J. *Early Broadway Sheet Music: A Comprehensive Listing of Published Music from Broadway and Other Stage Shows, 1843–1918.* Jefferson, N.C.: McFarland, 2002.

Sullivan, Jack. *New World Symphonies: How American Culture Changed European Music.* New Haven, Conn.: Yale University Press, 1999.

Tarkington, Booth, and Harry Leon Wilson. "Mrs. Jim: A Comedy of American Life, Dealing in a Satirical Vein with the Prevailing Pursuit of Love and Money, with Its Attendant Embarrassments and Evils." Condensed by Lucy France Pierce. *The World Today* 19, no. 2 (August 1910): 897–904.

Tawa, Nicholas E. *Mainstream Music of Early Twentieth-Century America: The Composers, Their Times, and Their Works.* Westport, Conn.: Greenwood Press, 1992.

"Theatrical Notes." *New York Times*, 3 November 1915.

Tick, Judith. "Women in Music, §II, 4: Western Classical Traditions since 1800." *The New Grove Dictionary of Music and Musicians*, edited by S. Sadie and J. Tyrell, 27:527–31. London: Macmillan, 2001.

Tischler, Barbara L. *An American Music: The Search for an American Musical Identity.* New York: Oxford University Press, 1986.

Turk, Edward Baron. "Deriding the Voice of Jeanette MacDonald: Notes on Psychoanalysis and the American Film Musical." In *Embodied Voices: Representing Female Vocality in Western Culture*, edited by Leslie C. Dunn and Nancy A. Jones, 103–119. Cambridge: Cambridge University Press, 1994.

Van, Gilles de. "Fin de Siècle Exoticism and the Meaning of the Far Away." Translated by William Ashbrook. *Opera Quarterly* 11, no. 3 (1995): 77–94.

Van der Merwe, Peter. *Origins of the Popular Style: The Antecedents of Twentieth-Century Popular Music.* Oxford: Clarendon Press, 1989.

Van Vechten, Carl. "Communication." Letter. *Seven Arts* 2, no. 11 (September 1917): 669–70.

Walker, Juliet E. K. "African Americans." In *A Nation of Peoples: A Sourcebook on America's Multicultural Heritage*, edited by Elliot Robert Barkan, 19–47. Westport, Conn.: Greenwood Press, 1999.

Waters, Edward N. *Victor Herbert: A Life in Music.* New York: Macmillan, 1955.

"Weber and Fields: A New Hotch-Potch of Music and Nonsense Produced." *New York Times*, 6 September 1901.

Weber and Fields' Funny Sayings: Comprising Funny Things Said by Weber and Fields, and Other Noted Humorists. New York: Ogilvie, 1904. [Thus on title page. The cover reads *Weber and Field Stage Whispers*.]

"What It Means to Present 'Salome': An Eloquent Description of Difficult Problems by Those Who Ought to Know: Rehearsals before This Week's Final Battle." *New York Times*, 24 January 1909.

Wilde, Oscar. *Salome: A Tragedy in One Act.* London: Elkin Mathews & John Lane, 1894; electronic reprint, Electronic Text Center, University of Virginia Library, March 2000, http://etext.lib.virginia.edu/toc/modeng/public/WilSalo.html.

Wilder, Alec. *American Popular Song: The Great Innovators, 1900–1950.* Edited by James T. Maher. 2nd ed. New York: Oxford University Press, 1990.

Woodress, James. *Booth Tarkington: Gentleman from Indiana.* New York: Greenwood Press, 1954.

Yoshihara, Mari. "The Flight of the Japanese Butterfly: Orientalism, Nationalism, and Performances of Japanese Womanhood." *American Quarterly* 56 (2004): 975–1001.

Video and Audio Resources

Alda, Frances. *The Complete Victor Recordings, 1909–1915.* CD. Romophone 81034, 1999.

Ari Petros Sings "The Galli-Curci Rag": A Treasury of Opera-Inspired Americana. 12-inch LP. Jennifer Records, GH111, n.d.

Art of Singing, The: Golden Voices of the Century. Video cassette. NVC Arts 0630–15898–3, 1996.

Bard, Wilkie. *She Sells Seashells.* CD. Windyridge CDR 13, 2002.

Bel Canto: The Tenors of the 78 Era. Vol. 1. *Caruso, Gigli, Schipa.* Video cassette. West Long Branch, N.J.: Kultur, 1997.

Broadway through the Gramophone (1844–1929): New York in European Footsteps. Vol. 1. *1844–1909.* CD. Pearl GMS 0082 Mono ADD, n.d.

Caruso, Enrico. *Complete Recordings.* Vol. 12. *1902–1920.* Naxos 8.110753, 2004.

Comic Songs by Billy Murray and Company. Vol. 6. *The Ragtime Era, 1913–1916.* Audio cassette. West Palm Beach, Fla.: Vintage Recordings, n.d.

From Avenue A to the Great White Way: Yiddish and American Popular Songs. 2 CDs. Columbia Legacy, 2002.

Green, Stanley. "Hits from Early Musical Comedies." In liner notes to *"I Wants to Be a Actor Lady" and Other Hits from Early Musical Comedies.* New World Records NW221, 1978; reissued on CD, 1993.

Hits of 1920: Whispering. CD. Naxos CD 8.120635. 2004.

"I Wants to Be a Actor Lady" and Other Hits from Early Musical Comedies. New World Records NW221, 1978; reissued on CD, 1993.

La Paloma. 6 CDs. Munich: Trikont CD US-0220, 0227, 0241, 0272, 0327, 0328, 1995–2008.

Marx Brothers Collection, The. 4 DVDs. Warner Home Video, 2004.

Micro-Phonies. In *The Three Stooges.* Vol. 2. Video cassette. Columbia, 1987.

Movies Begin, The: A Treasury of Early Cinema, 1894–1913. 5 DVDs. Vol. 1. *"The Great Train Robbery" and Other Primary Works.* Kino International, 2002.

Music from the New York Stage, 1890–1920. Vol. 1. *1890–1908.* 3 CDs. Vol. 2. *1908–1913.* 3 CDs. Wadhurst, England: Pearl, 1993.

Phonograph Pioneers. Audio cassette. St. Johnsbury, Vt.: Vintage Recording, n.d.

Ragtime Showcase. Vol. 1. *Anna Chandler, Marguerite Farrell, Elsie Janis.* Audio cassette. West Palm Beach, Fla.: Vintage Recordings, n.d.

Scheele, Carl H. Liner notes to *Come Josephine in My Flying Machine: Inventions and Topics in Popular Song, 1910–1929*. New York: New World Records, 1977; reissued on CD.

South Shore Concert Band. *Sounds of the Circus*. Vol. 18. CD. Whitmarsh Recordings, n.d.

Squareheads of the Round Table. In *The Three Stooges: I'm a Monkey's Uncle*. Video cassette. Columbia, 1993.

Vintage George Gershwin. Audio cassette. St. Johnsbury, Vt.: Vintage Recording, n.d.

Waxman, Franz. *Sunset Boulevard*. Scottish National Orchestra conducted by Joel McNeely. Varese Sarabande 302 066 316 2, 2002.

Index